Here's What the Reviewers Say...

"Fine series.... Extensive background on the island's history, economics, and politics, flora and fauna, and culture and religion; the daily practicalities of life (e.g., recycling requirements, boating conduct, buying land); what to see and do." – *Library Journal*

"As the Caribbean's second largest nation's recent success in marketing itself as a holiday haven attests, a 250-year economic slump can mean a big payoff for visitors – notably a trove of historic Spanish buildings from the 1500s (including the Americas' oldest cathedral) plus spectacular beaches and jungles no developers were motivated enough to ruin. This guide to the isle's treasures is geared to independent travelers." – *NY Daily News*

"A frank and thorough rundown of the Caribbean country which can help prospective travelers plan their journeys and enrich their stays. Covers the various areas and cities, as well as a substantial roster of useful subjects, including language, arts and crafts, food (broken down by drinks, fruits and dining practicalities), sports and recreation, accommodations, transportation, etc. Descriptions of the people take in such aspects as racial prejudice, male and female relationships, and attitutdes toward Americans. Maps and a Spanish vocabulary embellish the down-to-earth text." – Jack Adler, *Prodigy Travel Board*

"A wonderfully succinct and powerful description of the island from Columbus to post-Trujillo. The section on Trujillo's rule is outstanding." – Howard Zinn, author, *A People's History of the United States*

Other books by Harry S. Pariser
available from Hunter Publishing

Adventure Guide to Barbados, 2nd Ed. 1-55650-707-0 $15.95
Adventure Guide to Costa Rica, 3rd Ed. 1-55650-722-4 $16.95
Adventure Guide to Puerto Rico, 3rd Ed. 1-55650-749-6 $15.95
Adventure Guide to the Virgin Islands, 4th Ed. 1-55650-746-1 $16.95
Explore Belize, 4th Ed. 1-55650-785-2 $16.95

Available in bookstores nationwide, or directly from the publisher. To order, send a check for the title(s) desired, plus $3 shipping & handling, to:

Hunter Publishing, Inc., 130 Campus Drive, Edison, NJ 08818

Explore
the
Dominican
Republic

3rd Edition

Harry S. Pariser

HUNTER

Hunter Publishing, Inc.
130 Campus Drive
Edison, NJ 08818
(732) 225 1900 / (800) 255 0343   Fax (732) 417 1744
hunterpub@emi.net
Visit our Web site at
www.hunterpublishing.com

In Canada:
1220 Nicholson Road
Newmarket, Ontario
Canada L3Y 7V1
(800) 399-6858   Fax (800) 363 2665

ISBN 1-55650-814-X

© Harry S. Pariser (3rd Edition)

Cover photo: *Church in Altos de Chavón*, Tony Arruza
All other photos by author.

Maps by Joyce Huber and Kim André
© 1998 Hunter Publishing

This guide focuses on recreational activities. As all such activities contain
elements of risk, the publisher, author, affiliated individuals and companies disclaim any responsibility for any injury, harm, or illness that may
occur to anyone through, or by use of, the information in this book. Every
effort was made to insure the accuracy of information in this book, but the
publisher and author do not assume, and hereby disclaim, any liability for
any loss or damage caused by errors, omissions, misleading information or
potential travel problems caused by this guide, even if such errors or omissions result from negligence, accident or any other cause.

4 3 2 1

WE LOVE TO GET MAIL

Things change so rapidly that it's impossible to keep up with everything. Like automobiles, travel books require fine tuning if they are to stay in top condition. We need input from readers so that we can continue to provide the best, most current information possible. Please write to let us know about any inaccuracies or new information. Although we try to make our maps as accurate as possible, errors can occur. If you have suggestions for improvement or places that should be included, please let us know.

READER'S RESPONSE FORM

Explore the Dominican Republic, 3rd Edition

I found your book rewarding because:

Your book could be improved by:

The best places I stayed in were (explain why):

I found the best food at:

Some good and bad experiences I had were:

Will you return to the Dominican Republic?

If so, where do you plan to go? If not, why not?

I purchased this book at:

Please include any other comments on a separate sheet. Mail to Harry S. Pariser, c/o Hunter Publishing, 130 Campus Drive, Edison NJ 08818 USA; fax to (561) 546 7986 or e-mail comments to the author at vudu@jps.net.

About the Author

Harry S. Pariser was born in Pittsburgh and grew up in a small town in southwestern Pennsylvania. After graduating from Boston University with a B.S. in Public Communications in 1975, Harry hitched and camped his way through Europe, traveled down the Nile by steamer, and by train through Sudan. Visiting Uganda, Rwanda, and Tanzania, he traveled by ship from Mombasa to Bombay, and then on through South and Southeast Asia before settling down in Kyoto, Japan. There he studied Japanese and ceramics while supporting himself by teaching English to everyone from tiny tots to Buddhist priests. Using Japan as a base, he traveled to other parts of Asia: trekking to the vicinity of Mt. Everest in Nepal, taking tramp steamers to Indonesian islands like Adonara, Timor, Sulawesi, and Ternate, and visiting rural areas in China. He returned to the United States in 1984 from Kanazawa, Japan, via the Caribbean, where he did research for two travel guides: *Guide to Jamaica* and *Guide to Puerto Rico and the Virgin Islands*, both published in 1986. That same year he returned to Japan, and lived in Kagoshima, a city at the southern tip of Kyushu, across the bay from an active volcano. During that year and part of the next, he taught English and wrote numerous articles for *The Japan Times*.

Harry has written for the *San Jose Mercury News*, *Belize First*, and other journals. His *Adventure Guide to Barbados, 2nd Edition*, won a Silver Award from the Society of American Travel Writers in their 1996 Lowell Thomas Travel Journalism Competition. He currently resides in San Francisco. Besides traveling and writing, his other pursuits include printmaking, painting, cooking, backpacking and hiking, photography, reading, and listening to music – especially jazz, salsa, calypso, and African pop. He may be found on the Web at www.catch22.com/ ~vudu/ and www.jps.net/vudu, or e-mailed at vudu@jps.net.

Acknowledgments

Thanks go out to Michael Hunter and his staff, mapmakers Joyce Huber and Kim André, and a very special thanks to Angie Jimenex and J.J. O'Connell for their suggestions on the manuscript. Thanks also to Marisol Ortiz, Jim Buehler, Joanne Peterson, Ramon Ortiz, informative Michael Ruge, Michael Reyes, Sjaiak Broers, Marie-Antoinette Piguet, Marlene Fretz, Sonia de Ginebra, Lise Pineau, Dr. Leonel Fernández, Pamela Graham, and to all of the Dominicans who were so friendly and open despite their adverse circumstances. A final thank you goes out to my mother, who always worries about me.

Abbreviations

AID – Agency for International Development

Av – Avenida

C – *calle* or street

d – double

E – east, eastern

ha – hectare(s)

km – kilometer

m – meter

N – north, northern

OAS – Organization of American States

ow – one way

pd – per day

pw – per week

RD$ – Dominican dollars (US$1 = RD$15)

rt – round trip

S – south, southern

s – single

W – west, western

GOING METRIC?

To make your travels in the Dominican Republic a little easier, we have provided the following charts that show metric equivalents for the measurements you are familiar with.

1 kilometer	=	.6124 miles
1 mile	=	1.6093 kilometers
1 foot	=	.304 meters
1 inch	=	2.54 centimeters
1 square mile	=	2.59 square kilometers
1 pound	=	.4536 kilograms
1 ounce	=	28.35 grams
1 imperial gallon	=	4.5459 liters
1 US gallon	=	3.7854 liters
1 quart	=	.94635 liters

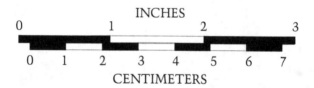

For Fahrenheit: Multiply Centigrade by 1.8 and add 32.

For Centigrade: Subtract 32 from Fahrenheit and divide by 1.8.

CENTIGRADE		FAHRENHEIT
40°	=	104°
35°	=	95°
30°	=	86°
25°	=	77°
20°	=	64°
15°	=	59°
10°	=	50°

Contents

Introduction   3
   The Land   3
   Climate   5
   Flora   7
   Fauna   12
        Marine Life   13
        The Coral Reef Ecosystem   18
   History   21
   Government   40
   Economy   42
   Agriculture   50
   The People   53
        Los Dominicanos (The Dominicans)   54
   Religion   61
        Catholicism   61
        Other Denominations   63
   Language   64
   Arts & Crafts   67
   Music & Dance   67
   Festivals & Events   69
   Food   75
        Fruit   78
        Drinks   79
        Eating Out   80
   Sports & Recreation   82
        Watersports   82
        Other Sports   85
   Practicalities   86
        Arrival   87
        Internal Transport   90
        Accommodations   95
        Visas, Services, & Health   98
        Money & Shopping   103
        Conduct   109
        Other Things You Should Know   113

Santo Domingo   119
   Introduction   119
   Old Santo Domingo Sights   124
   Metropolitan Sights   133

Santo Domingo Hotels   142
Santo Domingo Dining & Food   148
Santo Domingo Entertainment   154
     Santo Domingo Shopping   158
Other Resources & Services   164
     From Santo Domingo   168

The Costa Caribe   171
   Boca Chica   171
   Juan Dolio   176
   Parque Nacional Submarino La Caleta   178

The Southwest   179
   San Cristóbal   179
   Baní   183
   Barahona   185
   Parks of the Southwest   187
     Reserva Científica Natural Laguna de Rincón   187
     Parque Nacional Sierra de Bahoruco   188
     Laguna Enriquillo y Parque Nacional Isla Cabritos   188
     Parque Nacional Jaragua   190
   Onward to Haiti   191

The Cordillera Central Region   193
   Bonao   193
   La Vega   194
   Jarabacoa   196
   Constanza   198
   Reserva Científica Valle Nuevo   200
   Aguas Blancas   201
   Armando Bermúdez & José del Carmen Ramírez
   National Parks   201
     Pico Duarte   202

The Cibao   207
   Santiago de los Treinta Caballeros   207
   Vicinity of Santiago   215
     Moca   215
     San José de las Matas   215

Puerto Plata & the North   217
   Puerto Plata   217
     Puerto Plata Accommodations   223
     Food   228

Heading West From Puerto Plata 235
La Isabela 235
Monte Cristi 236
Parque Nacional Monte Cristi 237
Sosúa 238
Cabarete 249
Río San Juan 262
Playa Grande 264
Nagua 265

Samaná Peninsula 267
Santa Bárbara de Samaná 269
Vicinity of Santa Bárbara de Samaná 273
Cayo Levantado 273
Sánchez 274
Playa El Rincón 274
Playa Las Galeras 274
Limón 278
Las Terrenas 278
Leaving the Peninsula 285

The Southeast 287
Parque Nacional Los Haitises 287
Higüey 291
Costa del Coco 292
Punta Cana 292
La Romana 298
Vicinity of La Romana 299
Casa de Campo 299
Altos de Chavón 299
Boca de Yuma 300
Isla de Catalina 300
Bayahibe 301
Parque Nacional del Este 301
San Pedro de Macorís 302
Spanish Vocabulary 307
Dominican Republic Glossary 313
Booklist 316
Index 322

Maps

Caribbean Islands   6
Hispaniola Land Forms   8
The Dominican Republic   9
National Parks & Scientific Reserves   11
Metropolitan Santo Domingo   121
Old Santo Domingo   129
La Fortaleza   129
Cultural Plaza   135
Boca Chica   172
Southwestern Dominican Republic   183
Central Santiago   208
North Coast   217
Puerto Plata   220
Sosúa   239
Río San Juan   263
Samaná Peninsula   267
Las Terrenas   279
Southeastern Dominican Republic   288

Dominican Republic A-Z

Accommodations – Every type of hotel in every price range is available, as is camping. Many hotels are small, intimate affairs, while others are gigantic all-inclusive resorts.

Art and artists – There are a number of fine artists and craftspeople in the Dominican Republic.

Banks – Banks and moneychangers give the best rate. Hours are 9-3 for banks. Banco Popular will provide a cash advance on credit cards. The currency of choice is US dollars. Canadian dollars can be difficult to exchange.

Buses – Luxury coaches are available on the major routes (such as Santo Domingo – Puerto Plata).

Business hours – Generally 8-noon and 1-5. Many businesses close on Sunday, as do restaurants.

Camping – There are few organized campsites. Tent-supplied "gourmet" camping is an up-and-coming phenomenon.

Clothing – Informal is the rule. You won't need much, if any, in the way of warm clothing.

Car rental – Cars may be rented throughout the country.

Caveing – A few caves now have tours. Most require a permit from the Dept. of Archaeology.

Credit cards – Generally accepted but may be subject to a surcharge by hotels.

Currency – The Dominican peso (RD$1) is divided into 100 centavos. However, owing to inflation, centavos have become largely worthless. Supermarkets still use them, but they have no real value. You will get about US$1=RD$15.

Departure tax – US$10.

Driving – Driving is on the same side as in the US.

Electricity – 110 volts AC. Outages are common so resorts and hotels have backup generators. Make sure your hotel has one before you check in.

Faxes – Most hotels have fax machines. You can also receive and send faxes at the Codetel office in each town.

Guaguas – Passenger vans that run between towns. They tend to be ridiculously crowded.

Marriage – It is possible to get married here. Michael Jackson did it!

Motoconchos – Motorbikes provide transport in small towns. They rent for RD$5 during the day and RD$10 at night.

Population – There are eight million people; only 3% are over 65.

Restaurants – Gourmet restaurants are found in Santo Domingo, Puerto Plata, Sosúa, Cabarete, and at resorts. Italian immigrants have also opened inexpensive restaurants in many places. Local fare tends to be greasy and limited in variety.

Taxes – A 7% sales tax is added to your hotel bill, along with a 6% value-added tax, and all tourist-oriented hotels and resorts add a 10% service charge as well. The very cheapest hotels are tax- and service-charge-free (or they include the taxes in their rates). Restaurants charge 8% value-added tax, plus an additional 10% for "service."

Taxis – Cabs are meterless. Be sure to agree on the price before getting into one.

Telephones – Codetel centers are ideal for making phone calls and sending faxes. Phone cards are available and service is good. Internal calls are expensive. Pay phones are scarce. To call the Dominican Republic from the US, dial 1-809 and the number. Omit the internal area code when dialing within the same area.

Tipping – Not mandatory. Usually 10-15%. Some establishments include a service charge; however, it may not be distributed to personnel.

Visas – Payment of US$10 at the airport buys a Visitor's Card, valid for 90 days, which allows entry for all tourists.

Water – Not generally safe to drink. You should *definitely* stick to bottled water!

Introduction

The Dominican Republic, the second largest nation in the Caribbean (after Cuba), is internationally known for its old Spanish ruins, spectacular palm-lined beaches, lofty mountain peaks, and baseball players.

Only slightly larger than Vermont and New Hampshire combined, the country is divided into three diverse regions by its five mountain ranges. Still, it is small enough that nearly every point is readily accessible by vehicle.

Although portions of the nation have been developed for the mass tourist market, much remains unspoiled and virtually unvisited. The Dominican Republic offers the highest mountain in the Caribbean, the authentic Spanish atmosphere of Old Santo Domingo, the vast plains of sugarcane surrounding La Romana, deserted coasts and white sand beaches, and a very Latin lifestyle.

The Land

The country has served as a gateway to Central America and the Panama Canal as well as to the northernmost nations of South America. As a consequence, it has been a center of conflict since the era when the Spanish, French, and English fought to control Hispaniola straight through until the American economic and military interventions of the 20th century.

GEOGRAPHY: Covering the eastern two-thirds of Hispaniola, the island it shares with Haiti, the Dominican Republic lies 600 miles (1,000 km) SE of Florida and is separated from Puerto Rico to the E by the 68-mile-wide (110-km) Mona Passage. One of the world's most geographically diverse nations for its size, its 19,386 sq miles (50,210 sq km) comprise more than 20 distinct geographic regions with a remarkable variety of scenery: everything from lush tropical jungle to semi-arid deserts to some of the most agriculturally productive land in the entire Caribbean.

LOWLANDS AND VALLEYS: Agriculture and animal husbandry flourish in the fertile alluvial soils of the lowlands. The **Valle de Cibao**, which covers 2,000 sq miles (5,180 sq km) or 10% of the national territory, is the most fertile area. It stretches some 140 miles from Samaná Bay to the Haitian frontier, then continues in Haiti as the Northern Plain. Its E portion is known as the **Vega Real** (Royal Plain), and contains some of the most productive agricultural land. The 650-sq-mile (1,800-sq-km) **Valle de San Juan** lies to the S. It extends into Haiti as the Central Plateau. The other major valley, the **Neiba** or **Hoya de Enriquillo**, comprises 710 sq miles (1,839 sq km) of semi-arid to arid land below sea level. Largest of the other lowland regions is the **Llanura Costera del Caribe** (Caribbean Coastal Plain) to the N, which covers more than 1,100 sq miles (2,900 sq km) and is the center of cattle-raising and sugar production. There are a number of other small valleys and basins, including **Los Haitises**, a national park.

RIVERS AND LAKES: For the most part the rivers are shallow. The Valle de Cibao contains the 399-km **Yaque del Norte**, the longest river, as well as the 185-km **Yuna**. The Valle de San Juan, S of the Cordillera Central, is drained by a tributary of the **Artibonito** and, to the SE, by the **Yaque del Sur**. Among the numerous rivers to the E are the 87-km **Río Ozama**, which cuts through Santo Domingo, and the Río Macorís.

Lago Enriquillo, in the Valle de Neiba, is the largest natural lake in the nation and has the lowest elevation in the Caribbean islands; there are also a number of smaller lagoons. Artificial lakes have been created by the construction of dams on the Río

Yaque del Norte at Tavera and on the Nizao at Valdesia.

OFFSHORE ISLANDS: Of the many islands off the coast, only three are inhabited: **Isla Saona**, the largest, off the SE tip; **Isla Beata**, off Peninsula de Pedernales near the Haitian border; and tiny **Isla Catalina**, a few miles SW of La Romana.

MOUNTAINS: Four parallel mountain ranges dominate the nation's rough terrain, traversing it from the NW to the E, where they are crossed by a single range of low mountains. These largely unpopulated ranges divide the country and separate the capital city of Santo Domingo from the rich agricultural Valle de Cibao and the N coast. The main range is the **Cordillera Central**, extending from Santo Domingo NW into Haiti, where it becomes the Massif du Nord. Its ridges crest at 4,921-8,202 ft (1,500-2,500 m) and include Pico Duarte (10,417 ft, 3,175 m), and Pico La Pelona (10,393 ft, 3,168 m), the Caribbean's highest peaks. Taken together with its Haitian extension, the range makes up a third of the Hispaniolan landmass. Flanked along the N coast by the **Cordillera Septentrional** – a range rising from the W near Monte Cristi – the Cordillera Central is bordered on the S by the **Sierra de Neiba**. The E portion of the latter is separated from the similar range of **Sierra**

de Martin Garcia on the Samaná Peninsula by the swamps surrounding the mouth of the Río Yuna.

Still farther S, the **Sierra de Baoruco** extends from Haiti while the **Cordillera Oriental** forms a minor chain to the E. The latter is more of a narrow band of hills extending from the Cordillera Central than a proper mountain range.

Climate

As holds true for the rest of the Caribbean, the Dominican Republic has a delightful climate. Its mild, subtropical weather varies little throughout the year, with most of the temperature differences coming from changes in elevation. The coolest spots are in the Cordillera Central; the coastal extremities are warmest. There is little seasonal change. Generally, temperatures vary from 64° to 90°F (18° to 32°C), falling to 68°F (20°C) only in Dec. Humidity is frequently stifling.

RAINFALL: The rainy season runs from May to Nov. Rainfall is heaviest in the N and E and far lighter in the S and W, where the mountains remove much of the moisture from the NE trade winds. While areas such as Barahona and Monte Cristi are extremely arid, the town of Samaná near the tip of Samaná Peninsula may receive 100 inches (254 cm) or more annually; average rainfall is about 55 inches (139.7 cm). Much rain falls at night. The Republic averages 245 days of sunshine annually.

HURRICANES: These low-pressure zones are serious business and should not be taken lightly. Where buildings are poorly constructed, property damage from hurricanes may run into the hundreds of millions of dollars.

A hurricane begins as a relatively small tropical storm, known as a cyclone when its winds reach a velocity of 39 mph (62 kph). At 74 mph (118 kph) it is upgraded to hurricane status, with winds up to 200 mph (320 kph) and ranging in size from 60-1,000 miles (100-1,600 km) in diameter. A small hurricane releases energy equivalent to the explosions of six atomic bombs per second.

A hurricane is like an enormous, hovering engine, fueled by the moist air of the tropics, and carried hither and thither by prevailing air currents – generally trade winds that intensify as they move N across warm ocean waters. Cooler, drier northern air ultimately starves the hurricane of fuel, and it subsides.

Routes and patterns of such storms are unpredictable. As for their frequency: "June – too soon; July – stand by; August – it must;

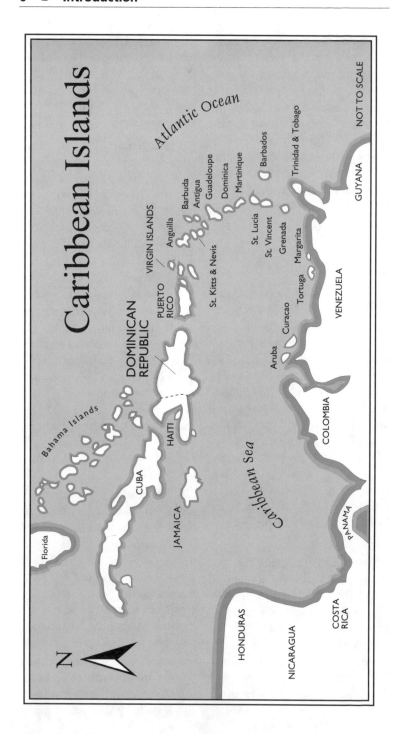

Caribbean Islands

September – remember." So goes the old rhyme. Those forming in Aug. and Sept. typically last for two weeks, while the ones that form in June, July, Oct., and Nov. (many of which originate in the Caribbean and the Gulf of Mexico) generally last only seven days. Approximately 70% of all hurricanes (known as Cabo Verde types) originate as embryonic storms coming from the W coast of Africa. Since record-keeping began, a number of hurricanes have wreaked havoc here. In 1930 a massive hurricane hit, killing 2,000 and changing the nation's history by allowing Trujillo to consolidate his power. Hurricane David struck in Aug. 1979, causing a billion dollars in damage, leaving more than 1,000 dead and as many as 10,000 homeless. Hurricane Frederick followed shortly thereafter.

Flora

The Dominican Republic has vegetation zones ranging from the coniferous forest lining the slopes of towering Pico Duarte and Pico La Pelona, the Caribbean's highest points, to the desertlike environment surrounding below-sea-level Lago Enriquillo. All in all, there are nine basic and seven transitional vegetation zones.

Subtropical moist forest predominates, covering nearly half of the nation. Occurring princi-

pally on mountain slopes, subtropical wet and **lower montane forest** covers most of the remainder. Sadly, less than 5% of the nation remains covered with pine. Much of the old-growth forest has vanished, removed for agriculture or charcoal-making. There are some 5,500 flowering plants and ferns.

HELICONIAS: Famous worldwide as an ornamental, the heliconia (*platanillo*) lends an infusion of bizarre color and shape to the tropical landscape. The name of these medium to large erect herbs comes from Helicon, a mountain in southern Greece which was believed to have been the home of the muses. They are a member of the order known as the *Zingiberales*, and there are thought to be around 200-250 species. Relatives within this category include bananas, birds-of-paradise, gingers, and prayer plants.

The family name *Zingiberales* comes from the Sanskrit word *sringavera*, which means "horn shaped," in reference to the rhizomes. Each erect shoot has a stem and leaves which are frequently (although not always) topped by an infloresence with yellow or red bracts. Each infloresence may produce up to 50 hermaphroditic flowers. Leaves are composed of stalk and blade and resemble banana leaves.

Hispaniola Land Features

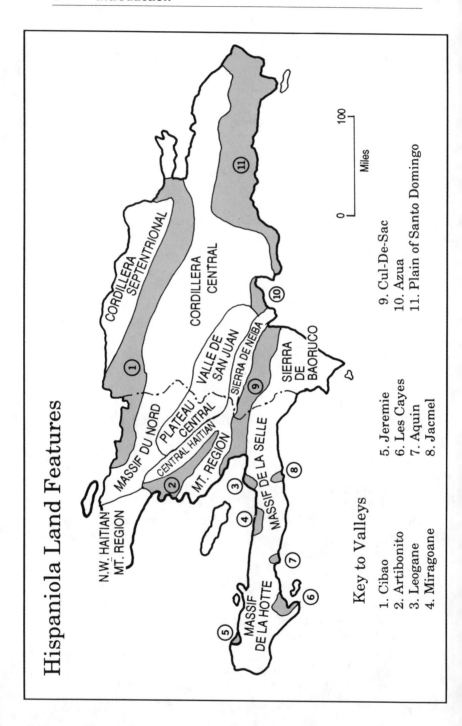

Key to Valleys

1. Cibao
2. Artibonito
3. Leogane
4. Miragoane
5. Jeremie
6. Les Cayes
7. Aquin
8. Jacmel
9. Cul-De-Sac
10. Azua
11. Plain of Santo Domingo

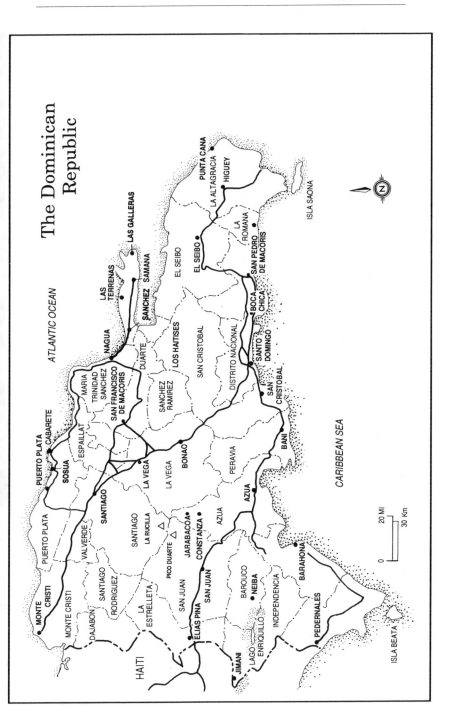

The Dominican Republic

Flowers produce a blue-colored fruit which has three seeds.

In the Dominican Republic you're most likely to find heliconias near rivers and along roads; they thrive in light gaps. Most are found in the tropical lowlands or in middle-elevation or cloud forest habitats. Lured by the bright flowers and bracts, hummingbirds pollinate the blooms as they fly from flower to flower in search of nectar.

CACTI: Any visitor to the nation's drier regions will notice the proliferation of cacti and other scrub vegetation. In these areas, you'll find numerous types of cactus, including the phallic dildo cactus and the prickly pear; several varieties of climbing cactus have night-blooming flowers.

Cacti were classified into a single genus comprising 24 species by Linnaeus in 1737. The name is Greek for "bristly plant." The oldest fossilized cacti are found in Colorado and Utah and date from the Eocene era, some 50 million years ago. Cacti have adapted to suit a hot, dry climate. Evolution has transformed their leaves into spines and their branches into areoles – localized regions which carry spines and/or bristles. The stems are responsible for photosynthesis. Shade and light diffusion is provided by bumps, warts, ribs, spines, and hairlike structures, which also serve to hinder evaporation and hold dew. The thick, leathery flesh stores water effectively, resists withering and can endure up to a 60% water loss without damage. Stomata (apertures) close during the day to stave off water loss and reopen at night. Blossoms generally last for only one day, and nearly all depend upon animals, especially bats, for pollination.

MANGROVES: Mangrove forests grow along the coasts; these water-rooted trees serve as a marine habitat for sponges, corals, oysters, and others around its roots – organisms which, in turn, attract a variety of other sealife. Some species live their entire lives in the shelter of the mangroves, and many fish use it as a shelter or feeding ground. Above the water level, they shelter seabirds and are important nesting sites. Their organic detritus, exported to the reef by the tides, is consumed by its inhabitants, providing the base of an extensive food web.

Mangroves also dampen high waves and winds generated by tropical storms. By trapping silt in their roots and catching leaves and other detritus which decompose to form soil, the red mangroves act as land builders. Eventually, they kill themselves off by building up enough soil for the black and white mangroves to take over. Meanwhile, the red mangroves have sent out progeny in the form of floating seedlings –

National Parks & Scientific Reserves

1. Reserva Cientificia Valle Nuevo
2. Parque Nacional Submarino La Caleta
3. Reserva Cientifica Laguna Rincón (Laguna Cabral)
4. Parque Nacional Sierra de Bahoruco
5. Parque Nacional Jaragua
6. Parque Nacional Isla Cabritos
7. Parque Nacional José del Carmen Ramírez
8. Parque Nacional Armando Bermudez
9. Parque Nacional Monte Cristi (El Morro)
10. Reserva Cientifica Natural de Villa Elisa
11. Reserva Cientifica Isabel de Torres
12. Parque Nacional Cabo Frances Viejo
13. Parque Nacional Los Haitises
14. To Sanctuario del Blanco de la Plata (125km. N of Puerto Plata)
15. Reserva Cientifica Lagunas Redonda y Limón
16. Parque Nacional del Este

bottom-heavy youngsters that grow on the tree until they reach six inches to a foot in length. Whenthey reach shallow water, the seeds touch bottom and implant themselves.

Unfortunately, mangroves are increasingly endangered in the Dominican Republic. Developers, concerned only with making as much money as possible, have cut the coastal groves illegally. Hardly a week goes by when some violation is not reported by the local media.

Most of these developments have been for tourism. In one 1997 case, workers secretly cut mangroves near La Romana in the middle of the night to expand a marina. The Costa Dorada, a new development near Puerto Plata financed by a Dominican senator, was also found to have cut mangroves illegally that same year. Other culprits include the Club Bahia del Principe (a hotel at Playa Grande on the N coast) and the "Natural Park," a new development at Punta Cana.

OTHER TREES: Mahogany, capá (used in shipbuilding), and **royal palm** predominate in the subtropical moist forest. The last is present almost everywhere, but abounds in the Vega Real. Its trunk may be used for soft lumber, its fronds (known as *yagua*) for thatch, and its nuts for hog feed. Secondary-growth trees found in pastures and along streams include the lancewood, cashew, yellowood, logwood, and the *jagua* palm. Ground oak and *malphigia* are among the trees found in pastures.

Fauna

The country hosts some 5,600 animal species, 36% of them indigenous. The indigenous mammal species are few, as holds true elsewhere in the Caribbean. The cattle, goats, pigs, chickens, and horses you will see were all introduced.

REPTILES: *Caiman* (**alligators**) are found only around Lake Enriquillo in the SW. They were introduced from the States. Other lizards include the **rhino iguana** and **Rocard's iguana**.

ⓘ *Did You Know?*
Taino children traditionally wore hats of dried leaf and straw, then they hid in trees whose branches had been covered with sticky resin. Each child held a live parrot as bait; other parrots would swoop in, drawn by the cries of their flockmates, and get stuck. The children then captured the birds using thin lassos.

BIRDS: The Hispaniolan **palmchat** or **palmthrush** (*cigua palmera*), declared the national bird in 1967, flocks in open areas, especially near royal palms. In low elevations, it builds a six-foot multi-compartmented nest high on a palm trunk. The **cotorra** (nicknamed *cotica* – "little parrot" – and *cuca*) was set on a path to extinction when the Tainos gave them as presents to arriving Spaniards. **Flamingos** are found in the Río Yuna delta and in Lake Enriquillo. Originally an African import, the Madam Sagá or **village weaver** builds unique woven nests.

THE SOLENODON: A relative of Madagascar's tenrec, the solenodon (*solenodonte*) is found only on Hispaniola and in Cuba. It is the Caribbean's only surviving insect eater. The brown, ratlike mammal has a rather strange way of walking, called "unglitude," in which it places only the edge of its foot on the ground. It sleeps by day in small caves and dry tree trunks. At night it prowls, preying on insects, worms, mollusks, and small vertebrates. Standing on hind legs and tail, the solenodon tears its quarry apart with its claws before dining. Despite the solenodon's multimillion-year history, the destruction of its natural environment, along with the advent of the mongoose, have greatly decreased its numbers. Many fear it may already be extinct.

THE HUTIA (JUTÍA): This endangered endemic rodent (*Plagidonita aedium*), measuring some 12 inches (30 cm) in length, resides in tree trunks and caves. It is a skillful climber and hunts at night. The hutia looks something like an anteater.

Marine Life

MANATEE (MANATÍ): This ungainly creature is elusive but is sometimes spotted offshore. It once ranged from South America up to North Carolina, but its numbers have dwindled dramatically – threatened by hunting, motor boat propellers, and careless use of herbicides. Currently inhabiting coastal waters from Florida to N Brazil, manatees move along the ocean floor at a maximum of six mph) searching for food. They surface every four or five minutes to breathe.

Surprisingly, the creature is thought to have been the model for the mermaid legend – perhaps because of the mother's habit of sheltering her offspring with her flipper as the infant feeds. Weighing 400-1,300 lbs, the pudgy creature is covered with finely wrinkled grey or brown skin decorated with barnacles and algae; it may reach 12 ft (four m) in length. Although to you they may appear ugly, with their small eyes, thick lips, bristly muzzles, and wrinkled necks, they are affectionate with each other, kissing and sometimes swimming flipper-to-flipper.

Manatees dwell in lagoons and brackish water, and may eat as much as 100 lbs (220 kg) of aquatic vegetables per day; they are strictly vegetarian. Their only enemy is man, who has hunted them since the time of the Tainos for their hides, oil, and meat. Today, some 60-80 manatees survive off the W coast of the Dominican Republic.

ⓘ *Did You Know?*
The manatee's nearest living relative is the elephant.

HUMPBACK WHALES: Humpback whales migrate every fall from the polar waters through the passage between Puerto Rico and the Virgin Islands, where they breed. Overhunting during the early to mid-19th century. has endangered them; they have been internationally protected since the mid-1960s. The Dominican Republic is the only nation that has established an offshore wildlife refuge specifically to protect humpbacks.

You may see these marine mammals offshore near Puerto Plata in the first few months of the year. Distinguished by their very long pectoral fins, which are scalloped on their forward edges, as well as by large knobs on their jaws and heads, the black-bodied, thickset humpbacks have white on their underbellies. They range from 30-40 ft (12-15 m) in length.

Watch them leap belly-up from the water, turn a somersault, and

arch backwards. They plunge headfirst back into the depths making a loud snapping noise in the process. While making deep dives, these whales hump their backs forward and bring their tails out of the water. They love vocalizing. Their moans, cries, groans, and snores are expressed in "songs" that can last up to 35 minutes. Humpbacks feed on small fish, plankton, and shrimp-like crustaceans – all of which they strain from the water with their baleen.

SEA TURTLES: All four types of sea turtle are found here. The large-finned, herbivorous **green turtle** (*tortuga blanca* or *tortuga verde*) has a total length of about three ft and weighs around 400 lbs. It lays eggs every two to three years, storming the beaches in massive groups called *barricadas*. Green turtles are readily identifiable by their short rounded heads.

The **hawksbill** (*tortuga carey*) is one of the smallest sea turtles, at 35 inches or less in length. It has a spindle-shaped shell and weighs around 220 lbs (100 kg). Because of its tortoise shell (a brown translucent layer of corneous gelatin that peels off the shell when processed) it has been pursued and slaughtered throughout the world. The hawksbill dines largely on sponges and seaweed. Worldwide demand for its shell, which sells for a fortune in Japan, appears to have condemned it to extinction.

The short-finned **loggerhead turtle** (*tortuga cabezona*) rarely exceeds four ft. Its head is large, narrow, and bird-jawed – twice the size of the green turtle's – and it dines on sea urchins, jellyfish, starfish, and crabs. The loggerhead is threatened with extinction from coastal development, egg gathering, and hunting by raccoons.

Black, with very narrow fins, the **leatherback's** name comes from the leathery hide that covers it in lieu of a shell. It can reach up to six ft in length and weigh as much as 1,500 lbs (3,300 kg). The leatherback's chief predator has always been the poacher.

REEF FISH: Common reef fish here include sergeant majors, blue tangs, blue chromis, blue-headed wrasses, yellowtail snappers, trumpet fish and French angelfish. Unfortunately, reef fish are being decimated by spearfishing.

ECHINODERMATA: Combining the Greek words for *echinos* (spiny) and *derma* (skin), this large division of the animal kingdom includes sea urchins, sea cucumbers, and starfish or sea stars. All share the ability to propel themselves with the help of "tube feet" or spines.

Known by the scientific name *Astrospecten*, **starfish** (*estrellas de mar*) are five-footed carnivores that use their modified tube feet to burrow into the sea.

Sluggish **sea cucumbers** ingest large quantities of sand, extract the organic matter, and excrete the rest. They have tentacles at their anterior end. Crustaceans and fish reside in the larger specimens.

Avoid trampling on that armed knight of the underwater sand dunes, the **sea urchin**, which has a semi-circular calcium carbonate shell and is protected by its brown, jointed barbs. It uses its mouth, situated and protected on its underside, to graze by scraping algae from rocks. Surprisingly to those uninitiated in its lore, sea urchins are considered a gastronomic delicacy in many countries. The ancient Greeks believed they held aphrodisiacal

---

⚡ Warning!

If a sea urchin spine breaks off inside your finger or toe, don't try to remove it. It's impossible! You might try the cure used in New Guinea. Mash up the spine inside your skin with a blunt object. Then dip your finger in urine; the ammonia helps trigger a process of disintegration. More safely, apply triple-antibiotic salve. Sea urchins often hide underneath corals.

and other properties beneficial to health. They are prized by the French and fetch a high price in Paris. The Spanish consume them raw, boiled, in *gratinés*, or in soups. In Barbados they are called "sea eggs," and the Japanese eat their guts raw as sushi. A disease in recent years has devastated the sea urchin population, but they are making a comeback.

SPONGES: Found in the ocean depths, reddish or brown sponges are among the simplest forms of multicellular life and have been around for more than a half-billion years. They pump large amounts of water through their internal filters to extract plankton. They come in numerous sizes, shapes, and colors, but they can all be recognized by their large, distinctive excurrent openings. Unlike other animals, they exhibit no reaction when disturbed.

CNIDARIANS: The members of this group – hydroids, anemones, corals, and jellyfish – are distingushed by their simple structure: a cup-shaped body terminating in a combination mouth-anus encircled by tentacles. Hydroids and corals (covered later in this

Unusual Facts About Humpback Whales

- **Whale spray** (or "blow") leaves a greasy film on whatever it comes into contact with.

- **Only the males vocalize.** All males "sing" the same "song." It is believed that one male dreams up a song to attract a female, and other males imitate it – forcing him to change his tune. Their songs may extend as far afield as 20 miles (32 km). By following their songs, scientists may determine the migratory routes.

- Marine mammals **conserve oxygen** while submerged by slowing their heart rate and reducing blood flow to less important organs.

- A **whale calf** feeds by swimming beneath its mother and feasting from her slit-concealed nipples. The milk has a yogurt-like consistency and contains 40-50% fat.

- A humpback is **sexually mature** at the age of four or five. Males compete aggressively to woo a fertile female for mating. However, no one has ever observed a copulating couple.

- While **migrating** between the Antarctic and the waters around the Dominican Republic, the whales do not eat but live off their blubber. They lose up to one-fifth of their weight during this journey.

section) are colonial, while jelly-fish and anemones are individual. The name *cnidarians* comes from the Greek word for another identifying characteristic: stinging capsules (or nematocysts) used for defense and capturing prey.

Hydroids ("water forms" in Greek) spend their youth as solitary medusas before settling down in colonies that resemble groups of ferns or feathers. Some sting, and the best-known hydroid is undoubtedly the floating **Portuguese Man-Of-War.** Its stinging tentacles can be extended or retracted. There have been reports of trailing tentacles reaching 50 feet! It belongs to the family of *siphonophores,* free-floating hydroid colonies that control their depth by means of a gas-filled float. The true jellyfish are identifiable by their domes, which vary in shape. Nematocysts are found in both the feeding tube and in their tentacles.

Box jellies, also known as sea wasps, can be identifed by their cube-shaped dome. From each corner a single tentacle extends. Many of them have a fierce sting; keep well away. The jellyfish season is Aug. to Oct.

Solitary bottom-dwellers, **sea anemones** are polyps with no skeleton. They use their tentacles to stun prey and force it to their mouths. Shrimp and crabs, immune to their sting, often live nearby for protection. Anemones' tentacles may retract when disturbed. One type of anemone lives in tubes buried in the muck or sand. Their tentacles only come out to play at night.

☞ *Traveler's Tip*
If you should get stung by any of the above, get out of the water and peel off any tentacles. Avoid rubbing the injured area. Wash it with alcohol and apply meat tenderizer for five to 10 minutes.

CRUSTACEANS: A class of arthropods, these are distinguished by their jointed legs and complex skeletons. The decapods (named for their 10 legs) are the largest order of crustaceans and include shrimp, crabs and lobsters. The ghost crab (*ocypode*) abounds on the beaches, tunneling down beneath the sand and emerging to feed at night. Although it can survive for 48 hrs. without contacting water, it must return to the sea to moisten its gill chambers as well as to lay its eggs, which hatch into planktonic larvae.

The hermit crab carries a discarded mollusc shell in order to protect its vulnerable abdomen. As it grows, it must find a larger home, and you may see two struggling over the same shell.

OTHER UNDERWATER HAZARDS AND CURES: Fire coral is not a true coral, but mimics its appearance; it takes many forms and has the ability to encrust nearly any object, taking on its host's shape. It is generally colored mustard-yellow to brown, and often has white finger-like tips. Its sting is quite painful. As with coral wounds, you should wash the affected area with soap and fresh water, then apply a triple-antibiotic salve.

The **spotted scorpionfish**, found on rocky or coral bottoms, is well camouflaged so it's easy to step on one. Although the Caribbean species is non-lethal, its bite can hurt.

Another cleverly camouflaged denizen of the deep is the **stingray**, which will whip its tail if stepped on – driving the serrated venomous spine into the offender. If this happens, see a doctor.

Fuzzy **bristle worms** have glass-like bristles that may break off in the skin, causing considerable pain. Apply tape to the skin and attempt to pull the bristles out; reduce the pain with rubbing alcohol.

Moray eels have a tendency to bite what is thrust at them; they have a tight grip and can be difficult to dislodge. Always exercise caution before reaching into a crevice!

The Coral Reef Ecosystem

The coral reef is one of the least appreciated of the world's innumerable wonders. This is, in part, because little has been known about it until recent decades. This wondrous environment is a delicate one – the only geological feature fashioned by living creatures. Many of the world's reefs – which took millions of years to form – have already suffered devastation at the hand of man.

Corals produce the calcium carbonate (limestone) responsible for most of the island's offlying cays and islets as well as most of the sand on the beaches. Bearing the brunt of waves, they also conserve the shoreline. Although reefs began forming millenia ago, they are in a constant state of flux. Seemingly solid, they actually depend upon a delicate ecological balance to survive. Deforestation, dredging, temperature change, an increase or decrease in salinity, silt, or sewage discharge may kill them.

Because temperatures must remain between 68° and 95°F for them to flourish, coral reefs are found only in the tropics and – because they require light to grow – only in shallow water. They are also intolerant of fresh water, so reefs cannot survive where rivers empty into the sea.

THE CORAL POLYP: Corals are actually animals, but botanists view them as being mostly plant, while geologists dub them "honorary rocks." The polyps do act more like plants than animals.

The algae inside them do the work of photosynthesis while they themselves secrete calcium carbonate and stick together for protection from waves and boring sponges.

A polyp bears a close structural resemblance to its relative the anemone. It feeds at night by using the ring or rings of tentacles surrounding its mouth to capture prey (such as plankton) with nematocysts, small stinging darts.

Coral polyps appear able to survive in such packed surroundings through their symbiotic relationship with the algae present in their tissues: Coral polyps exhale carbon dioxide and the algae consume it, producing needed oxygen. Although only half of the world's coral species possess such a relationship with these single-celled captive species of dinoflagellates (*Gymnodinium microdriaticum*), these species – called hermatypic corals – are the ones that build the reef. The nutritional benefits gained from their relationship with the algae enable them to grow a larger skeleton and to do so more rapidly than would otherwise be possible. Polyps have the ability to regulate the density of these cells in their tissues and they can expel some of them in a spew of mucus should they multiply too quickly. Looking at coral, you will see that the brownish-colored algal cells

show through transparent tissues.

Bacteria are an added and vital yet invisible component of the reef ecosystem. These microorganisms decompose and recycle all matter on which everything from worms to coral polyps feed. Other reef inhabitants range from crabs to barnacles, sea squirts to multicolored tropical fish. Remarkably, the polyps themselves are consumed by only a small percentage of the reef's citizens. Polyps often contain high levels of toxic substances and are also thought to sting fish and other animals that attempt to consume them. Corals also retract their polyps for protection during daylight hours when the fish can see them. Reefs originate as the polyps develop; the calcium secretions form a base as they grow. One polyp can have a 1,000-year lifespan.

CORAL TYPES: Corals may be divided into three groups. The hard or **stony corals** (such as staghorn, brain, star, or rose) secrete a limey skeleton.

The **horny corals** (for example, sea plumes, sea whips, sea fans, and gorgonians) have a supporting skeleton-like structure known as a gorgonin (after the head of Medusa). The shapes of these corals result from the ways the polyps and their connecting tissues excrete calcium carbonate; there are over a thousand different patterns – one specific to each species. Each also has its own method of budding. The giant elk-horn corals found in the Caribbean may contain over a million polyps and live for several hundred years or longer.

The last category consists of the **soft corals**. Although these too are colonies of polyps, their skeletons are composed of soft organic material, and their polyps always have eight tentacles instead of the six or multiples of six found in the stony corals. Unlike the hard corals, soft corals disintegrate after death and do not add to the reef's stony structure. Instead of depositing limestone crystals, they excrete a jelly-like matrix imbued with spicules (diminutive spikes) of stony material; the jelly-like substance gives these corals their flexibility. Sea fans and sea whips exhibit similar patterns.

A type of soft coral is the precious black coral. It is prized by jewelers because its branches may be cleaned and polished to high-gloss ebony-black. In the natural state it resembes a bush of fine grey-black twigs. Don't buy products made with this coral, however; doing so contributes to reef destruction.

COMPETITION: To the snorkeler, the reef appears to be a peaceful haven. The reality is that fierce competition for space has developed there. Some coral species have evolved sweeper tentacles with an especially high concentration of stinging cells. Reaching out to a competing coral, they sting and kill it. Other species dispatch digestive filaments that eat the competitor. Soft corals appear to leach out toxic chemicals (called terpines) that kill nearby organisms.

Because predation is so widespread, two-thirds of reef species are toxic. Others hide in stony outcrops or have formed protective relationships with other organisms. The classic example is the banded clown fish, which lives among the sea anemones, whose stingers protect it. Cleaner fish protect themselves from larger fish by setting up stations to pick parasites off their carnivorous customers. Mimicking the coloration and shape of the feeder fish, the sabre-toothed blenny is a false cleaner fish that takes a chunk out of the larger fish and runs off!

CORAL LOVE AFFAIRS: Polyps are not prone to celibacy or sexual prudery, and reproduce both sexually and asexually through budding. A polyp joins together with thousands and even millions of its neighbors to form a coral. (In a few cases, only one polyp forms a single coral.) During sexual reproduction polyps release millions of their spermatozoa into the water. Many species are dimorphic – with both male and female coral. Some species have internal, others external fertilization. Still others have both male and female polyps. As larvae develop, their "mother" expels them and they float off to found a new coral colony.

EXPLORING REEFS WITH CARE: As mentioned under "environmental conduct" in the *Practicalities* section later in the book, coral reefs are extremely fragile environments. Much damage has been done to reefs worldwide through human carelessness. Despite their size, reefs grow very slowly and it can take decades or even centuries to repair the effects of a few moments. In general, look but don't touch is the watchword.

UNDERWATER FLORA: Most of the plants you see below the surface are algae, primitive plants that can survive only underwater. Lacking roots, algae draw their minerals and water directly from the sea. One type, calcareous red algae, are very important for reef formation. Resembling rounded stones, they are 95% rock and only 5% living tissue. Sea grasses, plants returned to live in the sea, are found in relatively shallow water in sandy and muddy bays and flats; they have roots and small flowers. One species, dubbed "turtle grass," provides food for their namesake. In addition, sea grasses help to stabilize the sea floor, maintain water clar-

ity by trapping fine sediments from upland soil erosion, stave off beach erosion, and provide living space for numerous fish, crustaceans, and shellfish.

History

PRECOLUMBIAN ERA: Little is known of the island's original inhabitants. They were dominated by the **Taino**, who spoke a dialect of Arawak (a word believed to mean "meal-" or "cassava-eater"). There may have been other cultures on the island; it is not clear if the other groups were simply related tribes or entirely separate cultures. Although yucca was their staple food, the Taino also grew corn, sweet potatoes, chilis, and peanuts. They ate fish, turtles, shellfish, and manatee.

The Taino called their island Quisqueya ("Greatness") or Haiti ("Rugged Mountain"). The island was divided into five *caciazgos*, each ruled over by a *cacique* with a name like Higüey or Jaragua. Land was owned and cultivated communally, and there was little armed conflict. Gifted artists and craftsmen, the Taino carved sculptures, wove baskets, and produced pottery. Masks and necklaces were fashioned from gold, a practice that was to have unfortunate consequences later on. Also on the island were a group of Caribs settled around the Samaná peninsula.

ENTER COLUMBUS: Modern Dominican history began in 1492 with the arrival of Columbus and the Spanish. The admiral ran the *Santa Maria* aground at Navidad (present-day Cap Haitian in Haiti) on Christmas Day, 1492 and received a friendly reception. In his logbook Columbus described the Taino as "open hearted" and "fit to be ordered and made to work." On his return the next year, he found the colony of 39 men left there had been killed after they had taken to pillaging for gold and kidnapping the local lasses. Because the Taino told them there was gold in the area, a second settlement was established at Isabela, where the pioneers supplemented their farming activities with stealing gold ornaments, raping women, and capturing slaves for shipment to Spain.

ⓘ **Did You Know?**
The first recorded instance of the word Taino was noted by Columbus. The name derives from nitaino ("men of the good"), which was how the Taino sought to differentiate themselves from the Caribs and Ciguayos.

GENOCIDE: After the Isabela settlement ran into trouble in 1496, Bartolomew Columbus moved, along with most of the settlers, to the site of present-day Santo Domingo. It had some 300 inhabitants in 1498. Subsequently, Spain, the first great colonial power in the Americas, established Santo Domingo as its New World headquarters. Francisco Bobadilla, appointed by the Crown as chief justice and commissioner, took power and sent Columbus back in chains. Bobadilla was replaced by Nicolás de Ovando, who became governor and supreme justice. Because of his success in instituting the system of *ecomienda* (see below), he was made "Founder of Spain's Empire in the Indies."

Under the system of *repartimiento* ("distribution") established by Columbus, the Taino had been set to work in construction and in the mines or fields. Under the similar system of Crown control instituted in 1503, termed *ecomienda* ("commandery"), they were forcibly extracted from villages and set to labor for a *pátron* on his estate. Although the Indians were supposed to receive protection and learn about the wonders of Catholicism, this system was a thinly disguised form of slavery; the number of Taino shrank from as many as three million in 1492 to approximately 500 in 1548.

Along the way they left legendary martyrs. Among them was the valiant *cacique* Caonabo, who died while being shipped to Spain. Anacaona, his widow, considered to be the most beautiful woman of the island, was among the many murdered by Hitlerian-style humanist Gov. Nicolás de Ovando. Another famous Indian was Enriquill, the son of a *cacique* murdered at Jaragua by de Ovando's forces. He was educated by monks and, after being faced with re-enslavement under *repartimiento*, became the leader of an insurrection from 1520-33. It ended with him and his followers being resettled on a reserve. His legend is recorded in Manuel de Jesús Galván's classic novel *Enriquillo*, published in 1882. The importation of slaves began in 1503 as another de Ovando brainstorm. It put in place a race-regulated hierarchy that survives to this day.

THE AUDENCIA: In an attempt to put checks on Diego Columbus, who was appointed governor in 1509, the Crown devised the *audencia* in 1511, a three-judge tribunal whose authority extended all over the West Indies. The highest court of appeals, its influence expanded and it became the *Royal Audencia* in 1524, commanding jurisdiction over the Caribbean, Mexico, and the N coast of S America, including all of Venezuela and portions of Colombia. In 1526, a separate *audencia* for Mexico was established in an attempt to curb the power of Cortés.

Along with the government came the church. The first missionaries had arrived with Columbus on his second voyage in 1493, and the hemisphere's first bishopric was established in 1511; it was made the first archbishopric in 1547.

DECLINE OF IMPORTANCE: With the discovery of gold and silver in Mexico and Peru and the depletion of gold deposits in 1520, as well as the extermination of the island's indigenous people, Santo Domingo began to lose luster in the first part of the 16th century. In 1564, Santiago and Concepción de la Vega were destroyed by an earthquake, and Santo Domingo was sacked by Sir Francis Drake in 1586. Although the town repelled a British invasion in 1655, the Spaniards torched their settlements on the island's N coast in order to stave off smuggling and keep them from falling under French control. Under the Treaty of Ryswick in 1697, Spain ceded the western third of the island to France. This area, then known as "Hayti," became the most prosperous colony in the world, while Santo Domingo slipped into a 250-year slump. The Spanish colony grew to 150,000 by 1785. Approximately 40,000 were of Spanish ancestry, 40,000 were African slaves, and the rest were black or mulatto freedmen.

THE HAITIAN OCCUPATION: Haitian slaves, led by Toussaint L'Ouverture, revolted in 1791, sparking a confused civil war. Toussaint's forces fought with the Spanish against the French, until they heard of the emancipation of slaves by the French. Shifting his allegiance, Toussaint helped the French drive the Spanish from Saint-Dominique, the French name for Haiti. Toussaint was appointed governor of the French colony of Saint-Dominique by the French Convention. He marched into Santo Domingo in 1801. His new constitution freed slaves, causing the Spanish colony to lose one-third of its white elite, who migrated to Puerto Rico, Cuba, and Venezuela.

In 1802, French forces under the command of General Le Clerc (the brother-in-law of Napoleon) drove the Haitians back to the W, capturing Toussaint in the process. Toussaint was replaced by the despotic duo of Henri Christophe and Jean Jacques Dessalines. The latter declared Haiti's independence on Jan. 1, 1804. The French controlled Santo Domingo until 1809, when the Spanish drove them out with British help.

In 1821 colonial treasurer José Nuñez de Caceres declared Santo Domingo's independence, but he and other leaders made the mistake of looking for support from Haitian leader General Jean Pierre Boyer, who invaded. Meeting little resistance – Nuñez de Caceres handed over the keys to Santo Domingo on a silver platter – the Haitians stayed until 1844.

The Haitian occupation remains a bitter memory. Although the slaves were emancipated, emigration increased, sugar and tobacco production were paralyzed, all church properties were seized, and the economy staggered under the weight of a tyrannical bureaucracy and plundering by Haitian soldiers. An independence underground flourished under the leadership of Juan Pablo Duarte and his secret society, La Trinitaria. On Feb. 27, 1844, the Dominican rebels siezed Ozama fortress in Santo Domingo. Caught by surprise, the Haitians hastily exited, and a provisional government took control.

INDEPENDENCE: Duarte, however, was reluctant to take command of the presidency, and he soon found himself usurped and exiled by two self-appointed generals, Buenaventura Báez and Pedro Santana, a rancher with his own private army. Alternating as president over the next 45 years, these two dictators helped to fill their own pockets more than they helped anyone else. Taking control of the presidency in Nov. 1844, Santana began a quest to sell the country to the highest bidder. In particular, he held out as a crown jewel the Samaná Peninsula, which has a superb natural harbor. From 1848 to 1855, the nation was repeatedly threatened by the Haitian dictator, Faustin I. By 1861 the country was bankrupt and, now in his third term as president, Santana announced that the República Dominicana would again become a Spanish colony. By midsummer, Santo Domingo was once more swarming with Spaniards and, by mid-fall, the Dominicans were revolting again. This War of Restoration had begun to drive the Spanish back by 1863.

Independence was not reestablished until 1865 when Báez took his third crack at the presidency. He was, however, forced to leave the country five months later because of a revolt led by General Gregorio Luperón. Soon called back from exile, Báez convinced the Grant administration to sign a treaty annexing the country to the US. All Dominicans were to become US citizens and his government would be compensated to the tune of $1.5 billion. However, coming under stiff opposition led by Sen. Charles Sumner, the treaty failed to pass the US Senate by only 10 votes in 1870. But in 1872 Báez negotiated a 99-year lease of Samaná Bay to a New York company, and he was once again driven from office after the plebiscite called to ratify the contract was shown to have been rigged.

Báez was replaced from 1874-79 by reformist Ulises Espillat, who began issuing paper currency without backing. Unable to control the situation, he fell from power and Báez returned for his final fling at the presidency. But after only two months, he took US$300,000 and fled to Puerto Rico – leaving his country in shambles behind him.

ULISES HEUREUX: Following Báez, General Luperón took another turn at the presidency and was replaced by his lieutenant, Ulises Heureux, who was popularly known as "Lilís." Although he increased the large foreign debt tenfold, Heureux achieved political stability and modernized the economy during his 17 dictatorial years at the helm. All of this came at a high price. Despite a semblance of elections and a facade of constitutional government, he destroyed the party system, ruthlessly persecuted any opposition, and established a national and international network of spies and informers. As he became more ruthless and authoritarian, his popularity waned. It was finally greed that brought him down. Heureux negotiated an agreement lending Samaná Bay to a Dutch Bank and giving preferential treatment to the Americans. European criticism caused the agreement's collapse but led to the nation's bankruptcy in the late 1890s. The last of five coup attempts was successful when, in July 1899, Heureux was shot and killed at a public gathering by Ramon Cáceres, an opposition leader.

POLITICAL FACTIONALISM: Between 1899 and 1906, the country polarized into two competing factions: *Horacistas*, followers of Horacio Vásquez, and the *Jimenistas*, followers of Juan Isidro Jiménez. These were nicknamed *bolos* and *rabudos* after two types of fighting cocks. The conflict further reduced the economy. With the dawn of the 20th century, a new era of relations with the US began. In 1904 President Theodore "big stick" Roosevelt pronounced a new order of relations with the Caribbean. The Roosevelt Corollary to the Monroe Doctrine made the US an "international police power."

In 1907, the entire country was placed under receivership by Theodore Roosevelt who, sensing an opportunity to expand US influence, negotiated an agreement whereby the US would administer the now $40 million Dominican debt by collecting and distributing customs duties. Under its terms, the US would collect the export customs duties (the principal source of government revenue) and deliver 45% of them to the Dominican government while using the remainder to pay off the external debt. The 1905 agreement, signed by then-president Carlos Morales, was followed by a 1907 treaty, which required the US to approve any decision to expand the debt. Heureux's assassin, Ramón Cáceres, became president in 1908, bringing with him a brief era of reform and modernization. Following tradition, he too was assassinated in 1911. During the course of the ensuing civil war, Juan Isidro Jiménez became president.

THE US INVADES: Given the continued degeneration of the Dominican political system, coupled with the spread of German influence in Haiti, the Wilson administration was watching events carefully. On May 16, 1916, Jiménez was impeached by the Dominican Congress and a rebellion followed. That same year American troops landed and began an eight-year occupation under martial law. Divided, the Dominican politicians continued their fratricidal conflicts rather than banding together to oppose the invasion. Press freedom was restricted, and US publications with articles about the nation were banned. Although patriots rebelled, they were forcibly put down. Marines engaged in rape, murder and torture on numerous occasions. Many of the officers were from the South and faced an opposition largely black and mulatto.

US private investors supplied funds for schools and sanitation systems. A highway system was built. The Tariff Act of 1920 reduced tariffs dramatically, flooding the nation with US imports and costing the government badly needed revenue. Baseball was introduced, and social reforms were instituted, but most measures were short-lived. One legacy, which was to have unfortunate consequences, was the institution of a Marine-trained *Guardia Nacional Dominicana* (Dominican National Guard), the first formally trained and organized military force in the nation's history.

In 1921 Charles Evans Hughes, Harding's Secretary of State, negotiated the Hughes-Peynado agreement, which permitted US departure and the accession of sugar king Juan Batista Vicini to the head of a provisional government. After elections in 1924 that left newly elected but aging General Horacio Vásquez in charge, the Marines exited.

THE RISE OF TRUJILLO: For six years everything went relatively smoothly. Vásquez prolonged his term from four to six years, then repealed the ban on re-election. But in 1930 a revolt was spearheaded from Santiago. With the tacit support of the head of the new National Guard – a young but ruthlessly clever fellow named Rafael Trujillo – the rebels toppled Vásquez. Trujillo first encouraged rebel leader Rafael Estrella Ureña to run for president and then "convinced" him to run for vice-president. Winning the 1930 elections with more votes than there were eligible voters, Trujillo began his metamorphosis into the persona of Generalissimo Doctor Rafael Leonidas Trujillo Molina, Benefactor de la Patria y Padre de la Patria Nueva.

Trujillo was born in the little village of San Cristóbal in 1891. He worked first as a telegraph operator with a gang of hoods nicknamed "the 44," and then as a weigher at sugar estates before entering the National Guard in 1918. He had been promoted to Lieutenant Colonel and Chief of Staff by Vásquez in 1924, and he was further elevated to Brigadier General and Chief of the National Army – the successor to the National Guard – in 1927.

THE TRUJILLO ERA: After taking power, Trujillo established a reputation that made his name synonymous with totalitarianism. In the history of the Western Hemisphere there has never been a dictator more ruthless or bloodthirsty than Trujillo; it is estimated that more than half a million people were executed during his rule. One night in 1937, under Trujillo's orders, his troops massacred 12-25,000 Haitians whom he had invited in to work on his sugar plantations.

La Trinitaria

The Dominican liberation movement drew its inspiration directly from the Catholic Church. The structure of La Trinitaria, which had three-member cells, was based on the concept of the Holy Trinity. Their sacramental motto was "Dios, Patria y Libertad" – God, Country, and Liberty; this later became the motto on the republic's coat of arms. Its flag and shield featured a cross and an open bible. The leaders couched their struggle in religious terms.

More than any other leader in the history of the Dominican Republic, Trujillo shaped and, through his lasting legacy, continues to shape the nation's political, economic, and social fabric.

Trujillo dominated the nation from 1930-61 and turned it into his personal fiefdom. He amassed a fortune estimated at up to one billion dollars. Together with his family and friends, he came to control nearly 60% of the country's assets, including the majority of the sugar industry (80% of the mills), 50-60% of its arable lands, shipping lines, airlines, the national lottery, and dozens of other concerns. Approximately 60% of the labor force worked for Trujillo either directly or indirectly. As one of the two or three richest men in the world at the time of his death, he is said to have resembled Croesus more than Caesar, and a common joke was that if an enterprise lost money it belonged to the government, but if it made money it was Trujillo's.

One tragic aspect of his wealth was that the bulk of his profits were exported to Swiss banks, impoverishing the nation in the process. Although other Latin American dictators – Argentina's Juan Perón and Cuba's Batista – became incredibly wealthy and sent hundreds of millions of dollars out of the country, none was able to institutionalize fraud and monopolize economic control like Trujillo.

An incredible cult of adulation grew up around the man. Santo Domingo was renamed Ciudad Trujillo, the highest mountain was named Pico Trujillo, and the dictator became the godfather of scores of children brought to mass baptisms. El jefe's figure – in the form of busts, statues, and photos – became the regime's symbol, and time was measured in the "Era of Trujillo." All buildings were engraved with his name on their cornerstones, and excerpts from his speeches were engraved on their walls. Signs at village pumps read "Only Trujillo

Gives Us Drink" and those at hospitals informed visitors that "Only Trujillo Cures Us." A neon sign proclaiming "God and Trujillo" hung at the entrance to the capital's harbor. In retrospective appreciation of his megalomania, it appears surprising that God's name was placed first! An equally famous sign, displayed over the lunatic asylum at Nigua, read "We owe everything to Trujillo."

TRUJILLO'S MODUS OPER-ANDI: The massive hurricane of 1930 allowed Trujillo to buy up property from impoverished landowners and eliminate constitutional guarantees by claiming the need for strong centralized rule. Instituting a series of austere policies – renegotiating foreign debt, raising taxes, and cutting the budget – Trujillo channeled money into service and industrial enterprises that were controlled by him or his relatives. The Dominican Republic produced nearly a million tons of sugarcane for export to the US during the 1950s, placing it just behind number-one exporter, Cuba. In order to sustain the nation's sugar quota, Trujillo lobbied and bribed US officials. During his regime, he met with Franklin Delano Roosevelt at the White House and was praised by businessmen, a cardinal, supreme court justices, and congressmen – one of whom asserted that Latin America could use 20

men like him! Secretary of State Cordell Hull even proclaimed Trujillo "a splendid President, who is outstanding among all those in the American nations." Pan American World Airways took out full page newspaper ads in his honor. He hired lobbyists, PR agencies and law firms to propagandize for him, and even paid the Mutual Broadcasting System $750,000 to feature his propoganda as news; the story came out only when he sued because he was unhappy with the services he was receiving!

Ironically, in retrospect, this totalitarian tyrant also promoted himself as the world's "Number One Anticommunist." And, to Trujillo, all those who disagreed with his concept of "democracy" were "communists." The Mutual Security Act of 1951 permitted his regime to purchase US military equipment and weapons: the Dominican Republic received over US$6 million in arms from 1952-61. In 1953, the nation became the first in Latin America to sign a bilateral Mutual Defense Assistance Agreement with the US.

SOCIAL CONTROL: A genius at manipulation, Trujillo stacked the armed forces, like the goverment, with his friends and relatives. His son Ramfis (Rafael Trujillo Martinez), for example, became a brigadier general at the mature age of nine and later served as chief of staff of the air force. Over a hundred of his relatives served in the armed forces. Informants were everywhere, mail was censored, and phone tapping was commonplace. Santo Domingo featured armed traffic cops on nearly every streetcorner, despite a paucity of traffic, forts were built in each town of 15,000 or over, and checkpoints were established every 20 miles on roads throughout the country. In addition to carrying a *cedula* (identification card) – without which one could not drive, work, travel, marry, or vote – citizens had to carry a certificate of good conduct from the secret police.

Anyone standing in opposition to his regime was branded a communist, and even those neutral or apathetic towards the regime were persecuted as subversives. Political prisoners were arrested on the flimsiest of premises and harshly treated: a common method of discipline was to deny a prisoner any drink save his own urine. Torture techniques included electric shocks, nail extraction, castration, and immolation. No one knows how many were murdered. In order to keep the armed forces in line, firearms were secured under lock and key, and many soldiers used only clubs and machetes.

The serfs on *el jefe*'s sugarcane plantations were kept in line through membership in the Trujillo-created labor union *Confedración Dominicano del Trabajo* (CDT). "Freedom" existed only under Trujillo's eclectic definition of the word, which called for "private discernment" (i.e., restraint) under "norms of general convenience." To Trujillo, a society in which individuals were subordinated to the "common good" was one in which individuals were "truly free." Under the credo *trujillismo*, all loyalty was placed in *Dominicanismo*, a new political and social myth which identified nationalism with Trujillo. Under the "Dominican Revolution," Trujillo asserted that "all progress, to be effective, must be harmonious" – which meant stifling all dissent. These concepts gained legitimacy because, from youth, Dominicans were kept isolated and indoctrinated.

The elementary school primer, startling in its praise of the regime, was authored by Trujillo himself. It even encouraged children to turn in their parents: "If you should find in your home a man who wishes to disturb order, see that he is handed over to the police." Presented to the children as a great work of moral philosophy, Señora Trujillo's book, *Moral Meditations*, a compilation of newspaper columns of the Norman Vincent Peal genre, was compulsory reading. The entire news media was brought under

Trujillo's ownership, unsympathetic radio broadcasts from foreign shores were jammed, and the foreign news media were manipulated as well. Art was subordinated too, and artists willingly prostituted themselves. Poets, musicians, and painters represented Trujillo as God, Pegasus, the eagle, the sun, volcanic lava, and Plato. His infallibility was proclaimed in *merengues* and in a 10-part symphonic program featuring movements titled "Public Works" and "Struggle Against Communism".

GOVERNMENTAL STRUCTURE: The constitution, often termed a "parody," was amended and laws were passed to suit Trujillo's needs – even to expedite his desires for a divorce, to disown daughter Flor de Oro, and to legally enfranchise two of his bastard, but beloved, children. Government personnel were subject to extensive investigation by a "purification" commission prior to employment, continually shuffled and reshuffled; any appointed government employees, along with all judges, were forced to submit a signed but undated resignation letter upon their appointment. Similarly, few legislators were permitted to serve their full term without finding themselves "resigning." Voting was mandatory, and not voting was viewed as a subversive act.

Trujillo's *Partido Dominicano* was established in 1931, partially funded through automatic 10% deductions from the paychecks of government employees. In 1941, after Trujillo had joined the US as an ally in the fight against Axis fascism, he created an opposition party, the Trujillo Party. He then ran as its head and, when its ballots were tallied together with those of the *Partido Dominicano*, he again garnered 100% of the votes! Most of Trujillo's selected candidates were unanimously elected as well.

TRUJILLO'S OVERTHROW: Nothing resting under God's heaven lasts forever, not even dictators, and Trujillo's regime began to sag during the late 1950s. In 1956, Trujillo made a major mistake – killing Jesús de Galindez, a brilliant social critic and Columbia University professor living in exile. Several months later, Oregonian Gerald Murphy, who had flown Galindez to the US, was also killed mysteriously. The ensuing scandal made headlines all over the world. Tourism plummeted and attempts at PR damage control backfired. Plunging sugar prices and Trujillo's three unsuccessful plots to assassinate President Betancourt of Venezuela (which resulted in a trade and arms embargo by the OAS) increased the opposition's clout. Another incident, which sealed his demise, was the slaughter of the three Mirabel sisters, wives of prominent dissidents. They were murdered after they spurned Trujillo's advances.

The US, perhaps recognizing that it could not oppose Castro and still support Trujillo, began to move against Trujillo. Hypocritically, OAS sanctions were complied with while the sugar quota was quadrupled. Responding to criticism, the Eisenhower administration later levied a sugar excise tax which cost Trujillo $30 million in revenues. In order to arm himself against invasion, Trujillo borrowed from Canadian banks to the tune of $40 million – the first foreign indebtedness the nation's "Financial Emancipator" had incurred since 1947. A group of younger air force officers, who had been trained in the Canal Zone, where they came into contact with new ideas and officers from democratic Latin American nations, came to oppose Trujillo. New clerics in the heretofore sycophantic church, turned against him, breaking all ties in a pastoral letter dated Jan. 25, 1960. On May 30, 1961 Trujillo was assassinated by a seven-man hit team coached and armed by the CIA. The middle-class assassins – businessmen, politicians, and former generals – missed their opportunity to seize power and all but two of the two dozen conspirators were eventually murdered in retribution. Several were slowly tortured to death. Trujillo's iron fist was inherited by his son Ramfis, along with puppet president, Joaquin Balaguer.

FREE ELECTIONS: Under American pressure, Ramfis and Balaguer allowed exiles to return and permitted the growth of opposition parties. Instituting a series of cosmetic "democratization" reforms, Ramfis created more opposition and incurred the wrath of Trujillo's brothers, his "wicked uncles" Héctor and Arismendi. They returned from exile in Bermuda and attempted to supplant him. Taking $90 million, Ramfis and the rest of the family fled the country in Nov. 1961. A seven-man Council of State, which included Balaguer as well as two of Trujillo's assassins, was formed on Jan. 1, 1962, but was overturned by a military coup. Two days later, a counter-coup restored the Council but forced Balaguer into exile in New York City. During this period, the US poured in millions of dollars in aid and technical assistance, more per capita than to any other Latin American nation at the time. But the Council was criticized for failing to rid the nation of Trujillo-era bureaucrats, and for neglecting social welfare programs, social inequalities, and agrarian reforms.

A new spirit of democracy reigned and one of its chief beneficiaries was Juan Bosch, the fiery head of the social democratic *Partido Revolucionario Dominicano* (PRD, Dominican Revolutionary Party). Becoming the first democratically elected president in the nation's history on Dec. 20, 1962, his two-to-one win over Virato Fiallo's National Civic Union represented a victory of the people over the traditional ruling elites.

It all seemed to be too good to be true, and it was. Promising democratic, economic, and social reforms, his administration quickly ran into difficulties trying to fulfill its pledge. The Catholic Church and the army felt threatened by his administration, in particular by its promise to extend participation in the political process to Marxist groups. The Church was further alienated by his refusal to declare Catholicism as the state religion, and he also refused to snuggle up with the US Embassy. His parceling out of Trujillo's former estates to peasants enraged large landowners who worried that their properties might be next. He also offended some US officials by seeking investment and aid from Europe in an effort to liberate the nation from its slavish dependence on the US.

In Sept. 1963, after only seven months in office, Bosch was overthrown in a bloodless military coup led by Col. Elias Wessín y

Wessín. The military replaced Bosch with a three-man civilian junta dominated by Donald Reid Cabral, a local CIA agent nicknamed *El Americanito* ("the little American"). Reportedly, US President John. F. Kennedy dispatched his confidant, Colonel Reed, to the Dominican Republic to scout out prospects for a counter-coup. To his credit, Kennedy refused to recognize the "Triumvirate," withdrew his ambassador, and cut off aid. But Kennedy was assassinated only two months after the coup and his successor, Lyndon Johnson, restored aid and recognition. In exchange he received a promise of elections that would never take place.

THE SECOND AMERICAN INTERVENTION: On April 24, 1965, Bosch's supporters, the PRD and its allies – known as Constitutionalists – staged a rebellion. As the military prepared to counterattack, Constitutionalist leader Col. Francisco Caamaño Deñó sought to arrange a cease fire with US ambassador William Tapley Bennett. Bennett, a staunch anti-communist, believed that the Constitutionalists were attempting to create a "second Cuba."

With US encouragement, the military counterattacked, led by General Elías Wessín y Wessín, but on April 28 they were routed from Santo Domingo. Following the precedent set by Wilson 50 years before him, President Johnson – concerned with prevention at all costs of "another Cuba" and with sending a message to the North Vietnamese – ordered troops in that same day. Altogether, 23,000 American troops occupied the nation.

The invasion was justified to the American public by the need to protect American lives and, when that explanation didn't wash, the administration pulled from a hat a contrived list of 58 "communists" said to be hiding in the Constitutionalists' ranks. The US pressured OAS members into sending token units to comprise an InterAmerican Peace Force. But it compromised the OAS's integrity in the process by gerrymandering the vote tally through inclusion of a representative of the Dominican junta. With the exception of Costa Rica, only totalitarian OAS members such as Nicaragua and Paraguay agreed to send troops. Despite the US claim that the invasion was to protect and evacuate US citizens, its real intent was to prevent the return of Juan Bosch and the Constitutionalists.

On Aug. 31, 1965, after several thousand deaths, the war was halted when the US pressed Constitutionalist and conservative forces to sign an OAS-crafted Institutional Act and an Act of Reconciliation, which led to the appointment of Hector Garcia-Godoy as interim president. The US government showed the world how a strong nation can control the destiny of a weaker one, a heavy hand which continues right up to the present day.

BALAGUER RETURNS: Bosch was permitted to return from exile and run for the presidency, but threats to his life forced him to keep a low profile. Heading his *Partido Reformista* (PR, Reformist Party), Balaguer won 57% of the vote to Bosch's 39%, but he also spent $13 million on the campaign; the Americans – who had arrived to *prevent* Bosch from regaining power – were still occupying the nation, and there were widespread reports of fraud and intimidation. Officially, 25% more votes were cast in this election than the one previous, a statistic that curiously corresponded directly with Balaguer's margin of victory.

In a telling move, one of Balaguer's first acts after his election was to amend the constitution so that, as under Trujillo, unlimited presidential re-election was restored.

Ruling from 1966 to '78, the former Trujillo puppet president, often seen as a civilian *caudillo* (general), proved himself a shrewd administrator. His administration was characterized by graft and abuse, and he turned a blind eye to the mysterious right-wing death squad known as *La Banda*, whose 2,000 victims included three newsmen. The group, believed to have been partially composed of police and military officers in civilian garb, was allegedly controlled by national police commander Gen. Pérez y Pérez, and was disbanded after national and international pressures forced Balaguer to replace him. Re-elected twice in farcical plebiscites, Balaguer gave forth an image of exaggerated prosperity which in no way accorded with the underlying realities of a nation that was both socially and economically devastated. The US gave the nation over US$132 million during his first two years in office, and its sugar quota was upped as well. During the mid- to late 70s, he spent hundreds of millions of dollars on public works projects such as dams, roads, and tourist facilities. This "miracle" benefited the middle and upper classes, while denying pay increases to government workers, raising taxes, and stunting social welfare programs. Multinationals were given red carpet treatment – and gold mining, ferronickel, and bauxite production boomed along with tourism – but unemployment remained at an abysmal 20-25%. Peasants were forced to subsidize the "boom" through price controls on agricultural products.

On Feb. 3, 1973, former Constitutionalist force commander Francisco Caamaño Deñó, in the company of nine companions, staged an unsuccessful invasion attempt. At the commencement of the invasion, Balaguer declared a state of emergency, closing newspapers and radio and TV stations, sending troops onto streets and campuses, and detaining some 1,400 labor, political, and student leaders.

Later that year, defeated for his party's nomination, Juan Bosch formed his *Partido Liberacion Dominicano* (PLD, Dominican Liberation Party). The PRD, headed by Peña Gomez, nominated prosperous rancher Antonio Guzmán in both the 1974 elections – during which soldiers sported *Partido Reformista* flags from the ends of their bayonets – and did it again in 1978.

THE GUZMÁN PRESIDENCY: In the 1978 elections Balaguer and his clique pressured government workers to vote for him and instituted a massive PR campaign. When early returns showed Guzmán leading by 180,000 votes, military units seized the ballot boxes for the National District from the Central Electoral headquarters in Santo Domingo. Captain America, personified this time by the Carter Administration, came to the rescue. Secretary of State Cyrus Vance, together with the head of the Canal Zone-based US Southern Military Command, flew to

Santo Domingo. Under US pressure, and with the threat of a general strike over his head, Balaguer had no choice but to return the ballot boxes. After granting considerable concessions to the Balaguer camp, Guzmán became president.

The Guzmán years were undistinguished, and he was faced with rising oil prices and falling sugar revenues. Although he doubled the minimum wage – which had been frozen during the Balaguer years – the increase failed to compensate for inflation. After he doubled gas prices in July 1979, a protest by taxi drivers ended with several deaths. Guzmán then nationalized the public transportation system. In Aug. 1979 Hurricane David struck, causing a billion dollars in damage and leaving over 1,000 dead and as many as 10,000 homeless. Hurricane Frederick followed close on its heels. In Oct. 1979, the government purchased Rosario Dominicano, S.A., a gold mine.

THE JORGE BLANCO PRESIDENCY: Choosing not to run again, Guzmán was replaced by moderate-left lawyer Salvador Jorge Blanco. Running against Blanco were Joaquín Balaguer and Juan Bosch. Receiving 47% of the popular vote, the PRD victory was marred by Guzmán's suicide in the National Palace just a month before Blanco's inauguration. Through his death, he

staved off investigation of a corruption scandal involving his daughter Sonia, who served as his personal secretary. Unfortunately, he also missed the opportunity to become the first president in Dominican history to have been elected, to have completed his office without attempting to extend it, and to have turned over his office to a properly elected successor.

Sugar prices plunged to 4¢ a pound and the public debt skyrocketed to $4 billio. The International Monetary Fund agreed to loan the nation $599 million, contingent upon currency devaluation, import restrictions and budget cuts. After the government raised oil prices as dictated by the IMF in 1984, riots erupted in Santo Domingo in April, quickly spreading to 20 cities and towns. In three days of fighting, 7,000 were arrested, 500 were injured, and 100 died. Notably, the government employed the US-trained crack troops, the *Cazadores de la Montaña*, to shoot protesters. The administration disputed guidelines with the IMF for a year while an emergency $50 million loan from the US prevented the nation from defaulting on a number of major foreign loans.

In 1985 the IMF agreed to loosen its hangman's noose and lent $79 million, only a quarter of the $300 million which would have been given had the country complied with the prescribed austerity measures. In that same year judges walked out on a three-month strike in protest against the administration's failure to increase salaries and depoliticize the courtroom. On Feb. 11, in reaction to staggering price increases for food and gas, a general strike virtually shut down Santo Domingo, as well as at least five other cities. Rollbacks followed. During Blanco's tenure, despite his reputation as a defender of human rights and liberties, the government arrested and detained important labor leaders, attempted the licensing of journalists, and allegedly repressed left-wing activists. Unfortunately, despite pledges to the contrary, he failed to prune the government bureaucracy, and the number of employees shot up 40% to 250,000.

Although Blanco did not use it as a tool in the way Balaguer had allegedly done, corruption reached dismaying levels. Yet positive achievements of his administration were a low-income housing program and a literacy campaign. The final verdict on his administration is not in. On Aug. 8, 1991, Blanco was convicted of embezzling US$5 million through inflating the price of equipment purchased by the military and national police force during his last two years in office.

Along with his chief of armed forces, he has been sentenced to 20 years in jail. The sentences are under appeal, and Blanco maintains that he is being persecuted by the Balaguer administration.

BALAGUER RETURNS: For the 1986 elections, the PRD selected Jacobo Majluta, former interim president after Guzmán's suicide. Leftists within the party disputed the choice, charging that Majluta was but a carbon copy of Guzmán. The PLD again selected Juan Bosch. While smoothing over his rhetoric, he continued to champion the poor while attacking Balaguer's as well as the PRD's corruption. His 1986 campaign slogan was "Neither a murderer or a thief."

Balaguer headed the Reformist Social Christian party ticket, and brought reminiscences of "the good old days" to the minds of voters. Early returns showed Balaguer and Majluta running neck-and-neck, with Balaguer commanding a slim lead. When Balaguer claimed victory, Majluta demanded a recount. An independent commission headed by the Catholic archbishop of Santo Domingo verified Balaguer's win and persuaded Majluta that it would be in the nation's best interests to accept it. In the final count Balaguer had won by less than 50,000 votes, and Bosch had taken 18% of the vote.

Continuing to rule in his old clientelist, patrimonial fashion – granting land titles in the outback each weekend and ordering subsidized food dispensed from government trucks – the now nearly sightless 79-year-old Balaguer ran a "moralization campaign," which focused on the PRD opposition. The campaign forced ex-president Jorge Blanco into US exile.

Tourist visitations surpassed the one million mark in 1987 for the first time. New industrial duty-free zones opened but, because import-substitution industries were not expanded, basic goods became increasingly scarce, services deteriorated to the point where hundreds of people would stand in street corners to await transport, blackouts were frequent, and basic foodstuffs (eggs, flour, bread, sugar) were in short supply. Rioting began in early 1988, largely led by the nebulous *Coordinadora de Luchas Populares* (Coordinator of Popular Struggles). The organization lost support after the nation's major opposition parties and labor confederation criticized its violent approach. The Catholic Church stepped in and organized the Tripartite Dialogue; it forged a compromise that was ratified on May 28, 1988. However, business reneged on its promises and by mid-June labor confederations were again calling for a strike. The inflation rate soared to some 60% that year.

BALAGUER YET AGAIN: In May 1990, an 83-year-old Balaguer, garnering 35% of the vote, narrowly defeated an 80-year-old Juan Bosch. The extraordinary surge in Bosch's support during the 1990 campaign reflected the deep-seated dissatisfaction many Dominicans felt with the current regime and with the failure of a younger, capable leader to emerge in the nearly three decades since Bosch's overthrow.

Bosch cried foul and invoked a period of "national mourning." The controversy over the election, combined with increases in fuel and food prices, led to three strikes as well as rioting that shut down the nation for weeks. The same year saw inflation double from the year before, climbing to over 100% for the first time in the nation's history; the foreign debt climbed to more than $45 billion. Fuel became scarce and power blackouts frequent; basic foodstuffs became either unavailable or for sale only at black market prices.

In spite of it all, Balaguer continued his classic *caudillo* form of rule, spending billions on roads, housing, stadiums, the Columbus Lighthouse and the new aquarium. He remained a shadowy and iconoclastic figure. Always clad in a dark suit and fedora, he paid a visit to his mother's tomb every Sun.

THE 1994 ELECTIONS: The major candidates in this race were incumbent 86-year-old president Joaquin Balaguer, José Francisco Peña Gómez of the PRD, and another octogenarian, Juan Bosch of the PLD. Other candidates included Jacobo Majluta of the *Partido Revolucionario Independente*, who had served as president for a month after Guzmán's suicide, and controversial and outspoken priest Antonio Reynoso of the *Movimiento Nuevo Poder*, a grassroots coalition of minority parties. After he announced his candidacy, the Catholic Church suspended him as Jarabacoa's parish priest.

Balaguer took his time in formally announcing his candidacy. Donald Reid-Cabral – former Interim Government President after Juan Bosch's deposition, a member of Reverend Sun Myung Moon's "International Host Committee" – led the *Movimiento Lo Que Diga Balaguer*, a cheerleading squad exhorting him to run during the course of near-daily televised rallies.

During the campaign, Balaguer assaulted Peña Gómez's character – highlighting his Haitian ancestry. He showed news clips of him attending a spiritualist ritual (portrayed as "satanic"), and he warned that his supporters would rise up in anger should he be as-

sassinated. Television commercials portrayed a gesticulating Peña accompanied by frenzied drumming, and a map of Hispaniola in which a dark brown Haiti expanded to cover a bright green Dominican Republic. The campaign was assisted by a team of political consultants from the States. Bosch, who ran together with vice-presidential candidate Leonel Fernandez, also attacked Peña. However, Bosch's popularity had waned.

Balaguer was re-elected in May 1994, winning by a razor-thin margin of 22,281 votes. The final vote took an incredible 11 weeks to tally. Peña Gómez cried fraud and claimed that some 100,000 of his supporters were somehow omitted from the voting rolls. Independent observers cited irregularities. Balaguer's re-election proved bad news for the newly-announced total boycott of Haiti. Smuggling of oil and other goods had become widespread, and it was alleged that the same military charged with policing the smuggling were, in fact, engaging in it.

But the re-election fraud was so well documented this time that Balaguer could not get away with it. An investigation found that the names of more than 28,000 voters had been deliberately removed from the voter rolls. While Balaguer was permitted to re-assume the presidency, his term was to be limited to 1 ½ years, after which new elections were to be held. However, this was amended by the Congress to two years, which spurred a PLD walkout.

THE 1996 ELECTIONS: This time Balaguer agreed to disqualify himself as a candidate. At the time, the rightly infuriated Pena Gómez threatened to "burn the country to the ground" if he were defrauded again. The 42-year-old Leonel Fernandez – a lawyer who attended elementary and high school in New York – won the election in a runoff, defeating Pena Gómez, who received 48.75% of the vote to Fernandez's 51.25%. The margin came to a slim 72,000 votes.

Balaguer – who is blind, deaf, and cannot walk without assistance – still remains a political force to be reckoned with. In fact, President Fernandez has had a difficult time because his party has only one out of 30 senators and 12 out of 120 representatives in Congress.

THE FERNANDEZ YEARS: In 1997, Fernandez increased teachers' salaries by 92%, the highest increase recorded in the history of public education. Inflation soared that year as the government raised prices for petroleum products. Rice rose to US50¢ per pound and a poor harvest drove the price of onions to US$1.40 per pound. Power blackouts plagued the nation, and demonstrators in the towns of Naguabo and Salcedo hurled homemade bombs at police. One policeman was shot and another was wounded; six demonstrators were wounded by pellet guns. The demonstrators were demanding the construction of an aqueduct, the expansion of rural roads, and land grants for poor families.

The next elections, set for the year 2000, are likely to be contested by an incumbent Fernandez, wealthy businessman Jacinto Peynado (representing the PRSC), and an undetermined candidate from the PRD. Peña Gómez has annnounced that, owing to health reasons, he will not be running again. Balaguer may run again, if health permits, which would rule out a Peynado run.

Government

Historically, as just described, the Dominican Republic has been plagued by self-serving, megalomaniacal, and corrupt dictators who have provided the role models for political leadership up to the present. Although he has been dead for nearly a quarter-century, the shadow of Trujillo still looms large over the political scene. This *caudillo* on horseback, though despicable, nonetheless was a brilliant showman who brought a degree of order and organization to the country. Like a woman who cannot decide between two suitors, the nation remains continually torn between authoritarianism and democracy.

Today, Dominican political culture can be seen as a struggle between the authoritarian tradition of the *conquistadores* – typified by the *caudillo* and *personalismo* – and the US-influenced tradition of democratic legalism. Political parties remain dependent on a single leader and have not emerged as true institutions. No form of government has ever worked well in the Dominican Republic, but elections have been held since 1978, and democracy is now better established than ever.

POLITICAL STRUCTURE: The country is currently on its 25th constitution, one ratified in 1966. As in many other Latin American nations, the system of checks and balances, and citizens' rights that are associated with democracies, have been guaranteed by each constitution and cast aside as soon as the ink dried. The president is elected to a four-year term by direct vote, and heads the executive branch of government. He must not have been on active duty with the armed forces or the police within one year prior to the election.

Because the people have come to expect a personal and paternalistic approach from their leader,

extraordinary power is couched in the executive branch. The president is head of the public administration and supreme chief of the armed forces; he also appoints cabinet members.

The bicameral legislature, the National Assembly, is divided into the Senate and the Chamber of Deputies. One senator from each of the 26 provinces (and one from the National District of Santo Domingo) is elected by direct vote to a four-year term.

Also serving four years, the 120 members of the Chamber of Deputies are apportioned in accordance with the population of each province.

Congress meets for two 90-day sessions, beginning on Feb. 27 and Aug. 16. It commands broad legislative powers, including the ability to approve treaties, to regulate the national debt, to levy taxes, and to proclaim a state of national emergency. The president appoints a governor to head each of the 26 provinces (*provincias*). Provinces have no legislatures, nor much independence. They are divided into municipalities (*municipos*) – 96 in all.

The judicial branch is headed by the Supreme Court of Justice; its nine members are elected by the Senate. As all judges serve four-year terms, judicial independence is not maintained.

ELECTIONS: All citizens 18 years or older, and those who are under 18 but married, are entitled to vote. Voting is compulsory, but the law is not enforced. Elections are held for both local and national offices once every four years in May. The three members of the Central Electoral Board, a supervising body responsible for printing ballots, are elected by the Senate.

POLITICAL PARTIES: Although there are some 20 parties, only three are of consequence. The *Partido Reformista Social Cristiano* (PRSC, Christian Social Reformist Party) represents a fusion of former president Joaquín Balaguer's *Partido Reformista* (PR, Reformist Party) and the Christian Social Revolutionary Party (PRSC), a merger which cemented his surprise victory in 1986. While the alliance gave the Christian Socialists an opportunity to play a major role, Balaguer benefited from association with a party representing the Church and urban workers. It also helped that the party had ties with the Christian Democratic World Union and other organizations related to the international Christian Democratic Movement.

The *Partido Revolucionario Dominicano* (PRD, Dominican Revolutionary Party) offers a center-left face: it is social democratic and a member of the Socialist International. Since Juan Bosch left in 1973, it has been driven by José Francisco Peña Gómez, who headed his party's presidential ticket in 1990 and again in 1994. He is now semi-retired (for health reasons) and a new leader will emerge by the next presidential elections, scheduled for the year 2000.

The nation's third major party is the *Partido Liberacion Dominicano* (PLD, Dominican Liberation Party), which gained 18% of the votes in the 1986 election. The PLD would have won the 1990 election without voter fraud, and finally triumphed (as the result of a Bosch-Balaguer truce) in 1996. Founded by Juan Bosch in 1973, it is now let by the current Dominican president, Leonel Fernandez.

As the twin titans, Balaguer and Bosch, pass on in the coming years, the nation's major parties will probably face a shakeup. While both the PLD and PRSC spring from their *patrón's* support base, neither may survive intact in their present form. The future remains similarly cloudy for the PRD.

Economy

The Dominican Republic's export economy has historically revolved around a single crop, sugarcane, and one foreign nation, the United States. Although attempts have been made to diversify the economy, the country has been traditionally so dependent upon sugar that price fluctuations, imposed from abroad, have managed to topple many administrations. Second only to Puerto Rico as a market for US goods in the Caribbean, the country sells two-thirds of its exports to the US. One factor that has worked against the nation in recent years has been the rising cost of oil. And demand for sugar on the world market continues to decline, while internal comsumption of petroleum continues to grow.

PERSISTENT PROBLEMS: Despite the substantial sugar and import-export business, the Dominicans have remained impoverished. This is because only the elite and foreigners have benefited from the economy's largesse. Another problem has been that much of the nation's potential has been underdeveloped or undeveloped. Reasons for this include 300 years of colonial neglect under the Spanish, the political chaos of the 19th century, which continued unabated into the 20th, the chilling effects of the Trujillo years, the lack of investment capital, and a small population. The infrastructure has remained poor until recently.

BALANCE OF PAYMENTS: The Dominican Republic reported a current account surplus in 1995 of $51 million. Tourism contributed $1.5 billion in 1995. That same year, the nation's export trade volume reached $765 million, while imports rose to almost $3 billion.

A major underground source of income in the Dominican Republic has been from the transshipment of cocaine, which is first brought into Haiti from Colombia (to the tune of one metric ton per month) and then smuggled into the Dominican Republic, where it goes to Puerto Rico and then into the US. The Colombian operators, who are thought to have ties with the Cali drug cartel, have posed as Dominicans when crossing the border.

Another major source of foreign currency is the remittances sent by Dominicans living abroad; these climbed to US$1,350 million in 1997 and may grow to eclipse tourism as a source of revenue by 1998.

WAGES AND UNIONS: Despite calls by the labor unions for an increase to a reasonable RD$5,000 (US$350), the minimum wage stands at RD$1,450 a month (US$100)! Only about 15% of the nation's workers belong to organized unions. The Labor Code – in force since the Trujillo era – forbids public employees from striking. Lacking a strong financial base, unions are also divided, and many are often affiliated with political parties. The once-contentious situation at the Gulf & Western sugar refineries and tourist complex has been smoothed over since its takeover by Central Romana. At present an estimated 30% of Dominicans are unemployed and another 20% are underemployed. Over 40% of the population is between 18 and 29, and the lack of job opportunities has understandably led to social tension and instability.

THE PUBLIC SECTOR: An ironic inheritance of the Trujillo era is the extensive involvement by the government in industry, agriculture, and commerce. Although the government originally confiscated Trujillo's properties in order to sell them and terminate his family's influence, the state has ended up holding on to the properties and practicing a form of mismanaged socialism.

Today, government assets are divided into two major divisions. The *Consejo Estatal de Azúcar* (CEA – State Sugar Council) and the *Corporación de Fomento Industrial* (CFI – the State Enterprises Corporation). A deficit-laden white elephant, the *Corporación Dominicana de Electricidad* (CDE, Dominican Electricity Corporation) is legendary for its blackouts; it remains overstaffed, with poorly maintained facilities.

EMPLOYEES: Nearly half of all Dominicans are estimated to be government employees, for the most part in 23 state enterprises. Estimates in the late 1980s had the public sector generating nearly 20% of the GNP, 40% of all investment, and 40% of all finan-

cial activities. Much of the reason for the huge bureaucracy is that presidents have viewed the civil service as their private fiefdom and awarded posts galore to friends, family, and loyal party members. Despite rhetoric to the contrary, Guzmán increased the number of government employees by 50-60% and Jorge Blanco upped the ante by 40%.

THE PRIVATE SECTOR: One reason for the nation's dire straits is the attitude taken by businessmen. With no annual land tax, no property tax, no taxes on wealth, no taxes on capital gains, and loophole-laden corporate taxes, the Dominican Republic has been unable to generate revenues adequate to keep pace with its growing economy. Despite their recognition of the pressing need for fiscal and other reform, members of the aristocratic business class, appearing to lack a sense of social responsibility, remain firmly opposed to paying their share.

FOREIGN INVESTMENT: A growth in US investments has often followed US political/military intervention in the Dominican Republic. As a major source of investment capital, US firms operate some 414 subsidiaries in the country's numerous "free trade zones." These zones are not only the largest in the Caribbean, they are the fourth largest in the entire world. Most of the female workers receive no beneifts and are paid abysmally. Companies in these zones are now allowed to sell up to 20% of their products domestically. The minimum wage in the zones now stands at about US85¢ per hour, assuming a 40-hr. work week), although many workers make more than that.

Companies with substantial investments include Esso, Alcoa, 3M, Xerox, Gillette, Colgate-Palmolive, and Phillip Morris. Many fear these multinationals are striving to take over the government.

Under the Caribbean Basin Initiative's "twin-plant program," firms with operations in Puerto Rico are permitted to operate a second support facility. For example, Westinghouse employs some 800 Dominicans at around US70¢ per hour or less to work on circuit boards, circuit breakers, and other devices which are then shipped to Puerto Rico for assembly and calibration.

Although there are over 100 official trade unions in the zones, not one has ever negotiated a labor contract. The manufacturers claim that the Dominicans are happy with things as they are – low wages and poor working conditions. The AFL-CIO asserts that female employees are sexually harrassed, health and safety regulations are regularly violated, and clean drinking water and ba-

sic sanitary facilities are denied. An earlier petition in 1992 was turned down after the nation adopted a new labor code. It is generally agreed that this code is not being enforced. Although a commission (composed of government officials, workers, and employers) was instituted in August 1993, it has been wracked by internal conflict and has yet to meet!

ⓘ Did you know?
The Dominican Republic has been given an investment rating of "BB+" by both Duff & Phelps and Moody's! Dominican Republic bonds were issued in New York for the first time by Trinet in 1997 and 40% of Tricom, the nation's second largest telecommunications company, is owned by Motorola.

GULF & WESTERN: Until it sold its holdings in 1985 to the Fanjul family of Palm Beach, Florida, the name of Gulf & Western was synonymous with the evils of foreign control. Gulf & Western, through such activities as union-busting and bribery, managed to antagonize both the left and the right; many, including the Dominican Liberation Party, had called for its nationalization. Elements of its $200 million stake in the country ranged from sugar refineries to real estate and top hotels. Sometimes referred to as a "state within a state," its annual sales exceeded the nation's GNP. Acquiring the sugar plantations and refinery of South Puerto Rico Sugar Company in 1966, Gulf & Western moved to destroy the independent sugarcane workers' union. A company-controlled union was substituted. In a nation where only 14% of the land is arable and 75% of the population is either landless or cultivating subsistence plots, Gulf & Western owned a full 2% of the land area. Less than half of this was used for sugar; the rest was devoted to ranching and other export crops. The company also held a major share of the tourist industry, with its own multimillion-dollar resort complexes (Casa del Campo and Altos de Chavon) in La Romana. It also controlled luxury hotels in Santo Domingo.

In 1969, Gulf & Western set up an industrial free zone near La Romana – the first company to do so – under a 30-year government contract. About half of the companies operating in the zone were Gulf & Western subsidiaries.

frankly Fanjul: Having purchased Gulf & Western's Dominican and Florida holdings for an estimated $200-240 million, the new owners of the Gulf & Western properties have kept a lower profile. Cuban-born entrepreneurs Alfonso and José "Pepe" Fanjul made a fortune in the sugar business in Florida and maintain many ties to right-wing groups both in the US and in the

Dominican Republic. In addition to having Carlos Morales, the nation's vice-president, as a minority stockholder, they also have lent their Lear Jet to Balaguer on occasion. Pepe, who donated US$100,000 to Bush's election campaign, has dined at the White House. The Fanjuls have become notorious for their alleged underpayment of workers slaving in Florida sugarcane plantations. While conditions at their US plantations have been termed exploitative, the Dominican estates are said to provide the best working conditions in the country. "Best," of course, is relative compared to conditions on the government-run plantations, which human rights group Americas Watch has likened to slavery.

genealogy: The Fanjul's family history reads like a Cuban "Dynasty." André Goméz Mena arrived in Cuba as an impoverished teenager in the 1850s, built up a small fortune, became a prosperous landowner, and perished when he was shot by a cuckolded husband in 1917. One of his daughters married Alfonso Fanjul, Sr., a prosperous sugar broker. The Fanjul family had invested in New York City real estate and fled there after Batista's overthrow in 1959. For US$165,000 they bought a 25% stake in a company that moved a Louisiana sugar mill to 4,000

Important Dates In Dominican History

1492: Columbus lands on Hispaniola.

1564: Santiago and Concepcíon de la Vega rocked by earthquake.

1586: Santo Domingo sacked by Sir Francis Drake.

1655: Santo Domingo repels another British invasion.

1697: Under Treaty of Ryswick, Spain cedes the western third of the island to France.

1801: Toussaint invades Santo Domingo.

1809: The Spanish drive the French out.

1821: Haitians occupy the nation.

1844: Juan Pablo Duarte and La Trinitaria drive out the Haitians.

1861: President Pedro Santana announces that the nation will again become a Spanish colony.

1865: Dominican independence re-established.

1870: Bill authorizing annexation of Samaná Peninsula fails to pass the US Senate.

1882: Jesus Galván's classic novel *Enriquillo* is published. Ulises Heureux becomes president.

1899 President Ulises Heureux assassinated.

1907 The nation is placed under receivership by Theodore Roosevelt.

1911: President Ramón Cáceres assassinated.

1916: US troops land and begin an eight-year occupation.

1930: Trujillo wins the 1930 elections with more votes than there are eligible voters. Hurricane hits the nation hard.

1953: The Dominican Republic becomes first Latin American nation to sign a bilateral Mutual Defense Assistance Agreement with the US.

1961: Trujillo assassinated.

1962: Juan Bosch becomes the first democratically elected president in the nation's history.

1963: Juan Bosch overthrown.

1965: Constitutionalists lead a rebellion; US invades.

1966: Joaquin Balaguer elected president; he is re-elected in 1970 and 1974.

1978: Antonio Gúzman elected president.

1979: Hurricanes David and Frederick strike.

1982: Jorge Blanco elected.

1986: Joaquin Balaguer re-elected president; he is re-elected in 1990 and in 1994.

1996: Leonel Fernandez is elected president.

acres of remote Florida farmland just drained by the US Army Corps of Engineers. From that they built up a new sugar empire. Their net worth has been estimated by *Forbes* to be in the US$500 million range.

DUTY-FREE ZONES: First established in 1970, 300 firms operate in the nation's 25 duty-free zones. They are located in the vicinity of La Romana, San Pedro de Macorís, Puerto Plata, Santiago, Azua, Barahona, El Seibo, Higüey, San Francisco de Macorís, La Vega, Baní, and elsewhere. Foreign firms have been lured by attractive tax exemptions (75-100% on income), dirt cheap labor (37¢ per hour), the lack of unions, low-to-no customs duties, cheap rent (14¢ per sq ft per month), and other benefits. The multinational firms must pay for rent, salaries, and local supplies in US dollars through the Central Bank. Still, the duty-free zones contribute only slightly to reducing inflation and to the nation's balance of payments. Over 90% of exports go to the US; garments and textiles account for 60% of production, and footwear, leather goods, and electronic components are also manufactured. In 1990, the dduty-free zones employed some 120,000 and exports came to US$790 million.

TOURISM: Seen by some as the "new sugar," tourism has grown dramatically in recent decades, from near zero under Trujillo to 1.3 million visitors today, of whom 25% are returning Dominicans. The nation has some 25,000 hotel rooms and an additional 7,000 under construction. Today, tourism has surpassed sugarcane in importance, and now comprises some 13% of the GNP. Some leaders believe increased political stability is one of the benefits of tourism. Because civil strife or military coups scare away tourists, possibly plunging the economy into recession, politicians will be forced to negotiate rather than fight, and the constitution will take on new importance.

MANUFACTURING: Sugar refining accounts for half of the nation's manufacturing sector. Other major products are cement and other non-metallic minerals, leather goods, clothing, footwear, textiles, food, and drink. About 20% of the labor force works in manufacturing. Shamefully, in 1993, US Customs discovered illegally transhipped textile goods from China in 15 of 23 factories they inspected. China had been taking advantage of Section 907 to export duty-free goods to the US illegally.

MINERALS AND MINING: Ferro-nickel and doré, a gold-silver alloy, are the most profitable minerals. Ferro-nickel is mined by Falconridge at Bonao.

Panned since the early colonial days, gold is mined along with silver near Pueblo Viejo. The mine was established in 1973 as a joint US-Dominican venture and nationalized in 1979. Its reserves are rapidly being depleted.

About 24 miles W of Barahona in the Valle de Neiba are the major salt deposits, including a million tons of almost pure gypsum and some 250 million tons of salt. The world's largest salt deposit is 10-mile-long Salt Mountain. Salt is also reclaimed from sea water along the coast between Santo Domingo and Barahona.

Granite and marble are also mined in the Barahona region, and very high grade marble is found near Samaná. Other ornamental stones include travertine and onyx. Bauxite was once a mainstay averaging half a million tons per year, but production ceased in 1984 with the withdrawal of Alcoa. The government resumed mining in 1987; some 150,000-200,000 tons are now shipped to Surinam annually for refining. Oil deposits have been located in the Barahona region in the SW, but are as yet untapped.

LIVESTOCK: The nation has over a million cattle, many of which are descended from the smaller varieties introduced by the Spanish. One recent crossbreed is the Romana Red, devel-oped by the La Romana sugar estate. Most of the dairy-produced milk is used to make cheese. Although there are only a few commercial farms, pork is an important form of meat. Pigs dine on refuse and on nuts from the royal palm. Small sheep herds are used for meat rather than wool because the climate precludes the production of high quality wool. A source of meat and milk, goats roam the farms and *barrios*.

FORESTRY AND FISHING: An example of what unregulated logging can do, the Dominican Republic no longer has a forestry industry. Fires and indiscriminate cutting by landless farmers and loggers led to the criminalization of tree felling in 1967. Fishing is only small scale. The major fishing areas are in the Samaná Bay and off Monte Cristi where red snapper, mackerel, kingfish, and shrimp are found.

INCOME LEVELS: A 1997 survey by the newspaper *Hoy*, along with Gallup, revealed that 66.4% of Dominican households earn between RD$1,000 and RD$5,000 per month (US$70- $360). A mere 2.8% of Dominican families earn more than RD$20,000 a month (US$1,400); 2.2% of urban households have average monthly income ranging from RD$15,000 to RD$20,000 (US$1,100-$1,400).

Agriculture

THE FARMERS: Some 45% of the Dominican population are rural farmers who own small farms (*finquitas*) or sharecrop. Owing to unequal distribution of land – with the upper 10% of the rural farmers controlling 62.7% of the land – the majority must squat on private or government land. Per-acre production is among the lowest in Latin America. Wages are extremely low, and plantations that hire fewer than 10 workers are exempt from labor regulation, including minimum wage. Unemployment ranges upward from 70% in the outback, and average annual income is $700. As part of the lasting legacy imparted by 30 years of repressive Trujilloism, the farmers are fatalistic, but they have become more politically active in recent years.

SUGARCANE: Legend has it that sugarcane was introduced to the island by Christopher Columbus when he stopped off at Puerto Plata during his second visit. In fact, sugar has been grown since the 16th century, but only small quantities were grown until the end of the 19th century. Two events changed this. One was the Spanish reoccupation (1861-1865), which brought Spanish and Italian immigrants who moved into business and agriculture. Second and more important was Cuba's Ten Years War

(1868-1878), which resulted in the migration of displaced sugar planters to the Dominican Republic. Well capitalized and possessing the needed technical skills, they instituted mass production in the 1870s. Sugar rapidly became the cornerstone of the national economy.

In 1921, a banner year for production, sugar exports garnered $45 million – 423% more than all other exports combined! Sugar prices have always been susceptible to severe fluctuation. In just a few years leading up to the early 1920s the price dipped from 22¢ a pound to 2¢ a pound! The ups and downs in the market meant consolidation. By 1925, only 21 estates remained, 12 of which were US-owned, controlling over 81% of the total acreage.

All this development came with a price. Economic problems resulting have included the transfer of the domestic economy into foreign ownership, a greatly increased dependence on the international commodity market, and a decreasing capability to grow enough food for local consumption owing to the destruction of diversified agriculture in the cane-growing regions. Meanwhile, the populace in these areas were transformed from independent farmers with small holdings into a rural proletariat totally dependent on the sugar companies.

Politically disenfranchised and voiceless, the peasantry were powerless to prevent the takeover of their land and the destruction of their way of life. If the companies could not buy land, they could cheat or violently force peasants out of their tracts. Many did not have leases or held insufficient title; the land title system was chaotic and antiquated, to say the least. The legal system and laws favored large companies that could hire lawyers and surveyors. Sugar companies sometimes obtained title to whole villages. The Central Romana estate burned El Caimoní and Higüeral, two such small villages, in 1921, leaving 150 families homeless without compensation.

Even if a peasant consented to become an independent *colono* raising cane for the plantation, he would have to borrow from the sugar estate and put his land up as collateral in order to finance the transformation. One bad season and he could be ruined. Work conditions on the estates have always been bleak. The practice of importing labor (from Haiti and the Windwards) kept labor prices depressed and prevented workers from unionizing.

High levels of unemployment and underemployment have traditionally prevailed in the Dominican Republic. Despite this fact, it has been cheaper for companies to import more desperate workers from abroad – who might be paid even lower wages than Dominican *braceros* – rather than raise wages to a level which might attract Dominicans. The government-owned and -operated *Consejo Estatal de Azúcar* (CEA – State Sugar Council), which owns 12 of the sugarcane plantations, was formed to run properties expropriated from Trujillo. After building up debts of US$200 million by the late 1980s, it has launched a diversification program. The 1985 quota cutback strained relations with the US, and in 1988 the quota dropped to the lowest level since 1875.

Today, cane cutters are paid just US$1.50 per ton of cane cut, and they live under conditions that have been likened to slavery. They routinely work for 12-18 hrs. daily on the 14 *ingenios* (sugarcane plantations), 10 of which are government-owned and operated. Human rights violations are common. In 1991, William G. O'Neill, a consultant to the National Coalition for Haitian Refugees, testified that Dominican government recruiters in Haiti have duped children into working for them. These children are fed only one meal per day. It is also estimated that 9% of the nations' 250,000 cane cutters are HIV positive.

The Dominican Republic remains the largest employer of

Haitians on the entire island! The CEA remains in complete disarray, with the 1997 harvest having fallen to a fifth of its level in 1975. Rail lines and mills are in such poor shape that cane has been left to rot in the fields. Many independent sugar producers, under contract to the CEA, have stopped production because they have not been paid in the past few years.

COFFEE: The nation's second most important export crop was introduced in 1715. Most farms are located on steep or rolling hills between 1,000 and 3,000 ft (640-1,000 m) elevation. The three major growing areas are the mountainous slopes lining the Cibao Valley, the SE portion of the Cordillera Central between the towns of Baní and San José de Ocoa, and the NE slopes of the mountains S of Barahona. The nation's coffee, a variety of Arabica, is high quality but low yielding. The Dominican Republic failed to benefit from 1997's dramatic increase in prices because the crop for that year had already been sold and because production was down.

CACAO: Thought to have originated in the Amazon basin on the E equatorial slopes of the Andes, *Theobroma cacao*, the "food of the gods," has been cultivated for upwards of 2,000 years. After the Spanish conquest, *cacao* (known as chocolate or cocoa in its refined form) became an important crop and the Dominican Republic remains one of the world's biggest producers; it ranks as the third leading export crop. Much of the harvest comes from small farms in the Cibao and Yuna valleys and from the humid coastal lowlands near the towns of Sabana de la Mar and Miches.

OTHER VEGETABLES: Crops include rice, corn, red beans, peanuts, coconut palms for oil, *yuca* (manioc or cassava), sweet potatoes, limited quantities of white potatoes, pigeon peas, and *yautia* (taro). Grain sorghum is growing in popularity as an alternative animal feed. Vegetable fibers such as cotton, henequen, and sisal are also cultivated. Bananas and plantains are produced by small growers. Irrigated crops such as cabbage, tomatoes, scallions, onions, radishes, and garlic are intensively cultivated in the Constanza Valley.

Tobacco, the only other significant export crop, is indigenous and cultivation by settlers began in 1531. Production centers in the Cibao and it is famous for its quality. The Dominican Republic supplies around half of the world's cigars and, with the new fad for cigar smoking, exports have soared. The nation gained some US$100 million in 1996 and an estimated US$300 million in 1997.

AGROINDUSTRIES: Nontraditionals include citrus fruits, pineapples, chinola (passion fruit), oranges, melons, olives, cashews, and other vegetables. Dole's role is growing in the country. Dole Fresh Fruit International has invested another $41 million in the nation and intends to turn the country into a major pineapple exporter. Foreign Investment Law No. 61 limits foreign ownership of agroindustries to 49% of equity, a limit investors say hamstrings them. Ironically, despite the push to develop crops for export, the nation is not yet self-sufficient in very basic staples such as rice and beans.

The People

Caribbean culture is truly creole culture. The word "creole" comes from *criar* (Spanish for "to bring up" or "to rear"). In the New World, this term referred to children born in this hemisphere, implying that they were not quite authentic or pure. Later, creole came to connote "mixed blood," but not just blood has been mixed here. Cultures have been jumbled as well. Because of this extreme mixture, the Caribbean is a cultural goldmine. The culture of a specific island or nation depends upon its racial mix and historical circumstances. Brought over on slave ships – where differences of status were lost and cultural institutions shattered –

slaves had to begin anew. In a similar fashion but not nearly to such a degree, the European, indentured or otherwise, could not bring Europe with him. Beliefs were merged in a new blend born of the interaction between different cultures – African and European. Today, a new synthesis has arisen in language, society, crafts, and religion.

INDIGENOUS INFLUENCES: Although the Indians have long since vanished, their spirit lives on – in traditions, in the feeling of dramatic sunsets, and in the wafting of the cool breeze. Remaining cultural legacies include foods (*casabe*), place names (Jaragua, Canoa), and innumerable words (such as "hammock," an Indian invention), and in native medicines still in use. Even the Indian name for the island, *Quisqueya* (Mother of All Lands), is still in use. Many Spanish towns were built on old Indian sites; the *bateyes* of the Indians became the plazas of the Spanish. A few archaeological sites remain, including several with pictographs and petroglyphs.

AFRICAN INFLUENCES: This has been the strongest of all outside influences on those Caribbean islands with large black populations. Arriving slaves had been torn away from both tribe and culture, and that culture is reflected in everything from the primitive agricultural system to the African influence on religious sects and cults, mirroring the dynamic diversity of West Africa. Although the African influence is less pronounced than in neighboring Haiti, it has still been very powerful in shaping the culture.

SPANISH INFLUENCES: Spain was the original intruder here. Although the Spaniards exited the Dominican Republic in 1821 after more than 500 years, the island's culture is still predominantly Spanish – as in neighboring Cuba and Puerto Rico. Many Caribbean islands, whether the Spaniards ever settled there or not, still bear the names Columbus bestowed on them 500 years ago. And, although other European influences have had a powerful effect, Spanish continues to be the predominant language in the islands once controlled by Spain. Major Spanish architectural sites remain in the old parts of San Juan and in Santo Domingo. The Spanish legacy continues in the form of *personalismo*, the worship of leaders. Constitutions have often been ignored, elections have been contested, and often only lip service has been paid to democracy.

AMERICAN INFLUENCES: The history of the US is inextricably linked with the Caribbean in general and the Dominican Republic in particular. Although American influence predates American occupations, baseball, the national passion, was introduced by the Marines who also laid the path for the accession of Trujillo. Television and fast food continue to have their effect, as have the migration and return of Dominicans to the mainland. The nation also remains economically dependent on the US.

Los Dominicanos (The Dominicans)

As with so many of its neighboring islands, the Dominican Republic has forged a unique racial and cultural mix. The Taino Indians, the original inhabitants of the island, were forced into slavery by the Spanish *conquistadores* and exterminated. Other arrivals over the centuries have included Spanish, Italians, Germans, other Europeans, Africans brought in as slaves, escaped slaves from the US, Sephardic Jews from Curaçao, Jewish refugees from Europe, Canary Islanders, Puerto Ricans, Cubans, other West Indians, Chinese, Japanese, and Lebanese. All of these diverse ethnic groups, intermarrying and multiplying, have helped forge modern Dominican culture.

Although most Dominicans are of mixed racial ancestry, the upper class tended to be whiter and the lower class darker. Immigration of sugarcane workers has resulted in the *mulatización* of parts of the society ranging from food and religion to language. Each of the nation's different regions has developed its own special characteristics, and these may even be divided further into different subgroups.

THE NATIONAL PSYCHE: Throughout history, Dominicans have felt a sense of inferiority, fatalism, and despair. Some writers have gone as far as to argue that the Dominicans have a fatal flaw or congenital defect that prevents them from achieving democracy and civilization. Some maintain that the Dominican complex regarding their mulatto background has also handicapped them in their dealings with the outside world. Trujillo's success as a leader came partially as a result of his promise of a release from this karmic cycle.

POPULATION: Some 60% of the population is mulatto, with another 35% black and 5% white. Today, it is estimated that some half-million Haitians reside in the Dominican Republic. A large percentage of births are illegitimate. Population density stands at around 145 people per sq km. Although the current annual growth rate hovers at 2.7%, the population skyrocketed from three million in 1960 to 6.3 million in the mid-1980s and an estimated 7.5 million today. Another million-plus Dominicans live within the continental

United States. Most have been compelled to migrate by economic necessity. The large portion of the Dominican population defined as black is the fastest-growing racial category and is largely a result of increased Haitian immigration.

CLASS STRUCTURE: Owing to turbulence within the nation, a distinct ruling elite did not coalesce until the end of the 19th century. Up until the time of Trujillo a small, elite Spanish-blooded ruling class (today known as *de primera*) had controlled the nation's political, economic, and social life. Currently composed of about one hundred families, this group thrives in Santiago, where its members are businessmen and property owners; its Santo Domingan counterpart is composed of politicians and professionals. Traditionally, they have been joined by the *gente de segunda*, who are slightly less wealthy. To their ranks have been added those who prospered in the Trujillo years, as well as a more recent group who have prospered in light industry, banking, and tourism. Encouraged by Trujillo, a small middle class – composed of military officers, government employees, businessmen, and industrialists – sprang up and challenged the position of the elite. Today, the middle class comprises some 20% of the population.

The vast majority of the population remains composed of lower class, uneducated, impoverished, and disenfranchised blacks or mulattos. Many have inadequate diets or diets that are seriously deficient. Many have no potable water available. In the rural areas, most are illiterate and unemployment rises to 50%.

DOMINICANS ABROAD: Approximately one out of every seven Dominicans now lives outside the nation. New York City has a half-million to a million of these *dominicanos ausentes* (absent Dominicans), and it is now the second largest Dominican city. Many borrow $2,000-$10,000 for the trip and some finance it by mortgaging the family house at outrageous interest rates. Many men make the move, slave and save, and visit their families once a year. Under tremendous financial and social pressure to succeed, some have turned to drug dealing as a quick way to make lots of greenbacks. Others have established themselves as outstanding members of the New York community. Many have also emigrated illegally to Puerto Rico, where they blend in more readily.

The passage is not without its hazards. Shipwrecked Dominicans just 20 miles (13 km) off the nation's coast were eaten by sharks in 1987. Despite this, Dominicans continue to mount rickety *yolas* (small boats) and risk drowning and shark attacks to cross the dangerous Mona Passage. Paying up to US$500 each, the smuggling has proved a popular and profitable business: there are an estimated 100,000-300,000 Dominicans in Puerto Rico at any one time! Soon after arrival, they pick up a stolen or forged birth certificate and learn to talk like Puerto Ricans. Then it's a simple matter to migrate to the States. It is estimated that these émigrés remit some $500 million to one billion annually, an income which is now the nation's largest source of foreign exchange.

Although their influence is such that candidates for office in Santo Domingo now campaign in New York, emigrant Dominicans have not really assimilated into the US, and their main motivation for emigration has been the relatively increased economic opportunities found abroad. However, Dominicans are having their influences: Dominican newspapers are sold on New York streets on the day of publication and popular Dominican TV series are aired simultaneously in NY and on the island.

Returning Dominicans, however, are far from readily reassimilated. They are branded "Dominican Yorks" or called *cadenús* (after the gold chains popular with drug dealers), and their children are referred to as "Joes." They are seen as bad eggs bringing crime to the island.

THE HAITIANS: Since 1915, when the internal agricultural system broke down during the US occupation of Haiti, a steady stream of Haitians has crossed the border to harvest sugarcane (*zafra*). While many have returned, about half a million remain in the Dominican Republic. Forced to work an exhausting 12-hour day at wages below the minimum, they are provided barrack housing in *bateys* – concrete or wooden structures generally lacking in light, running water, or toilets. Food is lousy and bosses are abusive. For decades Haitians have been brought across the border in *kongos* (work teams) through an arrangement with the Haitian government, in exchange for a hefty recruitment fee. Trujillo initiated the process by signing an agreement with the Haitian government.

In 1983, acting upon the request of the British-based Anti-Slavery Society, the International Labour Office sent a mission to expose the scandalous circumstances. While the report that followed was embarrassing, it did little or nothing to improve their lot. That same year "Baby Doc" Duvalier, Haiti's president, was paid an estimated US$2.25 million for supplying the workers. After Duvalier's fall in 1986, many Haitians refused to return to Dominican cane fields. In an effort to entice Dominicans into work in the cane fields, President Jorge Blanco went out and cut cane in front of the TV cameras.

Today, some 20,000-30,000 Haitian *braceros* are lured (or even kidnapped) across the border by *buscones* (recruiters), who are paid US$7-$20 for each worker delivered. Under the first portion of Aristide's presidency (interrupted by a miliary coup), the Haitian government attacked Dominican abuses. President Balaguer responded in 1991 by ordering the roundup of some 10,000 Haitians under 16 and over 60, summarily expelling them from the country.

DOMINICAN ATTITUDES: Today, Haiti and the Dominican Republic are two countries with their backs turned to each other. The long domination of the Dominican Republic during the 19th century, combined with fear of racial dilution through "darkening" and "Africanizing," has spurred on antagonisms toward the Haitians. They are largely seen as inferior serfs whose destiny is to harvest the Dominicans' sugarcane.

One of the greatest proponents of racism against Haitians has been former President Balaguer, who once refused to open the borders and ignored Haitian accomplishments in a 1984 book about

Haiti and the Dominican "destiny." He blamed deforestation on Haitians, and his administration has blamed food shortages on the Haitian presence.

Today, the Haitians find themselves in a country that requires their labor yet rejects their presence. Ironically, many aspects of Haitian culture have become integrated into lower class Dominican life, including types of food, housing, and religious beliefs. Peña Gómez, leader of the PRD (and a presidential candidate in 1990, 1994, and 1996) is also of Haitian ancestry, the son of immigrants who died during Trujillo's 1937 massacre. A final irony is that Trujillo, who cemented Dominican attitudes towards Haitians during his iron-fisted rule, had a Haitian maternal great-grandmother who settled in the Dominican Republic during the Haitian occupation.

RACIAL PREJUDICE: Although Dominicans may maintain that racial discrimination is nonexistent, there is a distinctly positive value attached to being white, which accounts in part for the prejudice against Haitians. Women commonly apply color-lightening cosmetics, and facial features in photographs may be whitened. Expressions such as "Indian color," "light mulatto," and "good hair" betray a desire to be white. Still, a black can acquire status through education and fi-

nancial success, so color does not constitute an impenetrable barrier.

MALE AND FEMALE RELATIONSHIPS: Most lower class Dominicans live together in a common law union. Often the girl is 14, 15, or even younger and already pregnant or a mother when she moves in with her boyfriend. All that's required is the consent of parents on both sides. A man may prefer to wait until a woman of higher status or lighter color comes along before he marries, and he may also live with more than one woman before he marries, often in middle age.

COMPADRAZGO: Literally "co-parentage," this important practice of social bonding resembles the system of godparents found in the States, but is much more solemn. *Compadres* and *comadres*, selected when a child is baptized, can be counted on to help out financially in a pinch. A poor farmer may seek out a rich employer to be his child's *padrino*. The employer will assent because he knows that this will tighten the bonds between himself and his employee. Or such a relationship may be sought merely to cement a close friendship between males. It is considered treasonous to conspire against one's *compadre* or *padrino* – a belief crafty Trujillo exploited to his advantage by conducting mass baptisms at which he became the godfather of thousands of peasants' children.

MALES IN THE SOCIETY: The Dominican Republic is indisputably a male-dominated society (as are all Latin cultures). The male ethos rests on a trilogy of concepts: *personalismo*, the *patrón*, and *machismo*. Stressing the uniqueness of the individual, *personalismo* values dignity and honor above responsiblility to a group and personal integrity over abstract rights and institutions. An important corollary is idealism (with visionary ideals extolled) while a correspondingly low value is placed on compromise – seen as casting doubt on the purity of one's ideals. Because individual honor is so sensitive, encounters are polite and cordial. Individuals are believed to shape the country – as Dominican history has borne out – and politicians attempt to portray themselves as dramatic and dynamic leaders rather than public servants.

Although the *patrón* custom originated under the plantation system, it permeates the entire society. In return for his guidance, the *patrón* demands unquestioning loyalty. *Machismo* (maleness) reinforces these traditional values. Males are expected to be daring, forceful, virile, competitive, and to have a sense of humor and fatalism. This image is tied to the *caballero*, the gentleman-knight of 16th-century Spain. Deriding manual labor, the *caballero* styled himself as a cultured and artistic intellectual. Among the upper classes the *macho* ideal is fulfilled through leadership, while lower class males are at the bottom of the pecking order and must demonstrate their *machismo* through sexual and physical prowess.

FEMALES IN THE SOCIETY: The Dominican woman looks to the male for her definition, and the feminine ideal is the exact opposite of *machismo*. Traditional feminine ideals are gentleness, passivity, self-sacrifice, abnegation, and identification with her husband. A dedicated homemaker, her life is devoted to the welfare of her husband and children. Unlike the male, who is expected to be sexually promiscuous, a woman must be faithful – regardless of her husband's behavior. Despite this, Dominican women are generally hardworking and self-reliant. Many must rear their children without male support. Sadly, owing to the economic situation and the lack of male responsibility for the children they father, many women have been forced into prostitution. There are an estimated 60,000 prostitutes on the island, and prostitutes have become a major export. Some 7,000 Dominican prostitutes work in Amsterdam alone.

66 Reader's Comment

"Dominican women can be as you stated. But they can also be very bossy when they know they can get away with it." – D. G., Sunnyvale, CA.

ATTITUDES TO AMERICANS: Generally, Dominicans have a favorable attitude towards US citizens. Unfortunately, many have a false image of North America and Europe, believing the streets to be lined with gold. Despite a singularly unfortunate historical legacy, there is little or no resentment. Western women, and American women in particular, are often courted by Dominican males who covet them for their "three Bs": blonde hair, blue eyes, and (most importantly) a blue passport.

THE MILITARY: Once at the forefront of the nation during the Trujillo years, the military establishment has exercised a lower profile since the Guzmán administration. While there has been a focus on a new "professional" military in recent years, the army has also been increasing its individual and institutional economic clout. The military is legendary not only for budget misuse and corruption but also for its alleged involvement in the nation's burgeoning drug trade. During Balaguer's first terms of office, many generals became millionaires, and the process of self-enrichment has continued since, despite Guzmán's attempts to reform the military hierarchy. Perhaps this will be changed under Fernandez.

A US-subsidized "modernization" program has included training of an elite counter-insurgency unit known as the *Cazadores de la Montagne* (Highland Rangers), who were used to shoot the populace during the 1984 riots. While the military supports "democracy," such as it is, it may well have a different reaction should meaningful efforts be made to pull its hand out of the till.

OTHER GROUPS: Trujillo instituted an open-door policy toward Caucasian immigrants, and large numbers of Western Europeans arrived. He hoped that they would produce white babies as a bulwark against the burgeoning blacks. Hundreds of Japanese families were recruited by Trujillo in the 1950s. They settled in many areas, but today they remain only in the villages of Constanza and Jarabacoa. Chinese arrived during the mid-1960s and invested in real estate and tourism. Today, large numbers of Syrians, Lebanese, and Turkish immigrants run clothing stores and restaurants in the cities. Refugees include the descendants of a small number of Jews (who founded the north coast town of Sosúa), a colony of 5,000 refugees from the Spanish Civil War who arrived in 1940, and 600 Hungarians who fled the Soviet invasion following the 1956 elections.

Religion

Any visitor to the Dominican Republic will soon notice the importance of religion, particularly among the womenfolk. Churches abound, even in small villages, and the country practically grinds to a halt during the Christmas and Easter seasons. While the majority are Catholics, evangelicals are playing an increasingly prominent role, and there are a small number of Jews, Muslims, and Ba'hais. Other sects include Mennonites, Jehovahs Witnesses, Mormons, *Vudu* practitioners, and Soka Gakkai International (SGI) – a Japanese "Buddhist" cult.

Catholicism

Some 93% of Dominicans are Catholics, and the Church's influence resounds throughout Dominican society. Every town, large or small, has its Catholic church, and the clergy have had an important historical impact.

HISTORY: The Catholic Church, introduced with Columbus, became a major national force only with the accession of Trujillo. *El jefe* entered into a smooth, mutually beneficial relationship with the Church. Out of shrewdly en-

lightened self-interest, he helped finance and supervise church construction, changed marriage from a civil to religious institution, permitted the Society of Jesus to return for the first time since the colonial era, and allowed clerics to become armed forces chaplains. He also signed a concordat with the Vatican – the first in the nation's history – which greatly strengthened the powers of the Church. In return, Trujillo gained a flow of positive propaganda, and the Church annulled his second marriage, while obtaining a papal blessing for his third. To many Dominicans, the Church seemed to be another arm of his government. At the time of his assassination, the Church was as powerful in the Dominican Republic as anywhere in Latin America. At the top, the Catholic archbishop, as head of an electoral commission, prevented the controversy over the 1986 elections from erupting into civil war. At the local level, the Church operates hospitals, dispensaries, schools, homes for the elderly, and orphanages.

Some priests have even espoused Liberation Theology in the past, actively challenging the ruthless land acquisition policies of the Rosario Mining Company near the town of Pueblo Viejo and the expansionist policy of Gulf & Western in the eastern sugarcane fields. The government reacted negatively: the priests were subjected to police intimidation and repression. Unfortunately, priests of this high caliber are in the minority, and the bulk of the Church's energy has been directed towards combatting progressive governmental policies such as family planning and divorce liberalization. While the Church did not turn against against Trujillo – under whose sponsorship it prospered – until the near the end of his administration, its heirarchy wasted no time in branding Bosch a "communist" during his presidency.

On the other hand, the Church did speak openly against the paramilitary units that were terrorizing the urban *barrios*. In recent years, it has also been outspoken on the mistreatment of the Haitian cane cutters. Since Balaguer's re-election in 1990, the Church has come under attack for allegedly displaying little concern over the country's economic crisis and for serving as an apologist for Balaguer. However, just before the 1990 elections and again in Dec. 1990, the Church criticized the widespread corruption, labeling it as the basic cause of the present crisis, and offering a forthright indictment of the current system in which a few elite live in unbelievable luxury while the vast majority wallow in misery, cut off from basic necessities.

PRACTICE: Catholicism here is a far cry from the dogmatic religion practiced in countries such as Italy. Dominicans have selected the rules and regulations they wish to follow while conveniently ignoring the rest. To them, being a good Catholic does not mean being dogmatic. Many strict Catholic couples, for example, have civil or consensual marriages and practice birth control. Many men don't bother to turn up in church.

ROSARIOS: These religious processions are commonly organized to pray for rain or request divine intercession in a common dilemma. An image of a saint or madonna is carried at the parade's head, followed by a person who leads the singing and carries a large wooden rosary.

FORMULARIOS **AND** *ORACIONES:* Resulting from the synthesis of Catholic and African beliefs among the lower classes, these incantations may be used to stave off the evil eye or to draw good luck; they are generally sold in *botanicas*.

SANTOS **CULTS:** Another complement to Catholicism is the half-magical cult of the saints (*santos*). Most households have an image of one or two of these, usually St. Anthony and one of the Virgins. They are grouped together with the family crucifix and designated as the "Holy Family." Saints are selected in accordance with one's needs, and reciprocation is mandatory if devotions are to continue. The relation between saint and worshipper is one of *promesa* (promise or obligation); promises are made by the devotee and carried out if his wishes are granted by the saint. Certain goods are offered to the saint, who is expected to reciprocate by providing prosperity and good fortune. Rituals of devotion, termed *rosarios* (see above), are held to obtain relief from sickness or give thanks for recovery after an illness. *Noche Vela*, the "Night of the Saints," is used to call the Saints to earth.

Other Denominations

EVANGELICOS: In recent years Evangelical Protestantism has skyrocketed in popularity, attracting both immigrant Haitians and members of the lower and lower-middle classes. Associated with the middl eclass, Protestantism is popular among family members because spouses are taught not to beat their wives or offspring nor fritter away their earnings on prostitutes and booze. It also provides the rural and urban poor a sense of emotional security in the face of a rapidly changing world. Formed in 1960 through the merger of other groups, the Dominican Evangeli-

cal Church is influential and the only indigenous denomination. Other major sects include the Asssembly of God, the Seventh-Day Adventists, and the Protestant Episcopal Church. Many well meaning US born-again Christians have come to visit, leaving behind a trail of dependency.

VOODOO: *Liborista* and the Brotherhood of the Congo are cults found in the outback. Brought to the nation by Haitian immigrants, *Vudu* (Voodoo), however, is more prevalent. As in Haiti, its rejection by the establishment has driven it underground. No religion in the world has been so misunderstood and vilified as Voodoo. It is a complex blending of African religious beliefs with elements of Christianity. Its name comes from a Dahomean word meaning "god." Worship takes place in *houm-forts*, where sacrifices are made and believers are possessed by *loas* (spirits). Many Dominicans also practice a form of spiritualism which is similar (see above). A good introduction is to visit one of the many *botanicas*, the supermarkets of spiritualism, which sell plants, herbs, oils, rubbing water, and spiritualist literature.

Language

Although a number of Dominicans can speak English, the more

Spanish you speak the better. You will be more readily accepted. Dominican Spanish is laden with local idioms, along with numerous Indian and African words. Keep in mind that the *"tu"* form of address connotes a high degree of familiarity; don't jump from the more formal *"usted"* until the relationship warrants it. "S" sounds are muted and may even disappear (as in *graciah,* instead of *gracias*). The "ll" and "y" sounds are pronounced like the English "j." And the terminal "e" sound is often truncated (as in *noch,* instead of *noche*). As a consequence, Dominican Spanish can be difficult to understand; ask them to slow down.

HISTORY: The first settlers brought the dialect of Andalusia with them. Later arriving Castillian *caballeros* had little influence on speech patterns. The Taino language quickly vanished but has left many words in the vocabulary. Haitian Creole has affected the speech of lower-class Dominicans and those living near the border. Many English words have come into the language, especially terms (such as "bar" and "leader") with no Spanish equivalent. Today, there is a gulf between the speech of the unschooled rural poor and the urban elite. Of the three regional dialects, *Cibaeña* – spoken by rural lower-class of the N Cibao Valley – is the most widely spoken.

Dominican Colloquialisms

Abur	Goodbye
Agallú	A person who has responsibilities above his head.
Arete	Earring
Apagon	A blackout of electricity or power failure
Arretao	Daring, bold
Ahora	Right now
Ahorita	In a short while
Ahortita	Sometime
A su orden	It's nothing. (Reply to "thank you")
Auyama	Calabash
Avión	Loose woman
Bandera dominicana	Rice and beans

Bija	Yellow coloring
Bohío	Thatch hut
Bolsa	Scrotum (a "funda" is a bag)
Colmado	Small corner store
¡Cómo va a ser!	Typical expression of astonishment
Cotica	Parrot
Cuadro	One block of houses
Cuero	Prostitute
Caballo	Person who is the best in everything
Calíe	Baby goat
Carro	Car
Carros de concho	Routed shared taxis
Casabe	Cassava
Catibia	An empanada (meat pie) made from yucca and stuffed
Cocolo	African American
Con-con	Burnt rice on the bottom of the pan (a delicacy)
Cutáfora	An old and abandoned woman
Chichi	Baby
Chichigua	Kite
Chopa	Cleaning woman (impolite)
Dar una bola	To bring to someone in a car
Dar una pela	To beat someone
Dar muela	To convince someone
Dímelo?	How are you?
Dí que	A connective between phrases, similar to "uh"
Fajarse	To fight, to work hard
Fritos verdes	Portion of green fried platanos
Fucú	A thing that brings bad luck
Garpántaro	Ugly. Reckless or careless
Goma	Pneumatic tire
Guácara	Cueva
Guachiman	Watchman

Guagua	Bus or van that carries passengers
Guapo	Angry
Guarapo	Sugar cane juice
Guevo	Penis
Halar	To throw, to pull
Indio	Also used to connote mulattos
Jabao	Person of complexion ranging between white and brown
Jablador	Person who talks a lot and exaggerates
Jalao	Palm sugar
Jumo	A drunk
Mabí	Small tree with a bitter bark from which the beverage of the same name is made
Mamacita	Pretty girl
Manejar	To escort, to drive
Mascarilla	Hair conditioner
Medio pollo	A cut
Mimir	To sleep
Moreno	Person of dark skin who is not Black
Papaúpa	Very important person
Pariguayo	Foolish
Pín-pún	Exactly equal
Papichulo	Come-on to an attractive woman
Prender el carro	Start the car
Prieto	Negro
Rebú	Hassle, tumult, lawsuit
Una rumba	A lot
Una vaina	Thing, affair, subject
Saco	Sack, jacket, coat
Siempre	Think nothing of it
Taíta	Father
Timacle	Brave or valiant

Toto	Female gender
Yaguazo	Strong blow
Venganza de Caonabo	Caonab's Revenge (identical to Montezuma's Revenge)
Vidrio	Small window of a car

Arts & Crafts

Dominican culture is largely Spanish in origin but has many African elements. While the Dominican Republic in its role as "cradle of America" had a cultural headstart, the quality and quantity of its artistic and literary work began to wane by the end of the 16th century. The Haitian occupation reinforced its sense of *hispanidad* (Spanishness).

LITERATURE: A number of Dominican authors wrote fine novels in the romantic and modern styles during the late 19th and early 20th century. Unfortunately, the ascension of Trujillo, the Kim Il Sung of the Caribbean, stymied the nation's culture. Since the late 1960s a movement known as *la nueva ola*, the new wave, has emerged.

ART AND ARTISTS: Dominicans have been influenced by US trends and schools. Indian and African influences are also found in the work. Some Spanish-born painters have become naturalized Dominicans; the most famous is the late José Vela Zanetti. Clara Ledesema is renowned for her landscapes and portraits. Ada Balcácer is noted for her sculptural pen drawings. Others of note include painters Jaime Colson, Darío Suro, Mario Cruz, Aquiles Antonio Azar, Fernando Peña Defillo, Guillo Pérez, and wood sculptor Domingo Liz. A visit to the fine art museum in Santo Domingo is a must.

Music & Dance

As holds true on islands all over the Caribbean, Dominican music and dance combine African and European elements in a distinctive blend. Dancing is a popular pastime – indeed an avocation – and you may spot young boys laying down their *merengue* steps. Dominicans learn young!

MUSICAL INSTRUMENTS: Dominican musical history begins with the Taino. At least one instrument, the *güira*, has been handed down by the Indians, and musicologists speculate that *areytos* (Indian dance tunes) have also influenced the development of Dominican music. Traditionally a hollow, notched, bottle-shaped gourd played with a wire fork, today's *guira* resembles a metal scraper. The double-headed *tambora* drum is covered on one side with the skin of an elderly male goat and on the other with the hide of a young female goat who has never given birth. The drum is tightened by dousing it with local rum. The best place to hear these instruments is in the *perico ripiao* or *prí prí*, three-member bands of roving minstrels who play folk music.

Another traditional instrument, the *marumbula* (a large thumb piano which the musician sits at and plucks) is also used at times. Also of note, and used to accompany traditional dance, are the *balsié* (accordion) and *pandero* (tamborine).

MERENGUE: Dating in its modern form from around the end of WWI, the *merengue* is the Dominican Republic's contribution to Latin music. Popular in part because it is easier to dance to than *salsa*, the *merengue* has taken over many of the New York City dance clubs. It consists of three segments: a brief introduction (often deleted in practice) followed by two main sections – one of 16 bars and another African-derived segment consisting of two-bar phrases repeated over and over with slight variations.

In its rural form a *merengue* band's instrumentation consists of the *melodeon* (an accordion-like instrument which supplanted the guitar in the 16th

century), the *güira*, and the *tambora*. A *marumbula* is also sometimes used. The musical style can also be heard in Haiti, where it's known as the *méringue*. Its predecessor was the *upa*, a dance introduced by Cuban regimental bands stationed in Puerto Rico which offended the authorities and was banned in 1848. Consequently, the *upa* was matched with new steps adapted from the *contradanza*. The word "merengue" was used in songs of this form from about 1850. Nearly all merengues are fast and many are satirical or humorous. Vocals are either solo or call-and-response. It is played to a fast 2/4 rhythm and dancers move only below the waist.

Merengue típico is a form originating in the Cibao; it has some similarities to Cajun zydeco. It features accordion and *güira* as part of its lineup. The newest and most popular form is *bachata*, which combines the rhythm of the Cuban *son* with the emotion of the Mexican *ranchera*. The most famous *bachata* artists are Luis Dias, Sergio Vargas, and Anthony Santos.

Two of the most famous *merengue* bands are those of Wilfredo Vargas and Johnny Ventura. Current hot bands include La Coco Band, José Esteban y la Patrulla 15, and Roka Banda. New to the scene is Son Familia, a group that offers up a blend of *merengue*, son, *vallenato*, and techno pop. Its leader, Chichí Peralta, worked with Jean Luís Guerra, the most important Dominican performer. Guerra was born to a middle class family and won a scholarship to enter the National Conservancy. From there, he attended the Berklee School of Music in Boston, MA. Returning to the Dominican Republic, he won the Merengue of the Year for four years straight. His group combines *merengue*, *bachata*, *soca*, *salsa*, gospel, North American folk, and pop. He is now immensely popular in Spain as well as the rest of Europe. Recent albums include *Bachata Rosa* (winner of a Grammy in 1991), *Areito*, and *Fogareté*.

> *"My biggest influence is the surreal world I grew up seeing in Santo Domingo, during the time of the dictatorship of Rafael Trujillo.... I'm touched by merengue because it's the music I have in my heart, and I'm touched by surrealism because it's a belief in a perfect, impossible world."* – Juan Luís Guerra

OTHER DANCES AND MUSIC: The *pambiche* is a simpler version of the *merengue* which consists of only the last portion. Coming from the nation's south, the *mangualina* is similar to the *merengue*. The *sarandunga* is an Africanized version of the fast tap Spanish dance called the *zapateado*. *Palo* drums play during one section, and a group of dancers perform a shuffle step instead of one couple performing a tap dance. Generally it's accompanied by accordion, *güira*, and *tambora*.

Other forms also revolve around the *palos* or *congos* and the *cantos de hacho* (axe songs) of the south. The Cibao region features nearly pure, ancient Spanish *salves* and *tonados*. Their melodic qualities are similar to ancient Castilian vocal forms. A dance known as the he mountainous regions.

Festivals & Events

The nation's Latin nature comes to the fore in its celebrations. Dominicans really know how to relax and have a good time. Most celebrations have a religious basis. Many are famous, including those at Higüey and Samaná. Every town on the island has its *fiestas patronales* or patron saint festivals. They generally begin on a Frid*tumba* may still be found in some of tay, approximately a week before the date prescribed. Services are held twice a day and the atmosphere is anything but religious. Music, gambling, drinking, and dancing take place on the town plaza, and food stalls sell local specialties. On the Sunday nearest the main date, *imahenes* or wooden images of the patron saint are carried around the town by four men or (sometimes) women. Flowers conceal supporting wires, and the base is tied to the platform to prevent it from falling.

Official holidays are now celebrated on the following Monday. Exceptions to the rule are New Year's Day; January 21 (Nuestra

Fiestas Patronales – Patron Saint Festivals

Jan. 1:	Santo Cristo: Bayaguana
Jan. 21:	Nuestra Señora de la Altagracia: Higüey
Feb. 2:	Nuestra Señora de la Candelaria: Barrio de San Carlos (Santo Domingo)
Feb. 11:	Nuestra Señora de Lourdes: Distrito Nacional de Peralta (Azua)
Mar. 18, 19:	San José: Bani, San José de Ocoá, San José de las Matas, Altamira, Río Grande, and San José de los Llanos
May 1:	San José Obrero: Jaragua (Baoruco)
May 13:	Nuestra Señora de Fatima: Galván (Baoruco), Arenoso (San Francisco de Macorís), Hondo Valle (Estrelleta)
May 15:	San Isidro Laboral: Luperón (Puerto Plata), Guayabal (Azua), El Plantón (Barahona), Los Calvelinis y Uvilla (Baoruco), El Llano (Estrelleta), Sanate y La Enea (Higüey), Las Caobas (Santiago Rodriguez)
May 30:	San Fernando Rey: Monte Cristi
June 13:	San Antonio: Sosúa, El Bonao (Higüey), La Lanza (Barahona), Tamayo and El Estero (Baoruco), Villa Riva (San Francisco de Macorís), Monción (Santiago Rodriguez), Villa Bohechío (San Juan de la Manguana), Tenares, Monte Plata, Laguna Salada (Valverde) & Miches.
June 14-24:	San Juan Batista: San Juan de la Manguana, Baní
June 29:	San Pedro Apostol: San Pedro de Macorís, Las Salinas (Barahona), Pedro Sanchéz (El Seibo), Jobo Palmarejo (Santiago Rodríguez, El Cercado (San Juan de la Maguana), El Plátano (Cotuí)
June 30:	San Pedro and San Pablo: Villa González (Santiago) and Bonagua (Moca)

July 4:	Santa Isabel: Isabela (Puerto Plata)
July 5:	San Felipe: Puerto Plata
July 15 :	Nuestra Señora del Carmen: Jabaracoa, Padre las Casas (Azua), El Palmar (Baoruco), Trinitario (Djabón), Castillo (San Francisco de Macorís), Gaspar Hernandéz, José Contreras, and Cayetanao Germosén (Moca), Duvergé (Jimani), Los Amacigos (Santiago Rodríguez), Honduras and Majagual (Samaná), and Platanal (Cotuí)
July 22:	Santiago Apostol: Santiago, Paya (Baní)
July 25:	San Cristóbal: San Cristóbal
Aug. 2:	Nuestra Señora de Los Angeles: Atabelero (San Francisco de Macorís)
Aug. 3:	San Augustin: Bajos de Haina
Aug. 10:	San Lorenzo: Guayabín (Monte Cristi)
Aug. 11:	Santa Filomena: Rinconito (Estrelleta)
Aug. 15:	Nuestra Señora de Antigua: La Vega
	Nuestra Señora de Agua Santa: Sabana Grande de Boyá (San Cristobal)
Aug. 16:	San Roque: Jaibón Laguna Salada (Valverde)
Aug. 22:	Corazon de Maria: Chaquey Abajo (Cotuí)
Aug. 24:	San Bartolemé: Neiba (Baorucu)
Aug. 30:	Santa Rosa de Lima: La Romana
Aug. 31:	Santa Rosa and San Ramon: Partido (Dajabón)
Sept. 8:	Nuestra Señora de los Remedios: Azua, Cabral (Barahona), El Limón (Jimaní), Naranjo (San Juan de la Maguana)
Sept. 14:	Santisma Cruz: Mao (Valverde)
Oct. 1-4:	San Francisco: Bánica (Santiago Rodriguez)
Oct. 4:	San Francisco: Las Rosas (Dajabón), Azlor (San Francisco de Macorís) Nuestra Señora del Rosario: Barahona, Moca, Dajabón
Oct. 14:	Santa Rosa de Jesús: Elías Piña
Oct. 24:	San Rafael, Boca Chica
Oct. 15:	Santa Teresa de Avila: Comendador (Elías Piña)

Oct. 23-24:	Bambula (San Rafael): **Samaná**
Nov. 1:	Todos los Santos: Maguana (San Juan de Maguana)
Nov. 13:	Santa Lucia: Las Matas de Farfán (San Juan)
Nov. 18:	Nuestra Señora de la Esperanza: (Valverde)
	Virgen del Amparo: Polo (Barahona)
Nov. 21:	Nuestra Senora de Regla: Baní
Nov. 30:	San Andrés: Andrés (Boca Chica)

Señora de la Altagracia – the nation's patron saint); Independence Day (August 16); Restoration Day (February 27 – true only when it coincides with change of government every four years); Virgen de las Mercedes (September 24); Christmas Day (December 25); Corpus Christi (remains on a Thursday in May); and Good Friday. When Labor Day falls on a Sunday, the following Monday becomes a holiday.

JANUARY

New Year: The evening before *día de año nuevo*, the place to be is Santo Domingo, where thousands assemble along the Malecón, the capital's seaside boulevard. Bands blast *merengue*, fireworks explode overhead, and sirens sound. The partying continues until the sun rises over the Caribbean.

On New Year's Day, the town of Bayaguana (NE of Santo Domingo) holds the *Festividades del Santo Cristo de Bayaguana*, which includes a mass, procession, dancing, singing, and other folkloric activities.

Epifanía (Día de los Santos Reyes): Held on Jan. 6, this event denotes the end of the Christmas season. As with the North American Christmas, the parents lay out the gifts while the children sleep. In many places, including Santo Domingo, there are processions featuring the Three Kings. The night before, children traditionally place boxes of grass along with candies and cigarettes under their beds to await the arrival of the Three Kings: Gaspar, Melchor, and Baltazar. After the camels eat all the grass, the kings leave presents in the now-empty boxes.

Las Noches de Vela: A synthesis between the African-derived popular religion and formal Catholic liturgy, this night of vigil (*vela*) is performed in San José de Ocoa, Monte Plata, Villa Altagracia, Pedernales, Paraiso, and los Bajos de Haina around the 20th of Jan. In honor of the Virgin of Altagracia, the spiritual mother of Dominican *pueblos*, prayers are recited, hymns are sung, music is played, and everybody dances. Instruments used include *panderos* (tambourines), *güiras* (scrapers), *atabales* (kettledrums), *tamboras* (hand drums), and *maracas*. The next day is the festival of the **Virgin of Altagracia** in Higüey when thousands of pilgrims converge on the basilica. The following Saturday, services are held at Los Zapatos church in Río Arriba. *Salves* ("Hail Mary!" chants) here are accompanied by *panderos* and *güiras*.

Día de Duarte: The celebration of the birthday of this national hero, born in Santo Domingo on Jan. 26, 1814, involves 21-gun salutes, flying the Dominican flag, services, and floral offerings. A *Carnavál Popular* is held this day in Santiago, Samaná, La Vega, Cotuí, Monte Cristi, San Pedro de Macorís, Bonao, and La Romana.

FEBRUARY

Ga Gá: Of Haitian origin, the *gagá*, a carnival-like mystical religious celebration, takes place in the *bateyes* or sugarcane villages. Known in Haiti as *rara*, it has become especially popular in the areas around Haina, Boca Chica, and Barahona. Here it is celebrated not only by Haitians but by thousands of Dominicans and represents a synthesis of Haitian and Dominican cultures.

The celebration parallels *Miercoles de Ceniza* (Ash Wednesday) in February. Festivities also take place in selected locations (Barahona and Boca Chica to name a few) on or around Mar. 28 as part of Holy Week.

Carnavál: This is widely celebrated in the days surrounding Feb. 27, Independence Day, which often falls around Lent. Over half a million participate in

National Holidays

Jan. 1:.	New Year's Day · · · · · · · · · ·
Jan. 21:	Day of Our Lady of Altagracia · · · ·
Jan. 26:	Birthday of Juan Pablo Duarte · · · ·
Feb. 27:	Independence Day · · · · · · · · ·
Mar.-April:	Good Friday (movable) · · · · · · ·
May 1:	Labor Day · · · · · · · · · · ·
June 17:.	Corpus Christi · · · · · · · · · ·
July 16:	Foundation of Sociedad la Trinitaria ·
Aug. 16:.	Dominican Restoration Day · · · · ·
Sept. 24:	Feast of Our Lady of Mercy · · · · · ·
Dec. 25:.	Christmas Day · · · · · · · · ·

Santo Domingo, and the highlight is a parade of some 30,000 down Santo Domingo's Malecón. Another prominent celebration is held in Santiago and, every Sun. afternoon in Feb., colorfully costumed *diablos cojuelos* take to the streets in La Vega.

APRIL

Semana Santa: A generally somber atmosphere prevails during Holy Week (*Semana Santa*), the week surrounding Easter, when processions and pageants are held island-wide. In some places a gigantic and grotesque Judas Iscariot is burnt in effigy (*Quema de Judas*) to mark the culmination of Holy Week. *Los Cachúas*, a local version of the *Diablos Cojuelos*, takes place in the SW town of Cabral between Good Friday and Easter Monday. Costumed participants crack whips and bandy about.

JUNE

Espiritu Santo: Taking place around the first or second week of June, these celebrations involve African instruments like congo drums. The most interesting places to visit are Villa Mella (near Santo Domingo), Santa María (San Cristobal), and El Batey (San Juan del la Maguana).

JULY

Festival del Merengue: Generally held during the third week in July, this festival usually contin-

ues into Aug. so as to coincide with the founding of Santo Domingo on Aug. 4, 1496. In addition to innumerable live musical performances, events include artisan fairs, a "gastronomic" festival, the Waiter's Marathon along the Malecón, Bartender of the Year competition, and a motocross competition.

AUGUST

Fiesta Patria del la Restauración: Held Aug. 16, Restoration Day commemorates the regaining of independence from Spain in 1863. Although there are celebrations nationwide, the largest are held in Santo Domingo and Santiago.

OCTOBER

Puerto Plata Festival: Similar to the *Merengue* Festival, celebrations here, held every Oct., include live bands, tents serving food, parades, and the like.

Descubrimento de América: Held each Oct. 12, this celebrates the "discovery" of America by Columbus. Festivities are held at Columbus's tomb in the Faro a Colón and at the Cathedral in Santo Domingo.

Bambúla: Held in honor of St. Raphael on Oct. 24, the *bambúla* is a traditional African-derived dance seen only in the Samaná region. It commences in the house of the descendants of Doña Vertil a Peña. The dance can also be witnessed at the *fiestas patronales* of Santa Bárbara held on Dec. 4.

DECEMBER

Christmas: *Las Navidades* (the Christmas season) stretches approximately from Dec. 15 to Jan. 6 and is the liveliest time of the year. Marked by parties and prayers, it's a time to get together with friends. Everyone heads for *el campo* ("the country") to join in celebrating the occasion with friends and loved ones. Out in the countryside, groups of local musicians known as *trulla* roam from house to house singing *aguinaldos* or Christmas carols. *Nacimentos* (nativity scenes) are set up in homes and public places. On *Noche Buena* (Christmas Eve) most people attend midnight Mass (*Misa de Gallo*) before returning home to feast on the traditional large supper known as *cena*. Traditionally *campesinos* celebrated this holiday seated around a fire where a pig was roasted. *Manicongo* and *lerenes*, meat pies wrapped in plantain leaves and bread fruit, are eaten. Midnight mass is also attended.

The *Areito*: The vanished Taino, the first residents of the island, celebrated weddings, funerals, and conquests with an *areito*, a great celebration in which the entire village turned out. Wine (probably from fermented pineapples) was consumed along with plenty of food as the people danced and sang. Naturally, the Spaniards condemned this, particularly for the food that was wasted.

Food

Dominicans combine African, Indian, and Spanish cuisine into a distinctly refreshing mix, and the nation's island cuisine provides a unique culinary experience. It is similar to Puerto Rican, Cuban, and other Caribbean cuisines, but it has its own distinct flavor. Not one of world's haute cuisines, it is nevertheless hearty and tasteful – if a bit on the greasy side!

And there are plenty of places to eat, including a variety of restaurants large and small. There are the ubiquitous fast-food joints and a considerable number of pizzerias which serve it up Dominican style. While international cuisine is scarce outside of the resort areas, Chinese food (or an imitation thereof) can generally be found just about everywhere.

SOUPS AND SPECIALTIES: *Sancocho* is a stew made with a variety of tubers, some greens, and meat (beef, chicken, and/or pork). *Asopao* is a soup made with rice and meat or seafood. *Lechon asado* or roast pig is another specialty. Served in local *lechoneras*, it's tastiest when the pig's skin is truly crisp and golden. *Chicharrones*, chunks of crispy skin, are sold alongside. Other pork dishes include *cuchifrito* (pork innards stew), *mondongo* (an African stew of chopped tripe), and *gandinga* (liver, heart, and kidneys cooked with spices). *Carne mechada* is a beef roast garnished with ham, onion, and spices. *Locrio de cerdo* (meat and rice) is another typical dish.

TYPICAL FARE: Goat is also quite popular and *cabro* (young or kid goat) is considered a delicacy. *Fricase*, a dish made with stewed chicken, rabbit, or goat, is usually accompanied by *tostones*, plantains that have been fried twice. Another popular dish is *arroz con pollo* (rice with chicken). Similar but more savory, the *sopa criolla dominicana* includes stew meat, pasta, greens, onions, and seasoning. The *pastelón de vegetables* (vegetable pastry) is a baked conglomeration of garden vegetables and potatoes that have been seasoned and thickened with eggs and flour prior to being cooked with fat or butter.

As everywhere in the Caribbean, the staple dish is *arroz con habichuelas* (rice and beans), generally served with meat, chicken, or fish on the side, along with some semblance of a salad. While Jamaicans refer to their "rice and peas" as the Jamaican "coat of arms," Dominicans fondly dub their version "the Dominican flag." Rich in vitamins A, B, and C, plantains are boiled or mashed with a bit of oil to make *mangú* which is often served with rice and beans.

☞ *Traveler's Tip*

Budget travelers dining in local Dominican restaurants may wish to bring paper towels or napkins with them to soak up some of the grease from tostones or other fare.

VEGETABLES: The Dominican Republic has a unique range of *verduras* (vegetables), including *chayote* and *calabaza* (varieties of West Indian squash), *yuca*, *yautia* (tanier), *batata* (a type of sweet potato), and *ñame* (African yam). All are frequently served in local stews. The indigenous *yuca* (manioc, cassava) can kill you if eaten raw. It's generally boiled, fried or prepared as *casabe*, a form of bread which the first Europeans found to be an acceptable substitute. *Catibias* are *yuca* flour fritters made with meat.

OTHER DISHES: *Mofongo* are mashed and roasted plantain balls (*plátanos*) made with spices and *chicharrón* (crisp pork cracklings). *Cocido* is a soup made with meat, chickpeas, and vegetables. *Chicharrones de pollo* are small pieces of fried chicken. *Pipián* is goat's offal cooked as a stew.

SEAFOOD: Although some seafood like shrimp must be imported, many others like *chillo* (red snapper), *mero* (sea bass), *pulpo* (octopus), *lambi* (conch), and *chapin* (trunkfish) are available locally. Fish dishes served *en escabeche* have been pickled Spanish-style. *Ensalada de pulpo* is a tasty octopus salad. *Mojo isleno* is an elaborate sauce which includes olives, onions, tomatoes, capers, vinegar, garlic, and pimentos. The most famous dishes are *langosta* (local lobster), *cangejos* (crabs), and *ostiones* (miniature oysters which cling to the roots of mangrove trees).

⚡ Warning!

Lobsters are off-season between April 1 and Aug. 1. Even if you find it on the menu, do not order lobster during this time, which is their breeding period. If lobsters continue to be caught during this time of year, there will soon be none left.

FOREIGN FOOD: Although often bland, Chinese restaurants are found throughout the land. The quality varies from gourmet to grease galore, but most feature the same menu: egg foo young, chop suey, rice and beans, steak, and sandwiches. You may want to ask them to leave out the *ajinomoto* (monosodium glutamate, MSG), a Japanese flavor enhancer derived from soy sauce that, along with cornstarch, ruins the quality and flavor of traditional Chinese cuisine. Other nationalities have opened restaurants in Santo Domingo, Santiago, and La Romana. In the resort hotels and towns such as Sosúa and Puerto Plata you can find many varieties of cuisine; Santo Domingo's network of restaurants caters to the nation's elite as much as, or more than, to tourists.

☞ Traveler's Tip

If ordering at a local restaurant in non-tourist areas, be sure to ask for your seafood to be cooked sin sal. For unknown reasons, Dominican chefs appear to pour an entire shaker of salt on their fish! Also, what may be referred to on menus as "salmon" is actually red snapper.

CHEESE, SANDWICHES: *Queso de hoja* is the very milky, mild-flavored, local soft cheese. It must be eaten fresh, and is often combined with the local marmalade, *pasta de guayava* (guava paste). Many types of sandwiches are also available. A *cubano* contains ham, chicken, and cheese inside a long, crusty white loaf.

DESSERTS: Desserts are simple but tasty, if a bit too sweet. They include *arroz con dulce* (sweet rice pudding), *dulce de leche cortada*, a sour milk dessert, *majarete* (corn pudding), *gelatina* (Jello), *flan* (caramel custard), *quesillo de leche y piña* (milk and pineapple *flan*), *cocoyuca* (a *yuca* flan with coconut chunks), *bizcocho* (sponge cake), *cazuela* (rich pumpkin and coconut pudding), *tembleque* (coconut pudding), and *plátanos horneados* (baked bananas). Ice cream is also readily available in towns. Nestlé now owns the popular El Polo chain.

Fruit

Called *yayama* by the Tainos, the pineapple was brought by Columbus to Europe and was introduced from there to the rest of the world, reaching India in 1550. Dominican *piñas* are much sweeter than their exported counterpart because they are left on the stem to ripen. Thought to have been introduced around 1740, the mango has its season in May and June.

Light to medium-green in color, the Dominican orange is sweet and seedy but nearly non-acidic. Brought by the Spaniards in the 16th century, the sweet orange is known as *china* because the first seeds came from there. Vendors will peel off the skin with a knife to make a *chupon*, which you can pop into your mouth piece by piece. *Naranja* is the sour orange. Limes here are known as lemons. *Guineo* or (sweet) bananas, imported by the Spanish from Africa, come in all sizes, from the five-inch *niños* on up. Brought from southern Asia, the *platano* or plantain is inedible until cooked. The white interior of the *panapen* or breadfruit is roasted or boiled as a vegetable. Another fruit indigenous to the West Indies, *lechosa* or *papaya* is available much of the year. The oval *chinola* (passion fruit) has bright orange pulp and makes a delicious fruit drink. *Zapotes* are brown and similar to avocadoes

---

⚡ Warning!

Not all fruits are good to eat. If you see a tree with all the fruit on it, that alone should serve as a warning sign. Fruit here is invariably picked as soon as it is ready to eat. Generally, if you see unknown fruit on a tree, it is still there because it will give you a stomach ache if consumed!

---

but with a sweet orange pulp. Coconut palms arrived in 1549 from Cape Verde, Africa, via Dutch Guiana. Other island fruits include the *mamey* (mammee apple), *guanabana* (custard apple), *caimito* (star apple), *jobo* (hog-plum), and the *jagua* (genipap). The *quenepa* or "Spanish lime" is a Portuguese delicacy about the size of a large walnut; its brittle green skin cracks open to reveal a white pit surrounded by pinkish pulp. Island avocados are renowned for their thick pulp and small seeds. *Acerola*, the wild West Indian cherry, has from 20-50 times the vitamin C of orange juice.

Drinks

Delicious fruit drinks are made from *chinola* (passion fruit) and many others, including pineapple. These are generally found in small restaurants. Shaved ice is covered with tamarind or guava syrup and served in a paper cup. Cool *cocos frios* or green drinking coconuts are available just about anywhere. *Batidas* are milkshakes made with fruit. *Clamato* is clam juice mixed with water.

ALCOHOL: Locally brewed, high-quality beers include Presidente, Quisqueya, Soberante, and Bohemia. There are also a Dominican version of Heinecken and Miller, and other imported beers are actively being promoted as well. It is no coincidence that Miller is manufactured and distributed here: The Miller Brewing Company is owned by Philip Morris, the tobacco firm which is the principal shareholder in the Cerveceria Nacional Dominicana, the nation's largest brewer.

Presidente is the most popular beer and commands a premium price. It is definitely the best tasting. Others run specials: check the walls for posters.

Beers come in both large and small bottles. Prices are lowest at *colmados* (small stores), which are outside of tourist areas. Expect to pay about US$1 for a small Presidente and $1.40 for a large one. For some, the most enjoyable way to have a beer is to have it put in a paper bag and sit or stand outside the store as the Dominicans do.

The three most prominent types of rum are Brugal, Bermudez, and Barcelo. Others are Macorix and Carta Vieja. Blanco (light rum) is the driest. *Anejos* are select golden rums that have been aged several years in wooden casks. Richest and most flavorful of the rums, they are smooth and sometimes compared to brandy. If ordering in a local bar or disco, you should know that *un servicio* is 1/3 liter of rum with a bucket of ice and *refrescos* (soft drinks). Prices vary from city to countryside for this service. Whole bottles of rum sell for around $4/liter and up. Of the many brands, the author's favorite is Brugal's Viejo Anejo, which comes in a dark bottle covered with yellow netting.

Drinks such as piña coladas and banana daiquiris were developed especially for the tourist trade. Piña coladas are made by combining cream of coconut with pineapple juice, rum, and crushed ice. Brandy, gin and tonic, and cognac are also found.

CAFFEINE: Aside from alcohol, the most popular drink in the Dominican Republic must be coffee. It is served either as *café expresso* or *café con leche* (coffee essence with steamed milk), along with generous quantities of sugar. Another popular drink is *chocolate caliente* (hot chocolate). *Té Ingles* (English tea) is also available.

Eating Out

If you're only into fine dining, it's better not to leave Santo Domingo or Santiago unless you're traveling to a resort. However, if you pass up local eateries, you'll also miss some of the best food and hospitality the nation has to offer.

TAXES AND TIPS: Restaurants charge 8% value-added tax, plus an additional 10% for "service." When dining at small restaurants, locals sometimes leave an additional tip. You may do as you like; the poorly paid waitresses are sometimes genuinely surprised if you leave them something.

SOFT DRINKS: Colored sugared water is enormously popular in the nation; imbibers will find a choice selection practically everywhere. Brands include Sprite, Pepsi, 7-Up, Coke, Country Club, Mirinda, and Club Soda. *Extracto de Malta* is a malt extract drink. Milk is available in supermarkets, as is orange juice. Both are surprisingly expensive.

BUDGET DINING: You'll find no lack of places to eat. There are a number of restaurants in every town. It's best to ask locals for recommendations. In the cheapest eateries, expect to spend $2-$5 per meal. Tourist towns such as Sosúa are considerably more expensive. It's always best

to ask the price of food before consuming.

BUYING FOOD: There are markets in every town, and you can bargain for your veggies. Avocadoes and other delicacies are frequently sold on street corners. There are also plenty of supermarkets and small stores.

TIPS FOR VEGETARIANS: The Dominican Republic is most definitely a carnivorous society, so the more you are able to bend or compromise your principles, the easier time you'll have. If you're a vegan (non-dairy product user), unless you're cooking all of your own food, you will find it even more difficult. The local fruits may be your salvation. Rice and beans is a good staple, but can get monotonous after awhile. Salads (including ingredients as varied as avocado, tomato, cucumber, and string beans) are also widely available. Also try Chinese restaurants. If you do eat fish, you should be aware that locals eat it fried and that it, along with dishes such as *tostones* (green fried plantains), may have been fried in lard or in the same oil as chicken or pork. The best way to find out is to ask if something is *"sin aceite de jamon?"* An inadvertent positive result of the economic downturn is that pork has become so expensive that lard isn't used as much. If you eat a lot of nuts, plan on bringing your

Dominican Food A to Z

Arroz con dulce – sweet rice pudding.

Arroz con pollo – rice and chicken.

Arroz con habichuelas – rice and beans (generally served with meat, chicken, or fish on the side).

Asopao – a soup made with rice and meat or seafood.

Batata – a type of sweet potato.

Cabro – young or kid goat.

Calabaza – a type of squash.

Cangejo – crab.

Carne mechada – a beef roast garnished with ham, onion, and spices.

Catibias – yuca flour fritters made with meat.

Chapin – trunkfish.

Chayote – a type of squash.

Chicharrones – chunks of crispy pork skin.

Chicharrones de pollo – small pieces of fried chicken.

Chillo – red snapper.

China – sweet orange.

Chinola – passion fruit.

Cocido – soup made with meat, chickpeas, and vegetables.

Cocos frios – green drinking coconuts.

Cuchifrito – pork innards stew.

Dulce de leche cortada – a sour milk dessert.

En escabeche – dishes pickled Spanish-style.

Ensalada de pulpo – a tasty salad centering on octopus.

Flan – caramel custard.

Fricase – a dish made with stewed chicken, rabbit, or goat.

Gandinga – liver, heart, and kidneys cooked with spices.

Gelatina – Jello.

Guineo – banana.

Lambi – conch.

Langosta – local lobster.

Lechon asado – roast pig.

Lechosa – papaya.

Locrio de cerdo – meat and rice

Majarete – corn pudding.

Mero – sea bass.

Mofongo – mashed and roasted plantain balls (platános) made with spices and chicharrón.

Mondongo – an African stew of chopped tripe.

Name – African yam.

Naranja – sour orange.

Pastelón de vegetables – a vegetable pastry.

Piña – pineapple.

Pipián – goat's offal cooked as a stew.

Pulpo – octopus.

Sancocho – a stew made with a variety of tubers, some greens, and meat (beef, chicken, and/or pork).

Sopa criolla dominicana – a soup with stew meat, pasta, greens, onions, and seasoning.

Tostones – plantains that have been fried twice.

Yuca – manioc, cassava.

own because (except for peanuts) those available locally are expensive. The same goes for dried fruits such as raisins. **note:** Places serving vegetarian food are frequently listed in the text.

Sports & Recreation

Watersports

BEACHES AND SWIMMING: All beaches in the nation are public property, even if they are bordered by a resort or hotel. Some of the best beaches are found in the Samaná area. One of the better places here is Cayo de Levantado, a small island accessible by ferry from Samaná town. It is, however, a very popular tourist destination. On Bahía Rincón, Las

Galeras is a half-hour drive from Samaná town. Set to the NW of town, Las Terrenas is the peninsula's crown jewel. Both are now up-and-coming resort towns, although Las Terrenas is the most developed.

A large number of beach resorts have opened along the 20 miles E of Puerto Plata. On the E coast, the 15-mile stretch of white sand beaches from Macao to Punta Caña is punctuated by resorts at Bávaro and Punta Caña. The best beach near Casa de Campo is Playa Bayahibe. Although much of the S shore is coastal limestone shelf which lacks sandy beaches, there are several great beaches near Santo Domingo, including the popular surfing beach of Guibia along Santo Domingo's Malecón. In the vicinity of the airport and on to the E is the popular Dominican tourist spot of Boca Chica, and the resort areas of Juan Dolio and Guayacanes. SW of Santo Domingo are Playa Monte Río (S of Azua) and La Saladilla and Los Quemaditos (S of Barahona). Other beaches near Barahona, such as Playa San Rafael, can have dangerous undertows, strong waves, or steep drop-offs.

SAILING: Hotels rent out Hobie Cats and Sunfish. Marinas are located at Boca de Yuma and at La Romana of the S coast. At Boca Chica, some 45 min. E of Santo Domingo, the **Club Náutico de Santo Domingo** (☎ 566-4522) has a marina. The **Punta Cana Beach Resort** (☎ 686-0084/0886) also has a marina. Contact all of these for sailboat charters.

SCUBA AND SNORKELING: With coral reefs bordering all three coasts and over 400 wrecks, the Dominican Republic is made for scuba divers and snorkelers. There are few independent dive operators so you'll have to go through resorts. It's preferable to bring your own snorkeling equipment. Good spots for snorkeling are found along the E coast from Samaná Bay to Punta Cana (when the waves are not too strong).

dive spots: With a large reef and wrecks, the N coast at Monte

Cristi is one of the best places, but it may be off-limits on occasion from Dec. to March when strong northerlies blow. Other prime locations are the breakwater at the mouth of the Río Haina, the Silver Bank 85 miles NE of Puerta Plata, Isla de Beata (off the coast of Pedernales province), Las Terrenas on the N coast of the Samaná Peninsula, and in the Bahia de Samaná. Isla Catalina at La Romana is the SE coast's premier dive spot. You can also try Bayahibe, E of Casa de Campo. Parque Nacional Submarino La Caleta (La Caleta National Marine Park) is near the Santo Domingo airport and features the purposely sunk wreck of the *Hickory* and the reef which has sprung up around it. The reef slopes very gradually from 50-80 ft and then drops off to 120 ft. A similar artificial reef has been created in Bahía de Ocoa, W of Santo Domingo. For more information on these spots, see the areas concerned in the travel section.

scuba companies: These are listed in the specific travel sections below. Every major resort area has its own firms. If you can afford them, it is better to go with PADI five-star firms.

novice divers: Choose your dive school with care. A five-star PADI company offers better service. Your first lesson will be in the pool. The most difficult part is

Tips for Snorkelers

- Wear a T-shirt to protect your back from the sun's lethal □☺☒•.

- Place the mask on your face, suck your breath in, and inhale through your nose. While you continue to inhale, the mask should stay put. Try another shape if this does not work.

- Moustaches, a strand of hair, or suntan lotion may spoil the fit of your mask. Those with moustaches should use a bit of vaseline or lip balm to improve the seal. If necessary, shave the upper part of your moustache.

- The strap is to prevent the mask from falling off, not to tighten the seal; it should be set up high for comfort.

- Before submerging you should spit into your mask, spread the saliva over the lens with your finger, and then rinse; this will have an anti-fogging effect.

- Avoid exhaling through your nose: this may fog your lens.

- Consider bringing your own equipment or at least a mask you feel comfortable with. Of course, you will have to do so if you require a prescription mask.

- Don't overextend yourself.

learning to blow water out of your mask. You have to insert your tongue in the airpiece to block the flow and then push on the mask to expel air by exhaling through your nose. Remember, if you breathe a lot and move around unnecessarily you will consume more air and have to surface sooner. It is natural and healthy to be afraid before you dive.

SURFING: The best areas are Playa Grande near Río San Juan in the N and, less often, Sosúa, also on the N coast, as well as Macao on the W coast. The Atlantic waves at these locations are strongest during the winter.

WINDSURFING: The internationally known beach at Cabarete, 14 km (eight miles) E of Sosúa, is the nation's best site. Most resorts here will rent boards. However, prices are extremely high, and the hotels are largely all-inclusive. The E coast is also quite popular.

DEEP-SEA FISHING: A phantasmagorical variety of fish reside offshore. Permits are required for all fishing. World records have been broken. Blue marlin are most numerous on the S coast in June and Oct., and on the N from Aug. to Oct., but can be caught all year-round. White marlin abound in the waters from Punta Espada to Punta Macao along the E coast. They are most plentiful from March through June and one of the best spots for them is at Cabeza de Toro, offshore near Punta Cana, also on the E coast. While wahoo appear year-round, yellowfin tuna may sometimes be caught off the S coast during the winter, and white bonito, skipjack, and albacore appear during the spring months. Sailfish are caught on occasion. The prime area for deep-sea fishing is off the SE coast at Bahía de Yuma along the Mona Passage. A marina is found in Boca del Yuma, at the mouth of the Río Yuma, and the town holds an annual fishing tournament. Cabo Rojo and other areas off the SW tip are also good spots.

ANGLING: Bass and carp fishing is beginning to become popular in the dams and man-made lakes. Snook and tarpon can be found in river mouths and coastal estuaries. Bring your own gear.

Other Sports

HORSEBACK RIDING: In Santo Domingo contact the **Rancho School** (☎ 682-5482), the **International Horseback Riding Club** (☎ 533-6321), or the **National Horseback Riding School** (☎ 682-5482). **Casa de Campo** (☎ 523-3333, ext. 2249) has several thousand horses for trail rid-

ing and polo. The **Punta Cana Beach Resort** also features riding. The nation is well known for its Paso Fino horses, and competitions are held yearly at La Romana and at La Feria Ganadera in Santo Domingo.

POLO: Available only at Casa de Campo and in Puerto Plata. Facilities at Casa de Campo include two 300-yard fields plus two fields for stick and ball practice. Its stables hold over 100 polo horses, and lessons are offered.

GOLF: The nation has a large (and growing) number of golf courses. Two 18-hole courses designed by Pete Dye are at Casa de Campo at La Romana. Windy and therefore requiring control, **Dientes de Pierro** is a 6,774-yard course. The second course, known as the "Links," is inland and has narrow fairways. These two are said to be the Caribbean's finest. A third Dye-designed course has opened at **La Romana Country Club** to the E. All-inclusive packages are available. Another course is at the **Andres Country Club** in Andres, Boca Chica. The **Baváro Golf Resort** also has a course.

Playa Dorada's challenging 18-hole course, designed by Robert Trent Jones, runs along the ocean. Other Robert Trent Jones course are at **Punta Goleta** in Puerto Plata and at **Costambar**, on Puerto Plata's outskirts.

Access to **Santo Domingo Country Club's course may be gained through your hotel.**

The Los Marlins Golf Course is at the **Metro Country Club** in Juan Dolio. Santiago also has a golf course.

Two new courses are being constructed by Gary Player at **Talanquera** in SE Juan Dolio . The **Guavaberry Golf & Country Club** golf course in Juan Dolio will house Gary Player's golf school. Two others are also being planned for the **Resort Reina Cumayasa** near La Romana. Several are also planned for the Punta Cana-Bavaro area.

TENNIS: Tennis courts are a standard feature of all major hotels and resorts in the republic. Most courts are clay and many have night lights. Generally, pros are available for coaching. Although it probably won't be necessary, you might want to bring your own tennis balls. The major international tournament is the Marlboro Cup.

BASEBALL: This sport is the passionate and nearly obsessive national pastime, and the nation has supplied so many ballplayers to the US that currently there are more Dominican players on US major and minor league teams than from any single US state or any other Latin American nation. The game was introduced during the occupation and the Domini-

cans first took on Puerto Rico in 1922. San Pedro de Macorís is the nation's most famous baseball town and has become practically synonymous with the sport on the island.

Practicalities

WHO SHOULD COME: The Dominican Republic offers something for practically every type of visitor. Large resorts provide every amenity for the well-heeled tourist, and there are a number of inexpensive options for those on a budget as well. Hikers and naturalists will revel in the country's national parks; swimmers, snorkelers, and divers will love its waters. Most definitely a Latin American nation, the Dominican Republic is also a great place to study, improve, or use your Spanish. If you want to be in a resort area, that is no problem. But if you want to get off the beaten track, there are an incredible number of places to go.

WHEN TO COME: When you should come depends upon your motives for coming. The best time is definitely off-season when rates for hotels plummet and there are few visitors to be found in the more popular spots. The rain is heaviest from May through Sept. and in Nov., although this has been changing of late.

If hiking and/or good weather are important to you, it would

Introduction

definitely be preferable to arrive during the dry season. If you travel to the more inaccessible or untouristed towns, parks, and reserves, crowds shouldn't be a problem no matter what the season. The average visitor will *not* want to arrive at Christmas and Easter, when Dominicans themselves go on holiday or visit loved ones; hotel rooms and flights from the States are frequently fully booked at these times.

PLANNING EXPENSES: If you are planning to stay in tourist-oriented hotels and eat at resort-style restaurants, you'll be spending as much as you would for a similar trip in Florida. If you dine at local restaurants, you'll find your costs substantially reduced.

low-budget travel: Expect to spend from $15 pp, pd at a minimum for food and accommodation. Generally, you'll find yourself spending at least $30 total and, depending upon your needs, probably more. The more you can do without the cheaper you can travel. The best way to cut down on expenses is to stay in one relatively inexpensive location for a time. Also, remember that prices for imported goods are high, so bring what you need.

Arrival

BY AIR: International flights with the major carriers arrive at **Las Américas International Airport** in Punta Cauceda near Santo Domingo on the S coast and at **Puerto Plata International Airport** between Puerto Plata and Sosúa. There are four other "international" airports (La Romana's Cajuile, Punta Cana, Santo Domingo's Herrera, and Barahona), but these are limited to small aircraft. (American Eagle does fly to La Romana's Cajuile and to Punta Cana; Barahona's airport is scheduled for expansion, and an international airport will eventually be completed at Samaná.)

The best way to get a deal on airfares is by shopping around. A good travel agent should probe around to find the lowest fare; if he or she doesn't, find another agent, or try doing it yourself. Most airlines have toll-free numbers. In these days of airline deregulation, fares change quickly so it's best to check the prices well before departure – and then again before you buy the ticket. The more flexible you can be about when you wish to depart and return, the easier it will be to find a bargain. Whether dealing with a travel agent or directly with the airlines, let them know clearly what it is you want. Don't forget to check both the direct fare and the separate fare to the gateway city and then on to Santo Domingo or Puerto Plata; there can be a price differential. Although it might be more convenient to fly in to Santo Domingo and exit from Puerto Plata (for example), airlines generally will make you pay a hefty surcharge for this privilege. Taxes – amounting to some $60 – will be added to your ticket. Some of this will go to the Dominican government and the rest will, presumably, help pay off the S&L scandal. The fares advertised in newspapers can be very misleading; be sure to check them further and add the tax. Allow a minimum of two hours connecting time when scheduling.

Airlines flying here include **American Airlines** (☎ 800-433-7300), which flies daily from New York and Miami to Puerto Plata and Santo Domingo. **Continental** (☎ 800-231-0856) also flies to these destinations from Newark. **Carnival** (☎ 800-274-6140) leaves from Miami, NY, Orlando, and San Juan, PR, and **Pan Am World Airways** (☎ 800-359-7262) now flies three times per week from NYC's JFK to Santo Domingo; it also flies from Miami. **Air Atlantic** (☎ 800-879-0000) also flies from Miami to Santo Domingo.

charters: A subsidiary of Northwest Airlines, **MLT Vacations** (☎ 888-267-8349) offers winter season charter packages to the Puerto Plata area. Flights run from Minneapolis, Detroit, and St. Louis. Minneapolis-based **TransGlobal Tours** (☎ 800-338-2160) offers seasonal charters for $339-$429 RT, not including

taxes. Packages are available. While not a charter, **Inter Island Tours** (☎ 800-245-3434) offers affordable packages.

from Puerto Rico: American Airlines and **American Eagle** fly from San Juan to Santo Domingo. American Eagle also flies from San Juan to La Romana, Punta Cana, and Puerto Plata. **Air Puerto Rico** flies from San Juan and Mayaguez into Santo Domingo and also to La Romana.

from Canada: Charters are cheap and abundant; contact your travel agency. Charter companies flying to Puerto Plata include Montreal-based **Vacances Air Transat**, **Canada 3000**, and **Royal Aviation** (☎ 514-739-7000). Others are **Club Adventure Voyage** (☎ 418-687-9043; 935 ch., Sainte-Foy, Quebec), **Inter Voyage** (☎ 418-524-1414), **Vacances Tourbec** (☎ 418-522-2791, 514-288-4455), and **Voyage Paradis** (☎ 418-688-1813). The other alternative is to fly to the States first and then use American Airlines.

from Central and South America: With a connection or two, it's a cinch to get to the Dominican Republic from anywhere in Latin America. **Avianca, Dominicana, COPA, Viasa, ALM**, and others fly.

from Europe: Generally, you must fly to Miami or another gateway city and make connections. **Iberia** flies from Madrid four times a week. **Dominicana** flies from Vienna and Milan to Santo Domingo. **Air France** flies twice weekly from Paris. **Lufthansa** flies from Germany via San Juan, Miami, and NY. **KLM** and **Air Portugal** also fly.

from Britain: The Dominican Republic is among the most popular long haul destinations for British travelers. Most of the arriving Brits come with charters and package tours because these offer the best value. Check with your travel agent for deals, some of which can be incredibly cheap if you book at the last minute.

BY FERRY: A ferry service is planned between Sans Souci in Santo Domingo and Mayagüez in Puerto Rico. Contact the tourist board for details.

BY SEA: There is currently no regular service between Hispaniola and other islands. Cruise ships call at Puerto Plata and at Samaná, but these don't allow the freedom needed to explore the island. There have been repeated reports that the government plans to operate a ferry between Mayagüez (a city on the W coast of Puerto Rico) and a town (or towns) in the Dominican Republic. However, nothing has materialized to date.

PACKAGE TOURS: As they say, all that glitters is not gold. This cliché still applies when it comes to package tours. If you want to have your every whim catered to, then package tours may be the way to go. However, they do have at least two distinct disadvantages: Most decisions have already been made for you, which takes much of the thrill out of traveling, and you are more likely to be put up in a large characterless hotel (where the tour operators can get quantity discounts), rather than in a small inn (where you can get quality treatment). So think twice before you sign up. Also, read the fine print and see what's *really* included and what's not. Don't be taken in by useless freebies that gloss over the lack of important features such as paid meals.

If you want comfort, isolation, and familiar surroundings, as opposed to exploration, you may choose to stay at the all-inclusives – where you won't have to meet a Dominican who isn't waiting on you. But if you really want to experience Dominican life, you'll spend only part of your time in the resort areas and the rest traveling around and discovering the heartfelt hospitality of the Dominican people.

DEPARTING BY AIR: For some unknown reason, the $10 departure tax *must* be paid in US dollars. A similar policy dictates that you may only change up to 30% of the funds you have changed into pesos back into dollars. So, if you find yourself stuck with pesos, you will have to go out to the black market and change; be sure to bargain. With any luck, these regulations will have been modified by the time of your visit.

Internal Transport

BY AIR: Air Santo Domingo (☎ 683-8020, fax 683-8436; www.g-air-europa.es/air_sdo; e-mail info.air_sdo@g-air-europa. es), a new internal airline, began operating in July 1997 between Herrera airport (in Santo Domingo) and Punta Cana, Portillo (Samaná Peninsula), Santiago, La Romana, and Puerto Plata. Flights inter-connect between destinations. Rates are from RD$700 on up.

Columbus Air (☎ 320-6950, fax 320-6951) runs day tours between Puerto Plata and Santo Domingo. Local charters also fly between Santo Domingo's Herrera and locations as diverse as La

Romana, Casa de Campo, Puerto Plata, Barahona, and Santiago.

The major companies operating charter service from Herrera Airport in Santo Domingo are **Faxa Air Taxi** (☎ 567-1195), **Servicios Aereos Profesionales** (☎ 565-2448), **Servicios Aéreos Turísticos** (☎ 566-1696, 567-7406), **Transporte Aéreo** (☎ 566-2141), and **Uni Charter** (☎ 567-0481/0818). **Prieto Tours** (☎ 685-0102, 688-5715) operates an air taxi service to and from Portillo. **Agencia Portillo** (☎ 565-0832) provides air taxi services to Puerto Plata and Punta Cana for around $35, including transfers and a meal. A division of National Jets, the **Airborne Ambulance Service** (☎ 567-1101/4171; Av. Tiradentes 52) rents executive jets in addition to their 24-hr. ambulance service.

BY BUS: Regularly scheduled buses ply the main routes; these

Major Bus Company Phone Numbers

Caribe Tours
Santo Domingo	221-4422/5424/5518
Santiago	576-0790
Puerto Plata	596-4544
Sosúa	571-3808
Samaná	538-2229

Metro Servicios Turisticos
Santo Domingo	530-2854, 566-7126
Santiago	582-9111
Puerto Plata	586-6062
Nagua	584-2177
Samaná	538-2851

"Not only are motoconchos a prominent part of Dominican life with their abundance and ferocious noise, but tourists traveling independently and planning on doing some walking (as I was) should be aware that Dominicans find it hard, if not impossible, to believe that tourists can or should make their way around town without hiring a motoconcho to drive them. It may be difficult to get directions from people on locations farther away than a few blocks. It may be especially difficult if motoconcho drivers are close by hoping for a fare." – M.M., Minneapolis, MN

leave on time. Tickets are sold in advance. Minibuses, known as *guaguas*, run throughout the nation, though service is best along the main arteries. Passengers often sing along with the latest *merengue* and *salsa* tunes. On the rural routes, you might share the bus with chickens. Be at the stop half an hour before departure. The buses' back seat is known as *la cocina* (the kitchen) because it's a center for gossip. Buses share the roads with *públicos*, and to some destinations only *públicos* are available. Both are frequently jam-packed.

Públicos leave only when full and run from approximately dawn to dusk. Private cars (*car-*

ros) – painted red and blue or blue and white – are among the vehicles operating as *públicos*. *Público* rates are fixed by law. They'll give you a speedier ride but may cost slightly more. There are generally three of you in the front; your leg may be jammed against the stick shift. You'll ride along to the thumping rhythms of *merengue*. Be sure to settle the fare before accepting.

From Santo Domingo, expect to spend on bus fares around US$7 to Puerto Plata, US$4 to Santiago, US$4 to Barahona, US$1 to Boca Chica, US$6 to La Romana, US$7 to Rio San Juan, and US$5 to San Juan de la Maguana. Travel times anywhere within the country are reasonable, but regular buses are slow.

☞ Traveler's Tip

Be sure to have change for guaguas and motoconchos. Fees for the latter generally double at night. When taking small buses, pickup trucks and the like between towns, ask the locals what the price is and make sure you agree on the price before departure. Another technique is to guesstimate the price (through previous experience) and request a fare somewhat below that. For example, you might offer a 10-peso fare for a trip you expect to cost 15 or 20.

Keep a close watch on your things while in transit. Baggage

can be a problem. Although some buses may have storage below, many do not – including the local buses. Overhead racks inside won't hold large backpacks or suitcases so it's preferable to carry as little as possible. If you're planning to travel on weekends or during three-day holidays, obtain your tickets in advance.

bus routes: There is good bus service to all the major towns. On the rougher rural roads, fares and travel times escalate. You'll need patience! Your hotel and a shop, bar, or restaurant near the bus stop are good sources for information on bus departures. But, if you're on a tight schedule or have an early departure, you would do well to double-check.

The two largest bus companies are **Metro** and **Caribe Tours**. Because it has larger vehicles and drivers who are less inclined to speed, Metro is reputed to be the safer of the two.

BY TAXI: Cabs are meterless. Be sure to agree on the price before getting into one. If you have a group of people, taxis can also be a reasonable alternative to renting a car, but you should negotiate as well as ask around. A less expensive alternative to taxis, empty *guaguas*, hired by one person or a group, are known as *carreras*. Fares rise around Christmas. *Motoconchos* or *motocochas* are motorcyclists who take passengers – up to three on

pillion. In Samaná, *motoconchas* tow four-seat covered rickshaws. This is potentially a dangerous form of transportation: you ride at your own risk! Be careful not to get a "Dominican tattoo," a leg burn from the hot exhaust pipe.

TOURS: Those without much time or with an urge to savor a few different experiences may try a tour. Most of these include hotel pickup, meals, and drop-off and cost around $50/day. The advantage of tours is that you avoid crowded buses, you can cover a lot of territory, and your driver may be very informative. The disadvantages include the added expense, the isolation from locals, and the loss of flexibility. Tours do provide an easy way to visit some of the national parks and other attractions. In addition to those listed in the text, hotels may offer their own tours for guests.

RENTING A CAR: Owing to high import duties and operating costs, car rentals are very expensive here. A substantial deposit or a major credit card is necessary, and they may take an imprint from your credit card form with the amount of payment not specified. It's wiser to rent from the better-known companies in order to avoid getting a clunker. You can use a valid US or international driver's license here for up to 90 days, but you must be 25 to rent a car. Insurance, at around

$6 per day, is generally not comprehensive, and you may be expected to pay the first $500-$750 of a claim against you. Cars may be rented at the airports. Rates vary, but you can expect to pay around $50/day or $250/wk. for a good but inexpensive model. Don't rent a 4-wheel-drive vehicle unless you really need it to get where you're going. As you should do everywhere, read the contract thoroughly – especially the fine print. Ask about unlimited mileage, free gas, late return penalties, and drop-off fees. Check the car over for dents and scratches and make sure that the agent notes any damage so you won't be charged later.

Mopeds may be rented with ease for about $15/day in the tourist areas. Be sure to lock yours up at night, and challenge larger vehicles at your peril. Note that there is no insurance, and scooter stealing is popular in resort areas such as Sosúa.

DRIVING: The nation has an extensive network of roads. Major highways in good condition include the Carr. Duarte, from Santo Domingo to Puerto Plata (soon to be four lanes); the Santiago-Monte Cristi road; and

---

Innovative Dominican Tour Companies

Here's a partial list of companies that are taking a different approach to tourism from the booze, sun, and sex approach in vogue elsewhere.

Ecoturisa (☎ 221-4104/4105/4106, fax 685-154; C. Santiago No 203-B, Gazcue) has as its motto "to know is to conserve" and operates a number of innovative trips, including birdwatching.

Iguana Mama (☎ 571-0908, fax 571-0734; 800-849-4720; EPS - D#342, PO Box 02-55548, Miami, FL 33102; www.iguana-mama.com; e-mail iguanamama@codetel.net.do) is based in Cabarete; they offer mountain biking, hikes up Pico Duarte, and other trips.

Extra Tours (☎ 571-3106) is a German-owned tour company based in Sosúa. It runs specialized trips to select destinations for up to eight persons.

Rancho Baiguate (☎ 696-0318, 563-8005, fax 574-4940; e-mail ranchobaiguate@codetel.net.do) is a full-service hotel near Jarabacoa which offers a three-day Pico Duarte climb, whitewater rafting down the Yaque del Norte, canyoning and canoeing, horseback riding to the waterfall, trekking, mountain biking, paragliding, and tubing.

the Santiago-Dajabón road. Many of the others have potholes, broken pavement or gravel and dirt surfaces. Avoid driving at night if possible. Speed limits are 40 kph in the city, 60 kph in the suburbs, and 80 kph on the main roads. Dominican drivers can be crazy, and motorcyclists are the worst. Tolls are charged on all of the main roads from Santo Domingo. Always keep in mind that, with few exceptions, service stations (*bombas*) are not open late (most close at 6, others at 10), and many close on Sundays

66 *Reader's Comment*

"We rented a car in Puerto Plata, against your advice, I know. My husband drove a taxi to support us in graduate school, and he was exhilarated by the challenge to drive like a maniac without being arrested. My toes were perpendicularly curled for 235 km from Las Terrenas to Puerto Plata facing the setting sun. We had a big problem reading road signs and identifying the towns we were driving through. Not speaking Spanish, we at first thought most of the towns were named 'Comido.'" – N.H., Dearborn, MI.

or are open only half a day. Be sure to fill up at the main towns before heading out to the sticks where there may be no service stations. Bring a rag to wipe the inside windows in the rain. Gas is more than $2 per gallon for un-

66 *Reader's Comment*

"As I no longer have credit cards (divorce 10 years ago ended that), I am always concerned about the procedures for getting a rental. In the DR, I have rented cars and motorbikes without any problems and without a credit card or deposit, just by putting down an (expired) passport. And, yes, you are right about locking those motorbikes up in Sosúa. I know of many people who have had them stolen at night from in front of their hotel; I bring my own chain."

leaded; leaded gas is thankfully being phased out. Be sure to check the pump before they start pumping. Unscrupulous owners have been known to not start the pump at zero!

An excellent **road map** is the one produced by International Travel Maps (☎/fax 604-879-7895) of Vancouver. Unfortunately, it does not include city maps. It should be available at any good map or travel bookstore.

Road signs are few and far between, and it will be difficult to get around if you don't speak some Spanish. Road maps may be out of date, and you may find secondary stretches to be impassable. An essential reference tool is the topographic map from the **Instituto Geográfico Universitaria** (☎ 682-2680), Instituto Autonoma de Santo Domingo, Calle de las Damas, Old Santo

Domingo. You can expect to be stopped by police at the entrances and exits to towns. Sometimes you'll be expected to pay a few pesos bribe; fees rise around Christmas. All towns have unmarked speed bumps so beware!

BOATS AND FERRIES: There are ferry boats from Sabana la Mar across to Samaná town. To board or land from Sabana la Mar, you will need to transfer to and from a smaller boat. You may wish to rent a boat to explore the Samaná Peninsula. The *canoa* is a small dugout; the *yola* is a medium-sized rowboat that takes up to 10 people, while a *bote* takes 20 or more.

HITCHING: Owing to the lack of cars, hitchhiking is slow but very possible and a good way to pass the time while waiting for buses in the boonies. In places where there is no bus service, it may be the only way to get around, other than a rental car.

ON FOOT: Walking is unquestionably the best way to experience Dominican life. Old Santo Domingo is best explored on foot, and no place in the central area of any town is too far to walk. One thing you'll find everywhere is that the street names repeat themselves: Independencia, Beller, Separación, Duarte, Ariza, Sánchez, 12 de Julio, J. F. Kennedy, and so on.

Accommodations

The Dominican Republic has hundreds of hotels, with more than 26,000 rooms – everything from luxury resorts to simple inns. What you want you can definitely find. Rooms with a private bath run for a minimum of $6. The five-star hotels charge an average of $140 plus 23% for service and tax. Apart-hotels charge $50-$130 for two. If staying for a while, inquire about a lower weekly or monthly rate. If you're traveling on business, you should try to get the special *"la tarifa comercial"* rate. As the towns are small, it's not a problem to walk from hotel to hotel checking out the rooms. Some hotels and resorts will have their own generators.

TYPES: *Apart-hotels* (spelled varyingly "Aparta Hotel," "Apar-Hotel," "Apart-Hotel," or "Aparte Hotel") are rooms or suites that are fully equipped with a kitchen or kitchenette. *Cabañas* are generally cabins. A *pensión* is a low-cost hotel that may be family-run. Motels are for short-term sex and are for rent by the hour.

ALL-INCLUSIVE HOTELS: Since their inception, the all-inclusive hotels have grown in popularity tremendously. They differ from ordinary hotels in a number of ways. Whereas, ordinarily, you will pay for every meal and every drink and have to tip, in an all-inclusive you won't have to worry about handling money. You have a wide range of options available. Facilities are generally well maintained and the resorts are physically attractive. Generally speaking, the staff appears more cheerful than elsewhere, and they aren't always waiting around for a tip. If your idea of travel is relaxation and escape, all-inclusives may be your cup of tea.

But there is a down side to the all-inclusives. Because they include all meals, they deprive you of the motivation to sample other restaurants – local as well as touristic. The food may be served cafeteria-style and might not be what you would choose to have. Unless you are staying in a five-star resort, you generally won't find the highest quality rums or the nation's best beer (Presidente) served. Everything (excursions, for example) may not be included after all and there may be limits on other activities. Many all-inclusives prohibit outsiders from entering the grounds, which may be a disadvantage. The "games" and other programs can be rather irksome at times, as can the fawning, slurpy honeymoon couples – unless you happen to be one of them of course!

You should be one who wants what the resort offers. Vegetarian teetotalers can find better values elsewhere. Otherwise, you may be hard-pressed to do better. If you do stay in an all-inclusive, consider taking a few more days at the end to tour the island. If you don't, there's no reason to have come all the way to the Dominican Republic!

─────────────────────

☞ *Traveler's Tip*

If you are staying in a villa-type of resort (many of which have two stories), request the upper level for greater privacy.

─────────────────────

BUDGET HOTELS: If you're content to live simply, prices are inexpensive compared to the rest of the Caribbean or the States. Truly low-budget travelers will wish to avoid the resorts and stay in the cities, mountain towns, or less-developed coastal towns. Among the difficulties you might encounter in the very inexpensive hotels are blaring TVs, clucking chickens, mosquitoes, spiders, and cockroaches. Some of the rooms are dimly lit. Other difficulties are the irregular power supply and, less frequently, problems with the water.

In spite of these things, the smaller hotels offer a genuine Dominican experience, one which often brings you closer to the local people and their lives. Your neighbors will be ordinary hardworking folks, not tourists. Hoteliers are generally quite hospitable and, if you speak Spanish, you can have some remarkable conversations. If you try it, you'll find that you can survive quite well without a/c; a fan or sometimes no fan will suffice. Before staying in a cheap hotel, ask about the electricity (*la luz*), making sure that it has a backup generator (*planta*) and ask about continuity of the water supply. If they do not have a generator, you can expect blackouts, which are relatively frequent practically everywhere. Finally, you should be aware that some of the cheapest hotels are unmarked.

TAXES: A 7% sales tax is added to your bill along with a 6% value-added tax; all tourist-oriented hotels and resorts add a 10% service charge as well. The cheapest hotels are tax- and service-charge-free (or they include the taxes in their rates).

RESERVATIONS: Reservations should be made in advance during the Christmas season and are recommended during the rest of the winter. During the remainder of the year, they are a good idea, but you generally can have your pick of rooms. Couples should state if they prefer twin or double beds. Rooms with a shared bath down the hall are the least expensive. Most tourist-oriented hotels give a 20-30% discount during the low season. The major resorts and hotels have two or more sets of rates. The least expensive hotels often do not take reservations. Figure the total price when considering a hotel.

PRICING: Prices (generally inclusive of 13% tax and 10% service where applicable) are listed in US dollars. These fluctuate and should be used only as a guideline. Wherever you go, there are likely to be one or more newer places not listed in this guide. Local hotels generally charge per room. Tourist-oriented hotels generally price singles at the same rate or only slightly lower than doubles. Establishments for which no price is listed in the text are classified as follows (US$):

Low budget	$3-$10
Inexpensive	$11-$30
Moderate	$31-$50
Expensive	$51-$80
Luxury	over $80
Ultra-luxury	over $120

CAMPING: There are no organized campgrounds, but camping is possible. If you decide to camp, make sure that your things are kept in a safe place.

Visas, Services, & Health

VISAS: All visitors require an onward ticket. American and Canadian citizens may enter with a passport or proof of citizenship and stay for 90 days maximum. In lieu of a visa, a $10 "tourist card" for entry and departure is sold at the airport or from your airline. You may be able to avoid this charge by applying for a tourist visa at an embassy or consulate. Legal US residents who are not citizens must show an alien card in addition to their tourist card. Persons under 18 traveling alone or accompanied by only one parent/legal guardian or other adult(s) are required to present written, notarized consent from the absent parent(s) or guardian(s), granting permission to travel.

FOR NON-US CITIZENS: Citizens of Great Britain, Germany, Italy, Switzerland, Spain, Denmark, Sweden, Norway, Finland, Luxembourg, Liechtenstein, Israel, Costa Rica, Argentina, Aruba, Ecuador, Netherlands, and the Netherlands Antilles may stay for 90 days without a visa.

EXTENDING YOUR VISA: Go to the Immigration Office (☎ 685-2505) in the Huacal Bldg. in Santo Domingo. An extension costs a few dollars.

INFORMATION: Tourist information centers are in major towns. Unfortunately, they do not offer a great deal of information. The **Ministry of Tourism** main office in Santo Domingo (☎ 221-4660, fax 682-3806) is open weekdays 9 to 2:30. It's located at Av. Mexico and 30 Marzo inside a modern complex of buildings; go to the one on the far left. Note the sign in the offices: "ADVERTENCIA DEL PROCU-

RADOR GENERAL: El uso indebido de los bienes del Estado es castigado por la ley con penas de multa y carcél cometer actos de corrupcíon causea daños permanentes a la reputación de que los comete y su familia." (In a nutshell, taking bribes can have negative consequences, including imprisonment.)

For toll-free information from the US, ☎ 800-752-1151, from Germany, 800-815561, from Britain, 800-899805, from Spain, (900) 995087, and from Holland, (06) 022-3107.

LONG-TERM STAYS: Shannon Roxborough, the contact for American Citizens Abroad, may be reached at 5139 South Clarendon Ave., Detroit, MI 48204-2923 (include a SASE), or at globaltips@aol.com. He will provide free info and advice regarding rentals, buying property, business, or retirement.

STUDY: The Caribbean branch of **Oxfam International** (☎ 682-7585, 687-1010, fax 689-1001; Apdo. 20271, Santo Domingo) does a lot of good work in the country. **Earthwatch** is an organization that allows you to visit the country, participate actively in valuable research, and contribute financially at the same time. One project involved exploring a wrecked ship off the coast near Monte Cristi. For more information, ☎ 800-776-0188.

A project of Creighton University, a Jesuit-run medical school, **Latin American Concern** (☎ 402-280-3217) sends teams of medical students for five-week sojourns in the nation's outback, where they form close ties with locals as they help them with their health care. Each of the six teams generally includes two medical students, two dental students, one nursing student, and a pharmacy student. Each group is supervised by three or four professionals from these fields.

North Caribbean Research (North Caribbean Adventures, Inc. (☎ 954-989-6234, fax 954-989-6237; 800-653-7447; Box 6549, Hollywood, FL 33081; www.oldship.com; e-mail info@oldship.com) allows student participation on their diving salvage trips. You will help raise cannons, old bottles, silverware, and other artifacts. Students are in the company of a trained archaeologist. You will stay in what was once the "Las Caravelas" hotel. Plan to spend around US$2,500 pp for two weeks or US$1,500 for one week.

LAUNDRY: Laundry services are available only in major towns and cities, but your hotel can usually arrange to do laundry or hook you up with someone who will. Otherwise be prepared to do it yourself.

TELEPHONE SERVICE: Operating since 1930, *Compañia Dominicana de Teléfonos* (Codetel) is a GTE subsidiary, and international calls can be dialed directly. Probably because it is not run by the government, there are few problems with the service. However, it is quite expensive. Calls from pay phones and at Codetel centers cost RD$3 or US21¢ per minute.

Codetel is, understandably, one of the most profitable phone companies in the world. In recent years competition has appeared in the form of Tricom and All-America Cables and Radio; both of these companies offer cheaper long distance and internal fax service. They have a reasonable number of pay phones that charge one peso to make a call. Phone cards (see box) are also available.

A bilingual Spanish/English business phone book is available, and you can reach a bilingual operator by dialing "0." In case of emergency, ☎ 711. While collect overseas calls can generally be made from your hotel, you may have to go to the local telephone office if you wish to pay for the call. The number for local information is 411. Finally, where there is no pay phone available, there is generally a pay-by-time phone. Ask around.

Using Phone Cards

A wonderful new addition to the phone service are phone cards, which are available for RD$25 on up. They may be used with any phone. (Naturally, your hotel and competing firms will not be happy if you try to use one with their phone.) Here are the steps involved in using one:

❶ Buy a card at a Codetel office if they have them in stock.

❷ Remove the adhesive paper covering the back of the card.

❸ Dial 611 and wait to hear the instructions (in English) to key in the code number.

using Codetel: To make long distance calls both within the country and abroad, you should visit a Codetel branch office. Dialing is now direct and computerized. Enter a booth and dial "1." After you give the number, you will be connected to your party. When you finish your call, go up to the desk and pay the amount shown on their computer printout.

faxing: Local Codetel offices will also receive (RD$5) and send (RD$32) faxes. Many small hotels use their fax services. Competing agenies also offer service.

calling from abroad: Direct dial service is available from both the US and Canada. To call the Dominican Republic, the country code is 809.

e-mail: Suprisingly, e-mail and Internet access is available at many Codetel branches. You must be familiar with the Windows format, and basic Spanish is required. Prices are extremely reasonable. Some hotels may also let you use their Internet access, and there is one "cybercafe" in Cabarete.

POSTAL SERVICE: Window services at the General Post Office, run from 7-1:30 on weekdays and 7-noon on Sat. Other offices are located nationwide and are normally open weekdays from 7-1:30. Mail generally takes at least a week to the US, Canada, or Europe but may take months. Sea mail usually runs about four to six weeks to North America. To ensure prompt delivery, mail from your hotel desk or a main post office. Be sure to have your letters stamped at the PO because employees have been known to steam off the stamps and resell them for supplementary income. International mail and parcel services are available, but they are very expensive. It's worth it to use *entrega especial* (special delivery) for overseas mail. There is a special window for this. You can have mail sent to you at your hotel or to *Lista de Correos* (which will be held at the local PO) in any other town. Post boxes are unreliable. Postal rates are high.

There is now a new private mail service, charging an exhorbitant US$1.40 for postcards and US$2.80 for letters. It claims to deliver everything in a day or two but a reader writes that "everything I sent took 4-6 weeks to get to Canada."

BROADCASTING AND MEDIA: There are 10 daily newspapers. Seven are published in the morning and three in the afternoon. Among the morning papers are *Hoy*, *El Listin Diario*, *El Siglo*, and *El Caribe*. *El Nacional*, *La Noticia*, and *Ultima Hora* are published in the afternoon. *La Información* is published in Santiago in the morning. *Vanguardia del Pueblo* is a weekly put out by Juan Bosch's Dominican Liberation Party. The only English-language press is *The Santo Domingo News*, a weekly. *The Miami Herald*, *The New York Times*, and *The Wall Street Journal* are available, as are *Time* and *Newsweek*. There are eight TV stations. In additon to NBC and CNN, there are 18 other cable TV stations operating 24 hrs. a day. The most popular programs are *telenovelas* (soap operas) and variety shows, both locally produced and imported. Many hotels have their own satellite dishes. There are 179 AM and

FM stations. Melody FM, at 91.7, is an "adult contemporary" station serving the N coast.

HEALTH: The tap water is generally not safe to drink. Hotels will supply purified water (*agua filtrada*, *agua purificada*). Two brands of bottled water are Agua Sana and Agua Cristal. When uncertain or in the parks, water purification tablets should be utilized. Also take basic precautions such as washing both your hands and pocketknife before peeling fruit. For sunburn, apply locally manufactured Savila, which includes aloe. No immunizations are required, but you might want to catch up on your polio and tetanus injections. There's no malaria so pills are not needed. There are plenty of pharmacies around should you require medicine, but most medications are imported from Europe and the US so are expensive by Dominican standards.

HEALTH CARE: If you should get sick here, ask your hotel for a referral or go to one of the clinics listed in the text. There is only one doctor for every 1,700 Dominicans. In the past, public hospitals have been legendary for their horrific conditions and were considered a last resort. You once had to bring your own sheets, your own food, and your own medicine at times! Things have improved, but they are still less-than-wonderful places to be. In

Medical Emergencies – 24-Hour Service

SANTO DOMINGO
Ambulance, Fire, Civil Defense, Police. ☎ 711
Ambulancia Aérea y Terrestre. ☎ 567-1101/4171
Red Cross, Ensanche Miraflores. ☎ 682-4545
Centro Cardiovascular, Josefa Perdomo 152. ☎ 682-6071
Centro de Intoxicaciones. ☎ 532-6511
Centro Medico UCE, Máximo Gómez 66. ☎ 682-0171
Clinica Abreu, Independencia. ☎ 688-4411
Clinica Corazones Unidos, Fantino Falco 21. ☎ 567-4421
Clinica Gómez Patiño, Independencia 701. ☎ 685-9131
Pharmacies
Los Hidalgos, 27 de Febrero 241. ☎ 565-4848
San Judas Tadeo, Independencia 57. ☎ 689-6664
NORTE
Santiago
Hospital José Ma. Cabral y Báez, Av. Central. ☎ 583-4311
Puerto Plata
Centro Médico during Bournigal, Antera Mota. ☎ 586-2342
Hospital Ricardo Limardo, J.F. Kunhart. ☎ 586-2210
ESTE
San Pedro de Macoris
Hospital Oliver Pino. ☎ 529-3353
Hospital Oncológico de la UCE. ☎ 529-6111
La Romana
Centro Médico Oriental, Sta. Rosa. ☎ 556-2555

the countryside near the Haitian frontier, local healers known as *curiositas* practice. If you're adventurous, give it a try!

PROTECTION AGAINST INSECTS: Although scarce at higher altitudes, mosquitos are prevalent in the lowlands. For low-budget travelers staying in cheaper hotels, a mosquito net will come in handy, as will boxes of mosquito coils. Avoid inhaling their smoke. Try antihistamine cream, Euthrax, or Caladryl to help soothe bites. Repellents (with the possible exception of Avon's Skin So Soft) are ineffective against sand gnats; use some antibiotic ointment and, as is the case with all bites, avoid scratching or risk infection. In summary, prevention is the best cure. Take the precautions listed here, and wear adequate clothing.

GETTING DIVORCED: A cottage industry of the Dominican Republic is the quickie mutual-consent divorce – possible because of legislation designed to attract US citizens. Expect to spend $1,000-$1,500. One party needs to stay in the Dominican Republic for a minimum of two weekdays; the other must grant power of attorney to a Dominican lawyer. For more information, contact the American Chamber of Commerce (☎ 533-7292, 532-7414) or the US Embassy (☎ 682-2171) in Santo Domingo.

Money & Shopping

MONEY: Monetary unit is the Dominican peso. The current exchange rate is approximately US$1=RD$15; the peso will probably have devalued further by the time of your visit. The currency of choice is US dollars. Canadian dollars (and other currencies) can be difficult to exchange.

CHANGING MONEY: Change only as much money as you think you'll need because most banks are not permitted to change funds back into foreign currency. One way to do it is to present your exchange receipt, air ticket, and passport at the Banco de Reservas in Santo Domingo or at the airport. Paper money is issued in notes of 20, 50, 100, 500, 1000, and 5,000 pesos. With the exception of the one peso and an increasingly rare 50 centavos coin, you will see no others. Prices may

be listed in pesos and centavos, but pesos are likely to be the smallest currency you will use.

The easiest currency to change is the US dollar, to which the Dominican peso is tied to the dollar. Most banks are open Mon. to Fri. from 8:30 to 1:30. Moneychangers (not the ones on the street) provide a generally speedier alternative. Hotels will exchange travelers checks, but will not accept personal checks. You can exchange your dollars upon departure at the airport; you'll lose 2-3%. For some reason, you can change back only 30% of the amount you exchanged into local currency. Note that moneychangers may not offer forms valid for re-exchanging pesos.

BLACK MARKET: A once-flourishing black market died down in 1991. It may, however, be resurrected at some future date. Beware of street changers, who will definitely rip you off. They'll follow you down El Conde offering to change money at as much as 35% above the official rate. Don't do it! They are very fast and count very quickly. If you count the money, they'll

---

☞ *Traveler's Tip*
It is always a good idea to carry low-denomination bills (not higher than RD$100) and to save your change for buses and other transport. Be sure to carry plenty of smaller bills when visiting rural areas.

Useful Dominican Republic Web Sites

Web sites dealing with the Dominican Republic are far fewer than for other Caribbean and Central American nations. Some are only in Spanish. These are among the most useful:

www.dr1.com. The web site of the *Santo Domingo News*. Good information, news, hotel informtion, and archives.

www.iguana-mama.com. The home page of Iguana Mama, the nation's foremost adventure travel operator.

www.cabarete.com. Very useful for those visiting Cabarete.

medianet.nbnet.nb.ca/index.html. The Dominican Republic North Coast home page.

www.bboxbbs.ch/home/bamert. Carlos Bamert's hotel links.

travel.state.gov/dominican_republic.html. US Department of State travel information.

www.tricom.net/islav/espanol/i-virt.html. "Isla Virtual."

www.hispanet.com/index.html. HispaNet.

www.aacr.net. All-America Cables and radio.

www.codetel.net.do/dedom/. Codetel site.

www.consudom-ny.do/tourism.htm. New York City Dominican Consulate travel information.

www.jps.net/vudu/domrepnotes.html. Travel notes by the author of this guide.

www.dominicana.do. Secretary of Tourism.

www.nando.net/prof/caribe/caribe.com.html. Caribe.com, a resource center with information for travelers to the Dominican Republic and other Caribbean islands.

www.intellicast.com/weather/sdq. Weather in Santo Domingo.

www.arte-latino.com/casadeteatro. Variety of Dominican artists, concerts, exhibitions, concerts, etc.

www.nd.edu:80/~rvillaro/JLG. "Juan Luis Guerra's Home Page." Site devoted to the Dominican superstar as well as other *merengue* stars.

www-unix.oit.umass.edu/~urena/jlg/index.html. A second Juan Luis Guerra home page.

www.dorsai.org/~luis. Page dedicated to *bachata* star Anthony Riospar.

www.nethomes.com/said.musa. Artist Said Musa.

www.inx.de/~cielonaranja/Par@bola.htm. (Dominican literature).

www.arte-latino.com/dominicana/index.htm. Dominican paintings.

www.aaart.com/domrep. AAArt Dominican page.

www.firstview.com/designerlist/OscardelaRenta.html. Dominican fashion designer Oscar de la Renta.

www2.nando.net/baseball/felipe/index.html. Felipe Rojas (baseball player).

www.civila.com/acuario. National Aquarium.

www.sdq.com/botanico. Botanical Garden.

www.odci.gov/cia/publications/nsolo/factbook/dr.htm. CIA World Factbook.

www.business1.com/pcoptima/jorobada. Marine Mammal Sanctuary.

www.nando.net/prof/caribe/Listin/RedListin.html. Listin Diario Newspaper.

iadb6000.iadb.org/~http/rep_dom/drbsed.html. Inter-American Development Bank Data.

www.undp.org/undp/fodom/undp/gastdom.htm. United Nations Development Program.

www.georgetown.edu/LatAmerPolitical/Constitutions/dominicanrepublic.html. Dominican Republic Constitution.

Gurukul.ucc.american.edu/uiwww/fg6414a/embassy/embassy. htm. Embassy of the Dominican Republic, Washington, DC.

www.jce.do. Junta Central Electoral (Electoral Commission).

www.jps.net/vudu/drlinks.html. Dominican Republic links.

www.georgetown.edu/LatAmerPolitical/Parties/Resumen/DomRep/domrep.html. Dominican Republic Political Parties.

---

pull it back and count again and a hundred or so will disappear. A very popular tactic is to exclaim that "the police are coming," hand you back your money, and take off. You will unfold your $100 note to find it magically transformed into a dollar bill!

CREDIT CARDS: A large number of establishments accept credit cards, but don't rely on them as your chief source of cash. Cards are of limited use outside of Santo Domingo or major tourist areas and hotels. At the American Express office in Santo Domingo you may be able to write a personal check to purchase traveler's checks in dollars if you have one of their credit cards. You should also be able to get cash from any of the banks if you have a major credit card. Be sure you investigate *all* of the charges before going this route.

SHOPPING: Stores are generally open from 8 to noon or 1, Mon. through Fri., with most stores closing from noon or 1 to 3 in the afternoon and reopening at 2 or 3 until 6-6:30 PM. Most close down Sat. afternoons and Sundays. Since government workers must have an outside job in order to survive, offices have a *jornada único* from 7:30 to 1:30 or 2:30. Souvenirs you *won't* want to bring out are things fashioned from tortoise shell or black coral. Tortoise shell will be seized by US customs, and the harvesting of black coral destroys the reef. (Harvesting of black coral is prohibited under DR law.) You can bring back a bottle of local rum, cigars to destroy the lungs of a hated relative, or a doll. Probably the best buys are the rum – which you should purchase in town, rather than at the airport – and the local version of Amaretto. Other unusual and inexpensive souvenirs include cocoa, coffee beans (ground and whole, $1/lb.), cinnamon, and nutmeg. As is the case with all luxury items, there's an import tax on photographic equipment and accessories, so bring your own.

craft items: There is a good selection of craft items in the nation, and specifics and locations of shops are given under the destination sections below. Wood, wicker, and rattan furniture are well made here. Some handicrafts are imported and then sold at inflated prices. Haitian paintings and other crafts are common.

jewelry: The best place to shop for jewelry is **Harrison's** (www.harrisons.com), which has a large selection of jewelry made with larimar, black jade, and amber, as well as platinum jewelry. Designs are attractive, conservative, and are extremely popular with German visitors. Branches are found near practically every resort area or town, incuding Playa Dorada, Punta Cana, and outside of Puerto Plata.

duty-free shopping: There are a number of duty-free shops. When purchasing goods, you'll have to pay a couple of days before your departure and pick the things up at the airport on your way out of the country.

amber: This is a rock-like fossilized resin from the West Indian locust tre. Amber (*ambar* in Spanish) is mined from caves between Santiago and Puerto Plata in the N. Relatively abundant in the Dominican Republic, this lustrous resin is one of the most mysterious and magical substances known to man. It is warm to the touch and burns like

Introduction

wood. When rubbed against silk, it becomes charged with electricity – a property which caused the ancient Greeks to call it "electron." It has long had a place in legend. Roman gladiators used it for protection in the arena, while early Christians used it as a talisman against evil spirits. Aristotle was the first to classify it as fossilized tree resin. Over the centuries medicinal properties were attributed to amber, and it was used in treating asthma and fevers. About one piece in 100 found in the Dominican Republic contains an inclusion, a fossilized plant or insect trapped by the once-fluid sap. Possibly the most best-known inclusion yet unearthed is a *Coprintes Dominicana*, the earliest known gilled mushroom.

People have been using amber in jewelery for a long time. The most famous piece of amber jewelery, a good luck charm, was found near Hanover, Germany and has been dated at 30,000 years old. And this is one of thousands of European finds. Amber jewlery has been found in King Tut's tomb (1400 BC) and in ruins in Mesopotamia (900 BC). In *The Odyssey*, Homer tells of an amber necklace owned by a wealthy Phoenician merchant.

Be aware that amber embedded with plant or insect fossils technically requires an export permit from the Museum of Natural

☞ *Traveler's Tip*
If you are in Cabarete, contact Marcel Devaux at the Casa Laguna Hotel regarding trips to the amber mines. He also has a local amber specialist that comes and shows samples (and inclusions) to hotel guests.

History, though no one will check your bags upon departure. Traditionally used by artisans worldwide, Dominican amber – some of which dates back 120 million years – is famed for its resilience and its range of colors: clear white, ruby red, lemon yellow, caramel, near black, and cobalt blue. The rarest shade is milky white. Found in Sabana la Mar in 1979, the largest piece yet discovered weighs around 18 lbs (8 kg) and measures 18 by 8 inches. Amber is found in shops islandwide. In Santo Domingo be sure to visit **Joyas Criollas** at Plaza Criolla and in Puerto Plata the **Amber Museum**.

larimar: This semi-precious gemstone used in jewelry is a light blue rock similar to turquoise, which is mined in the Bahoruco mountains. Actually a variety of pectolite found only in the Dominican Republic, the cobalt oxide present during its formation accounts for its color. The stone got its name in 1974 when a Peace Corps volunteer brought a sample to jeweler Miguel Mendez. He named the stone by combining "Lari," for his daughter Larissa, with *mar* (sea).

black jade: Dominican black jade – a type of jadeite – seems soft to the touch but is actually quite hard. You may find black jade jewelry at branches of Harrison's.

bargaining: Although most of the stores have fixed prices, you can bargain in market stalls and in smaller stores. It's better to start with what you would consider to be a ridiculously low price and slowly work your way up.

AMERICAN CUSTOMS: Returning American citizens, under customs regulations, can lug back with them up to $600 worth of duty-free goods provided the stay abroad exceeds 48 hours and that no part of the allowance has been used during the past 30 days. Items sent by post may be included in this tally, thus allowing shoppers to have goods like glass and china shipped. Purchases are dutied at a flat 10% on the next $1,000. Above $1,400, duty applied will vary. Joint declarations are permissible for members of a family traveling together. Thus, a couple traveling with two children will be allowed up to $2,400 in duty-free goods. Undeclared gifts (one per person of up to $50 in value) may be sent to as many friends and relatives as you like. One fifth of liquor may be brought back duty-free as well as one carton of cigarettes. Plants in soil may not be brought to the US. If you're considering importing a large number of items, contact the customs agency before you travel.

CANADIAN CUSTOMS: Canadian citizens may make an oral declaration four times per year to claim C$100 worth of exemptions, which may include 200 cigarettes, 50 cigars, two lbs of tobacco, 40 fl oz of alcohol, and 24 12-oz cans/bottles of beer. In order to claim this exemption, Canadians must have been out of the country for at least 48 hours. A Canadian who's been away for at least seven days may make a written declaration once a year and claim C$300 worth of exemptions. After a trip of 48 hours or longer, Canadians receive a special duty rate of 20% on the value of goods up to C$300 in excess of the C$100 or C$300 exemption they claim This excess cannot be applied to liquor or cigarettes. Goods claimed under the C$300 exemption may follow, but merchandise claimed under all other exemptions must be accompanied.

BRITISH CUSTOMS: Each person over the age of 17 may bring in one liter of alcohol or two of champagne, port, sherry, or vermouth plus two liters of table wine; 200 cigarettes or 50 cigars or 250 gms of tobacco; 250 cc of toilet water; 50 gms (two fl oz) of perfume; and up to £28 of other goods.

GERMAN CUSTOMS: Residents may bring back 200 cigarettes, 50 cigars, 100 cigarillos, or 250 grams of tobacco; two liters of alcoholic beverages not exceeding 44 proof or one liter of alcohol over 44 proof; two liters of wine; 500 gms of coffeee; 50 gms of perfume; 0.25 liter of cologne water; and up to DM350 of other items.

Conduct

Christopher Columbus described the native Tainos as "very open hearted people who give what they are asked for with the best will in the world and, when asked, seem to regard themselves as having been greatly honored by the request."

You may find the same to be true of many Dominicans today. Maintain this good will by treating them respectfully and fairly.

DRESS: Try to keep in mind that Latin and other conservative cultural mores prevail here. Men and women alike tend to dress conservatively. If you want to be accepted and respected, dress respectably: skirts or slacks are appropriate attire for women in towns and villages. Bathing attire is unsuitable on main streets, as is revealing female attire, which will solicit unwanted attention.

CULTURAL DIFFERENCES: If you find yourself face-to-face with an urban Dominican who's making hand gestures and speaking loudly, it's not that he thinks you're deaf. The *el campo* tradition of speaking loudly to overcome distances has been passed on, unmodified, to city dwellers. If you ask someone directions out in the countryside and are told that it's *alli mismo* (right over there), bear in mind that it may be miles away.

⚡ *Warning*
If you wish to visit cathedrals, museums, or libraries, be forewarned that you may be refused admittance if you wear shorts.

HUSTLERS: As everywhere in the Caribbean and Latin America, prostitutes are accompanied by thieves and pimps. Hustlers, in the form of self-appointed "guides," sometimes won't leave you in peace, but dealing with them means trouble. If your tip is unsatisfactory, they may threaten to tell the police that you approached them to deal in drugs. They also work with street moneychangers who frequently defraud tourists.

DRUGS: With the exception of alcohol, coffee, and tobacco, all drugs – from marijuana to cocaine – are treated as narcotics. Penalties are severe, and you can expect to spend a few unpleasant weeks rotting in a cell before you see a judge. You would also do well to steer clear of terrorist activities. According to the government tourism guide, "if you are part of a group smuggling arms, explosives, or drugs, it is possible that you will meet face-to-face with an INTERPOL agent."

TIPPING: If a service charge is added to your restaurant, nightclub, or hotel bill, it's not necessary to leave a tip. Nor is it necessary in small, family-run restaurants, though tips are always appreciated. A doorman or porter should be tipped, as should taxi drivers.

NIGHTLIFE: If you are a teetotaller, there is not much to do here! Most Dominicans either smoke or drink or both. Tourist resorts have shows with fake voodoo ceremonies and the like. There are a number of discos all over that cater to locals.

WOMEN TRAVELING ALONE: Dominican men have a definite propensity for courting Western women.

You're likely to receive the most attention at beach resorts like Sosúa. Many local lads there specialize in bedding bored foreign tourists (especially German women) for money. Many are quite successful. Don't be a sucker. Relationships between Dominican men and Western women seldom work out long-term. If you want a fling, make sure the guy uses a condom; some

of the male prostitutes are reportedly bisexual. If you wish to deflect attention, talk about your boyfriend or husband and keep them at a distance.

___

❝ Reader Comment

One female reader writes: "My worst experiences were related to constantly being harassed by Dominican men. It is very difficult to deal with, and one of the unfortunate aspects of macho culture. Women travelers should be especially conscious of this aspect of Dominican life, because it can negatively affect one's feeling of personal security, even if the hoots, hisses and catcalls are actually harmless."

___

TRAVELING WITH CHILDREN: The Dominican Republic is as safe as anywhere for children, and locals love foreign kids. Just take care that they are not overexposed to sun and that they get enough liquids. Remember to bring whatever special equipment you'll need. Disposable diapers and baby food are available, but expensive. Inquire at your hotel as to extra charges for children and whether they'll even be wanted. Finally, keep an eye on the kids while they're in the water. Good places to visit with children include the zoo, aquarium, and botanical gardens in Santo Domingo, and the capital's Parque de Tres Ojos, the nation's most accessible national park.

ENVIRONMENTAL CONDUCT: Respect the natural environment. Take nothing and remember that corals are easily broken. Much damage has already been done to the reef through snorkelers either standing on coral or hanging onto outcroppings. It's wise to keep well away just for your own protection: many corals will retaliate with stings and the sharp ridges can cause slow-healing cuts. When diving or snorkeling, resist the temptation to touch fish. Many fish secrete a mucous coating that protects them from bacterial infection. Touching them removes the coating and may result in infection and death for the fish. Also avoid feeding fish.

Dispose of plastics properly. Remember that six-pack rings, plastic bags, and fishing lines can cause injury or prove fatal to sea turtles, fish, birds, and other marine life. Unable to regurgitate anything they swallow, turtles and other sea creatures may mis-take plastic bags for jellyfish or choke on fishing lines. Birds may starve to death after becoming entangled in lines, nets, and plastic rings. Remember that the parks and reserves were created to preserve the environment and refrain from carrying off plants, rocks, animals, or other materials. Buying black coral jewelry also serves to support reef destruction and turtle shell items come from an endangered species. Finally, remember to treat nature with respect.

BOATING CONDUCT: Always exercise caution while anchoring a boat. Improperly anchoring in seagrass beds can destroy wide swathes of seagrass which takes a long time to recover. If there's no buoy available, the best place to anchor is a sandy spot where relatively little environmental impact can occur. Tying your boat to mangroves can kill the trees, so it is acceptable to do so *only* during

Hallucinogenic Rituals

The Tainos, the vanished Dominicans of yesteryear, practiced hallucinogenic rituals which involved inhaling a powder through a cane pipe. The Taino would then worship and commune with their gods, who were present in their *cemis* (idols). The powder was also used after long hikes in order to relieve exhaustion. The Tainos would stick a spatula down their throat to induce vomiting before inhalation. This was probably a way to purify themselves and to prevent them from vomiting later in the presence of the idols.

Dos & Don'ts

- Don't condescend to locals. Treat the local people with the same respect your would like to receive yourself.

- Don't act as though there are no social problems in your country and make it clear that Western societies have their share of ills.

- Do try local food and patronize local restaurants.

- Try to speak Spanish – even if it is only a few words.

- Don't eat endangered species such as turtles.

- Don't make promises you don't intend to keep.

- Don't make local children into beggars by acting like Santa Claus, dispensing gifts and money. Never pay for photos. Giving out money creates a cycle of dependency and creates more problems than it solves.

- Don't just lounge around your hotel. Get out and explore. But don't overextend yourself and try to do too much. This is not a place for rushing around. There's always the next visit.

- Don't dump your garbage at sea or litter in town. Protect the environment and set a good example.

- Don't remove or injure coral, spear fish, remove tropical fish, annoy turtles or touch their eggs. Do not feed fish or disturb wildlife. Do visit archaeological sites but refrain from disturbing them.

- Refrain from eating lobster out of season (April 1 - Aug. 1).

- Do not go nude, ride horses or drive ATVs on the beaches.

a storm. In order to help eliminate the unnecessary discharge of oil, maintain the engine and keep the bilge clean. If you notice oil in your bilge, use oil-absorbent pads to soak it up. Be careful not to overfill the boat when fueling. Emulsions from petrochemical products stick to fishes' gills and suffocate them, and deposits in sediment impede the develop-

ment of marine life. Detergents affect plankton and other organisms, which throws off the food chain. When you approach seagrass beds, slow down because your propellor could strike a sea turtle. Avoid maneuvering your boat too close to coral reefs: Striking the reef can damage both your boat and the reef. Avoid stirring up sand in shallow coral areas.

The sand can be deposited in the coral and cause polyps to suffocate and die. If your boat has a sewage holding tank, empty it only at properly equipped marinas. Avoid using harsh chemicals such as ammonia and bleach while cleaning your boat; they pollute the water and kill marine life. Use environmentally safe cleaning products whenever possible. Boat owners should avoid paint containing lead, copper (which can make molluscs poisonous), mercury (highly toxic to fish and algae), or TBT. Finally, remember that a diver-down flag should be displayed while diving or snorkeling.

Other Things You Should Know

WHAT TO TAKE: Bring only what you need. It's easy to wash clothes in the sink and thus save lugging around a week's laundry. You can leave your hairdryer at home. The electricity can be counted on to fail at times, and a few minutes in the sun will effectively dry your hair. Remember, the simpler the better. Set your priorities according to your needs. With a light pack or bag, you can breeze through from one town, resort, or region to another easily. Confining yourself to carry-on luggage also saves waiting at the airport. And, if a second bag of luggage gets lost, at least you have the essentials until it

turns up. If you do pack a lot of clothes, you could leave things at your hotel and pick them up later. When packing, it's preferable to take loose clothing. If you plan to wear shorts, bring long and loose ones. If you're planning to dine in expensive restaurants or attend church, you may wish to bring along some formal clothes.

protectives: Avon's Skin-So-Soft bath oil, diluted 50% with water, serves as an excellent sand flea repellent. Sunscreen should have an 8-15 or greater protection level. A flashlight is essential, and you might want to bring two, a larger one and one to fit in your handbag or daypack. Feminine hygiene items are rarely found outside the major population centers; bring a good supply. Likewise, all prescription medicines, creams, and ointments should be brought with you.

miscellaneous items: Books are twice US prices so you'll also probably want to stock up before arrival. It's a good idea to have toilet paper with you; the least expensive hotels and some restrooms may not supply it. Plastic trash bags and an assortment of sized baggies will also come in handy.

budget travel: If you're a budget traveler, you'll want to bring along earplugs, some rope for a clothesline, towel, washcloth, toilet paper, cup, small mirror, a universal plug for the

What to Take

CLOTHING
socks and shoes
underwear
sandals, thongs, or
windsurfing thongs
T-shirts, shirts (or blouses)
skirts/pants, shorts
swimsuit
hat
light jacket/sweater
umbrella/poncho
rubber boots

TOILETRIES
soap
shampoo
towel, washcloth
toothpaste/toothbrush
comb/brush
prescription medicines
chapstick/other toiletries
insect repellent
suntan lotion/sunscreen
shaving kit
toilet paper
small mirror

nail clippers
hand lotion

OTHER ITEMS
passport/identification
driver's license
travelers checks
moneybelt
address book
notebook
Spanish-English dictionary
pens/pencils
books, maps
watch
camera/film
flashlight/batteries
snorkeling equipment
earplugs
compass
extra glasses
laundry bag
laundry soap/detergent
matches/lighter
frisbee/sports equipment
cooking supplies (if necessary

sink, and a cotton sheet. A small pack is preferable because a large one may not fit on the rack above the bus seats; there are luggage holds only in some buses, and the smaller vans may be awkward.

nature lovers: If nature is your focus, bring a rain parka, walking shoes or hiking boots, a day pack, canteen, hat, binoculars, and insect repellent as well as a bird book or two. Loose cotton trousers are recommended; jeans take a long time to dry.

anglers: Necessities include sleeved shirts and pants, raingear, a wide-brimmed hat, and effective sun protection. It's better to bring your own equipment. Bring a 20 lb or stronger line for saltwater fishing.

MEASUREMENTS: Electric current is 110-120 volts AC. You can expect periodic failures as a matter of course. Hotels may have backup generators; make sure yours has one *before* you check in. While some villages are with-

Practicalities ■ **115**

Introduction

out electricity, other villages (and resorts which have their own generators) have electricity only part of the day. The major reasons for the shortages are mismanagement and corruption; the electrical output produced in 1990 was only 70% of the output in 1987. Compounding the problem is the fact that only 40% of all users pay their bills.

Gasoline and motor oil are measured in US gallons, but cooking oil is sold by the pound. Fabrics are measured by the yard. While land in urban areas is measured in square meters, the outback employs the *terrea*. Colloquial measures also apply: *una rumba* is a lot, *un chin* is a little bit, and *un chin-chin* is a tiny bit.

conversions: A meter equals three feet, three inches. A kilometer equals .62 miles (about 6/10th of a mile), a square km equals about 3/8 of a square mile. To convert Centigrade to Farenheit, multiply the °C by 1.8 and add 32.

TIME: The Dominican Republic operates on Atlantic Standard Time (Eastern Daylight Savings Time) all year, but attitudes about time are different from those in North America or Europe. It may be wise to request something earlier than you need it, and to reconfirm requests.

BUYING LAND: Although it is possible for foreigners to buy land

here, don't expect to do so easily or quickly. Even Dominicans have a difficult time purchasing land; a foreigner is even worse off. Land titles are a problem: many have been falsified or are forgeries. You must check with a lawyer to make sure that they are correct. Beware of documents that resemble land deeds but actually aren't. Be sure you understand what's written in Spanish. Some of the land is sold two or three times over.

THEFT: Problems include pickpockets and hotel break-ins. Nevertheless, you should be fine if you take adequate precautions. The very best prevention is being aware that you might be a victim.

☞ *Traveler's Tip*
In the event that something happens, contact the Policia Turista toll-free at ☎ 1-200-3500.

PHOTOGRAPHY: Film is expensive here so you might want to bring your own. Kodachrome KR 36, ASA 64, is the best all around slide film. For prints, 100 or 200 ASA is preferred, while 1000 ASA is just the thing underwater. For underwater shots, use a polarizing filter to cut down on glare; a flash should be used in deep water. The best place to practice underwater photography is at La Caleta National Marine Park to the W of Santo Domingo. Avoid photographs between 10 and 2

Keeping Safe

- By all means avoid the slum areas, don't flash money or possessions around and, in general, keep a low profile – avoid looking affluent.

- Keep track of your possessions, and *never* leave anything unattended on the beach.

- Avoid carrying anything in your back pockets. Women should carry purses that can be secured under their upper arm.

- Never, never leave anything in an unoccupied vehicle, not even in a trunk.

- Make sure that you keep an eye on your bags at all times in the airport – never entrust them to anyone, and be certain to lock your bags before checking them in.

- Remember that locals who form sexual liaisons with foreigners often do so with pecuniary gain in mind. And, if you give one of them access to your hotel room, it can be a bit sticky to go to the police and make a charge afterwards!

- It's useful to photocopy your passport and keep it separately, along with the numbers of your travelers checks and any credit cards.

- A final useful precaution is to secure unnecessary valuables in the hotel safe; even better, leave your jewels and Rolex watch at home.

when there are harsh shadows. Photograph landscapes while keeping the sun to your rear. Set your camera a stop or a stop and a half down when photographing beaches to prevent overexposure from glare. A sunshade is useful. Keep your camera and film out of the heat. Silica gel packets stave off moisture and mildew. Replace your batteries before a trip or bring spares. Finally, do not to subject your exposed film of ASA 400 or greater to the X-ray ma-chines at the airport. Hand carry them through. Ask permission of soldiers before you photograph military installations.

film developing: Because local developing is very expensive and of generally poor quality, it's better to take your film home for developing. There are a number of places where you can have photos developed. **Planet Foto** is a chain which operates in Sosúa, Cabarete, Playa Dorada, Playa Grande, Jarabacoa, Juan Dolio, and Bayahibe, among other places. They offer one-hour developing.

VISITING NATIONAL PARKS AND RESERVES: These are among the nation's greatest attractions. They occupy more than 11% of the national territory, covering an area larger than Rhode Island. But they're difficult to reach if you don't have your own transportation. In most cases, you'll need to bring your own food as well. Trails in many parks are neither marked nor maintained. One alternative may be to visit the parks as part of a guided tour. Although it is not always charged, admission is officially RD$50 (US$4) for foreigners and RD$20 for Dominicans.

Categories for Reserves

■ The *Reserva Natural Estricta* is an area designated exclusively for scientific research.

■ An *Area Natural Silvestre* is a virgin expanse to be given maximum protection. A *Parque Nacional* is an area "dedicated to preservation, education and recreation."

■ A *Monumento Natural* is an area "conserved for educational and recreational purposes."

■ An *Area de Manejo de Habitat/Especies* is a natural area that serves to protect a specific species.

■ *Paisajes Terrestres y Marinos Protegidos* are areas set aside for recreation and educational purposes.

Santo Domingo

Introduction

A sprawling, thriving metropolis of 2½ million, Santo Domingo is more exciting than any other Caribbean capital. In this city of contrasts, Spanish ruins compete with large office buildings, and Porsches share streets with the *chiriperos* (pushcart vendors).

The city is the focus of wealth, banking, finance, shipping, and money, and serves as the seat of government. It is truly the nation's hub. With the largest concentration of people in the country, it also has the highest growth rate. The population has more than tripled in the past 30 years.

Old Santo Domingo retains much of the flavor it had when it was the first Spanish capital of the Americas. It is a pleasant place to explore. There are small museums to visit and numerous cafés and a pedestrian shopping street.

The new city overlaps with Old Santo Domingo and seems to sprawl endlessly. It contains the museums, numerous parks, and the *cinturon de miseria* ("belt of misery"), a vast, squalid slum that is home to thousands of Santo Domingo's poor.

The capital's modern sector, with its broad boulevards, ultra-modern museums, and embassies, is a world unto itself. Yesterday's soldiers of fortune and missionaries have given way to swarms of Japanese businessmen, Venezuelan oil salesmen, and people trying to make a buck from the cigar boom.

ARRIVING BY AIR: Las Américas, the international airport, is 14 miles (23 km) from the city. A tourist office is to your right after arrival and nearby is an office selling tourist cards. If you need one, be sure to pick it up here. A bank is just past immigration. It takes 30 minutes by taxi from Las Américas, and the fare is around RD$280 (US$20).

You can take a cab into town, of course. To get there by bus or *público*, walk to the R about 25 minutes until you reach the main highway and then cross it. The stop is at Restaurante La Caleta to the left. Buses pass every half-hour during the day, but are less frequent during the evening. Another alternative is to walk down to Av. de las Américas and try to stop any passing bus or *público*. *Públicos* also leave from the top level of the airport.

internal flights: Air Santo Domingo (☎ 683-8020, fax 683-8436; www.g-air-europa. es/air_sdo; e-mail info.air_sdo@ g-air-europa.es) operates between Herrera airport (in Santo Domingo) to and from Punta Cana, Portillo (Samaná Peninsula), Santiago, La Romana, and Puerto Plata. Flights inter-connect between destinations. Rates range from RD$700 on up.

GETTING AROUND: When feasible, walking is the thing to do. Public transportation is excellent but confusing. There is no local alive who knows all the routes.

Ontrate, the public bus company, has yellow *guaguas* (buses) running throughout the city, but they are rarely seen these days. A new set of buses is on order and may have arrived by the time of your visit. Private companies run on many routes. You must have exact change. *Guaguas* or *públicos* also run throughout the city. These may take the form of vans or ordinary passenger cars. Charges start at RD$2 for cars and RD$2.50 (or RD$3. if you don't have change) for buses.

A central location for public transportation is Parque Independencia which is surrounded by *públicos*. You must find out where to stand; ask a local. From Parque Independencia, *públicos* head E on Av. Bolivar and return via Av. Independencia.

When standing on Av. Bolivar or another main artery, signal to a passing *público* with your hand whether you wish to turn left, right or go straight ahead. If traveling on the other side of the Río Ozama, you have to catch a bus along Av. 27 de Febrero or Av. Paris. Again, ask a local. Note that you'll be asked to pay when you get off as the vehicle nears its terminal.

The one word that sums up the transportation system here is "chaotic."

CITY LAYOUT: Santo Domingo might best be seen as a collection of sprawling *barrios* rather than a distinct metropolis. Each *barrio* has its *colmados* where locals buy, beer, rum, and even plastic packets of water and sweets for the children. The *colmados* serve as the social centers for the *barrios*, and you will often see people take plastic chairs from the store and lounge around inside.

Of the *barrios*, there are only a few you are likely to visit. The colonial section is centered in the SE, and three bridges (the Mella, Duarte, and Sánchez) span the Río Ozama. On the other side are the Parque Mirador del Este, Faro a Colón (the Columbus "lighthouse"), and the aquarium. The major road heading E is Av. Las Américas.

The colonial area (Ciudad Colonia) is small enough to explore on foot, and you can also con-

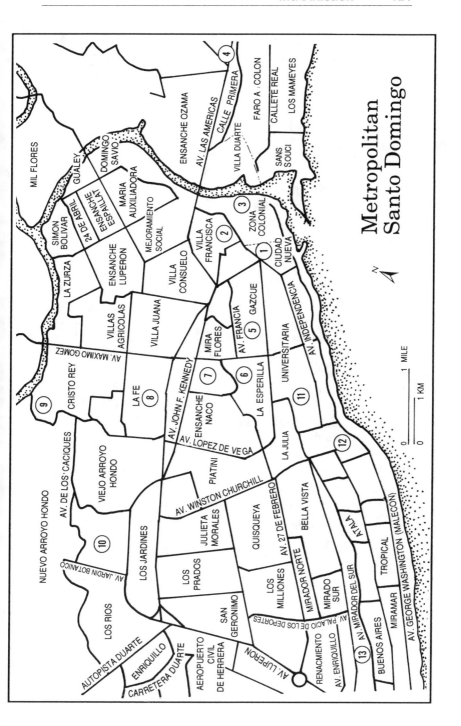

Metropolitan
Santo Domingo

tinue on to other areas such as C. Duarte (a shopping street) and the residential area of Gacúe.

Many major hotels such as the Jaragua are on the Malécon, a seaside boulevard formally known as Av. George Washington. It stretches clear along the coast from the old town through to the W and is the center of the Merengue Festival (held in July). It is bordered by restaurants and is the place for promenading.

Paralleling it, running closer in some places and farther in others, is Av. Independencia, which begins at Parque Independencia. The next major street running E-W is Av. Bolivar, which turns into Prolongación Av. Bolivar before becoming Av. Romulo Betancourt. Both are pleasant streets, lined with homes, political party headquarters, pharmacies, and hotels. The area they run through for the beginning of their stretch is known as Gazcúe.

Av. 27 de Febrero and Av. John F. Kennedy (which eventually becomes Autopista Duarte) are the two other main arteries. The major roads running N-S are Av. Duarte, Av. Máximo Gómez, Av. Abraham Lincoln, Av. Winston Churchill, and – farther out to the W – Av. Nuñez de Caceres and Av. Luperón.

TAXIS: Radio taxis are less expensive and safer than street taxis, and should be called 20-30 minutes in advance. They are: Taxi Apolo (☎ 537-1000), **Aero Taxi** (☎ 686-1212), **Taxi Fácil** (☎ 685-2202), **Tecni Taxi** (☎ 567-2010), **Mundi Taxi** (☎ 584-2222), **Taxi Radio** (☎ 562-1313), **Taxi Raffi** (☎ 689-5468), **Servbús** (☎ 686-6868), **La Paloma** (☎ 567-1412, 567-1437), and **Micromóvil** (☎ 689-2000). Most hotels have a set-fare taxi or limo service which goes through the city and to the airport. A hotel doorman will summon a taxi for you, and you can arrange to have one take you to a restaurant, wait, and then return you to your hotel. Taxis may also be rented by the hour, morning, or afternoon. *Motoconchos* are motorcyclists who take passengers – up to three on pillion! These are not found in the city center these days but operate on the outskirts.

Empty *públicos* are a less expensive alternative to taxis. Hired by one person or a group, they are known as *carreras*. Private cars are among the vehicles operating as *públicos*. Be sure to settle the fare before accepting; US$4 is average for trips within town, but they may well want more. Fares rise around Christmas.

TOURS: With desks in evidence at nearly every hotel, it's easy to find a city tour. Expect to spend around US$10 for a three-hour tour. The **Museum of History and Geography** (☎ 688-6952, 686-6668) offers city and other tours. **Edecanes Tours** (☎ 687-5245), C. Isabel la Católica 5, runs guided motorized trolley tours through the old town.

CAR RENTALS: Cars may be rented at the airport, on the road to Santo Domingo, and on the Malecón. Agencies include **Auto Rental** (☎ 565-7873), **Avis** (☎ 533-9295, Av. Abraham Lincoln), **Budget** (☎ 562-6812, Av. George Washington on the Malecón), **Ford** (☎ 565-1818), **Honda** (☎ 567-1015), **Nelly** (☎ 535-8800, Av. José Contreras 139), **Pueblo Rent-a-Car** (in front of Hotel Jaragua along Av. Independencia, ☎ 685-4127/4128, 689-9720/2000), **Rent-a-Matic** (☎ 685-6073), **Rentauto** (☎ 565-1140). Expect to spend US$60-170 per day including insurance; mileage is free. Most offer a shuttle service to your hotel.

HISTORY: Santo Domingo was founded On Aug. 4, 1496 by Columbus's brother Bartholomé, and was the first outpost of the Spanish in the New World. It was here that the first street, university, hospital, church, and mint were established. From here, Ponce de León sailed to colonize Puerto Rico, Hernando Cortez set out on his invasion of Mexico, and Diego de Velasquez departed to colonize Cuba. Originally known as Nuevo Isabella, the name of the town was changed either in honor of Columbus's father (whose name was Domingo) or for the day the town was founded (Sunday).

In 1502, it was destroyed by a hurricane and reestablished by Frey Nicolás de Ovando, who moved it to the W bank of what was later named the Río Ovando. In 1508 Santo Domingo became the first New World settlement to be declared a "city" and granted its own coat of arms. From 1509-1524 under Diego Columbus (Columbus's oldest son) as governor, the city reigned as the capital of the Indies and the New World's principal outpost.

After Columbus departed, the settlement slumped as Spanish explorers were lured toward the silver and gold mines of Mexico and Peru and as other nations arrived to put down stakes in the Caribbean. Santo Tomás de Aquino, the first university, was founded here in 1538. After a devastating earthquake in 1562, Santo Domingo was demoted to way-station status. In 1586, Sir Francis Drake and his crew of brigands sacked the city, burning much of it and departing with its jewels and other treasures. Trujillo changed the city's name to Ciudad Trujillo in 1936; it reverted to Santo Domingo after his assassination in 1961.

Santo Domingo

Old Santo Domingo Sights

This area is a gem. Most of the old buildings have been restored (at a cost of some US$10 million) by the government in cooperation with local residents. Walking is the best way to see the sights, and no place is too far to walk. Almost eerie at night, the town makes an immediate and indelible impression.

STREETS: Once known as C. Fortaleza because it runs past Ozama fortress, **C. Los Damas** ("Street of the Ladies") was named because the women of the viceroy's court lodged here. **El Conde**, the main shopping street, cuts right through the old town, and Av. Mella borders one side. Another main shopping street, **Av. Duarte**, traverses the old town at a perpendicular. The Malecón runs along the S edge of the area.

PARQUE INDEPENDENCIA (EL CONDE): This walled-in park is the first thing you come to if entering the old town area from the W. Formerly delineating the city's limits, **Puerta El Conde** (Gateway of the Count) was converted by the Count of Peñalva, Captain General of Hispaniola, into a bastion commemorating the Spanish victory he gained over an English incursion in 1655. Also known as the Baluarte de 27 de Febrero, the gate's Latin inscription roughly translates as "It is sweet and fitting to die for one's country." The carved bronze "nautical star" set into the walkway just past the gate contains the 32 directions in which the horizon is divided, as well as a mark indicating "kilometer zero" – still used as the point from which all distances to and from the city are measured. Standing in the center of Parque Independencia, the modern concrete and marble **mausoleum** was built in 1976 to house the remains of revolutionary heroes Duarte, Sánchez, and Mella. Its eternal flame is safeguarded by a military sentry.

NEARBY SIGHTS: The ruins of the fortress nearby were originally part of the city walls, and the main defense on the city's NW side. The **Puerta de la Misericordia** (Gateway of Mercy), corner of Palo Hincado and C. Arzibispo Portes, gave protection to the masses in the face of natural disasters. Here, Mella fired the first shot of the revolt against Haiti on Feb. 27, 1844. The ruins of **Fuerte de la Concepción** (1543) still stand at the corner of Av. Mella and C. Palo Hincado.

The entrance to El Conde – a large pedestrian mall – is marked by a hideous Burger King. The once-attractive mural above its entrance has been subtly altered. The new version appears to have a penis ejacuating blood! Be sure to check it out while you are in the area.

Farther S, the ruins of **Fuerte de San Gil** are on C. Padre Billini near the end of C. Piña.

CATEDRAL PRIMADA DE AMERICA (CATEDRAL DE SANTA MARIA LA MENOR): First and oldest in the Americas, this cathedral was constructed between 1523 and 1545. Its first stone was laid by Christopher's son Diego. Construction was begun by Bishop Alexandro Geraldini, but the building was completed by Rodrigo de Bastido's son, also a bishop, who used part of his inheritance to finance the structure. It stands in Parque Colón, which has a large statue of Columbus.

Installed in preparation for the 1992 celebrations, the new gargoyles and sculptures at the gates portray the Tainos at the time of conquest. Above the entrance, a remarkable frieze is decorated with horns and mythical figures. Pass through the 2½-ton main door. In the first chapel to the right of the altar, see where Sir Francis Drake nodded out in his hammock during his 1586 stay. He chopped off the hands of the bishop's statue and chipped off the nose of another during a fit of anger. Drake left the bishop's mahogany chair alone, and this is thought to have been the work of

Taino artisans. St. Peter's chapel was turned into a jail cell.

The remaining 13 chapels also contain Romanesque arches and Gothic vaults. Other items of note include life-sized wooden animals and a wonderfully abstract Jesus in a manger. The cathedral's treasury contains a large number of priceless religious artifacts and jewelry along with jewels donated by Simon Bolivar's great grandfather. It's open from 9-4.

Perpendicular to the cathedral, a separate building is undergoing renovation and may open as a museum this year or in 1999.

Exit via La Callejón de Los Curates, a small alleyway, to 308 C. Isabela la Católica where **Museo Duartino**, the former home of the independence leader, contains mementos of the revolution. In this house Maria Trinidad Sánchez, the Dominican Betsy Ross, sewed the first flag, which was unfurled over El Conde's gate on Feb. 27, 1844.

ALCAZAR DE COLON: This house was built without the use of a single nail. It was constructed in 1510-14 by order of Don Diego Columbus (Columbus's son) during his tenure as viceroy. It was once a crumbling ruin. Opened to the public on Columbus Day, 1957, it has been magnificently reconstructed at a cost of US$1 million, using stone of the same type as the original.

Inside, in the **Museo Virreinal** (Viceregal Museum), an armored knight rides a wooden horse; antique pottery, furniture, and musical instruments (including a 15th-century clavichord) abound. The authentic furnishings from Spain give you a real feeling for the Spanish colonial era. Note the three 17th-century tapestries depicting Columbus's story, the 16th-century tiled kitchen, and the ivory-encrusted desks. Also view the 16th-century Flemish carving of the death of the Virgin. It was shattered into some 40 pieces by gunfire during the 1965 civil war; experts toiled for a decade to piece it back together.

Open Mon. to Sat., 9-12; 2:30-5:30. The Alcázar is closed on Tues. and the *museo* on Mon.

FORTALEZA OZAMA: On **Calle las Damas**, oldest street in the New World, a children's library, and **Planarte**, a small but superb crafts shop, are located within the Casa de las Bastidas inside and to the left. Crafts fairs are held seasonally in Gonzales Fernandez de Oviedo Plaza here. Gonzales Fernandez de Oviedo's statue dominates the inner square. Oveido was the author of *Chronicle of the Indies* – the first history of the New World. He was once the warden here, and legend has it that the keys to the gaol

Old Santo Domingo

1. Catedral Primada del America (Santa María la Menor)
2. Fortaleza Ozama/Torre del Homenaje
3. Hostal Nicolás de Ovando
4. Panteón Nacional
5. Capilla de Nuestra Señora de los Remedios
7. Reloj de Sol
8. La Ataranza/Museo de Jamón
9. Alcázar de Colón/Museo Maritimo
10. Casa de Colón
11. Museo Duartino
12. Ruinas de Monasterio San Francisco
13. Iglesia Convento de Santa Clara
14. Casa de Tostado (Museum of the Dominican Family)
15. Convento de los Domenicanos
16. Capilla de la Tercera Order
17. Iglesia de la Regina Angelorum
18. Iglesia del Carmen
19. Puerta de la Misericordia
20. Puerta del Conde (Parque Independencia)
21. Iglesia de la Mercedes
22. Iglesia de Santa Barbara
23. Hotel Palacio de Colonia

Old Santo Domingo

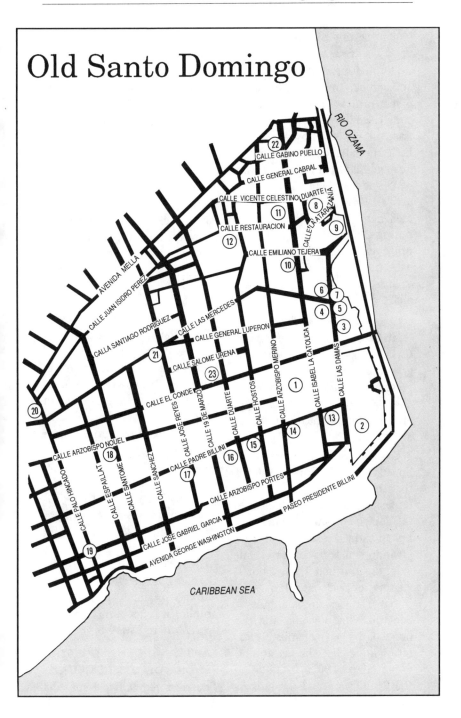

RIO OZAMA

CALLE GABINO PUELLO

CALLE GENERAL CABRAL

CALLE VICENTE CELESTINO DUARTE

CALLE RESTAURACION

CALLE EMILIANO TEJERA

CALLE LA ATARAZANA

AVENIDA MELLA

CALLE JUAN ISIDRO PEREZ

CALLA SANTIAGO RODRIGUEZ

CALLE LAS MERCEDES

CALLE GENERAL LUPERON

CALLE SALOME URENA

CALLE ARZOBISPO MERINO

CALLE ISABEL LA CATOLICA

CALLE LAS DAMAS

CALLE EL CONDE

CALLE JOSE REYES

CALLE 19 DE MARZO

CALLE DUARTE

CALLE HOSTOS

CALLE ARZOBISPO NOUEL

CALLE PALO HINCADO

CALLE ESPAILLAT

CALLE SANTOME

CALLE SANCHEZ

CALLE PADRE BILLINI

CALLE ARZOBISPO PORTES

PASEO PRESIDENTE BILLINI

CALLE JOSE GABRIEL GARCIA

AVENIDA GEORGE WASHINGTON

CARIBBEAN SEA

had to be pried from his hands upon his demise.

Dominating all this is the grim and somber **Torre de Homenaje**, oldest fortress in the Americas, constructed by Nicolás de Ovando in 1503. Ships were once hailed from its top. Diego Columbus and his wife lived in the warden's lodge here after their arrival. Prisoners were incarcerated here in the warden's lodge during the Trujillo era. It holds a museum/gallery with temporary exhibits. The tower is open Tues. to Sun., 8-7. Nominal admission charged.

Conquistador and explorer Rodrigo de Bastidas, who built **Casa de las Bastidas**, was also governor of Santa María (the present-day nation of Colombia). The structure's Romanesque arches surround the interior patio and garden.

Casa de Francia, known as the house of Hernan Cortes, is down the street on the left; it is now the home of the Alliance Francaise, the French cultural center. To the right nearby, **Hostal Nicolás de Ovando** is a 16th-century mansion transformed into a hotel; visitors are welcome. It is split into two houses: the colonial residence of Gov. Ovando and the home of the Davila family. Restoration united both homes around a central pool area overlooking the Río Ozama and the port. It once had its own private church and fort; the watchtower looks over the pool. Before and after pictures of the restoration process are on display upstairs. The hotel is currently closed; it may have reopened by the time of your visit.

Built in 1714, the **Panteón Nacional** (National Pantheon), across the street from the Hostal, was originally the Convento de San Ignacio de Loyola, a Jesuit Convent; after the Jesuits were expelled, it later served as a tobacco warehouse, and then as a theater. Now heroes and public figures are buried here, honored with a small eternal flame, a wall inscription, and an elaborate candelabra. During the Trujillo era, it was festooned with gifts received by Trujillo in commoration of its restoration. The Italian government donated marble tiles surrounding the eternal flame, Spain's Generalissimo Franco donated the imposing copper chandelier hanging in the cupola. Filled with Latin crosses – rumored to have been swastikas removed from a Nazi prison after the war – the iron grills on the second floor were donated by Germany. Although this memorial was originally prepared for Trujillo, he is not buried here. It's open Mon. to Sat., 9-6.

CAPILLA DE NUESTRA SEÑORA DE LOS REMEDIOS: The restored Chapel of the Remedies, where the earliest resi-

La Fortaleza

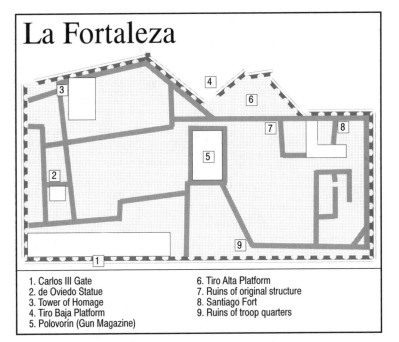

1. Carlos III Gate
2. de Oviedo Statue
3. Tower of Homage
4. Tiro Baja Platform
5. Polovorín (Gun Magazine)

6. Tiro Alta Platform
7. Ruins of original structure
8. Santiago Fort
9. Ruins of troop quarters

Santo Domingo

dents attended Mass, has a stark and simple interiors. It was built in the early 16th century. It's open Mon. to Sat., 9-6.

MUSEO DE LAS CASAS REALES: This Museum of the Royal Houses, also on C. las Damas, is one of the finest small museums in the Caribbean. An anchor from a salvaged Spanish galleon leans against one of its walls. During the colonial era, the building variously housed the Palace of Governors and Captains General, the Royal Audience and Court of Appeals, the Royal Counting House, and the Treasury. It was inaugurated by Balaguer in 1976, accompanied by Spain's King Juan Carlos I and Queen Sofia. Enter below the he-raldic shield of Emperor Charles V. See superb collections of hand-blown glass, armor, and weapons, intricately decorated crossbows – even samurai armor. There's also a beautiful apothecary shop, military dolls and models, and a monolith-sized milestone that delineated the border between the Spanish and French sides of Hispaniola. The **Voluntariado de Casa Reales** features contemporary art exhibits. (Open Tues. to Sun., 9-noon, 2:30-5:30).

Reloj de Sol, a sundial, is across the street and next to the Chapel of the Remedies. Built in 1753, it was positioned so the judges seated in the court across the way could always tell the time.

La Ataranza, first commercial center of the New World, is farther up the street next to the Alcázar. These eight 16th-century former warehouses have been turned into shops, restaurants, and bars. Stop in at **Drakes**, **Café Montesinos**, **Nancy's Snack Bar**, **Rita's Café**, or the **Museo de Jamón** here. One nice place to have a bite to eat is the attractive **Salon de Te**, just across from the Museo Maritimo.

MUSEO MARITIMO: This maritime museum highlights sunken treasure – artifacts and treasures salvaged from the *Guadeloupe* and *Conde de Tolosa* galleons, both of which were wrecked off of Samaná in a 1724 hurricane. Because they were carrying mercury, they have been nicknamed the "quicksilver" galleons. Only 40 of the 600 passengers lived to tell the tale of the disaster. Another major exhibit illustrates life on the *Concepción*, a Spanish galleon which capsized off the Dominican coast in 1641 en route back to Spain with a cargo of silver bullion and coins. Finds displayed here are absolutely enthralling. You'll find ceramic pipes, a brandy bottle, bars of silver, a lump of fused coins and pottery shards that weighs in at 14 lbs, silver bases used to hold then-exotic coconut cups, Ming Dynasty porcelain, copper bowls and pots, and contraband cargo including an eight-day bracket clock from London. It's open Wed. to Sat. 9-5 and Sun. 9-1.

CASA DEL CORDÓN: This "House of the Cord" is located opposite the Palacio de las Communicaciones building on C. Isabel de la Católica. Constructed in 1503 for Don Francisco de Garay – one of the early colonizers who later became governor of Jamaica – this was the first stone structure built in the New World. Its name stems from the belt of St. Francis engraved over the door. Diego Columbus and his wife lived here while they awaited construction of the Alcázar.

In 1586 Sir Francis Drake besieged and looted the capital, and then demanded a ransom of 25,000 ducats to return it to the Spanish. The rich brought their jewels here to be weighed, but they were not quick enough for Drake: he systematically burned and tore down parts of the town as well as looting churches and – for good measure – hanging several friars before setting sail for greener pastures. It's now the Banco Popular, and tours are free during business hours: Mon. to Fri., 8:30-4:30.

RUINAS DE SAN FRANCISCO: Located at Hostos at the cor. of Emilio Tejera. The carved white cord, symbol of St. Francis, also decorates this monumental 16th-century complex, first monastery in the Americas. It is believed to have had an underground passageway connecting it with the Alcázar and port, a characteristic shared with many other colonial structures. Sacked by Drake, it was devastated again by the 1673 and 1751 earthquakes. It was also damaged during the 1930s St. Zenon hurricane. An insane asylum was founded by Father Billini here in 1881. Portions of the cells remain, along with chains used to secure the inmates. Evenings are said to echo with the howls of deceased madmen on occasion. Interred here are the remains of Bartolomew Columbus and some other *conquistadores*. The Taino leader Enriquillo was educated here and artists, fleeing from the chaos of the Spanish Civil War, sought asylum within these walls. Today, ballets and concerts are sometimes performed here.

CALLE PADRE BILLINI: This street offers a number of sights as you head toward Palo Hincado. **Iglesia Convento de Santa Clara** was built in 1522 and served as asylum and church for the Clarissa sisters.

Early 16th-century **Casa de Tostado**, one of the most genteel colonial residences, has a unique geminated (double) window. Once this was the home of scribe Francisco Tostado. Inside is the Museo de la Familia Dominicana (Museum of the Dominican Family). In its collection are 19th-century mahogany antiques and Victorian wicker furniture. Be sure to visit the well in the garden. Inexpensive admission.

The **Convento de los Dominicanos**, popularly known as "El Convento," was founded in 1510 and was granted the title of University by Pope Paul III in 1538, making it the first in the Americas. It is now called the Universidad Autónoma de Santo Domingo, although the university has actually relocated to suburban surroundings. This formidable building is constructed of squared stone, faced with brick, and decorated with 16th-century Spanish tiles. Although the Gothic style predominates, it also employs early Renaissance and Plateresque decorative elements. Note the rose motif around the window and the decorative vines. Its altar was a gift of Ferdinand and Isabela's grandson, Spain's Emperor Charles I. Its altarpiece features the Hapsburg eagle because Charles simultaneously served as Emperor Charles V of Germany! Be sure to visit the Rosary Chapel, whose unique ceiling illustrates the medieval concept linking the elements of the universe, Christian icons, and classical gods in one unified system. The four evangelists represent Mars, Mercury, Jupiter, and Saturn, while the Sun personifies

God. Also portrayed, the 12 signs of the zodiac are believed to represent the 12 apostles. It's open Tues. to Sun., 9-6.

The 18th-century **Chapel of the Third Order** is where Eugenio María de Hostos founded the Escuela Normal, a teacher training school, at the end of the 19th century. The chapel is next to the **Iglesia de la Regina Angelorum** (1537), corner of C. Padre Billini and C. José Reyes, where the remains of philanthropist Father Billini are interred; the latter has a wall of silver near one of its altars. The first female poets in the New World, Leonor de Ovando and Elvira de Mendoza, lived here. To enter you must ask permission of the resident nuns. It's open Mon. to Sat., 9-6.

The small **Museo de la Porcelan**a, devoted to antique ceramics, is at C. José Reyes 6. It's open Tues. to Sun. from 10-6. Inexpensive admission charged.

IGLESIA DEL CARMEN: This 18th-century church contains an interesting wooden sculpture of the Nazareno (Nazarene), a type of Christ. It's on C. Arzobispo Nouel at the side of Capilla de San Andrés. It was christened the Plazoleta de La Trinitaria because its atrium served as a meeting ground for the Dominicans who led the revolt against the Haitian occupying forces in 1844. **Capilla de San Andrés** contains a statue

of this saint, to which miraculous qualities are attributed. If the chapel is closed, enter through the Padre Billini Hospital next door.

OTHER CHURCHES: Iglesia de las Mercedes (the Church and Convent of Our Lady of Mercy), corner of C. Mercedes and C. José Reyes, was built in 1555 and sacked during Drake's 1586 attack.

Far to the N, off Ave. Mella to the left near C. J. Parra, are the unique uneven towers and accompanying fort of **Iglesia de Santa Bárbara**. The curch was built in 1574 to honor the patron saint of the military. It was sacked by Drake in 1586 and, in the usual pattern, destroyed by the 1591 hurricane. It was reconstructed at the beginning of the 17th century. Visit the ruins of the fort, which command a good view. Although the fort has been restored, maintenance has been lax, to say the least. It's open Mon. to Fri., 8-noon.

The ruins of **Iglesia de San Antón** are off Av. Mella at the corner of C. Vincente Celestino Duarte.

CAPILLA DE LA VIRGEN DE ROSARIO: This church is on the other side of the Río Ozama towards the Molinos Dominicanos at the end of Av. Olegario Vargas. It was the first church built in the

Americas and was restored in 1943.

HOSPITAL-IGLESIA DE SAN NICOLAS DE BARI: This structure was built at the behest of Nicolás de Ovando between 1509 and 1552; it is located on Hostos between Mercedes and C. Luperón, Legend has it that it was built on the former home of a black woman who had once nursed the sick. This church's hospital was the first stone-built hospital in the Americas; it was sacked by Drake. Its walls were demolished in 1911 because they endangered passersby. The chapel has become incorporated into the Church of Our Lady of Altagracia. Today, pigeons reign supreme here!

MUSEO MUNDO DE AMBAR: This small museum was established in 1996 by Jorge Caridad, founder and past president of a national amber association. It offers a number of exhibits showing the origin and formation of amber, its uses, a number of amber inclusions as well as video monitors and even Internet access. Amber World (☎ 682-3309; e-mail m.ambar@codetel.net.do) is at Arz. Merino 450 at Restauracíon.

☞ *Traveler's Tip:*
Edecanes Tours (☎ 687-5245), C. Isabel la Católica 5, offers guided motorized trolley tours through this part of town. If you have limited time, this is a good way to visit all of the sites.

Metropolitan Sights

GAZCUE: Stretching W of the Zona Colonial as far as Av. Máximo Gómez, this serene residential area contains the houses of the rich dating from the 1930s and '40s, incorporating Spanish, Republican, Tudor, and Victorian styles. It's a great place to walk around if you want to get away from the hubbub of city life. To get here follow Av. César Nicolas Penson, which runs in a straight line just S of the Palacio Nacional to the Plaza de la Cultura.

PALACIO NACIONAL: Following the traffic flow from the park, you come to Av. Bolivár. Turn R on C. Dr. Delgado to find the National Palace. Used as executive and administrative offices and to house visiting foreign dignitaries, it has never been the presidential residence. Designed by Italian architect Guido D'Alessandro, this castle-like rose-colored marble structure was inauguarated in 1947. Inside, the palace was furnished with old mahogany, gold inlays, Samaná marble in various shades, beautiful mirrors, and

Santo Domingo

elaborate crystal. Its best known room is the "Room of the Caryatids," in which 44 draped sculptured women rise column-like in a hall decked with mirrors and Baccarat chandeliers. To make an appointment for a free guided tour (available on Mon., Wed., and Fri.) ☎ 686-4771, ext. 340 and 360. However, the building may not be open to just *anyone*, so you should think up a good excuse.

PLAZA DE LA CULTURA: Take a *público* along Av. Máximo Gómez or turn R on C. Bolivar and then left onto César Nicolas Penson until you reach this complex of ultramodern buildings in a park-like setting. This area was once the personal property of Trujillo. You can easily spend the better part of a day here roaming about, sharing it only with the staff. Even on Sundays, it doesn't seem to attract a crowd.

MUSEO DEL HOMBRE DO-MINICANO: This "Museum of the Dominican Man" is the best of the lot. It contains poignant photos of life in a sugarcane village, the unique throne cars the pope rode during his 1979 visit, an extensive collection of Taino artifacts, carnival displays, and more. It serves as a good introduction to the pulse and tempo of the crazy pastiche of African, Spanish, and Taino cultures that make up Dominicana. The first floor has a bookstore (good maps of the nation) and a room with Taino monoliths. From there you take an elevator up to the third floor, which has numerous Taino artifacts such as grinding stones, axes, carved necklaces, pottery, and a burial site under glass. There's also the stone head of Mictantecuhti, the god of the region of the dead. A diorama shows the slaughter of a beleaguered manatee, and another shows women cooking while the men lounge in hammocks; even way back then the Dominican women were doing most of the work. One section depicts the ways and means of hallucinogenic intoxication. A diorama shows men snorting and a chief in a trance. *Duhos*, thrones for sitting and inhaling, are shown, along with related paraphernalia.

The fourth floor illustrates Spanish and African influences on the island. There's a *Vudu Dominicano* altar, a collection of *oraciones*, depictions of *santos* (saints), and a display of musical instruments. Photos show ceremonies at such cultish churches as the Iglesia Maravillosa o de Boca de Mai at Villa Altagracia. There's also a model *casa de un campesino* and a display illustrating similarities to African architecture. One section shows *carnavál* costumes from all across the land. In direct contrast is a portrait of a stiff German couple posing in front of their Hotel Aleman in Sánchez on the

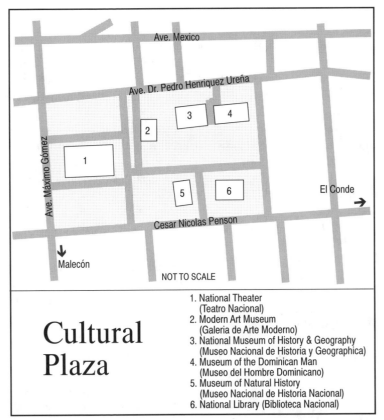

Ave. Mexico

Ave. Dr. Pedro Henriquez Ureña

Ave. Máximo Gómez

El Conde →

Cesar Nicolas Penson

↓ Malecón

NOT TO SCALE

Cultural Plaza

1. National Theater
   (Teatro Nacional)
2. Modern Art Museum
   (Galeria de Arte Moderno)
3. National Museum of History & Geography
   (Museo Nacional de Historia y Geographica)
4. Museum of the Dominican Man
   (Museo del Hombre Dominicano)
5. Museum of Natural History
   (Museo Nacional de Historia Nacional)
6. National Library (Biblioteca Nacional)

Samaná Peninsula. It's open Tues. to Sun., 10-5, ☎ 687-3622. Inexpensive admission.

GALERIA DE ARTE MODERNO: Located on Pedro Henriquez Ureña, this gallery contains fantastic woodcarvings, oils, mixed media works, and photographs. The display and arrangement here is excellent. The collection's highlights include Antonio Guadalupe's Tilapia, Manolo Pascual's portrait of a squid, Adolfo Piantini's "Sadismo-Masoquismo," Santiago Sosa's futuristic oils, and Alberto Ulloa's "Lamento

Americano." Its fourth floor features rotating exhibits that may range from stained glass to moving wooden sculptures. There's also a library open from Mon. to Sat. The museum itself is open Tues. to Sun., 10-5, ☎ 682-8280. Inexpensive admission charged; Tuesdays are free.

MUSEO NACIONAL DE HISTORIA Y GEOGRAPHICA: Right nearby on César Nicolas Penson, this museum is worthwhile chiefly for its comprehensive collection of Trujillo memorabilia on display in *sala* three. It's one of the few places, you'll see this despot's name mentioned directly. One of the first things you'll come to is the *gírocóptero* that Tirso Garcia flew from Bayamon, Puerto Rico to Santo Domingo in 1983. Sala de Historia 1 (1822-1861) features a ship model, weapons, depictions of the Haitian occupation, including details of various battles, and a coffee cup designed with moustaches in mind. The next room covers 1861-1916 and offers more weapons, memorabilia relating to dictator Ulises Heureux, old uniforms and money, and Juan Isidro Jiménez's presidential sash. Sala de Historia 3 (1916-1961) contains photos of the American occupation, including a legendary portrait of a torture victim, a reproduction of an electric chair, and a stupendous collection of Trujillo artifacts: his wallet, passport, *cedula* (identification card), medals, shoes, an ivory straight edge razor with his name inscribed on it, sashes, combs, briefcase, death mask, and a finely polished thick slice of a mahogany tree trunk with Trujillo's portrait etched on it; one of the three cars used in Trujillo's assassination is right behind the ticket desk as you enter. The museum is open Tues. to Sun. 10-5. Inexpensive admission is charged.

MUSEO DE HISTORIA NACIONAL: This museum's exhib-

its are labelled in Spanish and encompass space, geology, and zoology. There are dioramas, a gemstone section, and an amber collection. It also has whale skeletons, stuffed animals, and displays of the cosmos. If you want to familiarize yourself with the nation's birds. this is the place. It has a cafeteria on its upper level. It's open Tues. to Sun., 10:30-5:30. Inexpensive admission charged.

BIBLIOTECA NACIONAL: Right on César Nicolas Penson, the national library operates Mon. to Fri. from 9AM to 11PM. It houses tons of books along with a small art gallery.

TEATRO NACIONAL: This center for opera and symphony is on Av. Máximo Gómez (☎ 682-7255). Its main hall holds 1,600 people, and a smaller one holds 170.

MUSEO NUMISMATICO: The Numismatic and Philatelic Museum contains one of the Caribbean's most valuable and comprehensive coin and stamp collections. It's on Pedro Henriquez Ureña at Leopoldo Navarro and housed in the Central Bank, Open Tues. through Sat. from 9 to 5.

JARDIN BOTANICO NACIONAL (NATIONAL BOTANIC GARDENS): Set in the city's NW corner, this large park is a favorite picnic spot. The **Aquatic Plant**

Pavilion, just off the central plaza, features displays of plants in tanks and in pools. You'll find water lilies, marsilea, cattails, azolla, horsetails, pickerel-weed, and over 200 species of palm, along with West Indian mahogany, the national flower featured on the currency. A series of artificial ponds, the **Gran Canada** is great for birdwatching. Ducks share the water with rented rowboats, and heliconia and ginger bloom along the banks. The gardens' national herbarium has displays of medicinal and poisonous plants along with a small library. The **Bromeliad Pavilion** features guess what? Open Tues. to Sat. from 9-5. Inexpensive admission charged.

PARQUE ZOOLOGICO NACIONAL: This is one of the largest and most majestic zoological parks in the Americas, with the beautiful landscaped gardens where animals can roam freely over a 400-acre area. Monkeys swing from poles on an artificial island across from dromedaries munching on grass. There's an authentic African feel to the place. Beautifully designed and covered with netting, the walkthrough aviary features native and exotic species, including the Hispaniolan parrot and palmchat. Be sure to visit the serpent and reptile house, where you can see hutias and solenodons. The zoo's amiable chimpanzee es-caped in 1997 when a tree limb fell into his cage, opening a bridge to the outside. He was shot twice, operated on, and then returned to his cage, traumatized and shaken by his encounter. The zoo is open Tues. to Sat., 9-5. Inexpensive admission charged

PARQUE MIRADOR DEL SUR/PASEO DE LOS INDIOS: Located on a narrow stretch of land between Ave. Anaconda and Ave. Mirador Del Sur, this five-mile tree-lined boulevard and park was built to commemorate the Indians. It's situated atop a long limestone terrace – it's perfect for viewing the city, jogging, cycling, picnicking, and watching sunsets. Kite-flying contests sometimes take place here.

One of the park's largest caves, the **Cueva del Paseo de Los Indios** was formed when the limestone underlying the terrace dissolved. Bats are occasionally found in one of its large domed rooms. Visit here during the daytime. For refreshments try the food stands or the **Mesón de la Cueva**, a restaurant and nightspot. Newer and more celebrated is the **Guacara Taina** disco (see *entertainment*, page 155). It now offers day tours for groups of 100 or more.

PARQUE LOS TRES OJOS DE AGUA (THE THREE EYES OF WATER): This is a series of four interconnected underwater ponds of volcanic origin with numerous stalactite and stalagmite formation. It's one of the city's major natural attractions, set in the **Parque Mirador del Este** which borders the airport road. The large and spectacular *cenotes* (sinkholes), set in a limestone terrace facing the sea, account for its name.

Each cavern's *cenote* is colored differently. You can walk around the circumference of the largest and then descend the steps to a boat that takes you across to the other side. There's also a recently discovered fourth lake. Outside, vendors flog sculptures carved from stalactites. From the park, the Avenida de las Américas, running to Boca Chica, is lined with flags from all the western hemisphere's nations.

To get here from El Conde take a *público* along Av. Bolivar to Winston Churchill and from there take one in the direction of the sea.

⚡ Warning
Guides here are notorious for taking advantage of visitors. The price for a boat trip is included in the admission. You may tip them if you wish, but don't let them pull the "RD$300 for two according to my rate sheet" scam!

ACUARIO NACIONAL: A product of the Balaguer administration, this small aquarium features tanks you can walk *un-der:* an arched passageway leads beneath the tropical-fish-filled tanks. Open concrete ponds contain turtles, starfish, and anemones. There's also a small outdoor cafeteria. Open 9:30-6 from Tues. to Sun., it's located in the Parque Littoral del Sur, which is between C. Cuarta and 28 de Enero along the coast just to the S of Parque Mirador del Este.

FARO A COLÓN: Also across the Río Ozama, most of this monstrous lighthouse – a huge hunk of fortress-like reinforced concrete – is impossible to ignore. It is perhaps Balaguer's attempt to mimic Java's Borobudor or Cambodia's Angkor Wat. It contains the remains of Christopher Columbus. The six museums and libraries within are dedicated to Columbus, and its searchlight shines over a 60-mile radius with 149 Xenon Skytrack lasers projecting a cross onto the city skyline. Naturally, in a nation with chronic shortages of electricity, it has its own generator; plans call for it to converted to solar power.

history: The project was first dreamed up in the 19th-century by Dominican writer and historian Antonio Delmonte y Tejada who called for "a statue... a colossus, like that of Rhodes" in his *History of Santo Domingo*, published in 1852. In 1923 the Fifth International American Conference, held in Santiago de Chile, resolved that a lighthouse should be constructed in Santo Domingo. One J. Gleave, an architectural student from Manchester, submitted the winning design in an international contest.

A four-airplane goodwill flight – designed to promote the lighthouse construction – set out on a grand tour of the Americas in 1937. Unfortunately the three Cuban planes crashed into a mountain while flying from Colombia to Ecuador; only the Dominican craft. was spared. Although ground was broken under Trujillo in 1939, WWII intervened and construction was abandoned; some say that he had heard the story of a jinx on Columbus's name and events such as the plane crash and the earthquake that commenced during the 1946 Columbus pageant convinced him of its veracity. To this day, Dominicans refer to the *fucu* (Arawak for "curse" of Columbus) and refer to him only as "The Discoverer" and "The Admiral." Balaguer ordered renewed construction in 1987. The project is estimated to have cost more than US$70 million, and parts of the interior remain uncompleted.

the inauguration: The government had intended the lighthouse to serve as a beacon for tourism and to assert the Dominican Republic's place in the Western Hemisphere. That proved to be a major miscalcula-

tion. In an attempt to forge a religious connection, the government termed the event a celebration of "The Discovery and Evengelization of America."

The event was intended to attracti luminaries such as American right wing comedian Bob Hope (who had originally been scheduled to emcee a variety show) and the King and Queen of Spain. In fact, Argentina's Carlos Menem was the only head of state to attend the dedication. Although he later conducted a mass from behind the structure on the day before Columbus Day, the Pope disassociated his visit from the celebrations. The dedication was moved up from Oct. 12 (Columbus Day) to Oct. 6. After Balaguer's 73-year-old sister Emma Vallejo suffered a fatal heart attack just after touring the lighthouse, Balaguer cancelled his appearance at the dedication!

The celebration was marked by nationwide protests with demonstrators chanting "Colón Ladron" ("Columbus is a thief"). A group of priests protested, a protester was shot in Azua by an undercover cop, and a human rights lawyer was shot dead by six police officers from the secret service branch of the national police. In preparation for the dedication, some 50,000 residents of the area were evicted and 10-ft.-high walls erected along the road to the site in an attempt to camouflage the poverty. Dubbed the "Wall of Shame," it has aroused great controversy. As one resident said, "It shows that we are still Indians, symbolically speaking. We are still the people Columbus came to kill." Another asserted that "the government is treating us as garbage that must be swept under the rug."

sights: The first thing that comes into view as you enter is the elaborate marble and bronze tomb of Christopher Columbus, which was formerly housed in the cathedral. No one knows if it actually contains the bones of the 15th-century navigator; another elaborate chapel in Seville, Spain makes the same claim. Believed to have been first brought here by his daughter-in-law in 1544, the alleged remains were found during restoration work in 1877 by Padre Francisco Billini, and the tomb (donated by the Spanish government) was made in 1898. Friezes around the base depict important episodes in Columbus's life. Passing by the tomb, you come to a long outdoor passageway flanked on either side by beautiful mahogany doors with brass handles. These lead to the museums. They depict the history of the lighthouse, with a library dedicated to Columbus and his voyages, maps of the Americas, a Columbus museum, one on underwater archaeology, and a sixth displaying 15th-century ceramics. The monument is covered with thousands of crosses: Juan Bosch held that there is one cross for every Indian killed!

In 1997, Cardinal Nicolás López Rodríguez inagaurated the new **Capilla Santa María de la Rábida**. The chapel's name has its roots in medieval history. When Columbus failed to get backing from the King of Portugal for his voyage, he stayed at the Monasterio de la Rábida until he was able to contact the monarch of Spain and propose the voyage. There he reportedly prayed to Santa María de la Rábida.

THE BIBLE PARK: Believe it or not, a "Disney-style biblical

The Santo Domingo 2000 Project

The dream of a group of Florida architects, the plan is to develop the Sans Souci area adjacent to the Faro a Colón. The Molinos Dominicanos flour mill will be demolished. The sponsoring firm will obtain a 50-year lease on the area. Three hotels, with a combined 2,500 rooms would be constructed, each with its own casino. A new bridge, a monorail, shopping mall, and conference center would be built as well. Under the plan, the cruise ship port at Sans Souci will also be remodeled.

park" is currently under construction in Santo Domingo! The brainchild of Father Manuel Ruiz, the park is intended to utilize new technologies to literally shine a new light on Bible stories. Visiting families will be greeted by a giant open bible at the entrance. A boat will take them through technological reenactments of legends found in the Bible. The park will be funded by the Catholic church, the Dominican government, and by donations from Catholics in the Dominican Republic and around the world. Walt Disney and Universal Studios are consulting on the project. They will train staff and provide contacts with the requisite specialized firms. The Dominican government has donated land for the park, which is near the Avenida Ecologica, in the city's SW. The government will fund 60% of the project's cost. It may open as soon as the year 2000.

MALECÓN SIGHTS: The titanic scupture along the *Malecón* (waterfront) is of Fray Anton de Montecrios who protested the Spanish exploitation of the Indians. It was a gift. from Mexico in Oct. 1982. Two obelisks are farther down. The first commemorates payment of the national debt to the US during the negotiations between Trujillo and US Secretary of State Cordell Hull. It has been repainted with murals.

The second and larger one commemorates the renaming of the city as Ciudad Trujillo during the height of the despot's reign. Constructed in a record 17 days, it is popularly known as "Obelisco Macho." Located on one side of the street, Parque Eugenio María de Hostos has been restored to its 1940-era design. Though it was originally designed as the Plaza Columbiana where Columbus's remains were to be interred, plans were changed and it became Parque Infantil Ramfis after Trujillo's oldest son.

⚡ **Warning!**
Exercise caution along the Malecón at night. Reader M. M. relates "Only 100 m or so separate restaurants and bright lights from a dimly lit playground populated by thieves. I came within a hair's breadth of being mugged and losing my camera, film, etc. while walking there shortly after sundown."

OTHER SIGHTS: The **Museo de Trujillo** is a private museum in Store 7 at Plaza Criolla. Housing pre-Columbian artifacts, the **Museo Pre-hispanico** is set at Av. San Martin 279 (near the intersection of Máximo Gómez and 27 de Febrero). Run by the 7-Up Company; this small museum is open 8-noon, Mon. to Sat.

Past the Santo Domingo Hotel, **Centro de Los Héroes**, presently a collection of rundown government office buildings, was the setting for the 1955-56 Feria de Confraternidad (Fair of Peace and Fraternity of the Free World), on which Trujillo squandered an incredible US$40 million, a third of that year's national budget. It now houses the Senate and Congress. At the opening of the fair, the dictator's 16-year-old daughter Maria was crowned Queen Angelita I. She wore a US$80,000 satin coat with a 75-ft. Russian ermine train. These days, the area turns into red light central after hours!

If you wish to see a dramatic counterpart to the Faro a Colón, you should visit the Ciudad Universidad to the W of Gazcue. The **Universidad Autonomal Santo Domingo** (UASD) here has a large but delapidated campus. Never popular with Balaguer (he was ousted from a professorship here), the university is virtually free but vastly underfunded. Posters display protest demands, and conditions are quite bad. It shows where the government puts its priorities.

Santo Domingo Hotels

With so many places to choose from, it's not an easy task to decide upon a hotel. Factors include your pocketbook and your interests. The place to be is in Old Santo Domingo, but accommodations there is limited to a few hotels. Another nice area to stay in is Gazcue.

LUXURY AND ULTRA-LUXURY: Most of the accommodations listed in this section are priced at over US$100 pn. Many are located along Av. George Washington, the seaside boulevard popularly known as the Malecón.

At Av. George Washington 218 (corner of Pasteur), the **V Centenario's** (☎ 687-2933, 800-223-5652) 230 rooms include 30 suites; all rooms face the sea. Facilities include restaurants, tennis, squash, pool, gym, sauna, disco, casino, and piano bar.

The 260-rm. **Sheraton Santo Domingo Hotel and Casino** (☎ 221-6666, 688-0823, fax 687-8150, 686-0125, 800-325-3535; Box 8326) is at Av. George Washington 365. Rooms here have cable TV with remote control and most command views of the sea. Its facilities include gym, sauna, pool, tennis court, convention rooms, disco, casino, and three restaurants. A recently renovated classic, the 355-rm. **Jaragua Renaissance Resort and**

Casino (☎ 221-2222, fax 686-0528) is on Av. George Washington 367 and is set on 14 acres. The hotel's rooms have marble bathrooms, hair dryers, color TVs, and computerized door locks. Other facilities include a nightclub, ballroom, the nation's largest casino, a European-style spa, five restaurants, an Olympic-style pool, four tennis courts, and a convention center that can service up to 1,000. Prices range from US$110 for a "standard" room to US$1,500 for the penthouse, and this does not include 23% tax and service. You can ☎ 800-228-9898 toll free in the US or 800-331-3542 toll free in the Dominican Republic.

The 316-room a/c **Dominican Fiesta** (☎ 562-8222) is on Av. Anaconda and has two restaurants, an Olympic-sized pool, an attractive casino, and eight tennis courts.

The 316-room a/c **Hotel El Embajador** (☎ 533-2131, 800-457-0067, fax 532-4494/5306) is on Av. Sarasota. Its rooms are equipped with radio and cable TV. Facilities include a restaurant, coffeeshop, nightclub, casino, pool, shopping arcade, beauty parlor, massage and sauna services, car rental, babysitting services, and taxi service. It can accommodate up to 350 conventioneers.

Set right next to each other on the W side of the Malecón, the Hotels Santo Domingo and Hispaniola share common owners, and their meal plans are interchangeable.

The colonial-style 220-rm. **Hotel Santo Domingo** (☎ 221-7111), Av. Independencia and Av. Abraham Lincoln, offers elegant interior decoration by designer Oscar de la Renta. The rooms have lots of lush red lacquer work and Dominican mahogany furniture. With 69 rooms, its "premier floor" is designed for executives and features a breakfast lounge along with additional facilities in the rooms such as a hairdryer and TV remote control. Renting for around US$725 pn, the huge presidential suite on this level includes a business meeting room. Facilities include restaurant, pool, night club, tennis and volleyball courts, sauna and massage, beauty parlor, and boutique. ☎ 800-223-6620 in the US.

The 160-rm **Hotel Hispaniola** (☎ 535-7111), Independencia at Av. Lincoln, is the Santo Domingo's less elegant and less expensive sister; it has comfortable a/c rooms with cable TV and radio, a restaurant, bar, disco, pool, three tennis courts, beauty parlor, car rental, gift. shop, and massage. Built in 1956, it still has manual elevators with operators – a nice blast from the past. ☎ 800-223-6620 in the US.

EXPENSIVE: There are a number of choices in this price

range. The seafront 72-rm. a/c **Hotel Napolitano** (☎ 687-1131, fax 689-2714) is on Av. George Washington. It has a terrace restaurant, 24-hr. cafeteria, disco, pool, and a beauty salon.

The 180-rm. a/c **Hotel Cervantes** (☎ 686-8161, fax 686-5754; Apdo. 2768), C. Cervantes 202, has a swimming pool, steakhouse, and nightclub. Rooms come with cable TV, a/c, and radios.

The 87-rm. **Hotel Comodoro** (☎ 541-2277), Av. Bólivar 193, has a pool; rooms are a/c with cable TV and refrigerators; other facilities include a French restaurant, cafeteria, nightclub, car rental, taxi service, and convention facilities for up to 300.

The 39-rm. **Hotel Caribe I** (☎ 688-8141), Av. Máximo Gómez (corner of Ramirez), has a pool and an Italian restaurant. Rooms have radio, cable TV, and are a/c.

The 100-rm. **Hotel Continental** (☎ 688-1840, 689-1151-59), Av. Máximo Gómez 16, offers a/c rooms with radio and cable TV. Its facilities include a French restaurant, disco, bar, small pool, and babysitting service. In the US ☎ 800-223-1900.

The 72-rm. **Hotel San Geronimo and Casino** (☎ 535-1000/8851), Av. Independencia 1076, has a/c rooms with cable TV and radio. There's also car rental, pool, cafeteria, and restaurant. Rooms run around US$40 d.

Centrally located in the old part of town at C. Las Damas 53, **Hostal Nicolás de Ovando** (☎ 688-9220) is a restored 16th-century mansion which once belonged to the famous *conquistador* and Hispaniolan governor of the same name. It has a pool and is a/c. **note:** It was closed at the time of publication. One reader writes: "The room I stayed in was run-down and the service was poor." Hopefully, the remodeled version will be new and improved.

MODERATE: The a/c **Hotel Palacio** (☎ 682-4730, fax 6875535; www.codetel.net.do/Hotel_Palacio/Welcome.html, www.dominican-rep.com; email h.palacio@codetel.net.do; Apdo. 20541, Santo Domingo) is set in the heart of the old town at C. Duarte 106 (corner of Salome Ureña).

Opened in the fall of 1991, its 10 rooms are furnished Castilian-style. There are also two single rooms and a large suite, with a private Jacuzzi. The seven regular rooms feature remote-control color cable TV, wardrobe, phones (one for the room and one for the bath), furnished kitchenette, and minibar. Other facilities include secretarial service, fax, tourist guide service, bar, and small gym/Jacuzzi. The hotel is actually a restored home, once the private house of the offspring of Buenaventura Báez who served five times as president between 1848 and 1878. It has a pleasant patio facing a courtyard. Rates run from around US$50 s, US$60 d. Coffee and tea are complimentary; a continental breakfast is served at additional cost. A 10% discount is offered to readers of this book. E-mail reservations are accepted. The hotel is run by Joachim Wagner, a German expat who has resided in the Dominican Republic for almost two decades; he also owns Hotel Atlantis at Punta Bonita in Las Terrenas.

Just up the street is the **Hostal Nicolas Nader** (☎ 687-6674, 687-7887, fax 541-2404), C. Luperón 151 at C. Duarte, which is another refurbished home. An art gallery is downstairs. Algerian food is served some nights, and there is a bar.

Priced at around US$50 s or d, including tax and service, the 75-rm. a/c **Hotel Comercial** (☎ 682-8161; Apdo. 787, Santo Domingo) is at C. El Conde 201 at Hostos. It has a cafeteria and bar and all of its rooms come with private bath. It is reportedly not in the best of condition.

On C. Danae in the Gazcue area, 24-rm. a/c **Hotel la Residence** (☎ 682-4178, 686-2828) is a European-style hotel with TV, a/c, wall-to-wall carpeting, and your choice of bed size – from double to king.

Duque de Wellington Hotel (☎/fax 682-4525), in Gazcue, is

an attractive hotel with a restaurant. Rooms have cable TV, phone, hair dryers, and "walking" closets.

Newly opened in 1993, **Hotel Restaurante La Casona Dorada** (☎ 221-3535, fax 682-1832) is a small, elegant hotel at Av. Independencia 255 (cor. C. Osvaldo Báez). Rates run from around US$40 d.

Finally, **Hotel Delta** (☎ 535-0800/9722, fax 535-6957), Av. Sarasota 53, has 75 a/c rooms with TV, refrigerator, bar and restaurant, along with a solarium and Jacuzzi. In the DR ☎ toll free 1-200-1288 or write Apdo. 1818, Santo Domingo.

INEXPENSIVE: At C. Presidente Vicini Burgos 58 in Gazcue, a half-block from the obelisk on the Malecón, 13-rm. **Hotel El Señorial** (☎ 687-4367, fax 687-0600) is renowned for its relaxed and social atmosphere. Its comfortable rooms (priced at around US$30 s or d) are a/c, with cable TV. It has a nice dining room and good food.

The **Hotel Ocean Inn** (☎ 688-8242) has rooms for around US$25-30 d. The entrance is at Independencia 654; the official address is at Av. George Washington 555. It charges around US$25. Rooms have a/c and phones. The staff are affable and easygoing.

Priced from around US$20 s and US$27 d, **Hotel Palmeras**

del Caribe (☎ 689-3872, 682-0959) is on the Malecón at C. Cambronal 1. It has small but attractive rooms with b&w TVs. The Dominican management is very friendly, and the location is ideal.

In Gazcue at C. Danae 26, **La Mansion** (☎ 686-5562, 682-2033, 689-8758) has rooms for about US$20 and up. **Hotel La Residence** (☎ 682-4178), C. Danae 62, is a dollar or so more expensive but better value.

Priced at US$20 s and US$28 d., **Hotel Alameda** (☎ 685-5121/5122) is at C. Cervantés 157.

Hotel Anacaona (☎ 688-6888), Palo Hincado 303, has rooms with a/c, private bath, and hot water.

Hotel Bolivar (☎ 685-2200), Av. Bolivar 62, has rooms with bath, fan, and TV.

Maison Gautreaux (☎ 687-4856), Félix Mariano Lluberas 8 in Gazcue, is a small guesthouse with 14 a/c rooms for around US$30.

On the old town's Malecón above the restaurant of the same name, the **Llave del Mar** (☎ 682-5761) offers rooms for about US$18 s or d.

Back in the old town, attractive, extremely atmospheric, but aging **Hotel David** (☎ 688-8538, 685-9121/9123, fax 688-8056), Arz. Nouel 308), offers a TV and refrigerator in its rooms, which are priced at around US$40 s or d. Inexpensive **Hotel Aida** (☎ 685-7692, 687-2880), El Conde 464 at Espaillat, has a/c rooms and less expensive ones with fans.

Offering a terrace restaurant with Jacuzzi, at Av. Duarte and Teniente Amado Garcia, the **Royal Hotel** (☎ 686-5852/1717, fax 686-6536) offers 64 a/c rooms with phones for US$32 s, US$35 d, US$40 t.

Located near the Terra Bus terminal, **Hotel Rosal** (☎ 596-5033, 597-2066) is at C. Marginal 9, Alma Rosa 2.

La Luna del Norte (☎ 687-0124), Benito González 89 at Duarte, charges around US$15 for rooms with a/c. With TV and a/c, rooms run about US$20. It is not in the best of neighborhoods.

LOW-BUDGET: Set at Estrelleta 267 near Arzobispo Nouel and Parque Independencia, the seedy **Independencia** (☎ 686-1663) has rooms for US$15 d.

The **Hotel Rafael** (☎ 685-0084), Av. Independencia 19 (100 m from Parque Independencia) has rooms with fans and baths for US$11.

Aparta Hotel Ponce (☎ 688-6347), Palo Hincado 204, charges US$14 for rooms with a hotplate. The only sink is in the bathroom, and the hotel accepts short-term guests.

The **Hotel Montesino** (☎ 688-3346), José Gabriel No. 111 (altos), is near the Malecón in the old town. It charges around US$15.

You may also try the **Pensión Dominicana** (☎ 689-0722) at El Conde 454 and **Pensión Ginette** (☎ 685-7815); around US$15), El Conde 505. Also try to look for rooms in *casas de pensión* and in hotels by consulting the classified listings in the daily *Listin Diario*. Finally, be aware that many of the cheapest places are unmarked, so ask around.

APART-HOTELS: If you would like to do some cooking, you have a wide variety of choices. Featuring 28 suites fully a/c with color TV and kitchenettes, **Apart-Hotel Drake** (☎ 567-4427) is at Augustin Lara 29 near Plaza Naco.

At Plaza Naco, the **Plaza Hotel and Casino** (☎ 541-6226) is administered by the Naco chain. The tallest hotel, it features 54 suites and 165 efficiencies, all with kitchenettes. At Av. Tiradentes 22, a convenient midtown location, its rooms also include cable TV, radio, and a complete kitchenette; other facilities include a pool, cafeteria, restaurant, casino, and babysitting service. In the US ☎ 800-223-6510 and in Canada call 800-424-5500.

The **Apart-Hotel Aladino** (☎ 567-0144/0140), H. Pieter 34 (Ens. Naco), has both fan and a/c rooms available.

At Av. Bolivár 230, **Plaza Florida** (☎ 541-3957/4742, fax 540-5582) offers 32 spacious a/c and fully equipped one-bedroom apartments.

The **Aparta-Hotel Plaza del Sol** (☎ 688-5596/5497/5686, fax 542-5454), José Contreras 25-A, offers fully furnished studios.

On Av. 27 de Febrero, **Apart-Hotel Arak** (☎ 567-4267) offers fully equipped a/c apartments with power plant, maid, elevators, and 24-hr. security.

In Gazcue, **Apart-Hotel Plaza Colonial** (☎ 687-9111, 685-9171, fax 686-2877), C. Luisa Pellerano at the cor. of Av. Jules Verne, offers a/c fully equipped one- and two-bedroom apartments, pool, and restaurant.

Located near the Olympic Center, at C. Gustavo Mejia Ricart 8-A, **Aparta-Hotel Turey** (☎ 562-5271/5446) provides tasteful a/c studios and one-bedrooms with kitchenettes. There's also a pool and snack bar.

At the intersection of Av. 27th de Febrero and Av. Winston Churchill, **Plaza Central** (☎ 565-6905/6706) has 25 "Club Plaza" executive suites for business travelers, offerings telex, secretarial services, and seminar facilities.

Aby has three apartment hotels; one is at C. Padre Pina 104 (☎ 685-9729); another is at C. 23 Este Esq.; 25 Este la Castellana, Los Prados (☎ 541-0876/7116); and a third at C. 6 No. 9 Ens. Evaristo Morales, near the corner of Winston Churchill and 27 de Febrero (☎ 565-7184). **Aparta-Hotel Laurel** (☎ 530-4724/3859), C. Caonabo 41, features color TV in all apartments, a/c, and a restaurant.

Set on the edge of the Malecón, **Apart-Hotel Sea-View** (☎ 221-4420/4319/4119) has units from around US$45. Others include **Apart-Hotel Plaza Florida** (☎ 541-3650, Av. Lara 29) and **Apart-Hotel Mi Retiro** (☎ 598-0028, Del Pez 13).

In the old town, inexpensive and spartan **La Arcada** (☎ 686-7456), C. Arz. Meriño 360, has apartments with cooking facilities from around US$12 pn; a discount is offered for longer stays.

📖 *Suggested Reading*

If you're planning on sticking around town long-term, try to pick up a copy of Living in Santo Domingo, *published by the Santo Domingo News (1995).*

OUT OF TOWN: Staying in Boca Chica (see the following section) is an alternative to the capital. Public transportation to and fro is quite good during the day. The 54-room Italian-run **Hotel**

Acuarium (☎ 595-6755/fax 593-4484) is outside of town on the way to the airport. It has a restaurant, bar, pool, and conference rooms.

Santo Domingo Dining & Food

The more expensive restaurants here may require that men wear a jacket.

HOTEL DINING: Each of the major hotels has its own special restaurant. At the Santo Domingo and designed by Oscar de la Renta, the **Alcázar**, with its 20-ft. tented ceiling, resembles a Moroccan palace. It's known for its fish dishes; buffet lunches here are less expensive, and a champagne brunch is featured on Sun. Also try Las Palmas here. **La Piazetta** at the Hispaniola features Italian specialties. The **Hotel Comodoro**, Av. Bolivar 193, has **Le Gourmet**, which serves international and Dominican dishes. **note:** Many of the hotels offer lunchtime *buffets ejecutivos* for about US$10.

OLD TOWN DINING: At the end of El Conde between Damas and Parque Colón, Argentinean-owned **Ché Bandoneón** (☎ 689-2105) features elegant Argentinean, French, and Dominican food served outdoors to the accompaniment of tangos. **La Cocina** is nearby. Serving local and international cuisine, the **Fonda La**

Ataranza (☎ 689-2900) is at La Ataranza 5. The **Meson de la Ataranza** offers outdoor gourmet dining; naturally enough, it's also near the Ataranza.

Italian **La Bricola** (☎ 688-5055; reservations required), Arz. Meriño 152, is one of the finest restaurants in this part of town.

If it has been reopened, the Hostal Nicólas de Ovando's **Extremadura**, C. Las Damas 52, serves Spanish food. Also with Spanish-style cuisine, **América** (☎ 682-7194), is at C. Santome 201 and Arzobispo Nouel.

Serving English-style food in a formal setting, **Café Coco** (☎ 687-9624; reservations required) is at C. Padre Billini 53 off of El Conde.

Down at the Malecón on the old town side are a number of restaurants, including **Restaurant del Mar** and the **Restaurant la Llave del Mar** which offers piano music and decor including a stuffed crocodile, sea turtles, birds on the ceiling, corals, and stuffed fish. It claims to be a "paradise," but it's a marine life lover's nightmare.

Classy outdoor **Manresa** is across the road. The a/c **Les Jardines de Bagatelle** is next door and **La Bahía** is farther down the road. If none of these last few appeal to you, you can always snack it up at the **Pizza Capri**.

An intimate bar and restaurant, the **Meson de Bari**, C. Hostos and C. Salome Ureña, serves good Dominican and Spanish dishes.

Jardines De San Pedro (☎ 221-8850, ext. 228), C. Mercedes 155, is in Edificio San Pedro. Enter at the corner of Hostos and Duarte.

Less expensive options are the **Bar Restaurant América** (☎ 682-7124), C. Santome 201, which serves Spanish food, and **Rita's Café** (☎ 688-9400), C. Ataranza 27.

ON THE MALECÓN: At Av. George Washington 1, **La Bahía** is renowned for its seafood, including conch, lobster, and shrimp. Specializing in steak and seafood, **El Castillo del Mar** is at Av. George Washington 2. Serving French cuisine, **Les Jardins del Bagatelle** are at Av. George Washington 39. Folkloric shows are presented on the patio from time to time. With two locations at 459 and 123, spacious **Restaurant El Caserio** specializes in seafood.

The Sheraton's **Antoine's**, George Washington 365, features international and seafood dishes. A classic restaurant and continually bustling, **Vesuvio I**, Av. George Washington 521, serves Italian and international cuisine. A great location for peoplewatching, its outdoor section is the place to see and be seen. Smaller and similar, though less atmospheric, **Vesuvio II**, a second establishment, is at Av. Tiradentes 17. Outdoors on the Malecón at Av. George Washington 553, **La Parilla** specializes in BBQ.

NEAR THE MALECÓN: Featuring Peruvian-style seafood and local cuisine, the renowned **Jai-Alai** (☎ 685-2409) is at Av. Independencia 411, to the rear of the Jaragua and Sheraton hotels.

Also behind the Jaragua and Sheraton hotels at Av. Independencia 407, **La Mezquita** offers Spanish food in an informal but comfortable environment.

Serving Dominican, Italian, French, and Spanish food, **Restaurante Tonde de Tasis** is also in the vicinity of the Jaragua.

Outdoors and overlooking the Malecón, **Le Café**, JM Heredia, offers light meals including crêpes and desserts.

Popular with baseball afficionadoes, the **Lucky Seven**, C. Pasteur 16, has steaks and seafood. Next to Lucky Seven on C. Pasteur at Casimiro de Moya, **Marbella** offers seafood specialties. Also with Spanish cuisine, multi-level **El Toledo**, C. Pasteur at the corner of Casimiro de Moya, serves seafood dishes and other specialties.

At C. Santiago at C. Pasteur, **Don Pepe** has Spanish atmosphere and cuisine.

The **Bronco Steak House** at the Hotel Cervantes, C. Cervantes 202 at Bolivar, serves American-style steaks and chops; it has an extensive wine list.

Another beautiful converted home in the Gazcue area, **D. Luis** (☎ 689-3534), C. Santiago 205, has an international menu and a separate bar.

La Reina de España, C. Cervantes 103, serves Castillian and international food as well as innovative cuisine such as sea bass served in apple cider.

OTHER LOCATIONS: Offering steaks and other grilled foods, **La Pyramide** is at Av. Romúlo Betancourt 352.

The **Delcías Diner** is also on Av. Romúlo Betancourt.

D'Agostini, Av. Máximo Gómez 9 near the Continental and Caribe hotels, serves very expensive international food. It's well known for its *ceviche* and its cooked *mero* (bass).

Juan Carlos (☎ 562-6444), C. Gustavo Mejia Ricart 7, has been transformed from a local eatery into a Spanish-style formal restaurant.

At Av. Abraham Lincoln 605, **Piccolo Gourmet** offers seafood, and pasta dishes in a congenial and casual setting.

Inside Plaza Criolla on Av. 27 de Febrero, **La Fromagerie** dishes up crêpes, fondues, and bouillabaisse.

At Centro Europa to the rear of the Palacio del Cine on Av. 27 de Febrero, **El Picnic** offers seafood dishes as well as a deli/pastry shop. A bit off the beaten track but very convenient if you're visiting the museums at the cultural plaza, **Maniqui** features Sunday all-you-can-eat buffets for US$6.

The Japanese **Restaurant Samurai** is at Av. Abraham Lincoln 102.

Probably the most unusually situated restaurant is **Mesón de la Cava** (☎ 533-2818), Parque Mirador, which is set in a cave and entered by a spiral staircase. Noted for its dancing and steaks, it's very popular so reservations are a must.

On Av. Anacaona across from the Dominican Concorde, the **Lago Enriquillo** is in the same park and features Oriental and international cuisine.

Apart-Hotel Plaza Florida's family-style **Boga-Boga**, Av. Bolivar 203, serves up Spanish dishes, including seafood; tapas are served at five.

For pastas and snacks try **Café Atlantico**, Av. México 152.

Specializing in intriguing dishes such as BBQ rabbit, **Asaderos los Argentinos** is at Av. Independencia 809 (near Av. Máximo Gómez).

On the second level of Galerias Comerciales at Av. 27 de Febrero, **Café Galeria** combines displays of artwork with crêpes.

CHINESE FOOD: One of the best restaurants, reasonably priced, accessible, and attractively designed, **Salon de Te** is at C. Duarte just by the Maritime Museum in the old town. It's run by exceedingly friendly Anita and her sisters, who all speak fluent English.

More down to earth is the **Canton**, a 24-hr. greasy spoon. It is quite a production; the Dominican waiters serve, clear tables, gather up and replace tablecloths, and the Chinese management collects the cash and cooks in the behind-the-scenes kitchen. Entire Chinese families gather to dine here; you can watch the awkward Dominican lad as he tries to fit in with the family he has married (or will marry) into. It's more fun to watch here than to eat.

The **Restaurant Mandarín**, at Av. George Washington 516 on the Malecón, has daily lunch specials weekdays for around US$8. Entrée prices are reasonable.

At C. Gustavo Mejia Ricart 64, **Lee's Kitchen** is an informal eatery which offers N Chinese and Taiwanese food.

PIZZA: **Pizza Capri** is in the old town part of the Malecón, and there are a number of pizza joints along El Conde. On Av. George Washington, **Il Capo del Malecón**, offers pasta as well as pizza. Another pizza place is in the Embajador Gardens. Featuring *tacos* and *tamales* in addition to pizza, **Taqueria Antojiots** is at Av. Lope de Vega 49. Located at the Merengue Plaza on the corner of Av. 27 de Febrero and Av. Tiradentes, open air **Pala Pizza** has a second location on Winston Churchill.

LOCAL FOOD: Good and inexpensive, **Cafeteria Dumbo** is on C. Nouel behind Parque Independencia.

For those on a budget, **D. Yacky Mariscos**, on C. El Numero just up from Hotel Napolitano, serves inexpensive seafood dishes prepared Dominican-style.

At. C. Hostos 153 between C. Arz. Nouel and El Conde, **El Sarten** has a great atmosphere and red and white decor. On Arz. Nouel at Hostos, the **De Nosotros Empanadas** offers fast-food *empanadas* – just the thing for a snack.

The **Naiboa** is at Av. Bolivar 730 near Av. Máximo Gómez. On Felix E. Mejia, the **Comedor "Franklin"** offers creole cuisine. Less pricey are **El Burén**, on Padre Billini, and **Pacos Café** near Parque Independencia.

One reasonably priced restaurant is the **El Conuco** on Casimiro de Moya, situated approximately behind the entrance to the Jaragua. One reader writes: "It serves typical Dominican food in an atmosphere that reminds young Dominicans of their grandparents in the campo.

There is a buffet, a full array of fresh juices, all the local specialties, and dancing too. It is a fun place to eat for both tourists and locals."

Palacio de Mofongo (Av. Independencia, ☎ 688-8121) or the **Casa del Mofongo**, more distant on Av. 27 de Febrero, specialize in *mofongo*. For traditional Dominican sweets and cider, visit **Dulces Criollos Doña María** at Plaza Criolla, Av. 27 de Febrero. At Lea de Castro 205 in the old town, **Casita Dulce** has *pasteles in hoja*, *dulces*, and desserts. **Delicatesa**, across the street, sells pastries and bread. *Chimchurri* (spiced sausage) is sold from stands all over the city.

VEGETARIAN DINING: Your best bet is the cafeteria-style **Ananda** (☎ 682-4465) which is at Casimiro de Moya 7 at Pasteur and is open Mon. to Sat. for lunch and dinner (until 10). It is a sponsored by a worldwide Indian guru sect. The food is plentiful and quite good. They also have a set lunch of three items for less than US$2, but it's more fun to mix and match on your own. You can order and combine your own dishes. The easiest way to find it is to locate the Villar Hnos. shops on Ave. Independencia and walk N (away from the water); you'll come directly to Casmiro de Moya.

Bechtel, C. Luperón, is open from 12-2 on weekdays.

Run by Seventh Day Adventists, **Country Life** (☎ 686-7825), José Contreras # 28, is behind UTESA University. This vegan restaurant is open 12:30-3:30, Mon. to Fri.

Run by an even more eclectic sect, **Govinda** (☎ 686-5665), Cayetano Rodriguez 254, is one of those Hare Krishna places. It offers a daily special from 12:15-1:30. Nearby at C. Cayetano 153 (at Santiago), **Restaurante Naturalista Vida Silvestre** serves meals weekdays until 3 PM.

For gourmet dining, **Las Ojas** (☎ 682-3940) is in C. Jonas Salk near Bolivar and is within walking distance from the Plaza Cultural. Food here is exceedingly delicious but the accent on cream and cheese in many dishes is a bit heavy for cholesterol and fat watchers. One good alternative is the gluten shish kebab. Entrées are US$2-3. Lunches (US$4) are served all-you-can-eat cafeteria-style. It's open 12-3 and 6-9, but is closed Sat. evening.

Also try **El Terrenal** (☎ 689-3161), Malecón and Estrelleta, which features some vegetarian dishes.

To buy wholewheat bread, head for the **Panaderia Integral** on Padre Billini.

BUDGET FOOD: Many *cafeterias* clustered around the vicinity of El Conde are open late. Seedy in appearance (and therefore redolent in atmosphere), **Cafeteria Colonial** is on C. El Conde and is good for breakfast and lunch. **Cafeteria Viejo Roma**, Av. Bolivar across from Puerto El Conde, serves great lunches and dinners. Street vendors hawk peanut brittle, *dulce de leche* (a traditional sweet), and other goodies. **Nuevo Café Restaurante Mundo Europeo** serves Italian and local dishes at reasonable prices. You can also get a slice of pizza (or a whole one) at a variety of places in El Conde, but you may not find it to your taste.

FOOD STORES: At C. Luperón 9 (corner Arzobispo Meriño), **Restaurant Bethel** (closed Sat.) sells good whole wheat bread and sugary peanut butter in its shop; it's also good for lunch in a pinch but is hardly *haute cuisine*; you do get a free Jehovah's Witness pamphlet with lunch however. At the junction of a small park with Luperón, **Vita Naturaleza**, C. Mercedes 255, sells health food. There's also a health food shop along the side street garage entrance at Plaza Naco. The best place to buy vegetables is at the back of the **Mercado Modelo** on Av. Mella.

SUPERMARKETS: In the old part of town, a medium-sized good grocery store is the **Casa Velasquez** at Gran Luperón and Arzobispo Meriño. The **Supermercado Colonial**, C. Duarte and Nouel, has a good selection of items. **Supermercado Extra** is at Nicolás de Ovando 385 (corner of Av. Máximo Gómez). **Supermercado Avenida** is at Av. Duarte 379. Opposite Parque Independencia and near the Cafeteria Dumbo, **Casa Perez** is a small supermarket. In Gazcue, **Serpermercado Savica** is at Benito Moncíon 51.

Supermercado Nacional has locations at Av. Mella 119, Av. Abraham Lincoln at Av. 27 de Febrero, and on Av Nuñez de Caceres. The **Super Asturias** is in Centro Commercial Naco, Av. Tiradentes, and at Av. 27 de Febrero at Juan Baron Fajardo. Innumerable others are listed in the yellow pages.

Santo Domingo Entertainment

There's plenty of good nightlife here although the frequent blackouts can make getting around a pain. Be sure to bring a flashlight with you before venturing out at night. *Perico ripeao*, groups of three or four street musicians, serenade all up and down the *Malecón*, the waterfront boulevard. Dominicans traditionally welcome in the New Year here; the *carnavál* and Mardi Gras festivals also take place here, and the wide stretch is lined with cafés, bars, restaurants, and clubs. You can snack on everything from pizza to cashews as you stroll or

take a horse and buggy ride. Dominicans cruise along the stretch in Toyota convertibles.

CONCERTS AND THEATER: The **Teatro Nacional**, Av. Máximo Gómez, offers musical and other events, including performances by the National Symphony. Recitals and chamber music performances are held in the smaller Sala Ravelo. The ticket office (☎ 682-7255) is open from 9:30-noon daily, and tickets are inexpensive.

Local and international performances are also held in the **Palacio de Bellas Artes** (Palace of Fine Arts, ☎ 682-6384) on Av. Independencia at the corner of Máximo Gómez.

Located at the corner of El Conde and Las Damas, the **Casa de Francia** (☎ 685-0840) offers concerts, films, and other activities. The **Instituto Cultural Dominicano Americano** (☎ 533-4191), Av. Abraham Lincoln 21, offers theater performances and concerts.

Casa de Teatro (☎ 689-3430, 686-7840), a drama workshop and experimental theater formed in 1975, is at C. Arzobispo Meriño 110. It also has regular art exhibits and performances. The **Teatro Nuevo** in Barrio Don Bosco has performances all year. Set in the Parque Mirador Sur, the **Guacara Taina** (☎ 530-2666) offers folkloric dances on Tues. to Fri. from 7-10 PM.

DISCOS: There are many discoteques in town. Largest and most luxurious, the **Babilon disco** is at Av. George Washington 1005. Nearby, **Le Regine** also presents occasional fashion shows and live music. Inside the Jaragua, the Jubilee is a grandiose, classy disco in the Napoleonic style.

Also on Av. George Washington and at No. 165, elegant **Bella Blue** (next to Vesuvio's) features loads of *merengue* and sometimes has fashion shows and live bands.

Luxurious, with *merengue* groups on occasion, the Hotel Sheraton's **Omni** spins *merengue*, *salsa*, ballads, and rock. At the Hotel Hispaniola, **Neon 2002** caters to a young crowd.

At. C. La Guardia 25, **Kuora Disco** has "sensurrom" sound.

On Robert Pastoriza near the cor. of Av. Abraham Lincoln, the two-story **Gasolina** resembles a 1950s gas station; half of a car is attached to a wall on its first level.

At Av. Máximo Gómez 60 across from the National Theater, **Columbus/Club 60** features *merengue*, rock, and ballads.

Set atop the Plaza Naco Hotel and commanding a breathtaking view of the capital, **Top's** is another classy and popular disco.

The Hotel Continental has the **Tiffany Club**, a bar and disco.

With three bars on three levels and two dance floors, **Guácara**

Taina is the largest disco around. It's set in Parque Mirador Sur near Nuñez de Caceres. Music pounds from 9 or 11 to dawn.

others: You can also try Hotel El Embajador's **Hipocampo** and **Opus Discoteca** (*merengue, salsa*, etc.), Av. Independencia 624. Featuring daily live entertainment, **Bottom's Lounge** is on the first floor of the Plaza Naco Hotel on Av. Tiradentes at C. Presidente González.

At Sánchez Valverde y Balthazar de los Reyes in Villa Consuelo, **El Rincón Habanero** has Cuban *son* music from the 40s and 50s. At Baltazar de los Reyes and Pimentel, one block away, the **Secreto Musical Bar** is similar. It's the headquarters of the Club Nacional de Soneros. *Merengue*, rock, and ballads are also played here. Also try **La Vieja Habana** in Villa Mella on the city's N outskirts. **Lapsus** is at Av. Independencia 503.

BARS AND CLUBS: There are plenty of places to take others and display your sense of sophistication. Just down the street from the Hotel Palacio on C. Salome Ureña, **Ocho Puertas** is a great place to hang out. Visit on weekend evenings when the locals arrive for date night.

Another attractive place is the **Patio Bar** in Edificio San Pedro. The atmosphere is colonial and the restaurant here also serves lunch and dinner. It's at C. Mercedes and Hostos.

La Bachata Rosa (☎ 688-0969), Atraranza 9 near the Alcazar de Colón, is a posh bar for Juan Luis Guerra fans. **Drake's Pub** is across from the Alcázar nearby. **Café Montesino** is also here, as are **Nancy's Snack Bar**, **Rita's Café**, the **Candray Bar**, and the **Bar-Meson Museo de Jamón**, which features flamenco dancing to recorded music on Thurs. and Sun. at 10 PM. This "museum" takes its name from the batallions of smoked hams hanging from the ceiling – a surrealistic work worthy of Marcel Duchamp.

The **K-ramba Bar** is at 1 Isabel del Católica, at the beginning of Arz. Portes. It offers over 100 different mixed drinks and food. English, French, and German are spoken. A DJ spins pop and *merengue* tunes.

Just up the street at Isabel La Católica 7, **Henry's Bar and Grill** is a favorite expat hangout, one run by two American brothers whose mother (a US Embassy employee) introduced them to the joys of world travel. An amazing number of people that walk through the door have never heard of author Henry Miller, the bar's namesake!

Worthy of any city in the world, unforgettable **Chez Duke** has a living room atmosphere and a chess table; it's at Arz. Portes 99

at Meriño which is near the cathedral. Dark and romantic, **Disco Momento** is down the street. It's just the place for some hot petting. Similarly, **Sueños**, at Santomé 206 near El Conde, is a couples-only disco.

At Padre Billini and Las Damas, **La Taberna** features classical music. At the corner of Av. México and Av. Abraham Lincoln, **Café Atlantico** serves Mexican snacks during its happy hour, with occasional live bands and theme parties. It plays everything from jazz to samba to *salsa* to *merengue* to African pop.

On Av. Sarasota 53-8, inside the Delta Hotel, **Delta's Café** is where the white-collared come to relax after work. On C. Roberto Pastoriza 14, **D'Golden Club** is an upscale bar with a happy hour and live entertainment.

Set next to the Café San Michel on Av. Lope de Vega, the **Grand Café** caters to a younger crowd. Jazz, rock, and *merengue* bands perform here.

On Av. Independencia one block E of the Sheraton, the **Mento Bar** is a popular watering hole. **Ibiza** is at the corner of Av. Tiradentes and C. Roberto Pastoriza. **D'Golden** is next door.

Popular with Spaniards as well as university students, **No Lo Se** is on Av. Bolívar near the corner of Av. Máximo Gómez. Another popular venue is the **Stone Bar** in La Ataranza. Footballheads will want to visit the **Sports Center Bar/Restaurant** (☎ 688-3215/2369), 30 de Marzo 31, where you can watch international sporting events in season.

The **Berimbau** (☎ 567-2565), GM Ricart 120, is a Brazilian restaurant and bar.

Lapaus is a posh club with aggressive hookers; it is right behind the Hotel Jaragua on Independencia. "Las paws" would be a better name for the club. A similar "club" is next door.

One famous night club is the **Herminia** on Av. Mejia at Maximo Gómez.

hotel bars and clubs: The Hotel El Embajador's classy **Embassy Club** requires a jacket and sometimes has live entertainment. Another exclusive joint is the Sheraton's **El Yarey**, also with live entertainment. The **Sol Bar** is on the 12th F of the Hotel Naco. You can also try Hotel Jaragua's **Salon La Fiesta**, Hotel El Napolitano's **Disco Piano Bar**, Hotel Dominican Concorde's **La Azotea**, Hotel Comodoro's **Salón Rojo**, and the **Maunaloa Night Club and Casino** (Centro del los Héroes).

MOVIES: Movies in English are shown at theaters such as the **Broadway** (☎ 562-7171; Av. 27 de Febrero), **Cineplex** (☎ 562-2888), **Issfapol** (☎ 541-3255), **Manzana** (☎ 567-8554), **Palacio**

del Cine (☎ 565-0800), and the **Triple** (☎ 688-6844). Check the newspapers for listings and ask at your hotel or check the phone book for the exact locations.

GAMBLING: Casinos are found mostly at major hotels and are generally open from 4 to 4. Bets may be placed in US or Dominican currency, and Las Vegas odds and rules apply, with some variations. The staff is bilingual. Casinos are found at the **Hispaniola, V Centenario, Concorde, Santo Domingo, San Gerónimo, the Sheraton's Omni, El Embajador, Naco, Lina**, and in the **Jaragua**. You may also gamble at the **Maunaloa Night Club** in Centro de los Héroes.

BOAT TRIPS: The *Wonder* (☎ 221-4551) offers nightly excursions on the Río Ozama for DS$50 pp. Board the boat on the river in back of the Alcazar.

SPORTING EVENTS: Baseball games are held at the stadium. **Horseraces** are held year-round on Tues., Thurs., and Sun. at the Perla Antilla near the baseball stadium. **Greyhound** races are held on Wed. through Sat. at 7 and Sun. at 4 at Canodromo El Coco (☎ 567-4461, 565-8333), 15 min. N of Santo Domingo at Duarte Hwy. Km 13 (La Yuca, Av. Monumental). There are 400 dogs participating in 12 races an evening. Admission is minimal. **Cockfighting** can be found on

Av. Luperón; ☎ 566-3844. **Wrestling** events are held on occasion at Estadio Eugenio Maria de Hostos. For **racing** fans, the Autodromo Internacional Las Américas is under construction near the San Isidro Free Zone.

BOWLING: This can be found at the **Bolera Dominicana** (☎ 566-3818) in Plaza Naco. It's open from 9:30 to midnight.

JOGGING: Joggers may run at the **Olympic Center and Stadium** on Av. 27 de Febrero across from the Hotel Lina and the **Mirador/Paseo de los Indios** to the rear of the Hotel Embajador.

HEALTH CLUBS: These can be found at the **Jaragua**, **York Caribe**, **Lina**, and **Sheraton**. The most complete club is **Club Body Health** (☎ 565-5156) at Av. 27 de Febrero 102. Jazz, modern, and aerobic classes are offered by **Taller Dansa Moderna** (☎ 567-8261) at Centro Comercial Paraiso on Av. Winston Churchill.

Santo Domingo Shopping

Santo Domingo is by far the best place to shop in the nation and, perhaps, in the entire Caribbean. But if you go into a shop with a guide, you will pay more. Bargain hard and watch out for slick bag snatchers and pickpockets.

Around the old town, you'll find many stores along Aves. Duarte, Melia, and on C. El Conde (Street of the Count). Now a pedestrian mall, the last is the city's oldest shopping area, with a profusion of stores selling everything from furniture to records to clothing and toys. It's a good place to shop for shoes, jewelry, and hand-embroidered children's clothing. La Cafeteria Colonial here sells ground coffee. Av. Duarte also has a large number of stalls.

DUTY-FREE SHOPPING: In order make a purchase, you must shop a few days ahead and present your airplane ticket; your purchases will be available after you clear customs. You may shop for duty-frees in The Centro de los Héroes, La Ataranza, shops in the Santo Domingo, Sheraton, and Embajador hotels, and in the airport departure lounge. All purchases must be paid for in US currency.

MARKETS: Mercado Modelo, Av. Mella at Santomé, is chock full of stalls offering leatherwork, ceramics, *dulce* (sweets), boats made from cow's horn, and amber necklaces. *Merengue* tapes are less than US$2 after bargaining. Upstairs are huge sausages, whole barracudas, severed pigs heads and feet; the thump and crack of cold steel hitting bone reverberates throughout. A few *botanicas* sell Fortune Teller, Gambler's Amour, and other good luck seasonal sprays to believers in spiritualism. Out back, the market overflows with tomatoes, peppers, eggplants, cucumbers, potatoes, carrots, pumpkins, and tropical fruits.

La Sirena, Av. Mella 258, is a large discount store selling toiletries and innumerable household items. A plethora of other stores line Av. Duarte, up the hill from the old town.

Set on Av. Winston Churchill about three blocks N of the 27 de Febrero intersection, **La Hortaliza** is a smaller and quieter market. A bit more expensive, it sells produce, brass beds, baskets, ceramics, glazed decorative tiles, and other goods. Granix natural foods are also sold here.

⚡ Warning

Guides here extract a 5-10% commission from shops.

DEPARTMENT STORES: Puerto del Sol and **Gran Via** on El Conde. **La Opera** on El Conde and **González Ramos** at El Conde 252.

SHOPPING CENTERS: Located on 27 de Febrero at Máximo Gómez across from the Olympic Center, **Plaza Criolla** is a split-level arcade designed as a mock village, complete with clock tower. Its plaza houses a small fruit and vegetable market, and there are a wide variety of shops. On the plus side, it's air conditioned, you can use credit cards,

and there's a good selection. The downside is that it's very pricey, and you can't bargain as much.

On 27 de Febrero just a few blocks down, **Galerias Comerciales** features two levels of specialty shops. On C. Duarte, **Plaza Lama** offers a wide range of goods.

A combination market and supermarket, **Centro Comercial Nacional** is at the intersection of Av. Abraham Lincoln and Av. 27 de Febrero. One of its highlights is the flower market in its parking lot; it also has a supermarket. Just across the way, **Plaza Lincoln** specializes in high quality boutiques and home furnishing shops.

Nicknamed the "Golden Apple," the three-story **Plaza Central** is one of the Caribbean's largest malls, located at the corner of Av. 27 de Febrero and Av. Winston Churchill. Visitors may shop on its first two levels, feast on fast food, see a movie, or play sports on the third level. This is where the elite park their cars and shop; tellingly, there is no bookstore. **Café Benneton** here is quite popular. **Plaza Caribe** is at Av. 27 de Febrero and Leopoldo Navarro.

SPECIFIC SMALL SHOPS: At El Conde 153, **El Conde Gift Shop** sells unassembled rocking chairs for export.

At Arz. Nouel 151-1, **Musical Padilla** sells a wide variety of traditional musical instruments. **Mercantil Importada** is at El Conde 505. The **Novo Ataranza** is at Ataranza 21.

For high-quality crafts check out **Planarte** inside Casa de Bastidas. Sponsored by the Fundación de Desarollo Dominicano (Dominican Development Foundation), crafts found here include rag dolls, birds, and leather items.

At C. Nouel 53 (parallel to Conde), **Marialejos** carries ceramics and other crafts. You can have custom-designed pottery made by selecting a design from their portfolio. Government-owned-and-operated **Cendarte** (Centro Nacional de Artesania) sells the crafts of its students and local artisans. Goods here include macrame, pottery, furniture, jewelry, and leather items. To get here follow Av. Tiradentes by Plaza Naco and then cross Av. John F. Kennedy, continue to the Public Works Office and turn L. Cendarte is the second structure and is at the corner of C. San Cristóbal. It's open from 8 to 2.

Artessa, C. Roberto Pastoriza, offers a wide variety of crafts, both local and from Haiti and Latin America.

Set on a side street across from Plaza Naco, **Nuebo**, C. Fantino Falco 36, offers Haitian and Dominican crafts including pottery and handpainted birds.

Inside Plaza Lincoln, **Habitat**, Av. Abraham Lincoln near 27 de Febrero, sells handicrafts designed exclusively for this store.

At C. Cervantes 102, **Tu Espacio** features a wide selection of handicrafts, art, antiques, and furniture.

La Ferreteria Americana, a hardware store located at San Martin 175 and Av. Mella 413 (near the old town) has a wide variety of local handicrafts as well as items imported from all over the world.

On Av. John F. Kennedy, **Casa Hache** sells crafts and housewares.

On Av. Romulo Betancourt, between Av. Winston Churchill and Abraham Lincoln, **El Gallo** also sells housewares and other items.

Offering high-priced imported items, **Casa Virginia** is at Centro Commercial, and the shops **Mary** and **Alfonso** are at Plaza Naco. On the 2nd F of Plaza Naco, **Triana** offers a wide selection of crafts, both local and imported, from Central America and Spain.

The workshop of craftswoman **Maria del Carmen Ossaye** is at C. Cervantes 52, a street directly opposite the rear exit to the Sheraton's parking lot. Her specialty is handpainted mahogany handbags ranging in design from geometrical patterns to floral pastels.

Handcrafted guitars and furniture are also available here. At C.

Santiago 405, the **Dpiel** workshop manufactures a high-quality (and high-priced) selection of leather goods; they are sold elsewhere in boutiques. One place to buy them is **La Maleta** on Av. 27 de Febrero near Av. Abraham Lincoln. **Stained glass items** are found at Arte Vitral, C. Hatuey 151, in the Piantini area.

FLEA MARKETS: The flea market at Mercado de las Pulgas operates on Sun. at the Centro del los Héroes and at the Mercado de Oportunidades, 27 de Febrero. Another flea market is also sponsored by the office of Cultural Patrimony at the parking lot next to the Atarazana's parking lot. Everything from junk to antiques (including silver and pewter) can be found here.

FURNITURE AND HOME FURNISHING SHOPS: Santo Domingo is renowned for its finely crafted furniture. For budget furniture try **Ambiente Decoraciones**, corner of Independencia and Av. Dr. Delgado, which offers boxes, mirrors, birds, and hand-painted cushions; they will also make furniture to your specs.

Offering expensive but attractive items are **La Nueva Dimension** (C. Gustavo Mejia Ricart 79 in Plaza Naco), **Hipopotamo** (C. Max Enrique Urena 31), and the **Bonsai** (C. Fantino Falco near Plaza Naco). Featuring modern-style furniture, **D'Arquin** is at Plaza Paraiso. High-priced imported furnishings are found at **Domus** on Av. Tiradentes.

Artesania Rattan, on the ground level of the San Carlos Bldg., features a full range of home furnishings (including woven placemats, chests, and baskets). **Delgados**, at Av. Máximo Gómez 58 just around the corner from the US Consulate, shows wicker and rattan furniture. Offering special orders, **Casa Bibely**, C. Conde, offers wicker and rattan furniture and accessories. **Hogar de Mimbre** ("Home of Wicker"), Romulo Betancourt 1424, offers the same as does **Sauce**, down the street at No. 2056. At Av. 27 de Febrero at the corner of 30 de Marzo, **Gonzales Muebles** offers a vast array of furniture and furnishings. Also try **Alfonso's**, at Plaza Naco, which produces its own designs under its "mobleart" label.

At C. Jose de Jesus Ravelo 81, **Palacios** is an age-old name.

With a showroom at 27th de Febrero 503 and a factory in the Herrera Industrial Free Zone, **Von** has original and very contemporary designs in mahogany. **Rattan y Decoraciones**, in Av. Luperón's industrial zone, has a good selection. Set in the city's Alma Rosa district at C. Costa Rica 136, **Rattan Industrial** is another wicker and rattan furniture exporter.

FABRIC SHOPS: Although much of the fabric found is imported, some cotton and linen is made locally. One of the best places to buy is **Almacenes Doble A** on 19 de Marzo off El Conde. At Galerias Comerciales on 27 de Febrero, **Manikin** is a select and expensive fabric store, as is Plaza Lincoln's **Mundo Modas**.

TAILORS AND MENSWEAR: A few blocks from Av. 27 de Febrero at Av. Winston Churchill, high-priced couturier **La Coruña** has a wide selection. Ciprian, on the second floor of Plaza Naco, offers custom tailoring. At Av. Lope de Vega 18, **Cavalieri** has a wide variety of high-quality menswear, as does **Solo Para Hombre**, Av. Betancourt 1560. One block from the Merengue Hotel at C. Roberto Pastoriza 152, **Sunny** offers a contemporary selection.

TAILORS AND WOMEN'S WEAR: Ladies can have three-piece suits made at **Ciprian** on the second floor of Plaza Naco. Also at Plaza Naco you'll find **Abraxas**, **Marian Cristina Boutique**, and **Cachet Boutique**. **Mercy Jacquez's** boutique is across from the Supermercado Nacional on Av. Abraham Lincoln; tailoring is available upon request.

Next to the Salon Rosita at the corner of Av. Pasteur on Av. Independencia, **Mi Boutique** has a wide selection of fabrics and eveningwear. At the corner of C. Charles Sumner at C. Nicolas Ureña 101, **Velka's** workshop and boutique features her line of fashion. At C. Fantino Falcon 59 near Plaza Naco, **Mimosa** sells linen goods including blouses. At Centro Comercial Nacional, **Casa Virginia** is another notable boutique.

At Plaza Criolla, **Patapoof** offers swimwear, Danskins, shorts, and T-shirts. Another boutique **Babette Butti**, is located in Galeria Comercial on Av. 27 de Febrero. At Plaza Lincoln, **Le Pavilion Boutique** imports Italian shoes and sandals, as well as designer clothes. At 71 Gustavo Mejia, **Europa** sells a range of clothes from eveningwear to cottons. Specializing in lingerie, hand-embroidered nightgowns, and infant's clothing, **Natacha** is at C. Sánchez y Sánchez on the corner of Av. Lope de Vega. Larger-proportioned women might want to visit **La Dama Elegante**, 47-A C. Manuel de Js. Troncoso.

For sportswear try **D'Sport** at the corner of Alma Mater and Av. 27 de Febrero. The **Jaez Boutique** in the Sheraton's arcade also has a nice selection.

JEWELRY: El Conde is the center for jewelers, and **Di Carlo** is one of the preeminent dealers. For watches, gold chains, pearls, and other accessories, try **Seiko** in Centro Comercial Nacional. La Ataranza's gift. shops have local jewelry incorporating larimar

---

Major Shopping Malls in Santo Domingo

Galerias Commerciales
Av. 27 de Febrero;
entrance at Ortega y Gasset and Máximo Gómez

Plaza Andalucia
Av. Abraham Lincoln at Gustavo Mejia Ricart

Plaza Bolera
Av. Abraham Lincoln at Roberto Pastoriza

Plaza Central
Av. 27 de Febrero at Winston Churchill

Plaza Criolla
Av. 27 de Febrero at Máximo Gómez

Plaza Dorada
C. Roberto Pastoriza at Winston Churchill

Plaza La Lira I
C. Roberto Pastoriza; entrance at Abraham Lincoln and Winston Churchill

Plaza La Lira II
C. Roberto Pastoriza; entrance at Abraham Lincoln and Winston Churchill

Plaza Lincoln
Av. Abraham Lincoln at 27 de Febrero

Plaza Merengue
Av. 27 de Febrero at Tiradentes

Plaza Naco
Av. Av. Tiradentes

Unicentro Plaza
Av. 27 de Febrero at Abraham Lincoln

---

and amber. Try **Amber Tres** here. **Carlos Despradel** and **Eduardo Fiallo** design ceramic jewelery which can be found at select shops; try **Nouveau Gallery** next to the Sheraton on Av. Independencia and also ask at Plazoleta de las Curas's **Plaza Shop** behind the cathedral.

Other Resources & Services

ART GALLERIES: Galeria Plaza Toledo, Luperón at Isabel Catolica 163, is an art gallery worth visiting. **Institute Galerie de Arte Nouveau**, cor. of Aves. Independencia and Pasteur, is the best of the modern art galleries. With branches at El Conde 513 and at Av. Abraham Lincoln 904, the **San Ramón Art Gallery** features established artists. With an extensive representation of artists from all over the island, **Galeria de Arte Nader** is at La Ataranza 9. **George Nader's** gallery is at C. Gustavo Mejia Ricart 49, near Plaza Naco. Also, while in Gazcue, be sure to visit the **Centro de Arte Cándido Bido**, C. Dr. Baez 5, which is run by the renowned painter of the same name.

Guillo Perez's gallery and workshop is at C. Hatuey 302, just to the W of Av. Winston Churchill. At C. Espaillat 260, **Gallery Paiewonsky** features contemporary work. The **Casa de Teatro**, Arzobispo Meriño 110, and the **Casa de Francia** also have exhibits. Also try **Arawak** at Pasteur 104, **Auffant** at El Conde 513, **Candido Bido** at Av. Mella 9-B, **Rosa Maria** at La Ataranza 7, **Galeria El Greco** at Av. Tiradentes 16, **Nouveau** at Av. Independencia 354, **Galeria de Arte Sebelén** at Av. Hostos 209, and **Deniel's** at Independencia 120-A.

SERVICES: The **Ministry of Tourism** (☎ 221-4660, fax 682-3806) is open weekdays 9-2:30 at its main office in Santo Domingo. It's located at Av. México at 30 Marzo in new government offices. Unfortunately, they have little or no information available; their function appears to be more in attracting visitors to the island than with providing information.

The offices of the **Direccion Nacional de Parques** (☎ 682-7628) are at Av. Independencia 359. They're open Mon. to Fri., 7:30-2:30. It helps if you can speak Spanish, but don't expect much in the way of information!

The **American Chamber of Commerce** (☎ 533-7292, 532-7414, PO Box 95-2) operates inside the Hotel Santo Domingo. Large maps are sold in the **Instituto Geografico Universitario** around the corner from the Hostal Nicolas Ovando. A large selection of magazines can be found at **Geyda** in Centro Comerical Naco on Av. Tiradentes.

TOURS: Ecoturisa (☎ 221-4104/4105/4106, fax 685-1544; C. Santiago No 203-B, Gazcue) has the motto, "to know is to conserve." They operate a number of innovative trips that would be special anywhere. There is an eight-day birdwatching trip (Jan. to March in the national parks) a 10-day butterfly tour (offered year-round), a varied urban-and-rural nine-day "Route of the Rural Tern" trip, a seven-day "Route of the Galleons and Pirates" tour, and a 15-day "Green Paths of Quisqueya" tour. Custom designed trips are also available.

POST OFFICE: Mail letters at major hotels. Postage is relatively expensive, and your letters and postcards will take a *long* time to arrive. If you have their travelers' checks or credit card, you may have mail sent to **American Express** (☎ 532-2219) at Av. Lincoln 306. Other post offices are on the 2nd F. of El Haucal, a tall government building on Av. Padre Castellanos near Av. Duarte, and in the Hotel Embajador.

TELEPHONE SERVICE: Long distance, international, fax, and telex services are available at **Codetel**, Av. 30 de Marzo 12 near Parque Independencia, and at seven other locations citywide, including Av. Abraham Lincoln 1101 and at the airport. **Tricom** has three offices – at Av. Bolivar and Av. Nuñez de Caceres, on Av. Duarte at Santo Cura De Ars, and at Av. Lopé de Vega 95. Another competitor, **Larga Distancia**, is on the old town side of the Malecón. The Palacio de las Communicaciones next to the general post office does not have phone service.

TRAVEL AND TOUR AGENCIES: In the Gascue area try: Exotours (☎ 686-5141). C. Pasteur 55, Bibi Travel (☎ 532-7141), Dilia's Tours (☎ 682-1086), Dimargo Tours (☎ 582-3874), Dorado Travel (☎ 688-6661), Dormitur (☎ 567-5574), Gladys Tours (☎ 688-1069), Halcón Travel (☎ 566-

6116), Magna Tours (☎ 532-8267/7141), Merengue Tours (% 582-3373), Metro Tours (% 567-3138, Av. Winston Churchill), Omni Tours (☎ 566-4228), Pebeco Tours (☎ 567-8636), Portillo SA (☎ 565-3027), Prieto Tours (☎ 688-5715, Av. Francia 125), Santo Domingo Tours (☎ 562-4865/4870), Tanya Tours (☎ 565-5691), Thomas Tours (☎ 687-8645), Turinter (☎ 685-4020, Leopoldo Navarro 4), Viajes Barceló (☎ 685-8411), Viajes Continentes (☎ 532-0825), and Vimenca (☎ 533-9362).

CAR RENTALS: Rent cars from the major hotels, at the airport, or from **Avis** (☎ 533-9295/3530, 532-2969/2868), Av. Abraham Lincoln at Sarasota; **Budget** (☎ 567-0173/0174), Av. JF Kennedy at Lope de Vega; **Honda** (☎ 567-1015/1016, 541-8487), Av. JF Kennedy at Pepillo Salcedo; **Hertz** (☎ 533-9295/3520 or 532-2969/2868), Av. Independencia; Mc Deal (☎ 688-6518); **National Car Rental** (☎ 562-1444/1474, 565-5561), Nelly, Av. José Contreras 139; and **Rentauto** (☎ 566-7221), Av. 27 de Febrero 247. Check the yellow pages for others. Expect to spend US$60 pd on up.

DIVING: For information and reservations, contact **Mundo Submarino** (☎ 566-0340), C. Gustavo Mejia Ricart 99. They rent and sell equipment, teach classes, and organize trips. Another is **Buceo Dominicano** (☎ 567-0346), Av. Abraham Lincoln 960, which arranges dive trips, sailing, and snorkelling.

HAIRDRESSERS: All of the major hotels have beauty salons. Other reliable ones include **Salon Rosita** (Av. Independencia at C. Pasteur), **Hermanos Duenas** (Plaza Naco, 2F), **Salon Manolita** (Av. Independencia next to Hotel San Geronimo), **Los Gemelos** (Av. Tiradentes) and **Nolasko's** (Plaza Central).

LANGUAGE SCHOOLS: Offering Spanish classes are **APEC** (☎ 687-1000), Av. Máximo Gómez 55; **Instituto Cultural Dominicano Americano** (☎ 533-4191), Av. Abraham Lincoln 21; and **Instituto Superior de Idiomas** (☎ 688-5336), Av. 27 de Febrero 415. For French, study at the **Casa de Francia** on C. Las Damas in the old town.

HEALTH: Foreigners are recommended to go either to **Clinica Abréu** (☎ 688-4411/687-4922, Beller 42) or **Clinica Gómez Patiño** (☎ 685-9131/9141), at Av. Independencia and Beller, which offer high quality but expensive care on a 24-hr. basis. Also try **Clinica Abel González** on Av. Independencia or **Clinica Yunén** and **Clinica Centro Médico UCE** (☎ 682-0171) at Av. Máximo Gómez 66. Centro **Otorrinolaringología y Especi-**

alidades (☎ 682-0151), Av. 27 de Febrero, specializes in treating eye, ear, and throat ailments.

English speaking **physicians** include Dr. Jiordi Brossa (☎ 682-2090), and cardiologist Dr. Angel Contreras (☎ 688-0011).

PHARMACIES: The following offer 24-hr. service and delivery: **Farmacia Tiradentes** (☎ 565-1647), Av. Tiradentes 15 near Hotel Naco; **Farmacia Dr. Camilo** (☎ 566-5575), C. Paseo de los Locutores near Av. Winston Churchill; **Los Hidalgos** (☎ 565-4848), 27 de Febrero 24; and **Farmacia San Judas Tadeo** (☎ 689-6664), Av. Independencia 57, which has a complete selection of items. A list can be found in the phone book.

BANKS: Banks are open Mon. to Fri. from 8:30 to 2:30. Rates of exchange vary slightly; check the newspapers to find the best rates. Moneychangers are more convenient, but make sure that they give you a receipt.

Many banks line Isabel La Católica, including **Banco de la Reserva** next to the Palacio de las Communicaciones. At Ataranza and Emiliano Tejera opposite the Alcázar de Colón, **Banco Popular** has long hours. **Citibank** is at Av. John F. Kennedy 1, **Chase Manhattan** at John F. Kennedy and Av. Tiradentes, **Banco de Santander Dominicano** at John F. Kennedy and at Av. Lope de Vega,

Important Phone Numbers in Santo Domingo

Air Santo Domingo	683-8020
American Airlines	542-5151
Caribe Tours	221-4422
Continental Airlines	552-6688
Emergency	911
Information	1141
Metro Tours	566-7126,
	566-7129
Police	911
Terrabus	472-1080
Time	568-2222

and the **Bank of Nova Scotia** at Av. Lope de Vega and Av. John F. Kennedy.

Bancomercio has many branches, including ones at Duarte 58 and Duarte 322. They only change US dollars.

Exchange counters at the larger hotels are open until 9. Note that some banks do not accept traveler's checks. Changing money on the streets is illegal. In addition to the fact that you will definitely be cheated, there is also the chance that the black marketeer is in cahoots with a policeman who will swoop in and extract a substantial bribe in lieu of carting you off to jail.

LIBRARIES: The **Instituto Cultural Dominicano-Americano,** Av. Abraham Lincoln and C. Antonio de la Maza, has a fine library. (Open Mon. to Fri., 10-noon, and 3-7). Other libraries are in the **National Congress,** the **Pontificia Universidad Católica Madre y Maestra,** Uni-versidad **Autónoma de Santo Domingo),** and the **Instituto Tecnológico de Santo Domingo).**

BOOKSTORES: At the entrance to the Cathdral on Arz. Nouel, **Linea Studebaker** has a good collection of international newspapers and magazines as well as books. Soft drinks and traditional sweets are also available here. **Librería América,** Arz. Nouel at Sánchez in the old town, has a good selection of books; they also should have copies of this one. **Librería Avante** is at Arz. Nouel No. 53. Others include **Librería el Estudiante,** Av. Duarte 15; **Librería Pichardo,** Av. Duarte 271; and **Casa Cuello,** El Conde 201.

Cuesta Central del Libro (☎ 541-0551) is on Av. Tiradentes across from the Hotels Naco and Plaza. It is the city's largest bookstore.

EMBASSIES: The **American Embassy** (☎ 682-2171) is at the corner of C. César Nicolás Penson and C. Leopoldo Navarro.

The **Canadian Embassy** (☎ 689-0002) is at Av. Maximo Gómez 30. The **British Embassy** (☎ 682-3128) is at Ave. Independencia 506. The **German Embassy** (☎ 565-8811, 566-8047) is at C. Lic. Juan Tomás Mejia y Cotes 37 at the cor. of Eullides Morillo. The **Austrian Embassy** (☎ 532-2591, fax 535-3939) is at C. 1 ra No. 3, Sánchez, Bella Vista. The **Swiss Embassy** (☎ 689-4131) is at Ave. José Gabria Garcia 26. The **Belgian Embassy** is represented by Agencia Naverias Baez(☎ 544-2200) , Av. Abraham Lincoln 504.

From Santo Domingo

The nation's best (and fastest) bus company, **Metro** (☎ 566-7126/7129) departs from the corner of Av. Winston Churchill and Hatuey daily to Santiago (7, 9, 10, 1:30, 3, 5:30, and 6:30), Nagua (7:30 and 3:30), San Francisco de Macorís (7:30 and 3:30), Castillo (7:30 and 3:30), La Vega (7:30 and 4), Moca (7:30 and 4), and to Puerto Plata (7:30, 1, 4, and 7).

The only company running to Sosúa, **Caribe Tours** (☎ 221-5318) also runs a/c buses to Puerto Plata, Santiago, Bonao, Cabrera, Río San Juan, Nagua, Samaná, Dajabón, Monte Cristi, Jarabacoa, and San Francisco de Macorís. They're located at Av. 27 de Febrero and Leopoldo Navarro, not far from the old town. They also stop at Kilometro 9,

Lopé de Vega, and Máximo Gómez.

La Experiencia, located at C. Los Martires, and Av. Winston Churchill and Hatuey near Av. 27 de Febrero, runs to La Vega, Santiago, Nagua, Azua, San Juan, San Pedro de Macorís, and Puerto Plata.

Leaving from Plaza Criolla at Av. 27 de Febrero and Máximo Gómez, **Terra Bus** (☎ 472-1080) uses Mercedes Benz buses and employs uniformed hostesses who dispense free coffee and snacks. It runs to Santiago and also to Port Au Prince, Haiti.

Departing from Caracas 69 at Parque Enriquillo (Av. Duarte and Ravelo), **La Covacha** (☎ 686-1533) runs E to Higüey, Nagua, San Pedro de Macorís, Miches, and others.

Transportes de Cibao (☎ 685-7210, 689-5216), on C. Ravelo at Parque Enriquillo, runs to La Vega, Navarete, Mao, Santiago Rodriguez, Partido, Loma de Cabrera, Monte Cristi, Dajabón, Mamey, La Isabela, Sosúa, and Puerto Plata.

Located at Av. Independencia 7 near Parque Independencia, **Expreso Vegano** (☎ 686-8985) runs 21 buses daily to La Vega via Bonao from 6 AM to 6 PM (US$2.25). With this bus you can travel to Constanza (get off at Abanica and cross the road to find a pickup truck) or continue on to La Vega and change to go to

Jarabacoa, Santiago, and Puerto Plata.

Azua buses leave from Av. Bolivar near Parque Independencia.

Riviera del Caribe (☎ 566-1533/5400) runs to points SW from Av. Lincoln 703. Connect in Azua for Barahona, San Juan, and Padre las Casas.

Linea Sunchomiba (☎ 668-2411) at Av. Duarte and 30 de Marzo, leaves for Barahona (three hrs.) at 7:30, 10, 2, and 4.

For Constanza, **Linea Cobra** (☎ 412-7072, 566-5242, 565-7363) leaves from a small garage at Av. San Martín 197 at 5 AM; get there early as it fills up fast.

note: Check for times on all of these before traveling.

☞ *Traveler's Tip*

Even if your time is limited, it is worth the effort to hop on a bus and take a day trip. The most interesting route is to the W. You might go as far as Baní or as near at San Cristobal. If you go to the latter, get out in the main part of town, and then take a bus back later. You can learn a lot about the country just from what you see out the bus window!

GUAGUAS: These minibuses leave from Parque Enriquillo at the corner of Av. Duarte and C. Caracas to the N of the old town. Destinations include Higüey, Boca Chica, and Haina. Transportes de Cibao and La Covacha are also located here (see above).

FOR THE AIRPORT: Except for expensive (US$20) taxis, it's not easy to get to Las Américas. You must take a *público* from just N of Parque Enriquillo, Av. Duarte and Paris, to Boca Chica. Many of these stop at the airport; if not, you'll have to get off at the gate and walk in. Allow plenty of time if going this route.

DEPARTING BY AIR: In the main lobby you can make last minute phone calls at Codetel or buy ground coffee or other souvenirs if you have leftover *pesos*. Upon checking in you must pay your US$10 departure tax. Foreign visitors (as well as Dominican nationals) *must* pay in US currency – even if they are British or German! There are some duty-free shops after immigration, but if you're planning on buying rum, prices are 35% lower in town, and the selection is far better.

IN-COUNTRY FLIGHTS: Internal flights leave from **Herrera Airport** which has domestic charters. The airport is located in an area running perpendicular to Av. Luperón at the city's W end.

DRIVING: To leave the city toward the Cibao or the N, proceed from Parque Independencia heading N on C. 30 de Marzo, then cross 27 de Febrero and head straight to Av. John F. Kennedy, which becomes Duarte Hwy. at the intersection with Av. Lu-

Santo Domingo

perón. To reach the international airport and the E (Boca Chica, La Romana) you must cross the Río Ozama and continue straight along Las Américas.

BY AIR: Air Santo Domingo (☎ 683-8020, fax 683-8436; www.g-air-europa.es/air_sdo; e-mail info.air_sdo@g-air-europa.es) operates between Herrera airport (in Santo Domingo) to and from Punta Cana, Portillo (Samaná Peninsula), Santiago, La Romana, and Puerto Plata. Flights interconnect between destinations. Rates are from RD$700 on up.

The major companies operating charter service from Herrera Airport are **Faxa Air Taxi** (☎ 567-1195), **Servicios Aereos Profesionales** (☎ 565-2448), **Servicios Aéreos Turísticos** (☎ 566-1696, 567-7406), **Transporte Aéreo** (☎ 566-2141), and **Uni Charter** (☎ 567-0481, 567-0818). **Prieto Tours** (☎ 685-0102, 688-5715) operates an air taxi service to and from Portillo. A division of National Jets, **Airborne Ambulance Service** (☎ 567-1101/4171), Av. Tiradentes 52, rents executive jets and has a 24-hr. ambulance service.

FOR CUBA: Emely Tours (☎ 687-7114/7118; C. San Francisco de Macoris 58) runs package tours to Cuba. Costs run from US$400 for three days on up. Call toll-free ☎ 1-200-3262 or fax 686-0941.

BY FERRY: A ferry service is planned between Sans Souci in Santo Domingo and Mayagüez in Puerto Rico. Contact the tourist board for details.

The Costa Caribe

Boca Chica

The capital's resort area, Boca Chica is set around 19 miles (30 km) E of Santo Domingo and five min. from Las Américas International Airport. Initially developed as a port in the 1930s because of its sugar mill, Boca Chica came into vogue in the 1960s before declining in the 1970s with the rise to preeminence of Puerto Plata. In recent years, however, its popularity appears to be reviving – with some even calling it "Playa St. Tropez." Europeans and French Canadians flock here. It is best to avoid coming here on weekends.

Boca Chica has an attractive (albeit overdeveloped) beach and a shallow lagoon sheltered by reefs. At low tide you can walk out on to the reef or to the island of **La Matica** (The Little Tree). The larger **Los Piños** (The Pines) can be reached by swimming or by boat; it has its own private beach: La Escondida. watersports available here include jet skiing, wind surfing, snorkeling, and scuba. Catamarans and pedal boats can also be rented. For deep-sea fishing contact **Club Andres** (☎ 685-4940).

GETTING HERE: Frequent buses run from Parque Independencia to the main square in town (around 20 min.). The bus stops near the fruit vendors. You will probably have to change buses once. Be sure to get an *expreso*. If you are coming from Higüey or La Romana, get off on the main road and then walk or take a motoconcho into town.

GETTING AROUND: Nowhere is too far to go on foot. Otherwise, taxis or *motoconchos* will take you everywhere you need to go.

ACCOMMODATIONS: The three-rm. **L'Horizon Hotel and Restaurant** (☎ 523-4375) is owned by Swiss expats. Also with only a few rooms, **Neptune's Club** (☎ 523-6703), secluded at the E end of the lagoon, offers a bar and restaurant. **Pensión Pequena Suiza** (☎ 523-4619), Av. Duarte 56, is another small hotel.

At Caracol and 20 de Diciembre, the 40-rm. **Calypso Beach Hotel** (☎ 523-4666, 523-4849) has rooms with a/c or fans, and color TV. It has a restaurant, bar, and pool.

Facilities at the 75-rm. **Sunset Beach Resort** (☎ 523-4580/4590, fax 523-4975) include a restaurant, solarium, and pool. In Santo Domingo ☎ 523-4511 or fax 523-6422.

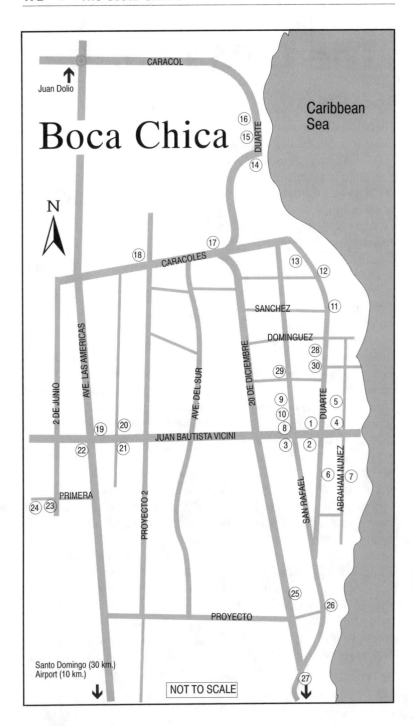

Boca Chica

Juan Dolio

CARACOL

Caribbean Sea

N

Santo Domingo (30 km.)
Airport (10 km.)

NOT TO SCALE

Hotel Discotec Burbujas (☎ 523-6813), C. Duarte 15, has a/c rooms for around US$35 s, US$45 d. Others include **Hotel Restaurant Macorís** (☎ 523-6242), C. Duarte 50; and **Hotel Caney** (☎ 523-4314), C. Duarte 21. **Mesón Isabela** (☎ 523-4224, fax 523-4136) is on C. Duarte 3.

Auberge La Fontaine de Soleil (☎ 523-4679), C. Juan Batista Vicini 11, offers a pool and meals.

Villa Sans Soucy (☎ 523-4461/4327, 800-463-0097, fax 523-4136) is at C. Juan Batista Vicini 48. It has a pool, bar, restaurant, and attractive rooms.

The 23-cabaña **Hotel Fiordaliso** (☎ 523-4453) is on Autopista las Américas at Km 32. If you prefer to stay near the airport, there are a number of places, including the a/c **Tropicana Night Club Hotel-Villas** (☎ 596-8885/8835),

Boca Chica

1. Central Park/express bus stop for Santo Domingo
2. Post Office
3. Le Calypso Restaurant
4. Don Paco Guest House
5. McDeal Rent-a-Car
6. Western Union
7. Don Juan Beach Resort
8. Church
9. Police
10. Auberge La Fontaine de Soleil
11. Pequeña Suiza Bar/Pensión
12. Portofino Bar & Restaurant
13. Codetel
14. Hamaca Resort
15. Mesón
16. Sunset Beach Resort
17. Pizzeria Dolce Vita
18. Taberna Alemana
19. Supermercado Santa Fe
20. Restaurant Terraza Quebec
21. Villa Sans Soucy
22. Don Juan Beach Resort
23. Alpha 3000 (auto rental)
24. Condominios Las Kasitas Del-Sol
25. Farmacia "Barbara María"
26. Boca Chica Resort & Beach Club
27. To Andrés (Boca Marina Yacht Club, DeMar Beach Club, Pop-eye Fisherman Club, Club Nautico)
28. Rte. 66 Restaurant

The Costa Caribe

Av. Las Américas Km 8, which boasts 50 d rooms, 12 suites with marble floors, four apartments and pool, Jacuzzi, nightclub, and BBQ.

resorts: Run by AMHSA, the huge, all-inclusive and ultra-luxury **Hotel Hamaca Beach Resort** (Santo Domingo ☎ 562-7475, fax 566-2436; 800-472-3985; www.worldhotel.com/AM-HSA; e-mail amhsa@codetel.net.do), C. Duarte, is another option.

The all-inclusive **Don Juan Beach Resort** (☎ 523-4511, 687-9157, fax 688-5271) has 111 rooms. Facilities include restaurant, bar, pool, disco, deep-sea fishing, scuba, and watersports. It has a good reputation. In the US ☎ 800-922-4272 or 212-432-1370.

The all-inclusive **Boca Chica Beach Resort** (☎ 523-4521/4529, fax 523-4438), C. Juan Batista Vicini at 20 de Diciembre, features 209 apartments. In the US ☎ 800-828-8895.

FOOD AND DINING: Many restaurants are located along C. Duarte, the main street. **Carlo and Anita's Pub** offer complimentary coffee with their breakfasts.

Restaurante Friisima III, on C. Duarte, serves Dominican and Italian dishes on its menu.

Set next to the Hotel Boca Chica Beach Resort, the **Punto**

☞ *Traveler's Tip*

The ***Boca Chica News*** *is an ad-filled German-published rag which is informative as well as cute to read: "It is a well-known fact that the Caribbean women and men hold a great attraction for the other white sex." A good place to get info and advice is at the* **Rolling Stone** *bar whose owners are well informed. They also have a large library of paperbacks which you may peruse on the premises.*

Central offers German beers, cappuccino, and German dishes.

El César, in front of Tricom, offers Dominican food. The nearby **Route 66** is a "rockcafe" which has its own flavor. It has cocktails as well as "American sound." The motto here is "If you're not having fun, don't blame us!"

Terraza Quebec, C. Juan Batista Vicini 45, serves international dishes, including seafood. On the same street, **Le Calypso** offers international specialties, including lobster.

At C. Caracol 15, **Dolce Vita** serves pizza and other Italian dishes. Try **L'Horizon** restaurant, which has fondues, or **Buxeda**, with excellent *centolla* (crab). **Portofino** is on C. Duarte. Popular watering hole, **Route 66** (☎ 523-5744), C. Duarte 41, serves Indonesian specialties. **La Criolla Bar & Restaurant** offers

Dominican food as well as entertainment.

Neptuno's (☎ 523-6534, 523-4703) is a long-running gourmet restaurant with dishes such as paella, lobster, and shrimp.

The **Pequeña Suiza**, is in a garden, a setting is intended to mimic the "Tinoco" style found in the Italian area of Switzerland. Fondues (including seafood), good coffee, and many other dishes are served.

The **Romagna Mia** (☎ 523-4647), 15 C. Duarte, is a Northern Italian-style restaurant with serves pasta, pizza, seafood, and wonderul desserts. Other Italian eateries include **Pizzeria D'Lucien** and **Pizzeria Italy & Italy**.

SHOPPING FOR FOOD AND SNACKS: Supermercado Santa Fe is at C. Juan Batista Vicini 65. Local food is sold at *fritureras* on the beach, including *yaniqueques* – johnny cakes. There is also an ice-cream shop in town.

ENTERTAINMENT: The Hamaca Beach Hotel has a **casino**. Rock bands play twice monthly at **Route 66** (☎ 523-5744) on C. Duarte.

On the main street, **Carlo and Anita's Pub** offers up oldies on the stereo as well as more than 20 beers from around the world. Nightly happy hour is held from 9-11.

La Yola Disco Club is at Don Juan Beach Resort. The **El Gua-camaya** is inside the Hotel Guamira, C. Abraham Nuñez 27.

Popular with Dominican couples, **Club Burbujas**, a disco, is just past the post office.

The **River Club** is near the main highway and is a "cavelike" disco that attempts to mimic the Guacara Taina in Santo Domingo. You will also meet Dominican couples here.

LOW LIFE: There are a large number of bars. There are three discos on the main street where, as the *Boca Chica News* so bluntly puts it, "the Dominican boys and girls try to earn their daily bread." This is the place to go for social anthropologists, amateur or professional. Come prepared to fend off ardent suitors whose priorities are pecuniary in nature.

The top three discos are the **Isla Bonita**, the **Miramar** ("unique and fantastic and absolutely tropical" according to its ad), and the **Alcatraz** – which attempts to resemble a prison. All are on C. Duarte, Boca Chica's main street.

The Costa Caribe

──────────────────
☞ *Traveler's Tip*
*The best deal in town (and perhaps in the entire nation) is the **Las Olas disco** at the Hotel Hamaca which offers entrance for US$7, including all you can drink from 11-2 (confined to local brands).*
──────────────────

☞ *Traveler's Tip*

There are a number of advantages to using Boca Chica as a base. A stay here puts you outside the city, yet a good bus system takes you into the beginning of the old town. Boca Chica is relatively near the airport. And it has some fairly good restaurants and places to stay. The downside is that it takes a long time to get into town and the beach is crowde, with a lot of vendors.

SERVICES: **Western Union** is at C. Duarte 65. You may change money at its counter or go to Banco Popular Dominicano, C. Duarte 43. **Codetel** has its offices on C. J.B. Vicini. Established in 1967, the marina of the **Santo Domingo Club Naútico** is at the W end of the beach. It also offers watersports. For car rental, contact **Alpha 3000** (☎ 523-6059) on C. Primera. **McDeal Rent-a-Car** (☎ 523-4414) is on C. Duarte near Juan Bautista Vicini.

DIVING: Contact **Treasure Divers** (☎ 523-5320, fax 523-4444) in the Hotel Don Juan Beach Resort.

HORSEBACK RIDING: Rancho Esmeralda (☎ 532-7424, 301-9770) offers both a one-hour tour and a "safari" tour.

SHOPPING: There are a number of souvenir shops around. For buys on things, you need to go into Santo Domingo. The Ha-maca Beach Hotel has a branch of **Harrison's**, the island's major jewelry store chain.

EVENTS: The town's *fiestas patronales* for San Rafael take place Oct. 24.

TOURS: Operating on the main street, **Quisqueya Tours** (☎ 523-4881) offers trips to Santo Domingo, Isla Saona, Lago Enriquillo and other destinations. **Kaona Tours** (☎/fax 526-2077) has similar trips.

NEARBY BEACHES: Guayacanes and Embassy are popular.

FROM BOCA CHICA: Express buses to Santo Domingo leave regularly from the main square. You will need to change at Andes where the a/c *expreso* bus is waiting. The bus should pass through Parque Enriquillo before terminating at Parque Independencia at the start of El Conde. To head E, walk up to the main highway and take a bus traveling to the R. You can catch buses to Higüey and La Romana on the main road. A taxi to the airport costs around US$11; to Santo Domingo, US$22.

Juan Dolio

Located E from Boca Chica, this resort has plenty of hotels. It began developing as a tourist destination only in 1987 and a development association was formed in 1991.

PRACTICALITIES: The 152-unit **Punta Garza Bungalows** (☎ 529-8331, 526-3411) offers 46 rooms (in two-storey houses or cabañas) with kitchenettes and your choice of a/c or fan. Managed by AMHSA (Santo Domingo ☎ 562 7475, fax 566 2436; 800-472-3985; www.worldhotel.com/AMHSA; e-mail amhsa@codetel.net.do), the all-inclusive **Decámeron Beach Resort** (☎ 529-8531, 526-2307) has 280 rooms, pool, disco, tennis, children's playground, and watersports. In the US ☎ 800-223-9815.

Both renting and selling one- and two-bedroom apartments, the 180-rm. **Metro Hotel** (☎ 526-1710/2811) is under the same management as the Embajador in Santo Domingo and Villas Doradas in Puerto Plata. Facilities include two restaurants, conference room, two swimming pools, Jacuzzi, lighted tennis courts, marina, and watersports. In the US ☎ 800-332-4872. or 212-838-3322.

The 295-rm. a/c all-inclusive **Occidental Playa Real** (☎ 526-1114, fax 526-1613) offers seaside swimming pool, coffeeshop, restaurant, tennis court, meeting rooms, banquest rooms, horseback riding, and a full range of watersports. Rates are around US$100 s, US$170 d.

The Occidental Hotels may be reached in North America and Canada (☎ 506-877-3160, 800-843-3311, fax 506-877-3160), in Belgium (☎ 30-235-0373, 09800-14596), in Denmark (☎ 8030 1031, 45 87 00 08, fax 45 87 22 49/93 21 41), in France (☎ 05 00 11, 4071 2121, fax 4071 2131), in Germany (☎ 0180-231 21 21, 06151-905760, fax 06151-905750), in Ireland (01 6605 000, fax 01 6605 540), and in Switzerland (☎ 155 5583, 715 1616, fax 715 5583).

The 275-rm. a/c **Talanquera Hotel and Villas** (☎ 526-1510/1018) offers sauna, Jacuzzi, restaurants, disco, game room, horseback riding, tennis courts, all watersports, Olympic-sized pool, archery, and riflery. Condos and homesites are available. The **Hotel and Beach Resort Costa Linda** (☎ 526-3011/2011, fax 526-3601) has rooms from around $60, as well as more expensive cabinas. The expensive **Caribbean Village Costa Linda** (☎ 526-2161) has a pool. The 137-rm. **Marena Beach Resort** (☎ 526-2121, fax 526-1213, in Santo Domingo 562-7475) is a "family-style" resort which has a pool and gardens.

Also try the 96-rm. **Hotel Embassy Beach Resort** at Playa Caribe (☎ 533-5401; José Contreras 98, Santo Domingo), the 77-room **Tropics** (☎ 526-2009), the 258-room **Villas Jubey Talanquera** (☎ 541-8431, 800-922-

The Costa Caribe

4272), **Sol y Mar** (☎ 529-8605), the **Hotel Ramada** (☎ 526-3310), and **Residencial Tamarindo** (☎ 526-1312).

At Guayacanes, the **Stone House Vacational** (☎ 526-3007) rents studios by the day or week.

FOOD: There are a number of restaurants around. Try the **Oasis**, **BBQ**, **El Bambu**, **JR's**, and the **Quisqueya**.

SERVICES: In Juan Dolio, **Codetel's** office is at Centro Commercial Plaza Quisqueya. For diving information contact the **Neptuno Dive Center** (☎ 526-1473, fax 526-14410) and **Jerry's Dive Center** (☎ 526-1242). For tours contact **Venus Tours** (☎ 526-1197, fax 526-1340), C. Central 48.

CAR RENTALS: Contact **Budget** (☎ 526-1907), **General** (☎ 529-8371), **Honda** (☎ 529-8221/4477), **Metro** (☎ 526-1706), or **National** (☎ 529-8656).

TOURS: Operating out of the Supermarket Lucas at Playa Oasis, **Quisqueya Tours** (☎ 523-4881) offers trips to Santo Domingo, Isla Saona, Lago Enriquillo and other destinations. **Kaona Tours** (☎/fax 526-2077) has similar trips.

Parque Nacional Submarino La Caleta

La Caleta National Marine Park, is 14 miles (22 km) E of Santo Domingo and near the Santo Domingo airport. It was created in 1987 to protect a three-mile stretch of coast; the *Hickory* was sunk here, some ancient cannon and anchors were deposited next to it, and a reef has sprung up around them. The intention was to create an artificial reef to attract fish and so restock the waters emptied by local fishermen. Its crystal clear waters make it especially popular with underwater photographers. There's a small beach and Taino burial tombs; imitation carved stone Taino artifacts are on sale. A similar artificial reef has been created in Bahía de Ocoa, W of Santo Domingo. Displaying artifacts of the indigenous people, the museum of the same name is at the airport entrance.

DIVING: To dive here, contact **Actividades Marinas Del Caribe** (☎ 530-1837, unit 45; 541-1022). A one-day notice is necessary for reservations.

The Southwest

This nation's SW corridor is sparsely populated. Despite nearby Santo Domingo's commanding presence as a center of finance and government, the area in the extreme SW near the Haitian border (which includes Laguna Enriquillo), is semi-desert terrain with few houses and minimal agriculture. Unemployment is rife, and the government is attempting to encourage tourism in the area.

EXPLORING: Carretera Sánchez, the main highway W of Santo Domingo, extends to San Cristóbal and Baní, traversing sugarane fields. Buses going along the S coast will drop you at the entrances to the beaches. Fine beaches are found at or near Las Salinas. Azua, and Barahona, and other beaches, accessible only by car, line the S coast, starting at Barahona. Heading W from Baní, the terrain turns to desert, with organ-pipe cacti mingling with acacias and mesquites. Irrigated vegetable farms are found as well. From Cruce de Ocoa, the turnoff for San José de Ocoa, a paved road heads for the Cordillera Central foothills before turning N to Constanza on a dirt track.

HAINA: Santo Domingo's main port, which also contains the world's largest sugarcane mill (built under Trujillo), is located just outside the capital. There's a country club here which has a swimming pool. Stay at the teacher's vacation center which has low-budget accommodations.

The **Club Naútico Haina** (☎ 532-3961) is on Carr. Sánchez at Km 131.5. Near the village of Nigua, the 17th-century **Capilla de San Gregorio Magno** is the chapel of a ruined 16th-century sugar mill. A bust of St. Gregory and a painting of the Virgen de la Altagracia are inside. Curiously, the Virgin wears earrings. The junction for the 18th-century **Ingenio Boca de Nigua**, a sugar mill, is just past the bridge over the Río Nigua.

Also in the area but farther to the S are the ruins of the 16th-century **Ingenio de Diego Caballero** and the **Hacienda María** where some of Trujillo's assassins were executed in 1961.

San Cristóbal

Farther to the W some 18 miles (30 km) from Santo Domingo, San Cristóbal, capital of the Province of San Cristóbal, was Trujillo's birthplace; as such it was designated a "Meretorious City" in 1939. First settled at around the end of the 15th century, it is believed that the town got its name after the Spaniards constructed a fortress to safeguard a hoard of gold and placed it under the protection of St. Christopher. Today, it is a small town with an attractive downtown area.

GETTING HERE: Buses (express and regular) leave from near Parque Independencia. If you take the bus to the terminal, Casa de Caoba and La Toma pools are straight ahead, a few km down a dirt road; you can generally get a ride (DS$4.32) on a vehicle. Casa de Caoba is on a hill down the road from the bus terminal outside of town and La Toma is farther down that same road as is the turnoff for the El Pomier caves.

SIGHTS: In town, the nation's first constitution was signed in the Palacio del Ayuntamiento (City Hall) in 1844. The 19th-century **Iglesia de San Cristóbal** contains Trujillo's mausoleum – although his remains were actually interred in France. A monument across from its entrance marks the spot where the house in which he was born once stood. The **market** is also worth a visit; it's just down the street from the main plaza.

ⓘ *Did You Know?*

Dominican dictator Trujillo wore pancake makeup in order to lighten his skin.

The **Casa de Caoba** (Mahogany House), Trujillo's former home, can be reached by Land Rover bus leaving from behind the market. Open 9-5. It's been falling apart but is currently under restoration – a process which will not be complete before the next century. From the road you have to walk up the hill along a very bad road; it's a beautiful, peaceful stroll past gumbo limbo and almond trees dripping with Spanish moss and bromeliads. The old caretaker Mario Rodriguez will give you a tour. Trujillo's quarters are under lock and key, but you can see Ramfis's bathroom. Although the original was constructed in mahogany, it's being restored in concrete, and it is intended to serve as a restaurant. Much of the mahogany furniture is still around. **Castillo del Cerro,** or El Cerro, is the luxurious six-story home he ordered built but never lived in. It is also under restoration.

Concrete pools at **Centro Turistico La Toma** are great for swimming. Although the pools themselves are not particularly interesting, there are some water slides and a restaurant. They're open Mon.-Fri., 9-7, and Sat. and Sun., 8-8. Admission is charged

Also be sure to visit **Iglesia de Piedras Vivas**, and the Santa María caves and church, which are the site of an African-influenced stick-and-drum festi-

Dominican girl

El Conde Entrance, Old Santo Domingo (above)
Old Santo Domigo (opposite)
Schoolgirls in Old Santo Domingo (below)

Las Terrenas (above)
On the Way to Constanza (opposite)
Constanza (below)

Rural Transport (above)
Casa de Caoba, San Cristobal (opposite)
Cathedral, Santo Domingo (below)

In San Cristobal (above)
House, Puerto Plata (opposite)
Getting Around in Puerto Plata (below)

Coast at Monte Cristi (above)
Constanza (opposite)
San Cristobal (below)

El Pomier Archaeological Reserve

It may come as a surprise for visitors to learn that a world-class archaeological site lies quite close to Santo Domingo. Four miles (seven km) NW of San Cristóbal, the caves at El Pomier remain virtually unknown and unvisited. Also known as the Cuevas de Borbón, the government has titled them the **Reserva Antropológica Cuevas de El Pomier**. The caves contain an astonishing quantity of Taino cave drawings. This is undoubtedly the Antilles' most important prehistoric legacy, with thousands of wall drawings and many petroglyphs. The main set of caves (and the only ones you may visit) contain some 590 pictographs.

The International Committee for Cave Art and the International Federation for Cave Art have initiated an international campaign to have the caves designated as a world heritage site by UNESCO. Scholars have ranked its importance for the Caribbean region in line with that of the Egyptian pyramids for the Middle East or the Altamira and Lascaux caves for Europe.

Dominican researcher Domingo Abreu Collado maintains that the quantity of carbon dioxide generated by quarrying operations here is contaminating the area, which results in the caves' continued deterioration. Environmentalists sensibly maintain that preserving this site makes better economic sense than quarrying it for limestone to be used in construction. The caves provide refuge to flocks of bats that keep insects under control, contribute to reforestation by spreading the seeds of wild fruits they consume, and pollinate plants in the area.

The reserve's area was extended in 1996 in order to protect the caves from limestone quarrying. The National Park may request that the protected area be extended. Some 12 companies have mining operations in the vicinity.

To get to the caves, you will need to approach via the same road that goes to La Toma. Take the last turnoff to the left before La Toma. If you miss it and reach La Toma, backtrack around one km. You will either want to hire a *motoconcho* (bargain hard!) for the ride or will face a stiff uphill walk. When you first see the mining activity, turn to the R and then follow the signs. The caves are right by a large field.

Near Constanza

El Pomier (continued)

The guide will meet you at the entrance. He will unlock the cave for you, and you must pay the fee before entering. A guide is mandatory, and you can tip him as you like. Be sure to bring water, a flashlight, and hiking boots or good shoes. Be forewarned that the ranger/guide speaks only Spanish. He will point out pictographs with his flashlight and help you get around.

In the main chamber, you will see graffiti covering some petroglyphs; these were here at the time of the cave's protection in 1975. You'll see a ceiling recess with a colony of bats; a second chamber has some "historical graffiti."

The remarkable paintings were created with a combination of manatee fat and charcoal. You can see large birds, representation of the Rain God, and multitudes of other unknown animals and flying creatures. All are simply executed but – given their location – totally extraordinary.

After proceeding through a number of chambers, you will be told that the way ahead is difficult and slippery; should you prefer, you may backtrack and re-enter at the end. First, you must hoist yourself up into a narrow crevice. Then, you begin descending, passing through a section where you you must either limbo down or crawl.

The reward is worth the effort. You will encounter stellar stalactites and stalagmites. Finally, you arrive at an exceptional group of drawings. One resembels a giant bird swooping down and carrying humans off!

Continuing on, you eventually exit the cave. Allow at least a full hour for the trip inside the cave and a full day for the excursion.

---

val and the El Pomier caves. The local *fiestas patronales* (San Cristóbal) are held on July 25. They feature the *carabiné* dance. While in the area, visit Playas Najayo, Palenque, and Nigua. The mountain town of **Cambita Carabitos** to the NW offers a cooler climate and an overview of the capital.

PRACTICALITIES: San Cristobal is not designed for tourism, but there are a few facilities. Stay at **Hotel Constitución** (☎ 528-3309), Av. Constitución 118 (around US$10 d), or **Hotel San Cristóbal** (☎ 528-3555/2364), Av. Libertad 32. Others in town include **Hotel Wing Kit** (☎ 528-3229), M T Sánchez 13; **Hotel**

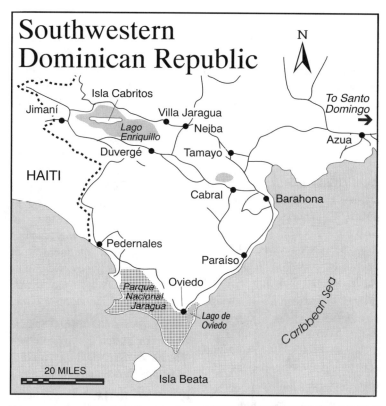

Southwestern Dominican Republic

N

Jimaní
Isla Cabritos
Villa Jaragua
Lago Enriquillo
Neiba
To Santo Domingo →
Azua
Duvergé
Tamayo
HAITI
Cabral
Barahona
Pedernales
Paraíso
Oviedo
Parque Nacional Jaragua
Lago de Oviedo
Caribbean Sea
20 MILES
Isla Beata

Formosa (☎ 528-3229), María Trinidad Sánchez; and **Hotel El Caminante** (☎ 528-3167), M. T. Sánchez 30. **Cafeteria Dulceria Airos, Restaurant Formosa**, and **Cafeteria Pica Pollo la Terraza** are on M. T. Sánchez; the Wing Kit also has a restaurant. *Pasteles en hojas*, a famous local dish, is made with *plátano*, minced meat, and other ingredients. **Codetel** (☎ 528-4196) is at Palo Hincado 14.

FROM SAN CRISTOBAL: Express minibuses to Santo Domingo leave from one corner of the plaza.

☞ *Traveler's Tip*

*The **Pizzaburger** on the main square combines pumping merengue with ice-cold large Heinekens and Presidentes. Sit at one of the tables on the sidewalk and watch as life streams by in front of the park. The giant pink square is another Trujillo legacy.*

Baní

Capital of Peravia Province, Baní is named after Cacique Caonabo's subordinate. The word means "an abundance of water."

The town is best known as the birthplace of 19th-century Cuban liberation fighter Máximo Gómez. The area is famous for its mangoes. Try the famous goats' milk sweets produced in Paya.

FESTIVALS AND EVENTS: Iglesia Nuestra Señora de Regla's *fiestas patronales* are held every Nov. 21.

PRACTICALITIES: In-town hotels include **Hotel Caribaní** (☎ 522-4400), C. Sánchez 12; **Hotel las BBB** (☎ 522-4422), Carr. Sánchez Km 1.5; inexpensive **Hotel Brisas del Sur** (☎ 522-2548); **Hotel Alba** (☎ 522-3590), C. Billini 13; **Hotel Sylvia** (☎ 522-4674), Carr. Sánchez at Km 2; and **Hotel la Posada** (☎ 522-4551), further down the same road. **Restaurant Heladeria Capri** is at C. Duarte 20.

VICINITY OF BANÍ: The beach at Los Almendros isn't much. Stay at the 78-rm. **Los Almendros** (☎ 571-3530/3515) which features restaurant, pool, Jacuzzi, watersports, and rooms with a/c and cable TV.

At Puerto Hermoso, you can stay at the **Las Salinas** (☎ 546-0794, 223-0621), which has rooms for around US$25. It is run by a Hollywood cinema freak and is near the beach.

SERVICES: For **information** contact City Hall (☎ 522-3515) and the Governor's Office (☎ 522-3316). **Codetel** is at Padre Billini 3.

PALMAR DE OCOA: There's a grey sand beach here, and a fishing tournament is held annually. Many wealthy Dominicans have built summer homes here. Azua

Lying 75 miles (121 km) W of Santo Domingo, the town of Azua was founded as Azua de Compostela in 1504 and named by Diego Velásquez, who went on to subdue Cuba. Granted a coat of arms by King Ferdinand in 1508, it became the capital of Azua Province in 1845. Azua has been set on fire numerous times during its history – by French corsairs as well as by invading and retreating Haitian forces.

FESTIVALS AND EVENTS: The Battle of March 1844, in which Dominicans repelled the invading Haitians, is celebrated Mar. 19.

GETTING HERE: You may wish to change buses for Barahona in town. It's two hours here from Santo Domingo, and less than two hours on to Barahona. Buses also run to San Juan and Padre las Casas.

SIGHTS: The ruins of the colonial town can be seen at **Pueblo Viejo**. Named for the battle that took place here between the Haitians and Dominicans, **El Número** offers a panoramic view. Travel on from here to **Corbanito**, an open cove with a couple of miles of white sand beaches and outlying coral reefs, on the E shore of the Bahia Ocoa.

Playa Chiquita is a grey sand beach with no waves. **Playa Monte Río** is another beach where rapacious conquistador Hernán Cortés hung out during his formative years. **Playa Blanca** is nearby, and there are also undeveloped **hotsprings** in the area.

EVENTS: The *fiestas patronales* for Nuestra Señora de los Remedios (Our Lady of Remedies) are held Sept. 8.

PRACTICALITIES: Modest **Hotel América**, C. Emilio Prudhomme, charges around US$12. Also try inexpensive **Hotel Restaurant San Ramon** (☎ 521-3529), Fco. R Sánchez at Km. 1.5; less expensive **Hotel Brisas del Mar** (☎ 521-3813), C. de Leones; or still cheaper **Hotel Altagracia** (☎ 521-3286), J P Duarte 59, and **Hotel El Familiar** (☎ 521-3556), C. Emilio Prudhomme. **Restaurant Patio Español el Jardin** is at C. Duarte 49, and **Restaurant El Gran Segovia** is at F del R Sánchez 31. **Codetel** is at Av. 19 de Marzo 118 and **Metrobus** (☎ 521-5366) is at Parque 19 de Marzo.

INFORMATION: Contact City Hall at ☎ 521-3302 and the Governor's Office at 521-3215.

SERVICES: Codetel is at Av. 19 de Marzo 118. *Metro's* terminal (☎ 521-5366) is at Parque 19 de Marzo.

Barahona

Barahona was founded in 1802 by Haitian General Toussaint L'Ouverture and is named after one of its earliest colonists. The town is three hours by car (or four hours by bus) from Santo Domingo on the S coast.

The opening of María Montez International Airport may mark a surge in tourism in the area. At least the government – given the area's chronic employment problems – would like to create a tourism boom. However, the area, while stunning in its beauty, does not possess the white standy beches that tourists love. The "international" airport has some major structural deficiencies, but it may yet attract international and charter flights.

Dominican President Leonel Fernandez on tourism: "He who drives by the coast of Barahona to Pedernales discovers that God placed special attention to the creation of this area of the world and I feel that if we have been blessed by nature in this magnitude, why not call the world to come here and at the same time invest, spend, and improve the living conditions of the local residents."

EVENTS: The town's *fiestas patronales*, in honor of Nuestra Señora del Rosario, are held Oct. 4. They feature the *carabiné* dance, accompanied by *balsié*

The Southwest

(accordion), *güira* (scraper), and *pandero* (tamborine).

SIGHTS: There's not much of specific interest in the town itself. There is a small public beach here, but stinging jelly fish are frequent visitors. Visit the Central Barahona sugar mill in the city. The nearby coffee-producing villages of Platon and Santa Elena are also worth a visit. Barahona may be used as a base to visit Lago Enriquillo and other areas in the SW.

ACCOMMODATIONS: Opened in 1993, the **Riviera Beach Hotel** (☎ 524-5111, fax 524-5798; Av. Enriquillo 6) has 108 a/c rooms with phone and satellite TV; there is a pool, tennis courts, and two restaurants. It's within walking distance of town and is run by the Spanish Continental hotel chain.

Simple and inexpensive 22-rm. a/c **Hotel Guarocuya** (☎ 524-2211) is on Av. Enriquillo at Playa Saladilla. It's priced at around US$20. The **Hotel Barahona** (☎ 524-3442) is at C. Jaime Mora 5. The Mencia (☎ 524-5611), 30 de Marzo, charges around US$9 d. The **Cacique** (☎ 524-4620), C. Uruguay 2, is less expensive. The **Hotel Victoria** (☎ 524-2392), Padre Billini 15-A (corner Uruguay), features d and s rooms with a/c. Also try the **Hotel Caribe** (☎ 524-2185), Av. Enriquillo; or the **Hotel Palace** (☎ 524-2500), C. Uruguay 18; **Hotel Brasil** (☎ 524-3661), C. Padre Billini 31; the **Hotel Las Magnolias** (☎ 524-2244), C. Anacaona 13; and the **Hotel Bohemia** (☎ 524-2109), C. Sánchez 72.

Located 11 miles (17 km) from Barahona to the SW between the coastal villages of Baoruco and Cienaga, the **Bahoruco Beach Club and Resort** (☎ 685-5184) combines an 84-rm. apart-hotel with a 90-suite hotel, along with 34 apartments distributed in five blocks. Its features include Jacuzzi, pool, restaurant, bars, satellite TV, horseback riding, tennis, watersports, and timeshares.

Another resort, the 36-rm. **Hotel Oasis**, is under construction and may have opened by your arrival.

FOOD: Options include the open-air **La Rocca** next door to Hotel Caribe, Av. Enriquillo, the **Restaurant Costa Sur** on the same street, or – for Chinese food – **Restaurant Brisas del Caribe** along Carr. Batey Central. There are also many small restaurants in the town center.

SERVICES: The **Codetel** office is at Nuestra Sra. del Rosario 36.

ENTERTAINMENT: Try the **Lotus Night Club** (near the main square), **Cindy**, and **Costa Azul** which is on the Malecón.

INFORMATION: For information contact the **tourist office** at C. Anacaona 8 or visit City Hall on C. 30 de Mayo.

FROM BARAHONA: If you have a car, you can explore the rocky but pretty beaches including the spectacular Paraiso. *Públicos* also run. The best scuba and snorkeling is found all along the white sand beaches of the S coast; still undeveloped for tourism, it's an area with beautiful inland scenery.

Between Baoruco and Enriquillo wet tropical forest abounds, and the small roadside settlements have fruit stands. From Enriquillo the drier lowlands of the Barahona peninsula begin. From Oviedo to Pedernales, thorny scrub alternates with karst outcrops. Cool freshwater lagoons are found behind several of the beaches, and Limón Lagoon is a flamingo reserve.

At **San Rafael** some 40 min. from Barahona, a freshwater swimming hole is in the river at the beach's end. You can camp here, and there's a small restaurant.

BEACHES: Most of the beaches in the area are rocky but beautiful. **Bahoruco** has large waves and over a mile of white sand beach. The 12-rm. **Casa Bonita** (☎ 687-5697, fax 686-3940) is just near the village and has gardens and a pool. Rates are around US$60 d. **El Pato** or Los Patos beach has smooth white pebbles and is suitable for surfing and swimming. Others are **La Cié-** naga, **Río Caño**, **El Quemaíto** (coconut palms), **El Defiladero de los Amargados**, and **San Rafael** (light brown sand).

SAN JUAN DE LA MAGUANA: On the main road to Haiti, you can visit the **Corral de los Indios**, an indigenous site several miles to the N of the town where a large circle of stones is set on a level plain.

OTHER DESTINATIONS: Also visit **Elias Piña**, one of the nation's frontier towns, which also has one of the dilapidated old houses built for Trujillo. At **Banica**, visit the church in the **Cerro de San Francisco**. People come here for a ceremony every year on Oct. 3 and 4.

Parks of the Southwest

Reserva Científica Natural Laguna de Rincón

Also known as Laguna de Cabral, **Rincón Lagoon** is the nation's largest freshwater lagoon and second largest lagoon of any kind (after Enriquillo). Set amidst sub-tropical forest, the lagoon harbors a large population of *jicotea* (freshwater slider turtles). Notable birds include the *pato espinoso* (ruddy duck), masked duck, fla-

The Southwest

mingo, Louisiana heron, northern jacana, and the glossy ibis.

Parque Nacional Sierra de Bahoruco

Rising as high as 7,766 ft. (2,367 m) near El Aguacate, next to the Haitian border, Sierra de Bahoruco National Park supports a wide variety of vegetation.

HISTORY: Formed some 50 mllion years ago in the Middle Eocene, the area is of note because Enriquillo (Guarocuya) declared his tribe's independence from its hilltops.

FLORA AND FAUNA: Vegetation varies from extensive stretches of pine forest to mixed forests to fields covered with latifoliats (broad-leaved plants). There are 166 species of orchids or over half those found within the country. Trees include the trumpet tree, creolan pine, West Indies laurel, West Indian sumac, and the Hispaniolan mahogany. One of the 49 species of birds present is the white-necked crow, which is extinct in neighboring Puerto Rico; others – found in the mountains – include the narrow-billed tody, the white-winged warbler, the Hispaniolan trogon, and the Antillean siskin. The white-crowned and red-necked pigeon, the Hispaniolan parakeet, the Hispaniolan lizard cuckoo, the Hispaniolan parrot, the white-winged dove,

vervain hummingbird, and the stolid flycatcher are found in its dry and humid forests.

Laguna Enriquillo y Parque Nacional Isla Cabritos

Set inside a national park, this 13-mile-long (21-km) inland saltwater lake is due W of Santo Domingo near the border with Haiti. Plummeting to 130 ft. (40 m) below sea level, its bottom is the Caribbean's lowest point. Rising sharply above the lake are two ranges: the Sierra de Neiba on the N and the Sierra de Baoruco (another national park) on the S.

SIGHTS: The largest of the three islands (and a reserve for the exotic American crocodile), five-mile-long **Isla Cabritos** (Goat Island) is in the lake's center. Flat with coral beaches, the island lacks fresh water. During a period of drought in the 1930s, it was connected to the mainland and goats were introduced. The American crocodile was introduced here by the Dominican government in the 1930s as part of a scheme to promote tourism. Currently, crocs are being propagated at the Zoo in Santo Domingo and are being released into the wild; fishermen are encouraged not to kill them or steal eggs. Herons, flamingoes, egrets, and royal terns may also be seen here.

The Las Marías sulfur **hot springs** are found in an oak forest by the village of La Descubierta in the lake's vicinity. Cold water baths are at **Las Barias**. A remarkable set of petroglyphs are inscribed on cliffs at **Cuevo Las Caritas** (Cave of the Little Faces) – a five min. climb from the road. These are a half-mile before the village of La Descubierta in the lake's NW corner. It is assumed that these are Taino, but nothing is known for certain.

HISTORY: Approximately a million years ago, the lake was part of a connecting channel from the Bay of Neiba through to the Bay of Port-au-Prince. Deposits from the Río Yaque del Sur at its mouth served to seal off the lake. Known as Guarizacca by the Indians, Cabrito served as the refuge for the legendary rebellious chief Enriquillo. He and his followers subsisted on dried fish. Between 1822 and 1824, the island and some of the surrounding territory was given to a French family by the occupying Haitians. The area became a national park in 1974.

FLORA AND FAUNA: The islands and surrounding hills are covered with short, dry thorn scrub, cacti, acacias, and mesquites. Some 62 species of birds include greater flamingos, herons, roseate spoonbills, terns, clapper rails, Hispaniolan parrots, village weavers, and burrowing owls. Numerous other species are found in the surrounding hills. Iguanas (rhinoceros and Ricord's) can only be seen on **Isla Cabritos**, which they share with American crocodiles. All three reptile species are endangered. Despite the island's name, goats no longer graze here.

GETTING HERE: From Santo Domingo via Barahona, it takes three hrs. by car to the lake. An additional hr. is required to drive around it. If visiting by bus, it will take you eight hrs. with *La Experiencia* and *Riviera del Caribe* companies. Get off at Los Ríos or La Descubierta; from here you can either walk or catch a ride to the lake.

VISITING GOAT ISLAND: Arrangements must be made in advance at the park office in La Descubierta. If the park motorboat is actually running, it takes less than an hour to get here; a rowboat requires two hrs. To get to the park, drive 2½ miles (four km) SE of town to La Zofrada. Arrangements are made in a building below the road (around US$15 for four). Bathe in the sulfur hot springs here. Bring water and expect high temperatures. Aside from a small shop in Descubierta, the nearest facilities are in Barahona. Development has been proposed in a big way for Pedernales, but it has yet to materialize.

The Southwest

PRACTICALITIES: At Jimaní, stay at low-budget **Hotel Jimaní**, **Hotel Quisqueya**, **Mellitzos** (facing the park), or others. You can also stay in one of several *dormitorios*. One is on the corner opposite the disco in the central square. There's also a fine *balneario* (swimming hole). It's possible to cross the Haitian border here and visit **Laguna del Fundo**, a saltwater lagoon inhabited by American crocodiles.

TOURS: Delia's Tours (☎ 682-1086 in Santo Domingo) offers tours to this region.

Parque Nacional Jaragua

Named after a Taino chieftain, **Jaragua National Park** is set in the nation's SW. It extends W from Oviedo to Cabo Rojo and, along with the accompanying small islands of Alto Velo and Beata, covers the S portion of Pedernales Province .

Extending over 520 sq. miles (1,350 sq. km), including 270 sq. miles (700 sq. km), of sea, this extremely arid park is generally hot. Covered with heavily weathered and sharp "dogtooth" limestone, cacti, and other rough vegetation, it can be a difficult place to walk around in. The several beaches along its coast can only be reached by long hikes or by boat. East of the town of Oviedo, **Lago Oviedo**, a six-mile-long saltwater lake, is separated from the Caribbean by a sandy barrier.

HISTORY: The mainland area was created in the Oligocene some 50 million years ago when land masses rose from the sea. The Laguna Oviedo and the outlying islands of Beata and Alto Vela, however, surfaced only a comparatively recent million years ago. Archaeological remains have been unearthed in the park from a settlement dating back to 2950 BC. The park's name is taken from that of the SW's *cacique*, Xaragua. The **caves** of Guanal, Mongó, and La Poza contain pre-Columbian pictographs and petroglyphs.

FLORA AND FAUNA: Cacti and other vegetation adapted to a hot, dry climate predominate. The forest contains trees like copey, Hispaniolan mahogany, lignum vitae, gumbo-limbo, and wild frangipani. Seagrapes are found at the beach and red, button, and white mangroves line the swamps. Solenodons and hutias reside here, as do 11 of the nation's 18 species of bats.

The 130 species of birds, half of which are aquatic, represent 60% of the nation's total number. The nation's largest population of flamingos live at the Oviedo Lagoon, while the common potoo inhabits the coastal mangroves. Boobies and brown pelicans are found around the beach where turtles also nest. Greater flamingos, pearly-eyed thrashers, willets, endemic green-tailed warblers, Antillean palm swifts, burrowing owls, and Ridgway's hawks all live on **Island Beata** off the park's S tip. You might also see great egrets, sooty terns, little blue herons, roseate spoonbills, and frigate birds. All four species of sea turtle (hawksbill, leatherback, green, and loggerhead) are found here. The rhinocerous iguana and Ricord's iguana also live in the area.

PRACTICALITIES: The road from Barahona to Pedernales passes by the park. You must have a truck or a jeep to get there, and you must bring whatever food and water you require. Pedernales has some small shops.

Onward to Haiti

Conditions in Haiti are such that visits are not now advised.

📖 *Suggested Reading*

For travel information on Haiti consult the current edition of Caribbean Islands Handbook. *A truly fascinating book to read before traveling is* The Rainy Season *by Amy Wilentz. It deals with Aristide and the political situation.*

PRACTICALITIES: Check to see if you need a visa from the Haitian Embassy (☎ 562-3519), C. Scout 11, Santo Domingo.

GETTING HERE: If the border is open, buses run from the Hotel San Tomé, Calle Santomé (next to the Mercado Modelo). ☎ 688-5100 and ask for Alejandro. Also call *Linea Sur* (☎ 682-1414). It's a six-hr. drive from Santo Domingo to Port-au-Prince.

by air: When and if conditions improve, there will be flights. **Aerolink** (☎ 567-0819, 320-0627) has offered air tours.

The Cordillera Central Region

The nearest thing the Dominican Republic has to an unexploited frontier, the Cordillera Central or "Dominican Alps" is a mountainous area that contains the nation's largest mountain range; the region is accessed via roads that intersect with Carretara Duarte, the main highway running between Santo Domingo and Santiago.

The two contiguous national parks here contain the nation's highest peaks, numerous waterfalls, the endangered *cotorra,* and the headwaters of its rivers. The gateway towns to the area are Bonao and La Vega.

⚡ *Warning*

If hiking in the mountains in this region, watch out for Mayas, miniature biting black flies. If you're allergic, your bites will swell up and last for weeks!

Bonao

Halfway between Santo Domingo and Santiago along Carr. Duarte, the discovery of mineral wealth (and the consequent arrival of the mining industry) has transformed Bonao (pop. 30,000) from a small village into sizable town; rich deposits of nickel, bauxite, silver, and gold were uncovered here during the early 1970s. Be sure to note the contrast between the shanties of the miners – who work long hours under dangerous conditions for low wages – and the transplanted suburban lifestyle of the American expatriate community in Barrio Gringo. The town is also known as "Villa de las Hortensias," and the nation's most famous bus stop is at the entrance to town.

Bonao is also of note for being the place where the first legal strike in the history of the nation's export-assembly industry was won. In 1996, the Bonahan Apparel Company consented to sign an agreement with the United Bonahan Worker's Union in the aftermath of a five-day strike. The Korean-owned firm was notorious for bad working conditions including two-way mirrors in restrooms, refusal to pay overtime or permit breaks, and the lack of adequate ventilation. The strike was made possible by a 1992 law which protects the collective bargaining rights of all workers.

PRACTICALITIES: Hotels here include **Hotel Bonao Inn**

(☎ 525-2727), Aut. Duarte at Km 85; **Hotel Viejo Madrid** (☎ 525-3558), just before it; **Hotel Restaurant Yaravi** (☎ 525-3267), C. Duarte 153; and **Hotel Plaza Nouel** (☎ 525-3518/2909), C. Duarte 128. Also try the **Elizabeth**, **Mi Provincia**, and **San Juan** (near market). Eat at **Restaurant Tipico Bonao**, Aut. Duarte at Km 83, **Restaurant San Rafael**, C. Duarte 182, or **Restaurant San Rafael**, C. Duarte 182. The **Codetel** office is at 27 de Febrero 69.

☞ Traveler's Tip

*Just before the town of Bonao is **Industrias Taveras**, a cheese market that sells queso fresco and other delights.*

La Vega

In the heart of the Cibao, the quiet valley town of La Vega (pop. 200,000) stands on the main highway between Santo Domingo and Santiago, near the junction of the road to Jabaracoa to the W. Neither extraordinarily dull nor enthralling, La Vega is best used as a transit point or as a base to explore the surrounding area.

HISTORY: La Vega's origin dates back to the 15th century, when Columbus mandated that a fort be built here. (Nothing remains of the original.) The nation's first commercial sugarcane crop was harvested in the environs, the New World's first mint set up shop here, and the first royally sanctioned brothel opened in this very town. Diego Columbus summered here, and the famous monk Bartolomé de las Casas also lived here. The original town's prosperity was shattered when it was destroyed by a hurricane in 1562; it was moved to the present location the next year.

EVENTS: The best time to visit the town is on Sun. afternoons in Feb. when colorfully costumed *diablos cojuelos* take to the streets in celebration of *carnával*. On Aug. 15, the *fiestas patronales* of Nuestra Señora de Antigua are held.

GETTING HERE: Departing from G. Godoy, *Expreso del Valle* (☎ 573-0722) has a number of runs. *Metro* (573-7099) runs twice daily at 7:30 and 4; they return at the same times from Santo Domingo.

SIGHTS: There's not much of note in the town itself. From La Vega on the R is the road to **Santa Cerro** and its convent where the Virgen de las Mercedes (Virgin of Mercy) is worshipped. Legend has it that Columbus placed the first cross here, one of which had been a bon voyage gift from Queen Isabella. During a bloody battle between the Spanish and Tainos led by Cacique Guarionex, the Indians attempted to burn the cross. It failed to catch fire and the Virgen de las Mercedes miraculously appeared on one of its arms; the Indians fled in terror. A piece of the cross has been preserved but is not on display. You can, however, see the **"Santo Hoyo"** – the "Sacred Hole" where Columbus is said to have planted a cross to mark the spot where the Virgin appeared. Situated inside **Iglesia Las Mercedes** (1860), it's covered with a square wire grill and is illuminated. There's a fine view from the multi-level terrace outside; see it in Jan. when thousands of coffee-shading *amapola* trees bloom and the vast valley turns coral pink. The festival of **Nuestra Señora de las Mercedes** is celebrated here around Sept. 24.

From here the entire Vega Real (Royal Valley) is unveiled. The road continues over the hill and into the valley where the ruins of **La Vega Vieja** – a small church and fort – stand. Founded by Columbus and destroyed by the 1564 earthquake, it has been undergoing restoration. The turnoff for Jarabacoa is straight ahead to the left from here.

Backtracking a bit towards La Vega, you will find the ruins of the **San Francisco monastery**. A number of skeletal remains have been unearthed here, and locals can lift the covers for your viewing pleasure.

ACCOMMODATIONS: The Hotel Restaurant "Quinto Patio" (☎ 573-6842; around US$11)) is at C. Restauración 48. **Hotel América** (☎ 573-2909), **Hotel Del Valle** (☎ 573-3974), and **Hotel Guariano** (☎ 573-2632) are all on Aut. Duarte. Cheapest (less than US$5) are the **Hotel Comedor** and the **Hotel Buenos Aires** (☎ 573-5120) next door; they're at Las Carreras and Ubaldo Gómez, not far from the bus stop.

Others include **Hotel Astral** (☎ 573-3535), C. N de Cáceres 18; **Hotel Real** (☎ 573-6487) nearby; **Hotel San Pedro** (☎ 573-2884), C. N de Cáceres 33; **Hotel Santa Clara** (☎ 573-2878), C. N de Cáceres 91; **Hotel Bello** (☎ 573-5282), Av. Rivas 67; **Hotel Cafeteria Genao** (☎ 573-4878), Av. Rivas 64; **Hotel Nueva Imagen** (☎ 573-7351), C. Restauración 3; and **Hotel Restaurant Royal Palace** (☎ 573-2738), C. Padre Adolfo.

FOOD: Eat at **Hotel Restaurant "Quinto Patio"** (☎ 573-6842) at C. Restauración 48; **Restaurant Maturijere** and **El Coche** on Aut. Duarte; **Restaurant Malecón** on Av. Imbert; **Restaurant Frito Lindo** on 18 de Abril; **Restaurant Cafeteria La Casona** at C. J. Gómez 127; and **Restaurant La Cocina** at C. Mella 29.

ENTERTAINMENT: The town's major disco, **Astromundo**, is on

Cordillera Central

Autopista Duarte. **Codetel** is on Juan Rodriguez at the corner of Duvergé.

FROM LA VEGA: *Públicos* leave for Santiago and Jabaracoa from the center of town. *Moto Saad* (☎ 573-2103) departs for Santo Domingo from Colón 37.

Jarabacoa

This popular resort town blossoms during the summer when locals arrive to beat the heat. The rest of the year it's pleasant, laid back, and very low key. And the presence of the nearby hydroelectric plant means that there's power practically all the time! The Río Jimenoa edges the town, which has only a few main streets and is surrounded by mountains. Jabaracoa may be used as a kickoff point for the trip up Pico Duarte, as a base to explore the area's waterfalls, or as just a pleasant place to kick back and relax in for a few days.

GETTING HERE: Take a *público* from La Vega or a Caribe Tours bus from Santo Domingo. From La Vega, it's an attractive ride along a two-lane asphalt road. As you climb higher, young pines line the road.

SIGHTS: Balneario La Poza is a short walk from town. It has a beautiful ambiance. More attractive but much less accessible, the *balneario* at "La Confluencia" on the Río Jimenoa offers somewhat

dangerous swimming and a restaurant. To get here you must follow a road lined with the houses of the elite. It's about an hour's pleasant walk.

WATERFALLS: Most accessible of the three waterfalls is **Salto de Biguate**. It's about a half-hour walk to the entrance, which is marked by a sign. Visit, if you can, between excursion groups of Germans on horseback. Allow an hour or two from the road both ways. Visit the upper and lower Río Jimenoa falls; the upper falls is three miles (five km) or so farther up the same road and down a steep slope. To get there, travel six miles (9.6 km) to the village of El Salto, where an unmarked trail from the road's edge leads to the falls. Look for the parking area on the R. While it's easy to get down, coming back up is a bit steep. The "lower" falls is several miles out of town along the road to Monabao; a suspension bridge is also nearby. Hire a *motoconcho* to get here.

ACCOMMODATIONS: About half a mile from town on the road towards Constanza, inexpensive **Pinar Dorado** (☎ 574-2820) features a small pool and restaurant. Very popular with Germans and other Europeans, its rooms have double beds and a balcony. Although aging, it's the plushest hotel within walking distance of town, and from here it's possible to walk to the Salto Biguate waterfall. Rooms here start from from around US$25 with fan; a/c is more expensive. In the US ☎ 800-843-3311.

Heading towards town along the road from la Vega, **Centro Turistico Alpos Dominicanos** is the first establishment you pass. Alpos Dominicanos features 132 rooms distributed in 11 villas and 66 apartments, with more on the way. It charges around US$35 d.

La Montaña (☎ 682-8181) charges around US$20 d.; it is a remnant of the Trujillo legacy. **Piños del Puerto**, and **Hotel Nacional** are also on the way. Charging about US$12 s or d, **Hotel Hogar** (☎ 574-2739) has rooms with a bath and fan. There is a nice courtyard and friendly management.

A way out of town on the road towards La Confluencia, **Anacaona Villas** (☎ 574-2686) offers concrete bungalows complete with fan and kitchen for US$120/wk. Farther on to the left down the same road, **Jabaracoa River Resort** (☎ 574-2772/2161) has units for around US$20 pn with TV and kitchen.

Iin La Joya near the Salto Baiguate, **Rancho Baiguate** (☎ 696-0318, 563-8005, fax 574-4940; e-mail ranchobaiguate@codetel.net.do) is a full-service hotel with restaurant, bar, volleyball court, and soccer and baseball fields. It also serves as a base for local adventure travel. These include a three-day Pico Duarte climb, white-water rafting down the Yaque del Norte, canyoning and canoeing, horseback riding to the waterfall, trekking, mountain biking, paragliding, and tubing.

low-budget: A cheap but unmarked hotel is on the cor. of Independencia. The **Dormitorio** is basic but clean and has a good *comedor.* **Hotel El Carmen** stands near it. Out of town, the Hotel Continental is for short-term sex. You can also **camp** at La Confluencia.

FOOD: Cafeteria Angel, Av. Independencia, has good coffee and is run by a sweet lady. **De Paolo Restaurant** has Italian food, as does **Restaurante Pizzeria El Cofre** which offers Dominican-style pizza. **Restaurant Brasilia**, C. Colón 26, has one of the nicest atmospheres. **Restaurant Sandy** is also good, but you can expect a large contingent of affluent Germans to arrive around 12:30 PM. A small market in town sells fruits and vegetables.

ENTERTAINMENT: You can play billiards at **Club Deportiv El Dugout**, next to the ballfield on the way to the Confluencia.

SERVICES: Codetel is on the upper part of Av. Independencia to the R in the direction of La Vega. **Rancho Baiguate** (see above) offers a number of tours. **Get Wet** (☎ 586-1170, 586-1655;

Cordillera Central

www.hispaniola.com/GetWet; e-mail getwet@codetel.net.do) offers rafting, caving, canyoning, and other adventurous activites. They take you to the Jarabacoa area and operate out of Puerto Plata.

Constanza

Set in a 4,000-ft.-high (1,219-m) mountain valley, Constanza is one of the nation's most pleasant towns – one virtually undeveloped for tourism. No one will offer to braid your hair, you won't be continually beeped at by *moto-concho* drivers, and no one will try to sell you a tour on the street!

Despite decades of international tourism in the nation, Constanza remains a haven, a great place to see what rural agricultural Dominican life is all about. Fresh vegetables (such as mushrooms, potatoes, and garlic), fruits (strawberries, raspberries, peaches, and pears) and flowers for export are grown in the area. There's also a Japanese emigrant farming community – descendants of some 30 Japanese families brought in during the 1950s at the behest of Trujillo.

The town itself is somewhat nondescript: your basic Dominican town. It boasts a giant military base and shows the dramatic contrasts between affluence and squalor.

Frequently, if somewhat mis-leadingly, billed as a bit of Japan or Switzerland in the tropics, the surrounding area is one of the nation's prettiest, with verdant forests, cool mountain air, and brisk streams and waterfalls. Reasonably pleasant during the days, temperatures may drop to freezing during the winter. View the cloud-covered peaks of the Cordillera Central from the high escarpment on the valley's S side. Constanza may be used as a base from which to explore the surrounding area, but – other than lush agricultural hillsides and the poor local inhabitants – there is little to see.

On June 14, 1959, a C-46 twin-engine transport landed here with 56 rebels on board. The plane was loaned by Venezuela, but it came from Cuba. Trujillo's forces swiftly defeated the rebels and later sunk two ships off the coast of Puerto Plata. This marked the end of Castro's one attempt to overthrow Trujillo. UFOs were sighted here during the mid-1970s; the latest was seen in 1991.

FESTIVALS AND EVENTS: The *fiestas patronales* of Nuestra Señora de las Mercedes are celebrated here around Sept. 24.

GETTING HERE: Constanza can be reached from Bonao by two *públicos. Linea Cobra* also runs. (See "From Santo Domingo" in the Santo Domingo section.) Direct transport between Constanza and Jarabacoa is only available in the morning. The alternative at other times is via the Santo Domingo-Santiago Hwy.

from Neiba: A time-consuming, difficult, but adventurous route is take a *guagua* to Cruce de Ocoa from Neiba (in the SW) and then take another from there to San José de Ocoa (NE of Azua). In **San José de Ocoa**, you can stay at low-budget **Hotel Marien** or at 10-bungalow **Rancho Francisco** (☎ 558-2291 or 565-7637/562-1930 in Santo Domingo), just outside the village. Its facilities include an Olympic-sized pool and a restaurant. From here there is only regularly scheduled transport three times per week (Mon., Wed., and Fri.). If you can get to Rancho Arriba by bus, it's possible to hire a motorcyclist to take you along an awful road to Piedra Blanca on the Santo Domingo-Santiago Hwy. From there you can get to Constanza.

by car: The road between Jarabacoa and San José de Ocoa passes through Constanza and Valle Nuevo. From Bonao, it's a more direct one-hour drive from the Carretera Duarte. The road's first part climbs into the mountains plying a ridge above **Laguna Rincón**, one of a chain of six man-made lakes found in the area. The area surrounding this lake was designated Refugio de Fauna Silvestre Laguna Rincón in 1996.

ACCOMMODATIONS: Hotels are friendly, but street noise can be high! Bring earplugs. Located on a sidestreet, pleasant **Hotel Brisas del Valle** (☎ 539-2365), C. Gratereaux 76, offers rooms for US$7.50 and up. The family-run **Hotel Casita Verde** charges around US$5 with bath. Low-budget (US$4) **Hotel Margarita** is on C. Luperón, the main street. Also try **Hotel El Gran Restaurant** (☎ 539-2675). C. G. Luperón 70. The **Hotel Restaurant Mi Cabaña** (539-2472), R. Espinosa 60, has rooms with shared bath for US$8; rooms with private baths are US$10. **Hotel Sara** (☎ 586-4834), C. Imbert, charges around US$7 for pleasant rooms with baths.

outlying: Outside the center of town are two others. **Cabañas de la Montana** (☎ 682-2410, 561-1131/1123/1439; e-mail cabamont@hotmail.com), C. San Francisco de Marcorís No. 99 in Sec. Don Bosco, has units with kitchens, and **Altocerro** (☎ 696-0202), Colonia Kennedy, offers 20 villas and 10 rooms. Prices run from around $16 s, $22 d, including tax.

FOOD: Popular with locals and offering a menu with a wide selection, **Lorenzo's** is the place to dine here. It has reasonble prices and an attractive atmosphere. It's right on the main street. **Restaurant Pizzeria y Heladeria Rey**, S. Ureña 22, has pizza and a wide selection of other goods. The **market** on C. Gratereux has a good assortment of fruits and vegetables. Many other shops are in the vicinity. There are also places to eat near the park.

ENTERTAINMENT: Evaldra is the local disco; it is active only on weekends. There are a number of video parlors around, including one off the main square. The Hamburger Shoppe Nintendo has Dominican youth mezmerized by video games.

FROM CONSTANZA: If you have not been there yet, the obvious place to head for is Jarabacoa. Head down to the Texaco station and get in or on one of the pickup trucks or cars.

Located near the market, **Linea Junior** (☎ 539-2777/2177) runs to Santiago. **Linea Cobra** (☎ 539-2415) runs to Santo Domingo; their offices are at C. Sánchez 37. To get to Santo Domingo, you must travel the road towards Bonao, which has truly spectacular scenery. If you don't take a direct bus, just get in a truck or whatever from the Texaco station and head down to the junction. You must cross the highway if headed towards Constanza and Puerto Plata.

There's regular but quite slow transport to San José de Ocoa three times per week (generally Mon., Wed., and Fri.) along a very rough road; ask around.

Reserva Científica Valle Nuevo

One of several areas in the country designated as a scientific reserve in 1983, Valle Nuevo extends from near the Valle Nuevo Military Post to the Pyramids, a local monument some 24 miles (39 km) S of Constanza. One of the nation's true virgin areas, the woods, at 7,000 ft. elevation (2,134 m), offer cool temperatures and solitary hiking trails. Two of the nation's major rivers, the Yuna and the Nizao, have their headwaters here.

FLORA AND FAUNA: Thought to have been sown by migrating birds, lyonia and holly are found only here in the Caribbean and flourish in the area's temperate climate. Dominican magnolia covers some western parts of the reserve. Of the 249 plant species, 97 are endemic. Unfortunately, a full third of the reserve burned during a 1983 forest fire and is just now recovering.

GETTING AROUND: Follow old logging roads into the forests. Some are driveable, but all deteriorate during the wet. Zigzagging through thick pine forest and fields of pine savannah, the route S climbs up to 8,000 ft. (2,438 m) before the Province of Peravia. On the way, the road traverses rocky crags and bluffs, the remains of what was once an extensive montane cloud forest, and then drops down to the Valle de Río Ocoa before ending at San José de Ocoa. A forest of acacia, mesquite, and mahogany lies to the S of town. Although the road is bad and rain is frequent here, this is one of the nation's loveliest areas. It takes about two hours by car to Santo Domingo. Allow a full day from Constanza for the trip.

Aguas Blancas

About six miles (9.6 km) S of town, "White Water Falls" is a two-staged waterfall with a chilly pool. Birdwatchers should keep an eye peeled for the Hispaniolan trogon, the gray-headed quail-dove, and the sharp-shinned hawk.

GETTING HERE: The best thing would be to have your own vehicle. If you do not, there's not much traffic, but you should be able to hitch. In Constanza, follow the road by the Texaco station marked "San José de Ocoa." The paved road degenerates into a dirt-and-gravel one just past the beginning of the Colonia Japonesa; keep to the R. You find absolutely stunning views along the way as you follow the main road past verdant hillside tracks. Impoverished villagers have their homes by the roadside. You'll rise up and then drop before coming to a junction with a sign marked "Aguas Blancas" to the L. The

steep, narrow, and winding track requires a four-wheel-drive vehicle, but it's less than a mile on foot. Young pines line the sides of the dirt road which climbs and descends, then arrives at the extraordinarily beautiful falls (S of the large pool). Unfortunately, the scenic beauty of these spectacular cascades is marred by garbage such as paper plates and soap suds in the lower pools.

FOOD: There are no restaurants. What *is* amazing in this area is that even out here in the boonies you will find stores selling Coke from gas-powered refrigerators, and Carnation milk is on the shelves. The multinationals are truly everywhere here.

Armando Bermúdez & José del Carmen Ramírez National Parks

These two national parks encompass the northern and southern slopes of the Cordillera Central. They have a combined area of 380,514 acres (153,994 ha). Here are the highest mountains in the Caribbean: Pico Duarte, 10,417 ft. (3,175 m); Pico La Pelona, 10,393 ft. (3,168 m); Pico La Rucilla, 10,003 ft. (3,049 m); Pico de Yaque del Norte, 9,826 ft. (2,995 m); and Pico del Gallo, 8,694 ft. (2,650 m), among others. Armando Bermúdez was es-

Cordillera Central

tablished by Trujillo and named in honor of the rum distillery owner who had funded expeditions in the area.

This area forms the gigantic watershed from which most of the rivers originate, including Yaque del Norte and a dozen others. Hydroelectric dams have been built at Taveras, Sabaneta, Sabana Yegu, and Bao. Pine forests are found in the regions surrounding Pico La Pelona up to Pico Duarte and from La Mediania hill in the S. Human life in this region scrapes by at subsistence level. Illegal squatting is an increasing problem. For an overview, check out the wonderful mural in Manobao depicting the park and the location of all the nation's national parks.

HISTORY: This area began forming some 60 million years ago during the Cretaceous period; a series of volcanoes erupted, and the lava blended with the earth's crust and solidified. The underlying rock is predominately igneous: volcanic limestone, slate, diorite, and marble. Armando Bermúdez was declared a protected area in 1956; Carmen Ramirez followed two years later.

FLORA AND FAUNA: Subtropical mountainous humid forest and rain forest predominate here. West Indian cedar, wild mountain olive, wild cane, palo amargo, and West Indian walnut are found at elevations up to 3,600 ft.; lirio, copey, sierra palm, and fiddlewood occur from 3,600 to 4,500 ft.; palo de viento, wild braziletto, wild avocado, and tree ferns grow from 4,500 ft. to 5,100 ft.; and creolan pine and a variety of bushes flourish at 5,100 ft. and above.

Wild boars (puerco cimarron) are abundant in Tetero Valley. Hutias also reside within the park. Birds include the Hispaniolan parrot, Hispaniolan woodpecker, the Hispaniolan trogon, the white-necked crow, palm chat, ruddy quail dove, mourning dove, and red-tailed hawk.

GETTING HERE: Access to the park is via the 20-mile (32-km) road from Jarabacoa (500 m) to La Ciénaga (1,000 m).

SIGHTS: The main activity here is climbing Pico Duarte. Pre-Columbian rock carvings are found in the Tetero Valley area of José del Carmen Ramírez National Park.

Pico Duarte

The brilliant Swedish botanist Erik Ekman ascertained that Pico Duarte was the highest mountain in the Antilles. Taking him at his word, Trujillo renamed it Pico Trujillo – replacing the former name of Pico La Pelona ("Baldy," for the treeless plain on its top). After Trujillo's fall, the mountain was renamed for the 19th-century revolutionary elder and founding father. The peak was not climbed until 1944, as part of the independence centennial celebrations.

CLIMBING PICO DUARTE: The dry season is a good time to undertake this venture. Begin at Jarabacoa and hitch to Manabao, then hitch or hike along the poor road to La Ciénaga (no public transportation) – stocking up on food along the way – and Casa Tabalone, at the entrance to the Parque Nacional Armando Bermúdez, where the trail begins. Follow the left bank of the Río Yaque del Norte for a few miles before turning up a steep mule track which winds its way around a series of ridges. Palms give way en route to coarse bracken ferns and *palo de cotorra* ("parrot tree"), a thin-stemmed tree with feathery leaves. At 5,900 ft. (1,800 m), the vegetation changes to jungle, congested with a variety of ferns, bromeliads, orchids, epiphytes, mosses, lichens, tree ferns, and conifers. Pine forest takes over near the crude bush shelter and spring at 2,650 m (7,900 ft.). From here follow a trail to the incredibly desolate summit. Allow two days from Casa Tabalone for this hike.

PRACTICALITIES: You must be in excellent physical condition for this demanding trek. In addition to all of your own food, you must bring warm clothing for the cold nights when temperatures may drop to freezing or below. Because of the entry fee and the necessity of hiring guides and mules, as well as purchasing food, the trip is not as cheap as you might imagine.

Entrance fee to the park is around US$10. Local guides and mules can be hired either in Monabao or in La Ciénaga; a guide is required for entry, and the National Park staff will help you locate them. Mules are not necessary no matter what you may be told, but they will take the burden off your back; in any case you will have to pay for at least one mule for your guide. You should arrive in La Ciénaga the day before to make preparations and ensure an early start the next day. You should purchase the majority of your supplies and provisions in Jabaracoa; in Manabao only things such as rice, beans, and spaghetti are available. The only accommodations here are the very reasonably priced rooms offered at Doña Patria's. She'll help you find a guide. You can also camp in fields outside the park, and there's a river for water and bathing. Otherwise, the nearest hotels and restaurants are at Jarabacoa, about an hour's drive on a rotten road. The park entrance is La Ciénaga.

At La Compartación, up the slopes from La Ciénaga (Boca del Río), there's a cabin. From there, it's a minimum of two hours (at a fast pace) to the top. Trekkers generally overnight at La Compartación again. The mostly downhill return trip takes seven hours or so. Overnight at Los Tablones on the first night. You can make it all the way down on the fourth day; it's possible to sleep at the park office. The last *camioneta* (pickup truck) leaves Manabao for Jarabacoa at around 2:30.

NOTE: Try to inquire in Santo Domingo about current conditions with the park service before undertaking this expedition. This is not an easy trip and is not for everyone. Bear in mind that it's 15 miles (25 km) from La Ciénaga (1,000 m) to the top of Pico Duarte (3,072 m). The park office may be reached at ☎ 472-4204.

TOURS: Both **Iguana Mama** (☎ 571-0908, fax 571-0734; 800-849-4720; EPS-D#342, PO Box 02-55548, Miami, FL 33102; www.iguana-mama.com; e-mail iguanamama@codetel.net.do) and **Rancho Baiguate** (☎ 696-0318, 563-8005, fax 574-4940; e-mail ranchobaiguate@codetel.net.do) offer organized treks up Pico Duarte. Iguana Mama's are pricier, more plush, and leave from Cabarete. Famed author Julia Alvarez made the trek in 1997 and wrote about it in *The New York Times Travel Section*.

Trekking in the Park

This long-haul journey from La Ciénaga to Mata Grande takes a minimum of six days.

An additional day, at least, must be added to this if you wish to visit Valle Tetero which adds an extra nine miles (14 km) RT.

From La Ciénaga to Pico Duarte (28 miles/46 km; the most popular route to climb the peak) requires three days RT. To climb Pico Duarte from the Mata Grande side (55 miles/89 km RT) takes a minimum of six days.

Here is a section-by-section trail description:

■ **La Ciénaga-Los Tablones** (1000-1200 m; 2½ miles/four km). Follow an old road along the Río Los Tablones. Vegetation is tropical broadleaf forest with patches of wild cane. Hikers may stay in a cabin at the park station at Los Tablones.

Trekking in the Park (continued)

- **Los Tablones-La Cotorra** (1200 m-1750 m; 2½ miles/four km). Follow the Río Los Tablones .3 miles (.5 km), then climb through mixed broadleaf and pine forest. The almond trees and sierra palms here provide food for the wild boars. The rest area is named La Cotorra because the endangered indigenous parrot may be spotted here. Great panoramas of the Valle La Ciénaga en route.

- **La Cotorra-La Laguna** (1720-2100 m; 1.2 miles/two km). Follow the natural ridgeline through a mixed forest of pine and broadleaf; many scenic outlooks. Water is available at the La Laguna rest area.

- **La Laguna-El Cruce** (2100-2200 m; .3 miles/.5 km). A steep climb to the trail junction for Pico Duarte and Valle Tetero. Ferns line the N slope.

- **La Cruce-Valle Tetero** (2200-1560 m; 4.2 miles/seven km). Trail runs to Valle Tetero, one of the Río Yaque del Sur's most important watersheds. Tremendous views and a cabin to spend the night. One large boulder has a Taino petroglyph. Backtrack from here to El Cruce.

- **El Cruce-Aguita Fria** (2200-2600 m; three miles/five km). Climb the ridgeline through a pine forest. Note the large bog just before the Aguita Fria rest area. It is the source of the Yacque del Norte and the Yacque del Sur. Keep to the N side (to your R) to avoid contaminating the waters.

- **Aguita Fria-La Compartición** (2600-2300 m; 2.2 miles/3½ km). Drop down along the pine-forest ridgeline to La Compartición, the start of the climb up Pico Duarte. Superb views. There is a cabin here.

- **La Compartición-Pico Duarte** (2350-3175 m; 2½ miles/four km). Climb thorugh pine forests along a wide ridge. From the junction at Vallecito de Lilís (a wide open meadow with spectacular panoramas of both Pico Duarte and La Pelona) continue straight ahead to climb Pico Duarte or head R to Valle de Bao. The final ascent to the peak is through pine trees interspersed with boulders. The summit itself is entirely rock and boulders. Returning to the junction at Vallecito de Lilís, head for Valle de Bao or return via La Compartición and Aguita Fria to La Ciénaga.

Cordillera Central

Trekking in the Park (continued)

- **Pico Duarte-Valle de Bao** (3175 m-1600 m; 7.2 miles/11.54 km). Trail departs Vallecito de Lilís and skirts around La Pelona. Follow the ridgeline down to the Río Bao basin where you will find a cabin at the valley's N end. This long trip runs the gamut in terms of vegetation from pine and broadleaf forest to Spanish moss and ferns galore!

- **Valle de Bao-La Guácara** (1600-1000 m; eight miles/13 km). Climb and descend several steep ridges and drainages along the Río Bao system. A cabin is found at La Guácara, the confluence of the Bao and La Guácara rivers.

- **La Guácara-Lomo de Loro** (1000-1900 m; 8.7 miles/14 km). Cross the Río La Guácara and climb up the ridge; termendous views of the Cordillera Central (central mountain range), including La Pelona. Pass by El Rodeo and Los Corrales cabins. Final portion of trail is along an old roadbed. Cabin is at Loma de Loro.

- **Lomo de Loro-Mata Grande** (1900-1000 m; 3.7 miles/six km). Follow an abandoned road; detour along last km before park office. Great panoramas of the Valle Cibao and Santiago.

The Cibao

Set between the Cordillera Central and the Septentrional, the Cibao is the nation's largest agricultural valley. It comprises the provinces of Santiago, Monsignor Nouel, Duarte, Espaillat, Sánchez Ramirez, and Salcedo. Famed for its coffee, cattle, rice, and bananas, this "food basket" has long attracted farmers and ranchers. Late in the 1800s, Cuban refugee *independentistas* settled in the region. Intermarrying with local landowners, they built up the export tobacco industry.

The region's folk are so prideful that other Dominicans refer to it as the "Republic of the Cibao." Its largest city, Santiago de los Caballeros, is Santo Domingo's main rival, which once played kingmaker in national politics. The nation's most Castillian Spanish is spoken here, locals use words common in the 16th-18th century, and they often substitute the consonant "r" for "l" or "i" when speaking.

Santiago de los Treinta Caballeros

Once the nation's largest city, "Santiago of the Thirty Noblemen" (pop. 500,000) has been relegated to a distant second place. Santiago is often regarded as Santo Domingo's alter ego. Unlike the capital, with its urban sprawl and frenzied pace, the pace here remains a bit slower. It has a reputation as a city of refinement where many of the most aristocratic and historic families live, but today Santiago appears to be losing its special character as "development" has razed many of the old houses and others are deteriorating through neglect. Still, ladies on mules compete for road space with taxicabs, and there are enough old gems around to make for some attractive pictures.

Located in the N-central part of the country in the heart of the lush and fertile Cibao, the local economy runs on rum and tobacco. Santiago may also be used as a base to visit the beautiful town of San José de las Matas to the SW, the town of Moca with its faceless dolls, and the national park of El Morro.

GETTING HERE: Santiago may be reached by express and regular bus from Santo Domingo. *Metro* runs seven times daily and also runs from Puerto Plata. Caribe Tours also runs here, as do a number of smaller companies.

by air: Air Santo Domingo (☎ 683-8020, fax 683-8436; www.g-air-europa.es/air_sdo; e-mail info.air_sdo@g-air-europa.es)

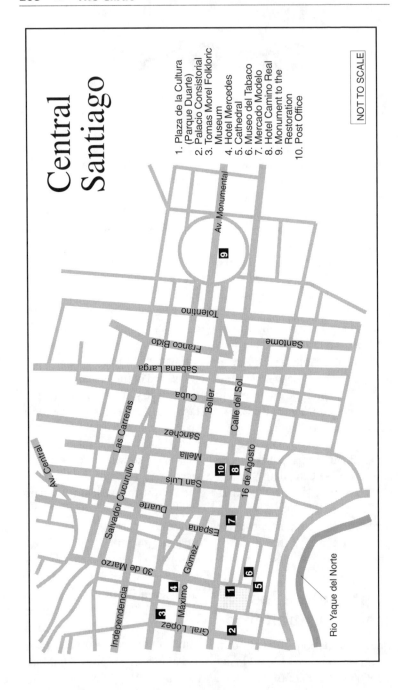

Central Santiago

1. Plaza de la Cultura (Parque Duarte)
2. Palacio Consistorial
3. Tomas Morel Folkloric Museum
4. Hotel Mercedes
5. Cathedral
6. Museo del Tabaco
7. Mercado Modelo
8. Hotel Camino Real
9. Monument to the Restoration
10. Post Office

NOT TO SCALE

operates between Herrera airport (in Santo Domingo) to and from Punta Cana, Portillo (Samaná Peninsula), Santiago, La Romana, and Puerto Plata. Flights interconnect between destinations. Rates are RD$700 on up.

HISTORY: Legend has it that Santiago was founded by 30 noblemen who named it after St. James, their patron saint. In fact the suffix "of the 30 noblemen" was probably added during the second half of the 16th century. There are conflicting stories as to who exactly founded the town and when. One holds that the brother of the notorious Christopher, Bartolomew Columbus founded Santiago on the Rio Yaque in 1495; another holds that Columbus himself did so in 1498 or 1499. This settlement disappeared, and the second Santiago was founded by Santo Domingo Gov. Frey Nicólas de Ovando, who granted land to recently arriving settlers from Spain and others relocating from La Isabela. This settlement was known as Jacagua. It was destroyed by the 1562 earthquake and rebuilt the next year on its present site. It then became known as Villa de Santiago. In 1970, at the behest of the Dominican Academy of History, the Spanish Royal Academy renamed the city's residents. They are now known as *santiaguenses*; formerly they were known as *santia-gueros* or *santiagueses*, which caused confusion with Santiago de Cuba and Santiago de Compostela. However, despite the Academy's dictum, locals still use the latter two terms.

ORIENTATION: The city itself sprawls, but the downtown area is small enough to walk around in. The major thoroughfares are Av. Salvador Estrella Sadhala, which cuts through the city's E side; Carr. Duarte which becomes Av. Central as it enters the city from the W and becomes Av. Franco Bido before it leaves to the E; Av. Central which heads into the city from the NW and turns into C. 30 de Marzo; C. Del Sol, the crowded main street which runs between the main plaza and the Restoration Monument (where it becomes Av. Monumental before turning into Autopista Duarte); and C. Restauración which runs parallel and a few blocks to the N of C. Del Sol. The Av. Circunavalación runs parallel to the Río Yaque del Norte which defines the city's SE perimeters. Finally, crossing the Río Yaque del Norte is the Puento de Hermanos Patino, a monstrous bridge and another Trujillo production.

GETTING AROUND: There's a large network of private shared taxis and public buses, but you'll have to ask locals which ones to take. It's easy enough to walk everywhere around the central part of town, but the blackouts make everything very gloomy at night. Taxis start from a bit less than US$5.

SIGHTS: The best place to start a tour of Santiago is at the centrally located **Plaza de Cultura**, also known as Parque Duarte. Located at the intersection of crosstreets C. Del Sol and 30 de Marzo, it's bordered by *frio frio* (ice cone) vendors and aspiring shoe shiners. You might see an old lady with a hair net sitting on a bench searching to see if she has a winning lottery ticket, a guy chasing his puppy, or a mother holding her unruly child.

Built with a combination of Neoclassical and Gothic styles between 1868 and 1895, the **Catedral de Santiago Apóstol**, at one side of the plaza, features an elaborate carved mahogany altar. It also contains the tomb of dictator Ulises Heureux, stained glass windows by Rincón Mora, as well as some heroes of the "Restoration," a revolt which re-established independence from Spain in 1865. It was renovated in 1991.

Another interesting old building in the plaza is the **Edificio del Centro de Recreo** (Recreational Center Building), an exclusive private club, which is built in Mudejar-style. The 19th-century **Palacio Consistorial**, which stands next door, is the former

town hall, now incorporated into the cultural center. A small museum of city history is inside.

Across from the cathedral on C. 30 de Marzo, the **Instituto de Tabaco** illustrates the harvest and production of the noxious carcinogenic weed that figures so prominently in the region's economy. Negotiate at this plaza for a carriage ride around the city – the drivers will find you – or head down bustling C. Del Sol, where you might see local lovelies window shopping, a guy selling puppies, men selling old coins, and cassette and other vendors plying their wares.

Set in a Victorian-style home, the **Museo de Artes Folkloricos Tomás Morel** contains a collection of carnival masks and other folk art. Note the masks of the *lechones*, mischievous imps from the town's *carnaval*. It's on C. Gen. Lopez, less than a 10-min. walk from the main plaza.

A sort of Dominican Eiffel Tower or Statue of Liberty, the aesthetically unappealing 220-ft.-high (67 m) **Monumento a los Héroes de la Restauración** is the city's highest point. Its interiors are adorned with murals by Spaniard Vela Zanetti. It was originally constructed by Trujillo in his own honor and named the Monumento a la Paz de Trujillo. You may or may not be able to enter, depending upon the current state of restoration of this monument, which now commemorates the Restoration, the nation's second independence from Spain. While no one would term it one of the great architectural wonders of the world, it certainly is imposing enough and provides a useful beacon for bearings.

Shaped something like a glassed-in high school gymnasium, the motley **Mercado Central** at the end of C. 6 de Septiembre (follow 30 de Marzo and cross the road) features a shop selling amber and a few small restaurants.

Founded in 1962, the **Universidad Católica Madre y Maestra** is on Aut. Duarte at Km 1.5. Although nothing spectacular, colonial ruins are found at Jacagua. The **Camp David Ranch** (☎ 583-5230/1543) has a number of old cars belonging to Trujillo.

TOURS: You can visit **La Aurora Tabaclero** (☎ 582-1131), 27 de Febrero, and the **Brugal Distillery** (☎ 575-1427), Av. 27 de Febrero 130.

GETTING AROUND: The central area with the sights is compact enough to easily walk around. Local buses have limited service. *Carros de concho* are the same price. Expensive *carreras* are also available. For a bit of local color, try a carriage ride.

ACCOMMODATIONS: Located at C. del Sol and Mella, one of the best places to stay is the 72-rm. a/c **Hotel Camino Real** (☎ 581-7000, fax 582-4566; Apdo. 459, Santiago). Its comfortable rooms are equipped with cable TV and private bath. Up on the top floor is the Olympus Restaurant, and the hotel's plush bar, which features entertainment nightly, is in the basement.

Many hotels are located near 30 de Marzo and Restauracíon. The white **Hotel Colonial** (☎ 247-3122), C. Cucurullo 115, has rooms with a TV and balcony for around US$15; the **Hotel Monte Rey** (☎ 582-4558) is at C. Cucurullo 92, and **Hotel Dorado** (☎ 582-7563), is at C. Cucurullo 88.

Alberto's Suite Apart-Hotel (☎ 971-6005) has a/c rooms with TVs; it is at V. Estrella 7.

Av. Estrella Sadhalá: A number of hotels are located on this important street. (Note that this is not in the downtown area.) The 40-rm. a/c **Don Diego** (☎ 575-4186; Apdo. 27, Santiago) features color TV, pool, tennis court, disco, and a Chinese-Creole-International restaurant. It charges around US$40 d. Also on Av. Estrella Sadhala, 36-rm. a/c **Hotel Ambar** (☎ 575-1957/4811) offers TV, bar, and restaurant. It charges around US$25 d.

Newest and largest, the **Hotel El Gran Almirante** (☎ 580-1992, fax 241-1492) is also on Av. Estrellas Sadhalá. It has a restaurant and is priced in the luxury range.

low-budget: There are a number of alternatives here, but one is particularly recommended. Reader H. R. writes: "Hostal Del Cibao at Calle Benito Moncion #40 581-7775 is a must stay for the budget traveler. It is just two blocks off of Parque Duarte. Lisa and I stayed for about US$12. No a/c but there is an a/c option. Carmen, the owner, runs a business and school on the first floor and is very accommodating and friendly. There is free drinking water, hot water for showers and cable TV in each room. They also have a generator. The rooms are very simple, but perfect for budget travelers. They have a small kitchen that sells soft drinks and beer."

The 40-rm. **Hotel Mercedes** (☎ 583-1171) on 30 de Marzo at Máximo Gómez charges about US$20 for rooms with fans; a/c rooms are double the price. This hotel, built in the 1920s, features an incredible spiralling marble staircase and balconies in each of its small rooms. It's truly like entering another era. Its restaurant serves Dominican dishes.

If that's full try the unmarked *pensión* on C. Restauracion, the **Hotel Alaska** (☎ 582-2764) at 16 de Augusto 129 at Benito Moncion, or search for other cheap hotels around Plaza Valerio, such as the **Santiago Plaza** and the **El Gallo de Oro**.

Another alternative is the **Hotel Dorado** (☎ 582-7563), Cucurallo 88. There are innumerable other small hotels in town.

outlying accommodations: A Dominican-style hotel built by Trujillo, the 52-rm. a/c **Matum** (☎ 581-3107) is at Las Carreras (altos) and features cable TV, pool, disco, and casino. **Hotel Canañas "La Posada"** (☎ 583-3291) is at Km 4.5 on the Aut. Duarte (Carr. Moca). The 35-unit **Cabañas Palmar** (☎ 583-7247/7248) is at Km 5 on Aut. Duarte (Carr. Canabacoa); it features a/c, TV, and an AM-FM stereo.

FOOD: There are many sandwich and pizza places in town, as well as restaurants. Good but not inexpensive, **El Dragón** on Av. Estrellas Sadhalá serves Chinese food. **Don Miguel**, on the Autopista Duarte opp. the Catholic University, has good food, including Cuban and *Norteamericano* dishes. In Parque Duarte, **Las Antillas** has meals from around US$4.

In Ensanche El Ensueño, **El Mexicano** has Mexican food. **Restaurant Yaque** is at Restauración 115. **Olé**, Juan Pablo Duarte and Independencia, has pizza. On Juan Pablo Duarte just past the Instituto de Tobaco, the

Roma has good Italian food and pizza. Also try the **Oriente**, C. 30 de Marzo 57. *Chimi* stands (esp. the *arepa* stands) behind the monument, are good for cheap dinners.

vegetarian: The **Restaurante Ananda** is just off Parque Duarte. They feature a daily lunch plate (US$1.75-2.25). For dinner they serve pizzas (vegan varieties are available), tasty vegetable burgers, and tofu sandwiches. The friendly staff also offers daily yoga classes.

formal dining: Try the **Restaurant Pez Dorado**, C. El Sol 43, which has Chinese and international cuisine including seafood. One of the town's most exclusive restaurants, **Restaurant Osteria**, Av. 27 de Febrero, specializes in Italian food. Set atop the Hotel Camino Real on C. El Sol, fancy **Restaurant Olympus** specializes in international cuisine. It has moderate prices, with some of the nation's best food and most attentive service.

ENTERTAINMENT: All the discos are high tech, but the Hotel Matum's **La Nuit** is that rare beast – a laser-equipped disco. Popular with locals, the **Hotel Camino Real**'s glitzy basement club features live bands nightly. Also try **La Mansión** (☎ 578-8404) in outlying San Jose de las Matas, **La Antorcha** (at Av. 27 de Febrero 58), and **Las Vegas**. The

Bosa Nova Bar Club is on Maximo Gomez, a block away from the Hotel Mercedes.

For information about events at the **Centro de la Cultura**, ☎ 971-5460. If you crave the sight of spilled blood, you can visit the **Gallera Municipal**, the local cockfighting venue. **El Baturro**, Av. Franco Bido 147 (Nibaje), has live nude shows from 9-4 nightly.

FESTIVALS AND EVENTS: Santiago has a reputation for putting on the best *carnavál* celebration in Feb., and another takes place in Aug. Representing mischievous devils, the pig-like *lechones* are the highlights of the celebration. Donning multicolored costumes adorned with mirrors and other ornamentation, these participants wear paper maché masks which, according to the shape of the horns, identify them as inhabitants of rival neighborhoods, Los Pepines and La Joya. The local *fiestas patronales* of Santiago Apostol are held around July 22.

INFORMATION: The **tourist office** is on the second floor of the *Ayuntamiento* (Town Hall) on Av. Juan Pablo Duarte. **services:** Codetel (☎ 582-8918) is on Estrella Sadhalá. The **PO** is on C. del Sol near the Mercado Modelo. **car rental:** Cars may be rented from Budget (☎ 575-2158), Av. 27 de Febrero; Honda, Av. Estrella Sadhalá at Av. Bartolomé

Colón, Nelly (☎ 583-6695), Av. Duarte 106; and Rentauto (☎ 582-3139/3130), Av. Bartolomé Colón 4.

HEALTH: The best bet is the **Clinica Corominas** (☎ 582-1171).

SHOPPING: There are rattan and wicker factories including **Artesania Rattan** on Carr. Duarte at Km. 4.5. **El Gallo**, Máximo Gómez 14, and **Casa Hache**, Av. Estrellas Sadhalá, sell housewares, and **Sirena** on C. Del Sol sells personal goods.

FROM SANTIAGO: Probably the best company, a/c *Metro* (☎ 582-9111/4611) runs frequently to Puerto Plata and to Santo Domingo (7, 8:15, 10, 12:45, 3, 4:30, 5:30, 6, and 7:30). To get here, take a carro marked "A" heading away from the park and ask to be let off at "frente de la Metro Bus." The exact location is on C. Maimón at Duarte.

At C. Restauración and Av. Juan Pablo Duarte, *Terrabus* (☎ 587-3000/5060/4554) serves Santo Domingo. Also in the vicinity, *Transporte de Cibao* has buses to Dajabón near the Haitian border. *Caribe Tours* (☎ 583-9198/9197) runs from Av. Sadhalá at C. 10 to Santo Domingo, Puerto Plata, Monte Cristi, and Dajabón.

66 *Reader's Comment*

Reader H. R. relates: "Outside of Santiago in San José de las Matas there is horseback riding at Hotel La Mansion. We paid DR$75 each for an hour. The ride was beautiful. When the guagua drops you off in San José de las Matas, take a motoconcho up to the hotel and ask the driver to return for you at a particular time. They are very accommodating and will take you back to the bus stop to return to Santiago. You can also use the pool at La Mansion if you come here to horseback ride."

An alternative is to take a bus from the area of 30 de Marzo. You can get express buses to Puerto Plata and Santo Domingo. If heading towards Constanza or Jarabacoa, change at the appropriate stops; ask the driver.

If driving to Puerto Plata, you should note that the reconstructed old Santiago-Puerto Plata highway has been closed to heavy vehicles in order to make it more attractive to tourists.

by air: Air Santo Domingo (☎ 683-8020, fax 683-8436; www.g-air-europa.es/air_sdo; e-mail info.air_sdo@g-air-europa.es) operates between Santiago airport and Santo Domingo, Punta Cana, Portillo (Samaná Peninsula), Santiago, La Romana, and Puerto Plata. Flights inter-connect between destinations. Rates are from RD$700 on up.

Vicinity of Santiago

Moca

To the E of Santiago, this coffee and *cacao* center makes an intriguing day trip. Be sure to see the splendid organ in the **Iglesia Corazón de Jesus**. The only other one of its ilk is in Brazil. The tourist office is located in the Ayuntamiento (Town Hall) on Av. Independencia and Antonio de la Maza. Outside the town on the road toward the Autopista Duarte, **El Higuero** is a center for the *muñeca sin rostro*, the popular "faceless" dolls portraying Dominican working women or flower or fruit vendors. Practically every building here is a cottage industry. Bargain hard. The latest gig in Moca is illegal pit bull fights, an activity popular among returned Dominican Yorks.

PRACTICALITIES: Stay at **Hotel Panorama** (☎ 578-2252), Av. Independencia 27, **Hotel El Dorado** (☎ 578-2113), **Hotel La Casona** (☎ 578-3465), C. Imbert 77, and **Hotel L'Niza** (☎ 578-2248), Carr. Santiago.

FROM MOCA: There's a beautiful road which winds through verdant hills to Caspar Hernández on the coast. You can also go from here to Sosúa by bus: change at Cruce de Veragua/Sa-

baneta. This is another spectacular trip with attractive views. *Metro* (☎ 578-2641) departs Moca from C. Morillo for Santo Domingo daily at 7 and at 3:30 .

San José de las Matas

Located to the SW, this attractive mountain town is near Santiago. Part of the Occidental Hotel Chain, the **Hotel Club Spa La Mansión** (☎ 578-8401, fax 581-9085) has 20 d rooms and 50 two-bedroom villas; all have a/c and phones. Rates are less than US$100 d with three meals. There is a restaurant, pool, horseback riding, stables and full spa facilities. The Occidental Hotels may be reached in North America and Canada (☎ 506-877-3160, 800-843-3311, fax 506-877-3160), in Belgium (☎ 30-235-0373, 09800-14596), in Denmark (☎ 8030 1031, 45 87 00 08, fax 45 87 22 49/93 21 41), in France (☎ 05 00 11, 4071 2121, fax 4071 2131), in Germany (☎ 0180-231 21 21, 06151-905760, fax 06151-905750), in Ireland (01 6605 000, fax 01 6605 540), and in Switzerland (☎ 155 5583, 715 1616, fax 715 5583).

Travelers on a tighter budget may stay at **Las Samanas** (☎ 578-8316), Av. Santiago 16, at **Hotel Restaurant Oasis** (☎ 578-8298), 30 de Marzo 51, or at **Hotel La Modenza**. Rates are around US$10 d.

Puerto Plata & the North

The N Coast has become one of the top the tourist attractions of the the Dominican Republic. Nearby is the upscale tourist mecca of Playa Dorada. Sosúa is another major tourist town.

EXPLORING: Puerto Plata is connected by bus with Santiago and Santo Domingo. Destinations such as Samaná, Nagua, Las Terrenas, and Sosúa can be reached directly by bus from Santo Domingo. If traveling between points on the N coast, you must take either small minibuses, crowded vans, or pickup trucks.

Puerto Plata

As with all Spanish colonial towns in the Americas, this old port – the major town on the Atlantic or "Amber" coast – centers around a plaza with gingerbread trim houses. The most promi-nent town in the N coast, Puerto Plata has become the island's major tourist resort town – the Ocho Rios of the Dominican Republic. Unlike the former, however, there is a comparative lack of hassle, and it's still a relatively laid back place.

Although a number of attractive 19th-century homes with overhanging balconies still stand, the majority have been torn down and replaced by specimens from the concrete box school of architecture. The second largest port in the nation, it handles 12% of exports and 2% of imports.

HISTORY: Puerto Plata was discovered by Columbus on his first voyage. Seeing a high mountain capped by a snow-like mist resembling silver, he dubbed the spot "Silver Port." (These were actually leaves of the grayumbo tree.) He commissioned Fray Nicolás de Ovando to establish a

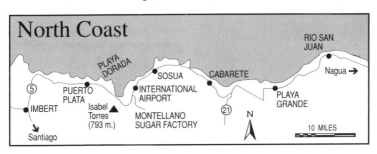

North Coast

settlement here in 1502. Becoming a leading port on the Spanish Main, it soon lived up to its name. By 1605, however, it had turned into a haven for smugglers and pirates and was destroyed by Spain. Bartolomé de las Casas, the celebrated monk of the Dominican order, began his epic tome, *Apologética Historia de las Indias (Historical Apology for the Indies)*, in a monastery here. Las Casas is considered to be the spiritual father of the once-trendy historical fashion known as *indigenismo* (Indianism) in which pre-conquest Indian civilization was portrayed as a golden age.

Re-established in 1750, Puerto Plata became a free port shortly afterwards. Infratur, a department of the Central Bank, began building tourist development in Sept. 1971. Today, with the arrival of cruise ships and the completion of the major tourism center at Playa Dorada, tourism is the major "industry" and with it have come the usual problems. The provincial economy is based on factories manufacturing alcohol, chocolate, and shoes, as well as production of dairy products, refined sugar, and sausages.

GETTING HERE: Puerto Plata can be reached by bus or *público* from Santo Domingo. Highly recommended *Metro Bus* (☎ 554-4580) runs via Santiago. *Caribe Tours* also runs. *Públicos* run from Sosúa and Cabarete. If driving, you will find the best scenery if you approach along the old road from Santiago or Sosúa.

by air: Air Santo Domingo (☎ 683-8020, fax 683-8436; www.g-air-europa.es/air_sdo; e-mail info.air_sdo@g-air-europa.es) operates between Herrera airport (in Santo Domingo) and Puerto Plata, Punta Cana, Portillo (Samaná Peninsula), Santiago, and La Romana. Flights inter-connect between destinations.

ARRIVING BY AIR: The recently renovated **Gregorio Luperón International Airport** lies midway between Puerto Plata and Sosúa. It's easy to get into town: just walk out to the main road and board a *público*. However, be sure you have the current fare. You may rent a car here or take a taxi. From the airport to Playa Dorada or to town it costs around US$11. From the airport to Sosúa it's around US$8 and to Cabarete it is US$14.

☞ *Traveler's Tip*

The parking lot attendant at the airport has been known to overcharge foreigners. Make sure that you pay the correct amount.

ORIENTATION: Unlike its congested cousin in Santo Domingo, Puerto Plata's Malecón is virtually free of traffic and is graced by a gentle sea breeze. Its most notable feature is the bronze statue of Neptune poised on an offshore rock – an aesthetic ad for the Puerto Plata Beach Resort. Long Beach is at the E corner of town: this long stretch of sand is popular with locals as well as tourists. Near its entrance is a plaza area with a concrete tower you can climb, a number of shops, and a few hotels.

GETTING AROUND: Nowhere in town is too far to walk. Otherwise, the best way to get around is the meandering city bus. Often painted white with blue or red markings, the small city buses have two routes. Both "A" and "B" run with variations from the main entrance to the Playa Dorada complex, down Av. Circunvalación, though Av. 27 de Febrero, up 12 de Julio, pass through downtown, loop through the W side, head S along Separación, pass through downtown again, and then head back to Playa Dorada. Buses run from 6 to 6, but some run as late as 7. Taxis can be found around the gazebo or ☎ 586-3454 (day) or 586-3458 (evening). As usual, make sure you have the fare straight before boarding.

Motoconchos, ubiqitous and awfully annoying at times, run out to Playa Dorada and will take you anywhere else you want to go. Expect to pay around 35¢ for a short ride inside the city; prices double at night when the buses are asleep.

SIGHTS: In **Parque Luperón** (Parque Central), the main square – bordered on its four sides by C. Del Castillo, C. John F. Kennedy, C. Separación, and C. Beller – stands the **gazebo** which was recreated from period drawings of the original.

Other buildings bordering the park include Victorian-style **Sociedad Fe en el Porvenir**, art deco-style **Catedral de San Felipe**, and **Club de Comercio**.

Set on the Malecón (waterfront) and surrounded by persistent hordes of salesmen, **Fortaleza de San Felipe** features a moat of sharp coral, and a variety of poorly-annotated artifacts and pictures – from coins to cannonballs – are displayed inside its cramped three rooms. The Fortaleza is worth a visit, however, for the views from its plazas. When construction began in 1541, the fortress was intended to defend against French buccaneers or other intruders. By the time it was completed in 1577, the town's strategic importance had been undermined by events. The nation's George Washington, Juan Pablo Duarte, was once held in one of its cells. Depicted forever frozen in bronze and on horseback out in the middle of the parking area, Gen. Gregorio Luperón fought to overthrow the Spanish from 1860 to 1865. This

Puerto Plata

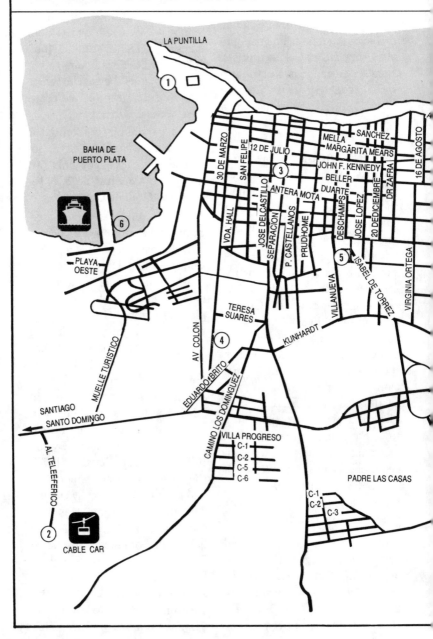

LA PUNTILLA

BAHIA DE
PUERTO PLATA

PLAYA
OESTE

MUELLE TURISTICO

SANTIAGO
SANTO DOMINGO

AL TELEEFERICO

CABLE CAR

30 DE MARZO
SAN FELIPE
12 DE JULIO
VDA. HALL
JOSE DELCASTILLO
SEPARACION
P. CASTELLANOS
PRUDHOME
ANTERA MOTA

MELLA
MARGARITA MEARS
SANCHEZ
JOHN F. KENNEDY
BELLER
DUARTE
DESCHAMPS
JOSE LOPEZ
20 DE DICIEMBRE
DR ZAFRA
16 DE AGOSTO

VILLANUEVA
ISABEL DE TORREZ
VIRGINIA ORTEGA

TERESA
SUARES

KUNHARDT

AV. COLON

EDUARDO BRITO

CAMINO LOS DOMINGUEZ

VILLA PROGRESO
C-1
C-2
C-5
C-6

PADRE LAS CASAS

C-1
C-2
C-3

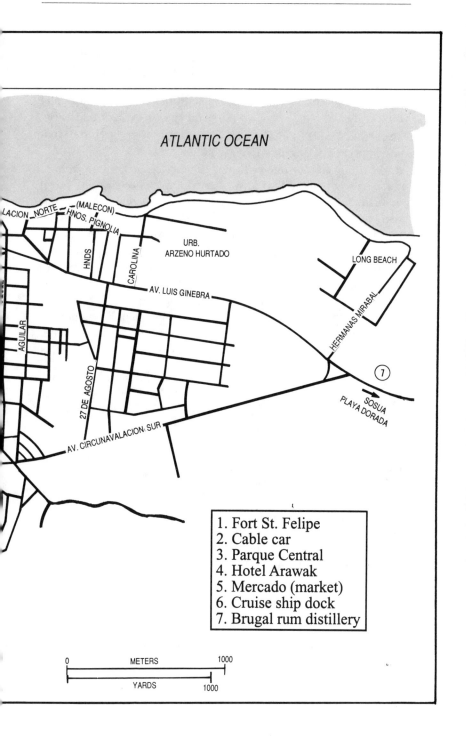

ATLANTIC OCEAN

LACION NORTE — (MALECON)
HNOS. PIGNOLIA
HNDS
CAROLINA

URB.
ARZENO HURTADO

LONG BEACH

AV. LUIS GINEBRA

AGUILAR

27 DE AGOSTO

HERMANAS MIRABAL

⑦

SOSUA
PLAYA DORADA

AV. CIRCUNAVALACION SUR

1. Fort St. Felipe
2. Cable car
3. Parque Central
4. Hotel Arawak
5. Mercado (market)
6. Cruise ship dock
7. Brugal rum distillery

0   METERS   1000
         YARDS   1000

museum-park honors Juan Pablo Duarte. The fort is open daily from 9-noon and 2-5 except Wed. A small admission fee is charged, and you should tip your guide if you use one.

Near the *plaza* at 61 C. Duarte, the compact **El Museo de Amber** (☎ 586-2848) houses one of the nation's largest collections of amber. It's a big draw with the tour buses, and downstairs is a large shop packed with every type of souvenir. Admission is charged to the upstairs museum (DS$25). A leaf, fly, mammalian hair, mating chinch bugs, a miniature walking stick, a cricket, and a centipede are all entombed in pieces of amber here. If you can get here between tour buses, you might have the museum to yourself.

Reached by the only *teleférico* (suspended cable car) in the Caribbean, **Loma Isabel de Torres** (2,565 ft., 789 m) is 30° F cooler than down below. Like its cousin at Rio de Janeiro, Christ the Redeemer spreads his arms above a fort built by Trujillo. Sip an expresso at the café and savor the view. This small park and scientific reserve (formally titled Reserva Científica Isabel de Torres) is surrounded by the heavily forested mountains of the Cordillera Septentrional. While in the area watch for 32 species of birds including the rufous-tailed solitaire, the Hispaniolan trogon, the Caribbean martin, the Hispaniolan parrot, the sparrow and redtailed hawk, and the smooth-billed ani. There are also 594 plant species including 11 varieties only discovered in recent years.

The *teleférico* to the mountain's top has often been out of order but may actually be operating again when you visit. You can also ride a horse up or hike (with Iguana Mama tours or on your own), and the road has been improved. Visit the ruins of the Vieja Logia and the Parque Central. Cool winds and fog are frequent here during the winter months.

BEACHES: Playa de Long Beach is at the E end of the oceanside avenue. It's crowded on weekends and not exactly the most spotless beach in the world. Watch your possessions here! Much better, but further W, is Punta Rucia, where you will find **La Orquidea de Sol** ("Sun Orchid") beach resort. Boat trips can be arranged from here to some of the more secluded beaches such as Playa Goya and La Encenada or to "La Laguna," a mangrove swamp. No buses run out here.

DIVING: The **Sea Pro** (☎ 320-2607) is in Playa Dorada.

Puerto Plata Accommodations

The tourist area known as Puerto Plata includes not only the town itself but also the tourist village of Playa Dorada and the smaller developments at Costambar, Cofresí, and Punta Rucia. (Another area, the Costa Dorada, is under development). The best value accommodation is in the town itself; one disadvantage is that Long Beach, the town's beach, is not the greatest and is on the outskirts. But staying in town allows increased access to Dominican life and culture – a distinct advantage in itself. Indeed, it's a simple matter to get off the tourist track here – something which is impossible to do in smaller places such as Sosúa and Cabarete.

IN TOWN ACCOMMODATIONS: Just a block from the main plaza, 22-rm. a/c **Hostal Jimesson** (☎ 586-5131, fax 586-6313), C. John F. Kennedy 41, is modern – yet its antiques and old furniture give it the feel of an old home. The house (1875) is attached to a more conventional modern building in the back. Rooms are quite comfortable and have attached bath; some have cable TV. Write Cafemba, C. Separación 12, Puerto Plata.

In Plaza Anacaona, **Hotel Restaurante El Indio** (☎/fax 586-1201) is at 30 de Marzo 94-98. The hotel is owned and operated by Wolf Wirth, an outgoing and extremely helpful German expatriate who is one of the founders of the Dominican Red Cross. El Indio is one of the best places to stay for the price. Rooms are clean and have bath and fans, and the restaurant is an attractive place to dine. It's very popular with Germans. The water comes from a spring and is specially filtered. Wolf knows the nation well and can make arrangements and offer suggestions. Note that Wolf may not be here during the off-season.

Hotel El Condado (☎ 586-3255) is on Av. Circunavalación Sur (M T Juto 45). The inexpensive (US$13 pp), centrally located **Hotel Castilla** (☎ 586-3736) is at J.F. Kennedy 36 at José del Carmen Ariza.

On Av. J.E. Kundhardt, 22-rm a/c **Mountain View Hotel** (☎ 586-5757/4093) features a pool, piano bar, and restaurant.

A bit out of town on the way to Long Beach and along the Malecón, **Hotel Puerto Plata Latin Quarter** (☎ 586-2770/3858, fax 586-1828) has comfortable rooms, a restaurant, and a pool. Rates are around US$35 s and US$42 d.

LONG BEACH ACCOMMODATIONS: Puerto Plata Beach Resort and Casino (☎ 586-4243) is on Av. Malecón, a short walk from Long Beach. It features 152 one-bedroom suites, 24 standard rooms, and 40 deluxe Victorian Club Suites. Its proximity to town makes it a much more desirable destination than other resorts at Playa Dorada for those who want to experience Dominican life. The resort features two restaurants, convention bar, a disco, jazz bar, a café, watersports, Jacuzzi, a pool, and a pool bar. Across the Malecón are its Neptuno restaurant, a mini-beach, and watersports facilities. Managed by AMHSA (Santo Domingo ☎ 562 7475, fax 566 2436; 800 472 3985; www.worldhotel. com/AMHSA; e-mail amhsa@ codetel.net.do).

Across from Long Beach, the moderately priced 104-rm. **Hotel Montemar** (☎ 586-2800; Box 38, Puerto Plata), Av. Hermanas Mirabal, offers rooms, suites, and bungalows. Facilities include a conference room, disco, restaurant, and a shuttle bus to Playa Mara Pica where there's a bar and a range of watersports. Reports about this hotel vary, and it may or may not be open when you visit.

LOW-BUDGET: One of the the better in-town values is the **Hotel Atlantico** (☎ 586-6108/2503) near Caribe Tours and on 12 de Julio. Rooms start as cheap as US$7 d with a fan and bath; a/c rooms are US$10 and up.

In the same area is the attractive **Hotel Victoriano** (☎ 586-9752), C. San Felipe at Restauración, which offers rooms with cable TV; it has a power plant. Rates run around US$10 with fan, US$13 with a/c.

Hotel llra (☎ 586-2337) is at Villanueva 25. Low-budget **Alfa** (☎ 586-2684) is at C. Padre Castellanos 20. **Hotel Comedor Glenn** (☎ 586-4644) is at Ortega 5 near C. Beller. **Hotel Doña Julia** (☎ 586-6640) is at San Felipe 11 **Hotel Guaronia** (☎ 586-2109) is at 12 de Julio 76. **Hotel Martin** (☎ 586-4616) is at 30 de Marzo 40. **Hotel Boutique Dilone** (☎ 586-4525) is at 30 de Marzo 100. **Hotel Cafeteria La 41** (☎ 586-4828), C. 6 No. 41, is in the Dubeau neighborhhod to the W of town. Finally, **Hotel España**, Duarte 13, is a "motel" used for short time sex.

⚡ **Warning**
Low-budget hotels in Puerto Plata are notorious for thievery. Stay at your own risk!

PLAYA DORADA ACCOMMODATIONS: Playa Dorada is a highly-developed resort complex E of town and 2½ miles (four km) from the airport. Sugarcane fields have given way here to resort development with some 4,000 hotel rooms, 35 restaurants, two casinos, numerous shops, and an 18-hole championship golf course. There are a large number of resorts here, and many of them change names and owners with frequency.

It all began with a World Bank loan in the 1970s, and Infratur (the Tourism Infrastructure Department of the Central Bank) supervised the construction. Horse-drawn carriages supply transportation within the complex. All the properties here are ultra-luxury class; the average price is over US$100 pn for two. For value, it's best to get a package tour here. The complex is for people who wish to insulate themselves rather than become involved in the realities of the Dominican Republic. For more information on accommodations here, write Asociación de Proprietarios de Hoteles y Condominios de Playa Dorada (☎ 586-3132, telex ITT 346-0360, fax 586-5301).

The first hotel ever to open at Playa Dorada, the 250-unit **Allegro's Jack Tar Village** (☎ 320-2554, ☎/fax 320-3800, 800-858-2258) is an "adults only" all-inclusive resort with a/c apartments and cable TV. Its facilities include casino, five restaurants, bar, tennis court, golf course, horseback riding, sauna, disco, and a variety of watersports. The target market is honeymooners, couples, and singles.

The 150-unit **Dorado Club Resort** (☎ 586-2019, Apdo. 56) features urban-style sophisticated apartments with wall-to-wall car-peting, complete kitchenette, and cable TV. Its facilities include pool and deck, golf course, and horseback riding.

Next door and formerly under the same management, the 428-rm. and 418-unit **Playa Naco Golf & Tennis Resort** (☎ 567-5281, fax 544-4112, 888-339-6226; e-mail h.naco@code-tel.net.do) opened in 1992. Facilities include restaurant, watersports, and a "Kids Club." It is now an all-inclusive. In the US ☎ 800-223-6510 and in Canada 800-424-5500.

With a total of 207 rms. ranging from standard to villas, the all-inclusive **Occidental Villas Doradas** (☎ 320-3000, 586-3000, fax 320-4790) offers a/c, cable TV, pool, restaurant, and watersports. Rates run around US$120 s, $190 d.

Larger and with a greater variety of sports, the all-inclusive 582-room **Hotel Occidental Flamenco Beach** (☎ 320-5084, 586-3660, fax 320-6319), its sister hotel, stands next door. It has double, jr. suites, and suites with a/c, phone, cable TV, and minibar. Its **Club Miguel Angel**, designed for business executives, has pool, solarium, Jacuzzi, and other services. Rates are around US$110 s, $120 d for the Flamenco and US$220 d for the Club Miguel Angel.

With some 351 rms. and suites by the beach, all-inclusive **Hotel**

Playa Dorada (☎ 320-3988, 586-3988, 562-5616, fax 320-1190; Box 272), is the third Occidental offering. It boasts a/c, cable TV, pool, restaurant, nightclub, disco, golf, tennis, horseback riding, watersports, convention facilities, and secretarial services. It has its own **Club Miguel Angel.** Rates are around US$130-$220 for the main hotel and US$150 s, $250 d for the Club Miguel Angel. (The latter rate only includes breakfast).

The Occidental Hotels may be reached in North America and Canada (☎ 506-877-3160, 800-843-3311, fax 506-877-3160), in Belgium (☎ 30-235-0373, 09800-14596), in Denmark (☎ 8030 1031, 45 87 00 08, fax 45 87 22 49/93 21 41), in France (☎ 05 00 11, 4071 2121, fax 4071 2131), in Germany (☎ 0180-231 21 21, 06151-905760, fax 06151-905750), in Ireland (01 6605 000, fax 01 6605 540), and in Switzerland (☎ 155 5583, 715 1616, fax 715 5583).

Uniquely designed 420-unit **Paradise Beach Resort and Casino** (☎ 567-5159) features eight different models of apartments ranging from studios to one- and two-bedroom suites. The property features murals by Dominican artist Ada Balcacer, and other touches include a Japanese-style garden with waterfall, and fantastic architectural design.

Villa Caraibe (☎ 562-8494) offers 200 well-appointed a/c apartments, with TV, and also provides tennis, horseback riding, watersports, and golf.

The 118-unit **Costa Dorada** features one-bedroom apartments with two double beds, a/c, TV, kitchenettes, and private balcony. Facilities include pool, golf, tennis, horseback riding, and a "Lagoon Club" set at the edge of a lagoon.

The 488-unit **Puerto Plata Village** (☎ 586-4012) offers two-rm. apartments and three-rm. villas done up Victorian-style. Its setting has a pseudo-plaza with gazebo, clock tower, and a town hall housing shops and services. There's also a concert and convention hall, golf course, horseback riding, spa, five tennis courts, two pools, disco, numerous restaurants, bars, and watersports.

A Caribbean Villages resort, the **Club on the Green** (☎ 320-5350) is spread over 16 acres and has 336 rooms, three restaurants, three bars, beach club with complimentary shuttle, scuba, horseback riding, and watersports.

A second Clubs International resort, the **Clubs International Tropicale** (☎ 586-4054) has 168 rooms, three restaurants, five bars, beach club with complimentary shuttle, two pools, disco, two tennis courts, and special children's programs. Rooms have a/c, cable TV, and phone; all-inclusive packages are available for both resorts.

Managed by AMHSA (Santo Domingo ☎ 562-7475, fax 566-2436; 800-472-3985; www.world-hotel.com/AMHSA; e-mail amhsa@codetel.net.do), **Heavens** (Box 576, ☎ 320-5250, 586-4739) is an all inclusive with 150 rooms and suites. It offers a/c, cable TV, an Olympic-sized pool, gym and spa, watersports, disco, and access to Playa Dorada's facilities. Another AMHSA property, the **Paradise Beach Club and Casino** (☎ 686-3663) has 436 rooms, three restaurants, three bars, pool, two tennis courts, shopping arcade, horseback riding, and watersports. Its a/c rooms have phone and TV.

COSTAMBAR: Set near the cable car station for Isabel de Torres, this new resort area features cottages and hotels as well as sports facilities. Featuring 100 condos, **Costambar** (☎ 568-3828) also has vacation homes for rent and residential sites for sale. Horseback riding is available. **Los Mangos** golf course is here as well as a club house with swimming pool and tennis.

The 14-unit **Apart-Hotel Condo Espanola** (☎/fax 320-0178), C. Penon 30-A, offers one- and two-bedroom a/c apartments which have large living rooms with terraces. It has a pool and restaurant.

Less than 200 ft. from the beach, 40-rm. a/c **Apart-Hotel Las Caobas** (☎ 562-4171/7461 in Santo Domingo) offers tennis and watersports. The 33-unit **Apart-Hotel Marlena** (☎ 586-3692) has studios, one- and two-bedroom apts. The **Apart-Hotel Atlantis** (☎ 586-3828/1353) also rents villas and houses.

Bayside Hill Resort & Tennis Resort here offered all-inclusive packages, two pools, restaurant, and – of course – golf courses. The hotel's operations came to a screeching halt in 1996 as a result of the construction of the Smith/Enron power plant. The resulting noise and soot caused bookings to collapse. In 1995, the hotel's owners received a payment of US$1 million in damages in tandem with a commitment to resolve the problems.

Although owners had opposed construction of the plant, forces inside the government pushed for its creation. Frank Rainieri, president of the Hotel & Restaurant Association opines that construction of the station was "an abusive and gross violation of the regulations applying to the area, evidencing how fragile the ordinances of our institutions are."

AT PLAYA COFRESI: This area is named after the 19th-century pirate. An intimate 18-room inn, **Club Paradise** (☎ 586-5551, fax 586-5552; Box 675, Puerto Plata) has gardens, pool, Jacuzzi, and a restaurant.

The 66-room **Club Hacienda-Cofresí** (☎ 586-6879, fax 686-6099) has rooms with phones, a/c, and TV, as well as a pool, tennis courts, horseback riding, and live entertainment.

A set of all-inclusives, the **Hacienda Resorts** (☎ 586-5724, fax 586-8537/8192) offer restaurants, tennis courts, golf course, pool, fitness center; units are for sale as well as rent. There are four different ones to choose from.

The **Riü Merengue** and **Riü Mambo** between Cofresi and Bahía de Maimon. These Spanish-run ultra-luxury all-inclusives cater to Germans who prepay in Europe.

PUNTA RUCIA: Right on the beach, 28-rm. **La Orquidia del Sol** (☎ 583-2825) features a choice of a/c or fans, restaurant, and watersports. It also has a family house on the beach.

Managed by AMHSA (Santo Domingo ☎ 562-7475, fax 566-2436; 800-472-3985; www.world hotel.com/AMHSA; e-mail amhsa@codetel.net.do), the 27-rm. **Discovery Bay Club** (☎ 586-5656) offers a/c rooms with cable TV, watersports, horseback riding, and nightly video movies.

───────────────

☞ *Traveler's Tip*

The Punta Rucia beach is notorious for sand fleas!

───────────────

LUPERÓN: The beach here is wide and has beautiful golden sand. It's an hour's drive W by car from Puerta Plata. Historically, its claim to fame is that an invading force intent on overthrowing Trujillo disembarked here in 1959. The 310-room and -suite **Luperón Beach Resort** (☎ 457-3211/9628) offers a/c, cable TV, four restaurants, bar, disco, conference room, video theater, adult and children's pool, golf course, horseback riding, jogging paths, heliport, and car and motorbike rentals.

Dally Restaurant and Pensión (☎ 571-8034, fax 571-8052) has restaurant and rooms with TVs. Puerto Blanco Marina (☎ 301-5490) bills itself as a "gringo hangout." It serves three meals daily.

Hosteleria Rancho de Sol (☎ 543-8172, fax 696-0325, 571-8052) is at El Castillo and has its own restaurant, beach, pool, tennis courts, and diving.

Vista Mar at El Castillo has a great view and houses Dimi's Diving Center (fax 571-8052).

Food

DINING OUT: There's plenty of fine dining here. The more expensive restaurants may require a jacket. Entrées are around US$10. **Restaurant Café Galeria**, on C. Separacíon, has good prices and desserts. At C. Diagonal 11, **Mamis Kneipe's** (Café

Margarita) offers family-style Austrian cuisine. Tea with marble cake and other pastries is served between 3 and 5. Call ☎ 586-4030 for mandatory reservations. On C. Luperón, Hotel Montemar's **La Isabella** offers fine dining.

At C. Separación 9, the romantic **Victorian Pub** serves seafood and international cuisine in an outdoor garden. Up the street from the movie theater of the same name, the **Roma II**, C. Beller at C. Emilio Prudhomme, serves local food in an attractive, formal atmosphere.

The **Aguaceros Bar & Grill** is on the Malecón. **Bar & Grill Para Continuar** (☎ 320-0728), C. Beller 103, serves Caribbean dishes

---

❝ Reader's Comment

"Your recommendation of Roma II was excellent for seafood. I think that was the nicest place we ate on the trip. For local food we enjoyed La Ponderosa on C. Beller, several blocks east of the town square.... Just west of Playa Dorada, we turned into a small market on the north side of the road. We went down concrete steps to an outdoor restaurant, Las Manguitas. The sign had a yellow mango on it. It was popular with the residents. We also found the atmosphere in the restaurant at the top of Isabel de Torres to be relaxing." – N.H., Dearborn, MI

---

including sea bass and other entrées including crêpes.

In Playa Dorada Plaza, **Hemingway's Café** (☎ 320-2230) has live music and serves everything from burritos to pasta.

OTHER DINING: The **Cafeteria La Economica**, perpendicular to the post office, has cheap breakfast coffee and sandwiches; it is popular with locals. If you can speak some Spanish, the **Pescaderia Mercedes,** C. Restauración, is excellent value. It is open from 7 AM-11 PM. They serve fish, crab, and other dishes, along with rice and beans or just *tostones.*

El Café de Francisco, next to the Atlantico, has budget-priced food in an attractive setting. The **Star Café** at C. Beller 87 serves seafood, omelettes, and other dishes. On the main road, **Pizzeria Internacional** serves seafood and other dishes. Featuring local cuisine, **El Chef Tipik** is at Luis Ginebra and Hnas. Mirabal. Two blocks N from the main square, **La Canasta** serves good lunches. An inexpensive place is **Plaza Los Messones**, off the side of Parque Luperón, which has lunch specials for less than US$2.

SNACKS: Branches of **Pepe Postre**, a pastry chain, are on 27 de Febrero and at Av. Colón 24. **El Sombrero** is on Playa Cofresí along the Autopista Santiago-Puerto Plata. **El Dorado**, a bakery, is at Duarte and San Felipe.

Unusual sweets are sold at a shop opposite the Listin Diario office on C. J.F. Kennedy.

SUPERMARKETS: Bellers Liquor, C. Beller and Emilio Prudhomme, is right near Parque Luperón and has a good selection. Pick up a beer or soft drink here and go out to the park. **Supermercado Italiano** is at Beller 110. **Supermercado Central** and **Supermercado José Luis** are on C. Monolo Travares Justo. Both the old market and the **Mercado Nuevo** (on C. Imbert two blocks NW of the main plaza) are good places to buy fruits and vegetables. **Erika**, C. Separación near the park and just down from the PO, sells cheese, meat, and other dairy products.

DINING NEAR LONG BEACH: If you're staying or visiting near Long Beach, you can dine at European-oriented **Don Pedro** or at **Restaurant Mozart**. In this area you'll also find **Café Terminus** (inq. about horseback safaris), **Tex Mex**, **El Cable**, **La Paella**, **Swiss Garden**, and the **Beach Club Restaurant**. **Marie Andres** here specializes in Spanish and Italian food. Up the next side road to the N, the very affordable **Portofino Restaurant** is run by affable Máximo Almondez Portofino. Right on the beach at Puerto Plata Beach Resort, expensive **Neptuno Bar & Grill** specializes in seafood. Waves crash on its windows and a statue of the sea god can be seen on a rocky outcrop; a wide variety of seafood dishes are served.

On the Malecón near the center of town are **Ristorante Barcos** and **Entre Amigo**.

PLAYA DORADA DINING: Most of the gourmet restaurants here are open exclusively for evening dining. The Radisson Puerto Plata's **La Condesa** serves continental food; a jacket is required. Eurotel's **América Restaurant** offers "light gourmet" dishes; a pianist plays evenings. **Porto Dorado** here offers seafood dining to the accompaniment of a guitar trio. At Villas Dorada Beach Resort, **El Pescador** offers fresh seafood dishes. **Jardin de Jade** serves Chinese food including Peking Duck.

Valentino's Italian Restaurant and Pizzeria is in the Playa Dorada complex near the Dorado Naco.

Serving dishes ranging from risotto to grilled chicken, the Flamingo Beach Resort's **El Cortijo** offers Spanish-style cuisine, including exotic seafood dishes and desserts. At Jack Tar Village, **Elaine's** serves up imported lamb chops and other US and Dominican-style dishes. Set on the upper floor of Victoria Resort's main building, **Jardin Victoria** offers international cuisine. At the Puerto Plata Club on the Green, **La Condesa** serves Caribbean-accented gourmet food. Playa Dorada Hotel's **La Palma** specializes in steak and lobster.

OTHER LOCALES: The Swiss-oriented **Blue Marlin** is at Aparthotel Elisabeth in Cofresi; **Mandy's** at Cofresi serves good local and Cajun dishes.

Near Playa Dorada is "**Otro Mundo**" (☎ 543-8116/8019: toll free), a restaurant set in a 120-yr.-old farmhouse. It features a small zoo as well as exotic dishes such as *tempura* frog legs and squid stuffed with shrimp.

Restaurant Primrose is in Apart-Hotel Barlovento in Costambar.

ENTERTAINMENT: The **Cine Mar** (☎ 320-1400) is a first-run movie theater in Playa Dorada Plaza. It's on the second level. The only downtown movie theater, the **Roma Cine**, is on C. Beller just up from the park.

Puerto Plata's only formal nightclub, the **Orion** is on 16 de Julio at 30 de Marzo. It has live music (cover charge) on weekends. Featuring a mix of *merengue*, *salsa*, disco, and rock, **Yellow Beard Pub** is on 30 de Marzo. Watch the local lovelies (and not-so-lovelies) pursue older Daddy Warbucks types.

Nearby on Av. Colón and perpendicular to the watefront, **Fat Eddy's** is a small bar popular with foreign visitors. **Hemingway's**, in Playa Dorada Plaza, is a popu-lar hangout with gringo expats in the area.

Up on Av. Hnas. Mirabal and off to the W from the Long Beach shop/restaurant area, **Paco's Bananas** is open 24 hrs.

For the bloodthirsty who thrive on cruelty to animals – or for those simply curious about a not-so-quaint aspect of Dominican life, **cockfights** are held Thurs. and Sat. from 1-6 and on Sun. from 2:30-6; the location is a small coliseum on C. Ramón Hernandez, a side street which connects to the Malecón. An afternoon may see as many as 30 feather-flying skirmishes.

discos: Puerto Plata Beach Resort features **Bogart's Disco**. Down the road towards town, the **Mermaid** is open all night.

Playa Dorada nightlife: Offering a range of music, from *merengue* to *salsa* to internatiional pop, **Andromeda** disco is in the Heavens Hotel. Playa Dorada Hotel also has a disco; Jack Tar's has **Charlie's Discotheque**; Playa Dorada Village has the **Disco Village**. **Tops** is in Playa Naco.

FESTIVALS AND EVENTS: An **Independence Carnival** is held at the end of Feb.; it celebrates the liberation of the area from the Haitians by Gen. Luperón. A **Fiesta de la Cultura** is held in June. Events include art exhibits, concerts, pupper shows, and sporting contests. The town's patron saint festival (for San Felipe) takes place July 5. Similar to Santo Domingo's *Merengue* Festival, the **Puerto Plata Festival**, held here in Oct., includes live bands, food tents, parades, and the like.

SERVICES: Set above the plaza at Long Beach, the **tourist office** (☎ 586-3676) doesn't appear to welcome visitors or be prepared to serve them. You may be able to pry a photocopy of a map out of them. Near the park, **Libreria Fenix** sells imported newspapers. It's open Mon. to Fri. from 9-2:30. **Codetel** has its offices at Beller 58, at Plaza Turisol, and at the airport. **Tricom** is on San Felipe at Beller. A third long distance company, **All America** (fax 586-6930), is at J. F. Kennedy 40. Open Mon. through Sat. from 8 to 5, the post office is at the corner of Separacíon and 12 de Julio. (Mail may also be dispatched from the front desk of the large hotels).

The **US Consulate** (☎ 686-3143) is at 12 de Julio 55. **Canadian citizens** can contact Tim Hall (☎ 586-5761); British can call on David Salem (☎ 586-4244). **Immigration** (☎ 586-2364) is at 12 de Julio 33.

tourguides: Unfortunately, there are a large number of unqualified and unscrupulous "guides" – including small boys, taxi drivers, and others – who are willing to steer you towards a certain shop or restaurant with

whom they have established a commission arrangement. Taxi drivers will go so far as to maintain falsely that a restaurant is closed or insist that they've never even heard of it. It's always preferable to go shopping on your own.

tours: Set to the W of town on Av. Luis Ginebra in the front of Plaza Turisol, **Brugal** offers distillery tours with free daiquiris from Mon. to Fri. 9-noon and 2 to 5. Drinks are on the house. There isn't much to see on the tour (only the bottling, which you watch from an overhead viewpoint), and it appears to be designed mainly to sell rum and overpriced Brugal souvenirs.

tour companies: Get Wet (☎ 586-1170, 586-1655; www.hispaniola.com/GetWet; e-mail getwet@codetel.net.do) offers rafting, caving, canyoning, and other adventurous activites. They take you to the Jarabacoa area. Out in Cabarete, **Iguana Mama** (☎ 571-0908, fax 571-0734; 800-849-4720; EPS-D#342, PO Box 02-55548, Miami, FL 33102; www.iguana-mama.com; e-mail iguanamama@codetel.net.do) offers hikes up Isabel de Torres peak. **Taino Jeep Adventure** (☎ 586-3911) offers trips out into the Dominican countryside, as does **Rum Runners** (☎ 586-6155, fax 586-2729; e-mail r.runners@codetel.net.do) who have their offices in Plaza Isabela but operate

---

Important Phone Numbers in Puerto Plata

American Airlines 542-5151
Caribe Tours 586-4544
Emergency 911
Information 1411
Police 571-2338

island-wide. **Aerolink** (☎ 567-0819, 320-0627) has air tours to Samaná, Santo Domingo, and (when conditions permit) to Haiti.

Most of the agencies offer the same variety of trips. Standard excursions are around Puerto Plata, to Santo Domingo (US$60), Santiago and the Cibao, to Samaná, to the Grí Grí Lagoon, and to Jarabacoa. Typical offerings include city tours (US$25), Santo Domingo tours, trips to Sosúa (US$15), Río San Juan and Playa Grande, and also to Santiago. **Agencia de Viajes Cafemba** (Cafemba Tours, 586-2177, C. Separación 12) is one of the island's premier travel agencies. **Go Dominican Tours** (☎ 586-6277/1101; fax 586-6652/4310; Av. J. F. Kennedy 47) is another. Another branch of **Go Dominican Tours** (☎ 586-5969) is in Plaza Turisol.

Other travel and tour agencies include **Prieto Tours** (☎ 586-3988, C. Marginal), **Puerto Plata Tours** (☎ 586-3858, Av. Beller 70), **Agencia de Viajes Victoria Tours** (☎ 586-3744/3773, C. Duarte 59) and **Vimenca Tours** (☎ 586-3883). **Columbus Air**

(☎ 586-6991) offers day-long tours of Santo Domingo. At Plaza José Augusto Puig, **Turinter** (☎ 586-3911, fax 586-4755) has the usual range of tours. **Go Caribic** (☎ 586-4075, fax 586-4073) deals with German tourists.

If you want something out of the ordinary, **Wolf Wirth** at the Hotel Restaurante El Indio (☎/fax 586-1201; 30 de Marzo 94-98) can put you in touch with options ranging from Pedro Brunschwiler's unique 14-day jeep trips around the island to boat trips to Los Haitises.

RENTALS: Cars can be rented at the airport or in town from **Puerto Plata Rent Car** (☎ 586-0215); **Rentauto Puerta Plata** (☎ 568-0240 or 800-631-0058); **Abby** (☎ 586-2516/3995) on Av. J.F. Kennedy; and **Budget** (☎ 586-4433) on Av. L. Ginebra. **Trixxy Rent-A-Car** rents motorcycles at reasonable cost. **Yuyo** (☎ 585-5440), 12 de Julio opposite Cosme Restaurant, rents scooters and "motorcicles." If renting scooters you should note that there is no insurance, and stealing scooters is a popular crime.

HEALTH: Clínica Dr. Brugal (☎ 586-2519), is at C. José del Carmen Ariza 15. **Grupo Medico Dr. Bournigal** (☎ 586-2342/3542) is on Av. Mota. **Farmacia Deleyte** (☎ 586-2583), Av. J. F. Kennedy 89 in front of Parque Luperón, is open 24 hrs. Others include **Farmacia Josefina** at C. Separación 62, **Farmacia Popular** at C. Beller 27, and **Farmacia Socorro** at C. Beller 41. A complete list can be found in the phone book.

SHOPPING: On C. Duarte, **Rancier Boutique** is a small department store featuring Dominican manufactured goods. The **Rainbow Gift Shop** is at C. Duarte 22. Featuring jewelry, hand-knitted blouses, ceramics, and dresses, **The Mine** is at C. San Felipe 32 at C. Duarte.

Macaluso, at C. Duarte 32, offers crafts and jewelry as well as rocking chairs. At C. J.F. Kennedy 3 at 30 de Marzo, **Centro Artesenal** offers jewelry by its students, handmade dolls, domino and chess sets, and wooden trays. For beauty-related items, **Casa Leonel** has two shops. One is on C. Beller and the other is across from the PO on 12 de Julio. The **Libreria Fenix** has imported newspapers as well as postcards. The **Tourist Bazaar** is at C. Duarte 6. **La Caona** has been recommended as a place to shop. On C. Separación, **Casa Nelson** offers a wide variety of goods. **Casa Colón** nearby has T-shirts and related clothing items. Near Playa Dorada on the road from Puerto Plata, **Plaza Isabela** offers a selection of gift shops and a small supermarket. **Plaza Turisol** is a small shopping mall largely housing tour company offices.

Harrison's, the nation's foremost jewelers, has a branch on the Puerto Plata-Sosúa road. **Playa Dorada** also has shopping in its mall.

FROM PUERTO PLATA: For Santiago and Santo Domingo, *Metro* (☎ 586-6063) runs from C. Beller, and *Caribe Tours* (☎ 586-0282) departs from C. 12 de Julio at José Carmen Ariza. Caribe also runs to Sosúa, Mao, Dajabón, and Manzanillo.

Transportes de Cibao (☎ 586-9408) has regular departures from a gravel lot next to Casa Criolla across from the Hotel Atlantico.

Carreras (chartered) run to Playa Dorado for around US$7, and to Sosúa, around US$11. From Playa Dorada to the airport, it costs US$11, and around US$7 to town. *Voladoras*, smaller minibuses, run all over and leave from La Javilla, the hospital, and from near Parque Luperón. If heading towards Sosúa, don't stand on the road but go to the terminal (near the hospital) or to Parque Luperón; most buses are packed when they pass, and every other vehicle will be offering itself up as a charter – even the city buses. These charge about 70¢ to Sosúa, Playa Dorada, and the airport, and about US$1 to Cabarete; ask a local to get the current price in *pesos* before boarding because many specialize in overcharging.

Motoconchos will also take you anywere you want to go, but, as with taxis, be sure to negotioate before leaving.

⚡ Warning

No matter where you are heading be sure to get an early start. It takes four hrs. to Nagua, and (allowing for frequent transfers) will take you a full day to get to Las Terrenas or Samaná. There are no big buses heading out this way, and the overload can be horrendous.

---

by air: **Air Santo Domingo** (☎ 683-8020, fax 683-8436; www.g-air-europa.es/air_sdo; e-mail info.air_sdo@g-air-europa.es) operates between Puerto Plata and Herrera airport (in Santo Domingo), Punta Cana, Portillo (Samaná Peninsula), Santiago, and La Romana.

Heading West From Puerto Plata

Well worth exploration, the nation's NW is still undervisited and undeservedly neglected.

Some of the country's best and most extensive coral reefs lie offshore between Monte Cristi and Punta Rucia. In addition, there is the major town of Monte Cristi as well as Monte Cristi National Park and Villa Elisa Scientific Reserve.

To get to Monte Cristi, you have to take a *público* from La Javilla (at the NW end of town on the main road) to the outskirts of Navarete and then one on to Monte Cristi.

La Isabela

This archaeological site lies to the W of Puerto Plata near the village of El Castillo. This particular site has generated great excitement among archaeologists because it may mark Columbus's first landfall in the New World on Oct. 12, 1492. The site is believed to be La Isabela, where a settlement was founded in 1493. However, it is no more certain than whether the ashes in Columbus's tomb in Santo Domingo are in fact those of the Great Navigator.

If this was, in fact, the site of Columbus's settlement, then this is the spot where he began his transformation from master mariner to bungling administrator and rapacious imperialist. In a misguided attempt at restoration during the 1960s, the site was bulldozed and countless artifacts were swept into the sea along with the topsoil. Despite this, the foundations of homes grouped around a central plaza have been unearthed, along with numerous potshards executed in the Moorish style common to 15th-century Spain and glazed a pink salmon color. Two ancillary sites, El Castillo and Los Coles, have been unearthed, but their exact connection with La Isabela is uncertain.

Monte Cristi

Reached via the Valle del Norte, the dusty coastal town of Monte Cristi is set in the nation's far NW and owing to its windswept, desert-like setting, it's known as *Estamosmoriendo de sed* ("We die of thirst"). Destroyed in 1605-1606, this small town – whose name is also sometimes spelled "Montecristy" – was resettled in the 18th century by German, Spanish, Italian, and English immigrants. It prospered during the 19th century and into the beginning of the 20th when it exported wood and agricultural products to Europe. It is seldom visited by travelers except on day trips.

Monte Cristi has as its major attractions an unusual town clock, the home of patriot Máximo Gómez (who played a key role in the Cuban independ-ence struggle and in the Dominican Restoration), and the spectacular national park within walking distance of town. A *balneario* is at Loma de Cabrera on the Haitian border.

ACCOMMODATIONS: Since few many tourists come here so there is a lack of upscale accommodations. **Montechico** (☎ 579-2441) is on Playa Bolaños; **Roalex** (☎ 579-2405) is on P.J. Bolaños, and **Hotel El Chic** (☎ 579-2316) is at C.B. Monción 44.

In the town of **Mao** to the SE, try inexpensive **Hotel Cahoba** (☎ 572-3357), E Reyes, **Hotel Céntrico** (☎ 572-5253), **San Pedro** (☎ 572-3134), and **Marién** (☎ 525-3558).

FOOD: El Parada is an inexpensive Italian restaurant right on the main road before town. There are a number of places to eat in town. **Heladeria and Pizzeria Kendy** is at C. Duarte 92. **Restaurant Coco Mar** is on PJ de Bolaños. **La Taberna de Rafua** is at Duarte 84. **Panifacadora Vitamina** is at S Fernando 18. Capped by a satellite dish, the **Restaurant Rabel** is on the main road to Dajabon.

SIGHTS AND ENTERTAINMENT: There's little to do in this town, which appears to have no true center. You may visit the **Casa Museo Generalisimo Máximo Gómez** – the house of patriot Máximo Gómez, which is now a small museum. Along with José Marti, Gómez penned the *Manifesto de Montecristi* here in March 25, 1895; it called for Cuban independence. Or see the **clock tower** – a cuckoo-clock-meets-the-Eiffel-Tower construction. Or hang out at one of the underpopulated and over-volumed discos. There's also a generator-powered movie theater, as well as the Academia de Music, which has the remains of old saxophones and tubas hanging on the walls.

SERVICES: Codetel is at Av. Duarte 85. **Alianza Francesa** is also on C. Duarte.

DIVE ARCHAEOLOGY: North **Caribbean Research** (North Caribbean Adventures, Inc. (☎ 954-989-6234, fax 954-989-6237; 800-653-7447; Box 6549, Hollywood, FL 33081; www.oldship. com; e-mail info@oldship.com) takes students on their diving salvage trips. Students help raise cannons, old bottles, silverware, and other artifacts. Students train in the company of an archaeologist and stay in what was once the "Las Caravelas" hotel.

FESTIVALS AND EVENTS: The town's patron saint festivities (for San Fernando Rey) take place around May 30.

FROM MONTE CRISTI: *Caribe Tours* runs to Puerto Plata via Dajaban. Be sure to get an early start.

There is no easy way to head S along here paralleling the Haitian border unless you have your own vehicle; a *carro* goes through to Pedro Santana a few times per week from Dajaban. You can get to Lomas de Cabrera (visit Balneario El Salto) and then take a truck to Restauracíon past breathtaking mountain scenery. Here you may get stuck. The road to Dajaban passes through cactus tree forests and by herds of goats. You might see a young boy herding cows followed by his even younger companion sporting a Batman T-shirt. In Dajaban check out the **Haitian market**. It is possible to cross over into Haiti, but the entry fee is US$25!

Parque Nacional Monte Cristi

This park, located in the NE near the border with Haiti, is also known as "El Morro" after its principal feature – a 900-ft.-high mesa overlooking the sea. Along with a nearby small hill called La Granja, El Morro is covered with windblown trees and shrubs on the ocean side, which turn to desert scrub inland. Reachable by swimming in many places, the park's inner portion lies in water seven-10 ft. deep, and its outer reaches range from 10 to 40 ft. deep. So far, 10 wrecks have been discovered here. There are also a number of small islands offshore known as the **Cayos Siete Her-**

manos (Cayes of the Seven Brothers).

GETTING HERE: A road runs from Monte Cristi via commercially exploited salt flats to the coast and up the mesa's side. You pass some restaurants along the way. The Club Náutico is adorned with red, white, and blue Brugal rum posters along with red and white Marlboro posters. A huge imitation bottle of Presidente adorns the building's roof. A rusting sign denotes "Villa del Morro," a tourist complex that – judging by the rust – will never come to fruition. Along the road, you might see legions of dragonflies suddenly pop out of bushes or fishermen casting their nets in the water. There are a number of expensive homes, some only partially constructed, which have been built within the park boundaries. They were illegally built by wealthy citizens of Santiago; construction has been halted.

EXPLORING: The area has been defaced with hideous white-painted metal crosses. Follow the path to the left all the way to the top to find an absolutely magnificent view. The visibility through the water is incredible. Back down the hill, you find more crosses and a sort of roadside altar with a set of stones like those of the 10 commandments. Follow this road to a small yet beautiful beach. If you branch off to the R,

the road passes by a lagoon with abundant mangroves.

FLORA AND FAUNA: Subtropical dry forest predominates here. Plant species include poisonwood, West Indian boxwood, wild frangipani, and waterlilies. The 163 species of birds include the magnificent frigatebird, great egret, yellow-crowned night heron, American kestrel, wood stork, American oystercatcher, gulls, five species of terns, plovers, willet, osprey, and brown noddy. There are 11 reptilian species, including the American crocodile, and three amphibians.

PRACTICALITIES: Stay and eat in Monte Cristi.

RESERVA CIENTIFICA NATURAL DE VILLA ELISA: Established in 1986, Villa Elisa Scientific Reserve lies in Guayubín municipality, near the village of Villa Elisa. This small stretch of subtropical forest features birds like the *cotorra* (parrot) and the *carpintero de sierra.* The 138 species of vegetation include a number of orchids and bromeliads.

Sosúa

Featuring a small beach on a bay, the very European town of Sosúa is set five miles (eight km) from the airport and around 16 miles (25 km) E of Puerto Plata. The town is divided into two areas: El Batey is the resort area featuring

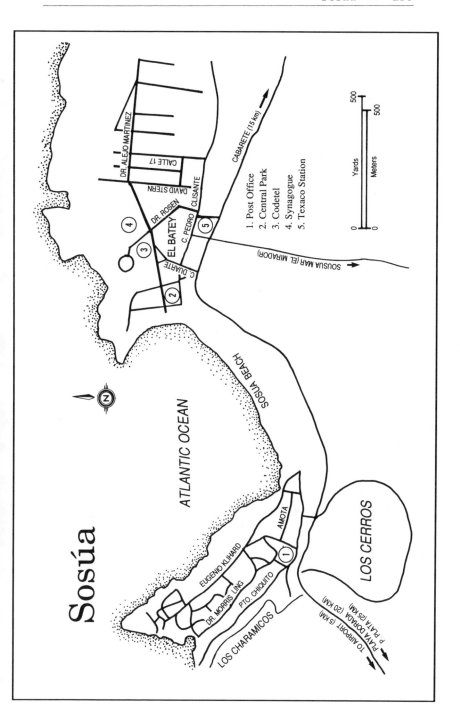

Sosúa

1. Post Office
2. Central Park
3. Codetel
4. Synagogue
5. Texaco Station

the majority of the area's tourist-oriented bars, restaurants, hotels, and hustlers. Much of it has sprung up recently, and it continues to expand.

Originally, El Batey's special character derived from the 600 Jewish refugees who settled here in 1940. Although only 100 actually put down roots, they developed the dairy and sausage plants. The synagogue still stands, and English, French, and German are commonly spoken in town.

Connected both by beach and road, Los Charamicos (pronounced Cha-ra-me-kohs) is the bustling Dominican area at the W end. Tin-roofed shacks predominate here, and the atmosphere is the same as you'll find elsewhere in the nation.

GETTING HERE: Take a *público* from Puerto Plata. *Caribe Tours* (☎ 221-4422) runs here via Puerto Plata. A taxi from the airport is around RD$200. Or you can walk to the road and take local transport for much less (RD$5) if you don't have much baggage.

by air: Air Santo Domingo flies. (See *Puerto Plata* for details.)

GETTING AROUND: It's easy to walk virtually anywhere. Los Charamicos is about 20 min. on foot; the most pleasant way is via the beach. The best way to stave

off hustlers is to ignore them! Be sure to have change for the *motoconchos*. They charge around 35¢ US during the day and 70¢ at night.

EVENTS: The town's *fiestas patronales* of San Antonio are held June 13, but the biggest time of the year is Easter week.

BEACHES AND SIGHTS: There are three beaches. To get to the main beach, follow the main drag (Pedro Clisante) and turn left at the end. Nearly the entire stretch is a huge outdoor market filled with vendors selling typical souvenirs – ranging from imitation Haitian paintings to T-shirts. They'll rent you beach chairs, braid your hair and add a bead on the end, sell you trips on glass bottomed boats, or take you on tours. They can get to be a nuisance; the best solution is to walk along the edge of the water. However, you'll soon find jewelry sellers and the like accosting you when you sit down. Give them a firm "no" if you're not interested and hope they go away.

The smaller **Casa Marina Beach** is in front of the Casa Marina Hotel. It's less spectacular but also has fewer vendors. A third, miniscule beach is in front of the **Larimar**. (Owing to the erosion caused by a breakwater, it has seen better days.)

Across from the Codetel on C. Martinez near C. Dr. Rosen, the

synagogue holds services every two weeks on Fri. at 7 PM.

Opened in 1997, the **Columbus Aquaparque** stands outside of town on the way to Puerto Plata. You'll recognize it by the unforgettable life-size fake caraval poised at the park entrance. Built at the cost of US$3.4 million, the park includes a giant twister, which bends and changes velocity, a "black hole," giant slides, and a "kiddie cove" with its own attractions.

ACCOMMODATIONS: Innumerable guest houses, hotels, and villas are in the area, and well over 2,000 rooms are available. The town's borders are expanding rapidly, and new construction is everywhere. By the time of your arrival, there will undoubtedly be a number of new additions, so ask around. None of the hotels here border the main beach, but most are only a short walk away.

Now in its second decade of operation, the **Hotel Tropix** (☎/fax 571-2291) is an attractive 10-cabaña resort that borders a swimming pool and gardens; inexpensive meals are served. Breakfast is served, as is dinner (by request). Use of the kitchen is available for guests after noon. Your host is Sylvie Papernik, a Sosúa native raised in the States; she runs the hotel along with partner Cory Price. Some of the attractive rooms have a/c and some have fans. It is ideal for

groups. Peace Corps volunteers and missionaries love the place. Rates are US$45 d plus tax. Student discounts are given. The hotel is on a side road to the S of town and is just a few min. walk from the Sosúa-Puerto Plata road.

One of the better inexpensive places to stay is the eight-rm. **Auberge/Village Inn of Sosua** (☎ 571-2569/3030, fax 571-2865/3750; EPS D-316, PO Box # 02-5548, Miami, FL 33102) run by semi-retired expatriate American lawyer J.J. O'Connell. It's at C. Dr. Rosen 8, just five min. or so on foot from the three beaches. It has a small pool. This inn features a restaurant, free ice and purified drinking water; the compact rooms are equipped with your choice of a/c or ceiling fan. You can also watch satellite TV with J.J.; he is well informed about the DR and will be happy to talk to you. However, you should note that he is out of the country during the low season. Rates run around US$20 s, US$30 d.

The 116-rm. **Casa Marina Beach Club** (☎ 571-3690, fax 571-3110, 800-874-4658; e-mail casamarina@codetel.net.do), Av. Dr. A. Martínez, offers three restaurants, a pool, Jacuzzi, and access to a small but nice beach, where you'll find windsurfing and sunfish sailing. An all-inclusive plan is available. They also own the nearby 32-rm. a/c **Club Marina** (☎ 571-3939, 867-9690), Av. Dr. A. Martínez, which offers executive and junior suites as well as a pool; it is decorated with beautiful stained glass and other artwork.

Facing a small beach, **Sosúa-by-the-Sea** (☎ 571-3222, fax 571-3020) offers a/c rooms with cable TV and refrigerator. Its facilities include pool, Jacuzzi, massage parlor, restaurant, and bar. In the US, ☎ 800-531-7043. **Villas Larimar** (☎ 571-2645), Av. Martinez 1, is under the same Austrian management.

On C. Pedro Clisante, the 210-room all-inclusive **La Esplanada Hotel-Sosúa** (☎ 571-3333, fax 571-3922) has a/c rooms with satellite TV, minibars, and phones. It also has a pool, two restaurants, three bars, two tennis courts, gift shop, and babysitting services. It caters to package tourists and is all-inclusive. It is a fair distance from the beach. This is a franchise belonging to the Occidental Hotels chain. The Occidental Hotels may be contacted in North America and Canada (☎ 506-877-3160, 800-843-3311, fax 506-877-3160), in Belgium (☎ 30-235-0373, 09800-14596), in Denmark (☎ 8030 1031, 45 87 00 08, fax 45 87 22 49/93 21 41), in France (☎ 05 00 11, 4071 2121, fax 4071 2131), in Germany (☎ 0180-231 21 21, 06151-905760, fax 06151-905750), in Ireland (01 6605 000, fax 01 6605 540), and in Switzerland (☎ 155 5583, 715 1616, fax 715 5583).

Featuring nine cabañas and four rooms, **Koch's Ocean Front Guest House** (☎ 571-2234) has two rooms (8 and 9) that command ocean views.

The 28-rm. **Hotel Sosúa** (☎ 571-2683, Av. Martinez) features a pool and kitchenettes in some rooms. You can have your choice of either ceiling fans or a/c rooms.

Offering your choice of a/c or fan-equipped rooms, 24-rm. a/c **Hotel Yaroa** (☎ 571-2578), C. Pedro Clisante, features a rooftop deck, French restaurant, and swimming pool.

Moderately priced 27-unit **On the Waterfront** (☎ 571-2690) offers simple rooms with fans and refrigerators; it has a steak and seafood restaurant next door which goes by the same name.

The **Sosúa Paradise Resort** (☎ 571-3438/3539), Av. Martinez 6, offers 28 a/c rooms with cable TV, balcony; junior suites have a refrigerator.

LOS CHARAMICOS ACCCOMMODATIONS: The only hotels that could be considered low-budget are found in this lively area. On C. Carmen, **Pension Gómez** (☎ 571-5159) has rooms for around US$9, which include bath and fan. Similarly priced and a bit superior, **Hotel El Bambú** (☎ 571-2379) has a nice sitting room and balcony; enter from the building's side. About half that price are **Pension La Cancilleria** (☎ 571-3594 – ask for Odé) at C. Charles Kinder #15, and **Pensión Tata**.

The 68-rm. **Sosúa "Sun Bay Club"** (☎ 571-0704) was once a "resort" and had three bars, restaurant, disco, pool, and other facilities. It is now a shell of its former self. The pool has been drained, and the rooms have been stripped: it gives the feeling of a post-disaster zone. The good news is that it is now cheap – around US$10 d.

For a more luxurious stay, try **Charamicos Beach Resort** (☎ 571-2675).

APART-HOTELS: These hotels are best if you are planning on cooking your own meals. On C. Dr. Alejo Martinez, the **Sea Breeze Hotel** (☎ 571-3858, 586-4132 in Puerto Plata, fax 571-2129) has 30 a/c rooms with balcony and kitchenette. Facilities include tour desk, pool, live entertainment, pool table and cable TV in an a/c game room, plus complimentary watersports and horseback riding. Prices are around US$40 pp.

The 55-unit **One Ocean Place** (☎ 571-3131) is an a/c apart-hotel with cable TV, phone, balconies, kitchenettes, pool, children's pool, and 24-hr. security.

Condos Sosúa (☎ 571-2504), C. Garcia, offers 15 one-bedroom apartments for short- or long-term rental.

Inexpensive 16-unit **Sosúa Sol** (☎ 571-2334, fax 571-2416; Box 55, Sosúa) has one- and two-bedroom bungalows with kitchenettes and ceiling fans. There is a pool.

At Pedro Clisante 11, **Apart Hotel Nuevosol** (☎ 571-2124) offers fully equipped apartments with a/c or fans, and private balcony. Restaurant and laundry facilities are also available.

Constructed with colonial arches, 12-unit **Apart-Hotel Alcázar** (☎ 571-2321) has a pool. **Condos Dominicanos Apart-Hotel** (☎ 571-2504) includes 12 studios, four one-bedrooms, and four two-bedrooms. It also has a pool and is not far from the beach.

Near the beach and eating and drinking spots, modern **Las Palmas Apart-Hotel** (☎ 571-2545) has two-bedroom apartments, a boutique, and a kiosk.

The 78-rm. **Tropiclub Los Almendros** (☎ 562-7461/3921/4171) is a fully equipped apart-hotel.

At La Puntilla in El Batey, **El Neptuno** (☎ 571-2664) offers 18 luxury two-bedroom apartments overlooking the ocean. Facilities include pool, Jacuzzi, and snack bar. The digs here are designed for long-term rental.

Puerto Plata & the North

Club Residential Aparthotel (☎ 571-3675, fax 571-1143), Pedro Clisante, offers attractive units for weekly and monthly rent. In the US, ☎ 800-831-1795.

With one- and two-bedroom apartments, **Don Andres Apart-Hotel** (☎ 571-3103) has pool, bar, and restaurant.

The **Tourist Studio** (☎ 572-2212), C. Dr. Rosen, has 12 one- or two-bedroom a/c furnished apartments in a convenient location.

The **Villas Carolina** (☎ 571-3626) offers 55 junior and six senior suites as well as two pools, bar, and restaurant.

OUTLYING ACCOMMODATIONS: On a beach just outside Sosúa, the 240-rm. **Sand Castle** (☎ 571-2420) is designed in pink Moorish style. It has three restaurants, shops, and watersports.

On the town's outskirts, the 180-rm. a/c **Hotel Playa Chiquita** (☎ 571-2800) has a pool, restaurant, and conference center. All rooms have kitchenettes.

The **Voramar Hotel** (☎ 571-3910, fax 571-3076), Playa Chiquita, has rooms for around US$25 d.

At Puerto Chiquito, **Coral Beach Resort** (☎ 571-2577, Box 711, Sosúa) is a four-star resort with a split-level Victorian design. Facilities include carpeted suites and cable TV.

The 72-room **Hotel Colina Sol y Mar** (☎ 571-3250, fax 571-3540) is just minutes away from the airport. Facilities include shuttle to the beach, pool, restaurant, disco, billiards, and an 18-hole mini-golf course.

With 209 rooms and all-inclusive (including booze), **Horizon Club** (☎ 571-2854/2856/2852) is in the hills. It features restaurants, pool, tennis, and a shuttle to the beach every 30 min.

Set between Sosúa and Cabarete, the **LTI Sol de Plata** (☎ 571-3600, fax 571-3389) is a four-star hotel with 216 a/c rooms in six three-story bldgs, and 134 rooms and 20 suites in 28 villas. All are equipped with phone, minibar, and satellite TV. The resort has three pools, four tennis courts, nearby golf courses, and shuttlebus to Sosúa.

An exclusive private development fronting 250 acres of seafront, pasture, and woods, **Sea Horse Ranch** (☎ 571-3880, fax 571-2374) includes homes, tennis courts, and a riding center.

EL BATEY DINING AND FOOD: There are a large number of gourmet and aspiring gourmet restaurants here; most are in the vicinity of C. Pedro Clisante. The best thing to do is to stroll along, look at menus and specials, and take your pick. Expect to spend less than US$10 to eat.

Sosúa by the Sea offers a breakfast buffet for around US$3. Hotel Annelise serves a traditional German breakfast. The Auberge/Village Inn's restaurant is on C. Dr. Rosen; it's also a good breakfast spot. Cheaper places are on the main road.

At C. Pedro Clisante No. 13, Don Juan's Restaurant offers good food and tries to please. Pollo Rico, Pedro Clisante, serves Dominican food. The Brittania and the a/c Schnitzel Hut are both on Pedro Clisante. Compact Café Mama Juana is open from breakfast on. At the town entrance, Café Sosúa offers snacks and light food.

Popular PJ's International, Pedro Clisante 5, serves US-style food, including soups and salads.

Featuring reggae and other Caribbean music, Casablanca Bar & Grill, Pedro Clisante 12, is a bar-eatery. Mauricio's serves seafood. Lorenzo's on C. Pedro Clisante serves pizza and Italian and Dominican specialties.

A gourmet Victorian-style Italian restaurant perched on a cliff, La Puntilla de Piergiorgio (☎ 571-2215) is the former summer home of an American diplomat. It will soon have its own 76-rm. hotel.

Sosúa-by-the-Sea's Sunset Place offers buffet on Wed. nights as well as all-you-can-eat breakfast buffets.

Serving steak and seafood, On the Waterfront also offers live entertainment.

Set on the main drag, Cyrano's Café serves French, German, English, European, and Caribbean cuisine in a Mediterranean atmosphere.

At No. 28 on C. Pedro Clisante, Restaurant Spaguetti House (☎ 571-3301) operates a wood-fired pizza oven.

Farther down Pedro Clisante away from the beach and off by itself, Restaurante Tipico Morena offers Dominican food at very reasonable prices.

Overlooking the beach, Pizzeria-by-the-Sea also serves mixed drinks. On the way to Los Charamicos on the beach, La Hispaniola offers dining in the evening by candlelight. Also on this beach, Carambar is run by Klaus Vormann who operates adventure tours to Samaná and Haiti.

FOOD SHOPPING: One supermarket is on C. Dr. Rosen, another is on the main road, and a third is at the corner of C. Pedro Clisante and C. Ayuntamiento. Aleman Panaderia is a German bakery offering baked goods at US prices. Right in the center of town, Swiss-run a/c Tanja's Pastry is handier and has a good selection. Supermercado El Batey, C. Pedro Clisante, offers a wide selection of items such as mosquito coils, cassava bread, and imported newspapers (US$3). **Messón Liquor Store** is at Av. Pedro Clisante 14. **Super Super** on Ayuntamiento has an excellent booze selection including wines (note that rum is cheaper than Gatorade!).

LANGUAGE STUDY: Goethe-Sosua (☎ 571-3174, 571-3285, fax 689-3241), La Puntilla 2, offers Spanish and German courses. **Premium International Language Center** (☎ 571-2151) gives courses in Spanish.

LOS CHARAMICOS DINING AND FOOD: Right in town, **La Peto** offers gourmet dining. **Restaurant Tortuga** serves local food at reasonable prices. Set atop a cliff on the Charamicos end, **Atlántico** offers great views and seafood. The lower-key **Michael's** is next door. **El Oasis** serves *comida criolla*. **Molinos Dominicanos** is the area's best local-style bakery.

ENTERTAINMENT: The chief activity here is at the discos. Owing to a government crackdown on prostitution, the ones in the center of town have all closed.

Despite a slight dip in numbers, high season still attracts hordes of prostitutes – both male and female. Known as "Sanky Pankies," the male versions are often basically homosexual: they just service the German women for the added income. Forced into prostituting themselves to survive, the females send their profits back home to their mothers and babies.

The action up until recently was at the **Oxy2** (a disco on the main road); it has a good sound system, a beautiful interior design which has the feel of a voodoo ritual ampitheater, drunken Poles, and females looking for nocturnal employment. However, the disco was shut down in the summer of 1997 after it was found to have held 14 underage girls "against their will" and "forced them to dance naked." It may have reopened by the time of your arrival. Down the street from the turnoff to Casa Marina, the **Copacabana** is a similar disco with live floor shows. Foreigners are hit up for DS$20 at both.

A quieter place to have a drink is at the **Tree Tops International Bar** in the center of town; it has an attractive atmosphere.

gambling: Over in Los Charamicos, you can catch **cockfights** on Sat. Opened in 1992, the **Casino Playa Chiquita** (☎ 571-3416) is the only casino in the area. Every type of gambling can be found here. It is open from 8 PM-4 AM.

SHOPPING: The most unusual shop is **Toe Rings**, C. Pedro Clisante, which offers an abundance of gems, fossils, crystals, and – you guessed it – toe rings. It's

Important Phone Numbers in Sosúa

American Airlines 542-5151
Caribe Tours 571-3808
Continental 541-2000
Emergency 911
Information 1411
Police 571-2338
Taxis 571-3097

worth a visit just to window shop. Visit the **Viva Art Gallery** on C. Alejo Martinez in El Batey. Patrick Silvermithy has been selling its wares for more than two decades. Saddles and other leather items are available at the workshop of **Juan Francisco de los Santos** near the Gran Parada on the Sosúa road. Heading towards Sosúa, it's on the R by the fork.

INFORMATION AND TOURS: **Extra Tours** (☎ 571-3106) is a German-owned tour company that operates tours in both German and English. They run specialized trips for up to eight persons to Montecristi and the Haitian border (with a visit to the Haitian market at Dajabon), to Samaná and Laguna Grí Grí (US$65), to Jarabacoa, and to Lago Enriquillo – a special two-day trip (US$219).

Their trips are unusual. For example, on the one-day Samaná trip, you are brought into a village and shown how people live, you take a personalized Grí Grí lagoon cruise, and points of interest along the route are explained.

Photo and video stops are available upon request. Some trips include food and beverages, others not.

German-owned and friendly **Melissa Tours** (☎ 571-2567) is on C. Duarte near C. Pedro Clisante. They offer a variety of trips.

SERVICES: One of the best rates is given by **Western Union** on the main road. Open Mon. to Fri. from 9-3, the **Banco de Reservas** is at Ayuntamiento and Pedro Clisante. A **Codetel** office is also on the main drag (C. Dr. Rosen at Av. Martinez); there's another Codetel office in Los Charamicos. Pay phones are outside. You can also try **Tricom** for overseas calls and internal faxes at discounted prices. Offering a whole range of facilities, the German-oriented **Plaza Tropical Club** is on the outskirts of town.

CAR RENTALS: **Sosúa Motors** (☎/fax: 571-3331) provides rentals from around US$30 pd. Rent-cars from **Honda** (☎ 571-3280) in the Hotel Los Almendros. **Elba**

Dive Sites Near Sosúa

The mini-wall is just off of Casa Marina's beach. It is a wall dive with coral gardens. The maximum depth is 60 ft. (20 m). Just E of it are the **Three Rocks**. This underwater canyon and wall dive has a depth of 60 ft. (20 m). **The Pyramids** are 18 miles N and have a depth of 40 ft. (16 m). With a maximum depth of 90 ft., the **Airport Wall** is near the airport, logically enough. An artificial reef created on a deliberately sunken vessel, the **Zingara Wreck** contains the remains of the boat of the same name; it is a maximum 12-ft. (4-m) dive. Finally, the **Paradise Reef** is a wall-dive in tiers; it averages 35-40 ft. (12-13 m).

Rent-A Bicycle can be contacted at ☎ 571-2050/2824.

SPORTS: For miniature golf (US$4 pp) or to work out, visit the **18 Hoyos** which combines the course with a health club (US$4 for one-time use). It has a sauna and Jacuzzi.

The **Golden Park Gym** (☎ 571-3243) is on the main road in back of Oxy2 Disco. It offers aerobic machines, karate, boxing, and aerobics classes.

DIVING: There are a number of outfits in town. Right in the center of town at Pedro Clisante 8, **Northern Coast Diving Aquasports** (☎ 571-1028, fax 571-3883; EPS-D 245, PO Box -2-5548, Miami, FL 33102; e-mail northern@codetel.net.do) is a five-star PADI dive center. A lesson and dive costs around US$45, with repeat dives at US$35. Certification and other PADI courses are available. The center is run by an American expat couple with an international staff. They do a fine job of instruction, and their store offers a wide variety of diving accessories. They also lead a snorkeling trip (two hrs., US$18). The **Big Blue Swiss Diving School** (☎ 571-2960, fax 571-2534; cellular 223-6868; e-mail a.marcel@codetel.net.do) runs courses as well as outings.

FROM SOSÚA: Taxis depart from the North Shore office, Av. Martinez, in El Batey. *Caribe Tours* (☎ 571-3808) is located at the entrance to Charamicos. They run a number of buses (around US$5) to Santo Domingo via Puerto Plata. To leave town, go out on the main road and ignore the persistent and obnoxious taxi drivers. Be sure you stand on the correct side of the road for the direction you're heading; Río San Juan-bound transport departs on the opposite side.

Cabarete

The beachside "village" of Cabarete runs along a two-km curving bay It has been crowned the "windsurfing capital" of the world.

Once offering only bare-bones accommodations, Cabarete has swiftly evolved during the course of the 1990s into a major resort town. It is around 15 miles (23 km) E of Sosúa, and some 15 min. by taxi (US$14) from the airport.

The main through-road doubles as the main street. Here you can still find authentic slices of Dominican life – from clucking chickens to the man on his donkey transporting clanking metal milk cans tied to the sides. You might see children eating in front of the evangelical church or dogs frolicking in the dust.

The main part of the town has now, however, been transformed. You can dine in chic bistros, listen to live jazz, and spend time with affluent Dominicanos who visit on the weekends: Cabarete has come into its own and is now *the* place to be.

Useful Web sites include www. caberete.com and www.hispaniola.com/Cabarete/indexframe. html.

HISTORY: The Cabarete area was first colonized by Don Francisco

☞ *Traveler's Tip*

When planning a trip to Cabarete for windsurfing, keep in mind that the wind is unpredictable. You should plan on staying for at least five days.

de Dávila y Coca who received a land grant near the Río Yásica in the 1500s. In the 1770s, it had some 14 homes with 500 inhabitants. During the 1800s, the invading Haitians gave it the name of Cabaret.The area remained relatively unpopulated and undeveloped for more than a century thereafter.

This town's surprising transformation came about after French Canadian windsurfing champion Jean Laporte arrived in search of unspoiled surfing spots. Today, the former village has grown to include some 75 restaurants, innumerable hotels, and a population of around 12,000 when you include tourists. Cabarete was originally popular with Quebecquois, but it now also lures lots of Germans as well as other Europeans.

Local residents have banded together to control development in the area, and, through their efforts, the lagoon has been granted official protection. Unlike many resort towns, locals have made a commitment here and are determined to avoid the mistakes that plague neighboring Sosúa.

Puerto Plata & the North

Tourism continues to grow at an exponential pace. A **Cabarete Race Week** has been instituted (the World Cup was held here in 1997), and the **Cabarete Kids Team**, a project that trains local Dominican youth to windsurf, was founded in 1991. It is also a center for mountain biking.

EVENTS: The **Cabarete Highwind Classic** is held in May. The **Chica La Costa** "bikini contest" generally takes place one Sat. in June as part of the **Cabarete Race Week** (information: Mike Braden, fax 571-3346; www.hispaniola.com/race; e-mail cabareterace@codetel.net.do). A **sandcastle contest** is also held annually, generally in June. A **jazz festival** is held in Dec.

GETTING HERE: Take a *público* from Puerto Plata or Sosúa. Determine the correct fare in advance and have change available. This *is* a tourist area! Charters are also available, but be sure to bargain.

by air: The same directions apply as with Puerto Plata. (See that section for information about internal air transport.) However, a taxi is DS$100 (or US$20 if you don't have *pesos*). While there is no direct bus service, you can come via Puerto Plata, Sosúa, or from the Samaná peninsula.

ACCOMMODATIONS: Hotels in this area continue to grow in number. More are being opened all the time, and you are certain to make your own discoveries. Hotels are listed from the direction of Sosúa.

Outside of town the 56-unit luxury **Coconut Palms** (☎ 571-1625, fax 571-1725) features one- and two-bedrooms with kitchens, bar, restaurants, tennis, and a pool.

Coming into town, you find the 196-rm., 100-acre **Punta Goleta Beach Resort** (☎ 571-0700/0705, 800-235-0695; Box 272, Puerto Plata) a few km. before the town; it caters to package tours. Its features include a pool, two tennis courts, two Jacuzzis, sauna, gym, jogging track, bicycle rental, and horseback riding. It has its own generator. Rooms have a/c and have balconies and satellite TVs.

The 20-rm. **Hotel Playa De Oro** (☎ 571-0880, fax 571-0871; e-mail playadeoro@cabarete.com; www.hispaniola.com/PlayaDe-Oro) faces the beach. Its restaurant has Indonesian dishes on the menu, and rooms have balconies. Facilities include licensed massage therapist, manicure, pedicure., diving lessons and PADI certification, snorkeling, beach and pool volleyball, shuffleboard, croquet, and horse shoes. Room rates are around US$60 s or d including tax. Meal plans are available.

The 20-unit luxury **Nanny Estate** (☎ 571-0744, fax 571-0655) is out of the center of town but close enough to walk back and forth. Its two-story, two-bedroom beach house condos are much more attractive inside than out. Each is individually owned and rented out. The first floor has a living room, toilet, and fully equipped kitchen; the second floor (accessed by a wonderful spiral staircase) has two comfortable bedrooms, one with a balcony, and a bath with two sinks and shower. The roof has a second open-air shower.

At prices ranging from US$75-100 pn, it is good value and comfortable, clean, and quiet. The grounds are immaculate, and a staircase leads down to the beach which is much more deserted than the in-town stretch. Tennis courts are on the premises, as are beach chairs and a medium-sized pool; babysitting service is available. The gourmet **Chez Cabarete** restaurant is right by the entrance.

Bahía de Arena (☎/fax:571-0523; www.hispaniola.com; e-mail sol.bonito@codetel.net.do) is another development near Nanny's. It has pool, Jacuzzi, and tennis court. Prices start at around $300 pw for a studio. Internet

reservations receive a 10% discount.

The AMHSA chain's **Estrella La Mar** (Santo Domingo ☎ 562 7475, fax 566 2436; 800-472-3985; www.worldhotel.com/AMHSA; e-mail amhsa@codetel.net.do) is an imposing and impressive all-inclusive which faces the beach.

The 21-rm. luxury **Hotel Condos Albatros** (☎ 571-0841, fax 571-0905; www.hispaniola.com/albatros; e-mail h.albatros@codetel.net.do) offers a pool, restaurant, babysitters, and other facilities. Rates start from around US$50 s or d not including tax. In Montreal ☎ or fax 514-674-4541.

With "jungle" gardens surrounding its 25 *bohio*-style bungalows and 31 rms., the **Hotel Kaoba** (☎/fax 571-0837; e-mail h.kaoba@codetel.net.do) has a pool, restaurant, and bar. It is on the other side of the road from the beach. Units are equipped with refrigerator, telephone, ceiling fan, sliding glass doors, balcony, and one double bed plus a single bed. Facilities include restaurant, bar, pool, Internet access. Rates start at around US$35 s or d including taxes and service.

town center hotels: The a/c **Villa Taina** (☎ 5710722, fax 571-0883; EDS-D 480, Box 02-5548, Miami, FL 33102;

www.hispaniola.com/VillaTaina; e-mail happy.cabarete@codetel.net.do) offers attractive a/c rooms and suites in a hotel designed with indigenous motifs. Its 11 rooms and four suites all have balcony or terrace, minibar and refrigerator. Breakfast buffet is US$5 pp; breakfast and dinner are US$18.00 pp.

The **Cita del Sol** (☎ 751-0720, fax 571-0795) has 48 one-bedroom units. Features include kitchenette, pool, and restaurant/bar. It stands across the road.

The 48-unit **Casa Laguna Hotel & Resort** (☎/fax 571-0725; www.cabarete.com/CasaLaguna; e-mail casalag@codetel.net.do) offers a pool, bar, and restaurant. While it continues to maintain an all-inclusive policy for some guests, Promotions Manager Delvaux is changing its focus to a "sports package hotel." Guests may windsurf for a day or so, and then move on to go horseback riding, dive, kayak, or pursue other activities. One activity is to be picked as a specialty and then others may be tried out. A bountiful breakfast buffet is served (strong coffee, tropical fruits, eggs cooked to your preference, etc.), and entertainment (even including Andean music) is offered. There is a pool, beauty salon, and business center. Attractive rooms have refrigerators and private patios. Currently a/c runs only at night, but there are plans to change this and make fans available.

The **Sun & Surf Hotel** (☎ 571-0522, fax 571-0573; www.cybercafe.com/sun&surf; e-mail sun.surf@cybercafe.com) has 48 rms.; each has satellite TV, phone, mini-bar, and balcony or terrace. A pool, access to the Cyber Café, and watersports are offered. Rates range from US$50-$135 to $80-$170, depending on the season and whether the room is standard or two- bedroom penthouse suite with kitchenette and Jacuzzi.

The **Hostal Maria Bonita** has a pool and offers rooms from around US$25.

The French Canadian-owned **Hostal de la Playa** (☎ 571-0930, fax 571-0931) is one of the oldest hotels here. It has 48 rms, pool, and rooms with phones and TVs. Rates are around US$45-$60.

El Pequeño Refugio Beach Hotel (☎/fax 571-0770; www.hispaniola.com/pequeno-refugio) has three buildings. The main building offers 29 beachside rooms with bath and shower. Rates start at around US$25 s or d. The "Pink House" (Beach House) has five rooms with either double beds or two single beds sharing two common bathrooms and one room with two beds and a private bathroom/shower. Rates start at around US$25 s or d. "Casa Verde" (The Surfer's lodge) has five rooms with two or three beds, each with two shared baths; rates start at US$10 s. Breakfast and dinner buffet spreads are offered in the beachside restaurant. In Germany, contact "WAVE-REISEN" (☎ 0202-771044. Fax 0202-771060) for a hotel and flight package.

eastern edge of town: The 24-rm. Swiss-run **Cabarete Beach Hotel** (☎ 751-0755/0832, fax 571-083; www.hispaniola.com; e-mail beach.hotel@cabarete.com) offers rooms with a/c or fan, two restaurants, a disco, and a gift shop. In Switzerland write Maria Bieri, Schoren 9, 3653 Oberhofen; ☎ 43-3040, or fax 43-5064. Rooms start from US$37 off-season and rise to around US$87 for the best room in-season.

The 171-rm. expensive all-inclusive **Camino del Sol** (☎ 571-0894/0893, fax 571-0892; e-mail camino.del.sol@codetel.net.do; www.hispaniola.com/camino-del-sol) faces the beach; it has Jacuzzis and a tennis court. A shuttle bus runs into town.

La Punta Apartamentos (☎ 571-0897, fax 571-0844; e-mail giampaolo@codetel.net.do; www.hispaniola.com/punta) are up a side road heading towards the ocean from the Caribe Surf; they charge around US$55 d, $70 t, and $82 quad. The apartments are one-bedroom units with closet, living

room, kitchen, refrigerator, two sofas, and bath.

Offering 24 fully equipped studios, one- and two-bedroom apartments, **Los Orquídeas de Cabarete** (☎ 571-0787, fax 571-0853) has a restaurant and a pool; it's toward the end of town and across the main road back. Its restaurant, **Basilic**, is reviewed below. Rates are around US$50 for a studio and US$80 for a two-bedroom.

Near Los Orquídeas, **Ali's Apartments** (☎ 571-0568, fax: 571-3346; dr@hispaniola.com, Cabarete) offer comfortable one-bedroom units with terrace/balcony. Rates are US$35 s or d.

Near Ali's, the **Hotel Residencia Dominicana** (☎/fax 571-0890; e-mail dr@hispaniola.com) offers 24 rooms; each has a sitting area, bath, small balcony; some units also have a small kitchenette and fridge. Three fully equipped apartments (kitchen-living room, separate bedroom and bathroom). Rates are from US$15 on up.

Casa Christa (☎/fax 571-0953; www.hispaniola.com/CasaChrista; e-mail l.costa@codetel.net.do) is an intimate resort with a mere four rooms. Facilities include restaurant, bar, pool, and garden. It's right near the beach. Weekly rates are around US$130 s, $190 d; meal-plans are also available.

other hotels: A beachside European-style condo hotel, luxury **Terrazas Las Palmas** (☎ 571-0780, fax 571-0781) has 78 rooms.

With 42 one- and two-bedroom units, **Villas del Atlántico** (☎ 571-0730, fax 571-0740) offers a restaurant, BBQ, bar, pool, and Jacuzzi.

Rooms at the intimate **Ocean Breeze Inn** (☎ 282-4026) include a poolside breakfast.

Set a few minutes from town by a complimentary shuttle, the 36-rm. **Hotel Bella Vista** (☎ 571-0759) features cafeteria, pool, and watersports.

At Vista del Caribe, 24-studio **Condos Val Maré** (☎ 571-3904, fax 571-3346) is 15 min. from the airport.

The **Hotel Caracol del Caribe** (☎ 571-0680, fax 571-0665; www.hispaniola.com/Caracol; e-mail caracol.caribe@codetel.net.do) has 46 one- and two-bedroom apartments with balconies, kitchen, and ceiling fans. They have a restaurant and offer a 10% discount for reservations made over the Internet. Rates are from around US$50 d.

Olas De Oro (www.hispaniola.com) is a beach house with tropical garden; it will hold up to five. Rates range from US$60 pd and rise according to the number of people. In Germany, ☎ (49) 7621-13635, fax (49) 7621-44616, or write Sabine Batt, P.O.

Box 1350 D-79603, Rheinfelden. In Switzerland, ☎ (41) 33-243-2725, fax (41) 33-243-2718, or write Beat Wyler, Trogenstraße 10, CH-3653, Oberhofen.

The luxury **Tropic Breeze Apartments** (☎ 571-0748, fax 571-3346) offer one- and two-person studios with large balconies and a three-bedroom house (available by the week or month).

Right on the beach, the **Cabarete Beach Studio Apartments** (☎ 571-0772, fax 571-3346) has rooms with kitchenettes; an attached restaurant serves German food. Rates are around US$30.

The 16-unit **Cabarete Palm Beach Condos** (☎ 571-0758, fax 571-0752; www.hispaniola.com; e-mail CPBCondos@codetel.net.do) has two-bedroom, two-bath apartments with kitchens and large patios. Rates are about US$160 for one to four occupants during the high season. Inexpensive rooms are also available.

The **First Class Resort** (☎ 571-0911, fax 571-0919) is on the main drag; it charges about US$50 d and has a pool.

others: Other hotels include the 30-rm. **California Beach Hotel** (☎ 571-0770), formerly the Auberge du Roi and in the town center, **Elsy's Apartamentos** (☎ 571-0717), **Hotel El Magnifico** (☎ 571-0686), C. del Cemeterio, **Hotel El Toro** (☎ 571-0878, C. Deportivos,

Windsurf Apartment Hotel (☎ 571-0710), **Guest House Casa Blanca** (☎ 571-0934), and **Villa Tranquila** (☎ 571-0751).

low-budget: Because it largely caters to affluent windsurfers, Cabarete isn't the best place for very low-budget accommodations. Plan on spending upwards of US$10 pp, pn. **El Bohío Taíno** (☎ 571-0683) offers rooms from US$10. The **Banana Boat Hotel** (☎ 771-0690) is another option. Check the bulletin boards in the center of town and ask around for other suggestions. Other possibilities include the Pink House and others mentioned above.

FOOD: With more 75 restaurants in the vicinity, the chances of going hungry here are nil! You can find everything from gourmet (see below) to little roadside stands frequented by poor Dominicans and economically minded Germans alike.

GOURMET DINING: Cabarete and Sosúa are, along with Santo Domingo, two places where you can find high-quality superbly prepared European cuisine. And, in Cabarete , the number of places that provide this is growing as the place expands.

An annex of the Los Orquídias de Cabarete hotel, **Basilic** opened its doors in 1997. One of the nation's finest gourmet restaurants, it offers charming and romantic dining on its covered veranda and open-air patio. Appetizers range from fried camembert in green shallot sauce to seafood shell to smoked salmon with capers. Salads may be ordered either to accompany the main course or as a side dish. Green salad with crab served with papaya pearls and ginger is a sample selection. Main courses include three types of linguini (RD$75-135), and a wider variety of seafood (RD$95-160) as well as other dishes. Deserts include frozen Grand Marnier soufflé (RD$45) and crêpe suzettes (RD$35). A wide selection of café flambées are available, as are wines (from RD$25/glass). This Quebequois-run establishment's *nouvelle*-French cuisine is prepared with homegrown spices in the company of garden-fresh vegetables. Vegetarian dishes are also on the menu, and there is an innovative children's menu as well. The restaurant is towards the E end of town and on the opposite side of the beach and back from the road. For reservations ☎ 571-0787.

Miro's on the Beach is another excellent place to dine. Run by ex-Torontonian Lydia Wazana, who arrived here originally to film a documentary on the jews of Sosúa, Miro's first gained distinction as a pizzeria. While it still serves pizza, the emphasis has shifted to such dishes as tricolored fetuccine, seafood linguine, *langostinas* in a pesto broth, and grilled snapper. Appetizers include tomato crab salad, grilled calamari, gazpacho, and spring rolls. A wide assortment of beverages are also available.

One of the finest gourmet bistros in the Republica, **El Viento** is the current home of Miro (of Miro's on the Beach). It was founded by Antonio, a North Italian who first came to the Dominican Republic in 1992 by fortuitous chance when he planned a Caribbean vacation, and the only flights open were to the Dominican Republic. He just happened to stop in Cabarete and fell in love with it! Appetizers include mussels gratin (US$5), seafoood bruschetta (US$5), marinated seafood on olive bread. Six different pasta dishes are offered including *al salmone*. Seafood entrées range from frutti di mare to steamed langostinos (small lobster) in white wine sauce. El Viento boasts an extensive wine list, and desserts include delights such as mango pie and chocolate mousse. The restaurant also offers Sunday specials for US$20.

The unpretentious **Casita de Don Alfredo** is run by a down-to-earth Frenchman from Strasbourg. "Papi del Playa," as he likes to be known, appears to have found his life's calling at long last. He merrily maneuvers large frying pans full of giant prawns and small lobsters (US$12.50), manipulating as many as four at a time (!) and serves them with bread or rice. His special French sauce includes white wine, spices, oil, and other goodies. Papi's fruit plates are truly legendary, and the other dishes are similarly up to par. He even offers aloe vera juice, crêpes, and shakes. It's quite an experience to sit at your table on the beach and have a frying pan full of giant shrimp delivered to you! He also has local musicians perform.

Leandro's is the only Dominican-owned restaurant.

L'Italiano serves authentic Italian cuisine including pizza baked in a brick oven; a buffet is served all day Fri.

Le Jasmin (☎ 571-0725) is set in the Casa Laguna Hotel; it offers nightly buffets, including lobster on Wed.

New Wave Café serves more than 40 baguettes and crêpes, fresh croissaints, and has a happy hour.

Island Pizzería Restaurant offers pizza and other dishes; it has a pool table.

The **Hotel Playa de Oro** serves Indonesian and other dishes.

Offering free transport to and from Cabarete, the **Chez Cabarete** (☎ 571-0744), at Nanny Estate, specializes in fondues.

In Villas del Atlantico, **El Taino** offers everything from pancakes stuffed with shrimp to mero filet and other delicacies.

Set in the Coconut Palms Resort, **The Palm Room** offers cuisine ranging from Creole to Cajun to continental.

Try **El Patio, Lucy Mar**, and the seafood restaurant **La Casa Del Pescador.**

Bar Restaurant Lucimar (☎ 571-0750) offers seafood and homemade pasta dishes.

☞*Traveler's Tip*

For a unique experience, dine at ***Blue Moon**, a restaurant in the hills run by a South African woman of East Indian ancestry. They serve authentic Indian food to groups. Ask around at Iguana Mama and other places.*

FOOD SHOPPING: In contrast to some years back when it was pretty much impossible to obtain anything, there is a much better selection these days. **La Casa Rosada** (☎ 571-0754) is open from 8-7. You will find the **Supermercado Albertico** down the street to the E and on the opposite side. The **Judith Mini Mart** is a bit farther. The **Argentina Bakery** is on the main road, as is another which is near the Casa Rosada. There are a variety of small colmados, mini marts, and fruit stands strung along the road at each end of town. **El Mercado del Mar**, to the W, sells frozen fish from around US$1.75/lb.

SHOPPING: CoTiCa sells amber and other crafts. It is next to La Criolla Plaza. There are also a number of other shops. For low priced goods go to Puerto Plata.

☞ *Traveler's Tip*

Conveniently located in the center of town, ***Iguana Mama*** *(☎ 571-0908, fax 571-0734; 800-849-4720; EPS-D#342, PO Box 02-55548, Miami, FL 33102; www.iguana-mama.com; e-mail iguana-mama@codetel.net.do) are open daily from 9-5; they will help you out and can also book tours for you. To be in the know, pick up a copy of* ***La Costa**, a free weekly that even has an entertainment schedule. It is written in Spanish as well as wonderfully iconoclastic English.*

ENTERTAINMENT: This village was once pretty dead at night. These days it's a lot livelier. In the best European fashion, many people make the evening meal their entertainment. And, this is one of the few places in the Caribbean where you can dine directly on the beach, place your feet on the sand, and enjoy gourmet dishes! It's a great way to spend an evening.

If you feel like socializing later, the liveliest spots are **Las Brisas,** the **Tiki Bar**, and **New Wave.** You'll find live bands here, and there is never a cover; all of these are along the main drag and in the village center. The **Hang Loose**

Bar, just down the road to the E, shows films in English, Dutch, and German. A schedule is posted outside.

Outside the main part of town to the W, **Buccanera** has a computerized dart board. Dominican males hang out at the wild **Happy Girls** bar on the edge of town towards Sosúa. It is one of those steamy and seamy places where you feel as if you are in on a movie set. There was a disco on the E outskirts of town, but it has closed down.

SERVICES: There is a Tricom office in the center of town; the Codetel office is farther up the highway toward Sosúa and about a 10 min. walk from the center of town. There are two perpetually broken pay phones in the center of town, and one functioning phone in front of Codetel.

The **Banco Commercial** offers one of the best exchange rates; there are a number of other places, including moneychangers.

The **CyberCafé** (☎ 571-0571, fax 571-0573; www.cyber-cafe.com; e-mail helpdesk@cybercafe.com) offers Internet access. For info on long-term rentals, employment, and other questions, visit the **All Services Public-Hall** across the street from the Hotel Casa Laguna. It is a set of covered bulletin boards with many useful postings.

Cabarete Sail & Board Repair will fix your board. All of the places listed under "Windsurfing" below also offer courses, renting boards and boogie boards.

Massage therapist Isabelle Prince is available through Los Orquídias de Cabarete (☎ 571-0787).

Alemania Tours (☎ 571-0505) offer the usual variety of tours.

Headquartered in Hotel Cabarete Surf, **For Fun** (☎ 224-3011, fax 571-0788) conducts trips on the Los Brazos, a small river running between mountainous bluffs by the road from Sabaneta to Moca. Guests swim and are offered a BBQ.

Motorbike and auto rentals are available from **Arcar** (☎/fax

---

Important Phone Numbers in Cabarete

American Airlines	542-5151
Caribe Tours	571-3808
Continental	541-2000
Emergency	911
Information	1411
Police	571-0810
Taxis	571-0767

571-1282; www.cabarete.com/
Arcar; e-mail arcar@cabarete.com);
Mauri (☎ 571-0660); **El Gitano**
(☎ 571-0951); and **Pivi** (☎ 571-
0653). Cars can be rented at
Puerto Plata airport. Call **Thrifty**
(☎ 586-0242); **Avis** (☎ 586-
0214); **National** (☎ 586-0285);
or **Nelly** (☎ 586-0505). For a **taxi,**
☎ 571-0767.

☞ *Traveler's Tip*
*La Costa (www.caribecom/la-
costa/costa.htm; e-mail l.costa@
codetel.net.do) is a free magazine
with articles in Spanish and effer-
vescent English. It is mainly of use
for its maps of Cabarete and Sosúa;
the ads are also informative.
Iguana Mama offers their services;
they will book any and all tours for
you. Farmacia San Rafael sells local and international papers.*

HEALTH: A 24-hr. clinic is run by
doctors speaking English, French,
German and Spanish. There are
pharmacies in town.

WINDSURFING: Although there
are few waves in summer, con-

☞ *Traveler's Tip*
*La Boca, a freshwater lagoon at the
end of the river and right across
from a turbulent sea, is a great
place for beginners to practice
windsurfing. It also is a fine swimming hole, but attracts hordes of
Dominicanos on Sundays.*

stant trade winds blow. In winter,
some days may be windless, but
on the days the wind does blow,
the waves are humongous. Expect to spend a hefty US$40 pd or
US$165 pw to rent a board. Here
are a few of the more prominent
companies:

The **Carib BIC Windsurfing
Center** is on the beach (☎ 571-
0640, fax 571-0649, 800-635-
1155/243-9675; EPS C-114
2898 NW, 79 Av., Miami, FL
33122; e-mail caribbic@code-
tel.net.do, caribic@tricom.net).
The Center provides private lock-
ers, showers, restrooms as well as
a club house. Attendants lug your
board to the water and fine-tune
the board before you take it out.
They are the only operation with

Windsurfing in Cabarete

- The two km of wide open bay provide both large and small waves.
- Average water temperature is 82°F (28°C).
- Trade winds prevail around midday.
- Skill level is rated from 1 to 6. The large shore break which arises during the winter months requires a skill level of 3 to 6.

a rescue boat. You need to reserve a specific type of board (when booking in advance), and you should bring your harness and booties. They have a gift and supply shop with loads of equipment. They are more expensive than their competition.

Happy Surf (☎/fax 571-0784) also offers lessons, as well as sales and rentals.

Managed by Udo Jansen, **Spin-Out Cabarete** (☎ 571-0805) is a high-tech windsurfing center.

Fanatic Board Center (☎/fax 571-7806; www.hispaniola.com/Fanatic) is another good place to go.

---

66 Reader's Comment

"We rigged up that morning and by midday we were attracting a lot of attention. By afternoon the whole town was on the beach looking at these strange 'mariposas.' They thought we were butterflies! Anyway, after two or three days of sailing, I had confirmed my suspicions that this was one of the biggest finds in the world and certainly the best sailboard destination in the Caribbean." – Jean Laporte remembering Dec. 9, 1984, the day when he first tested the waters of Cabarete with his sailboard.

BIKING: Iguana Mama (☎ 571-0908, fax 571-0734; 800-849-4720; EPS-D#342, PO Box 02-55548, Miami, FL 33102; www.iguana-mama.com; ˙ e-mail iguanamama@codetel.net.do) is definitely the place to go. They offer mountain bike tours and rentals; the office is in the center of Cabarete. The operation was started by lively and affable Tricia Thorndike de Surciel, a US citizen who first arrived in Cabarete for a vacation but ended up starting a business and raising a family. Tricia uses part of her profits to fund philanthropic efforts and always looks for ways to make tourism here benefit the locals.

In addition to guided mountain biking (with some 40 bikes on hand), Iguana Mama offers a three-day Pico Duarte hike, a seven-day Dominican Alps hike, and an eight-day Mountain Biking/Hiking/Rafting Adventure. Rates range from around US$40 to US$1,150 depending upon the trip.

HORSEBACK RIDING: Prices range from RD$200-600 depending upon the length of your ride. **Rancho Norte** (☎ 223-0660) is one good place to go horseback riding. **Rancho Montaña Verde** (☎ 571-0731; pager 1-200-6835) is in Gaspar Hernandez and offers both a full-moon party (held once a month) and a mountain and waterfall tour. **Rancho Sol y Mar** (☎ 571-0815), **Rancho Luisa** (☎ 310-4065), and **Rancho Gipsy** (☎ 545-0110) are others.

OTHER ACTIVITIES: A miniature golf course is on the main

The Jungle River Tour

A trip up the Río Yásica is one of the area's most stimulating excursions. Your host is Omar Mejia, a Dominican raised in the States. To get here, take a taxi (RD$60), *guagua* (RD$5), or *motoconcho* (RD$10) three miles (five km) from Cabarete to Islabon. It is right by the first bridge you come to. (Be sure to settle the fare beforehand.) Arriving on the site, you may visit with Omar's pet parrots, his cuddly tarantula, or his collection of boas and other nonpoisonous snakes; he extracts the snakes from a large clay urn to show you.

The tour itself is something of a misnomer because so little in the way of jungle remains. The voyage is really a chance to learn about the interaction of man with nature and its effects.

Before heading upriver, you duck under the bridge with the boat to see the nesting swallows. Heads of the adorable young birds poke out of their nests. By building the bridge, man has unwittingly provided them with shelter.

Heading upriver, you pass farm land and palm trees. Smooth-billed anis and snowy egrets are some of the birds you will see. The water hyacinth was first transplanted by a woman who admired its bloom. Because no animals consume it, it has proliferated to the point where it clogs the river. However, its roots do provide a nursery for fish and shrimp. Because tree cutting has been legally prohibited, there are still a number of local trees on and near the banks. Locals wait for a tree to fall before harvesting. The palm trees you see were brought to the area.

This trip is laced with anecdotes about local life. You see crab holes and perhaps a local lad toting the sticks used to harvest them. The crabs here dine on a poisonous local fruit (the *baga*) so that no one save the locals (who have developed an immunity) can eat them without developing a stomach ache. While the calabash tree provides gourds suitable for numerous utilitarian purposes, the breadfruit is a good source of nutrition. The first is a Caribbean native; the second, a S Pacific transplant.

The 2½-hr. tour costs RD$100. You make one stop for a walk along the bank and another to swim at La Boca. Bring plenty of sunscreen, snacks, a swimsuit and towel. A moonlight boat ride with a an all-you-can-eat-and-drink BBQ on the beach and a three-hr. lunch tour are also available. To reserve, ☎ 696-3253 or fax 571-3346.

street. A **kite shop** operates out of the Maestrale Bar and Snack at the La Punta Hotel towards the W end of town. They charge US$10/hr. for adult lessons and US$5/hr. for children. Kite rental runs from US$5-17/hr. The caverns may be visited, and there will probably be boat or kayak trips on the lagoon by the time of your visit to the area. For **Hobie Cat** rentals, ☎ 571-0848. Divers should contact the **Dolphin Dive Center** (☎ 571-0842).

DIVING: Dolphin Underwater Adventures (☎ 571-0842) is a five-star PADI center.

SHOPPING: On the main road, **Librería Daniela** (☎ 571-0775) sells books. **CoTiCa** is an amber and fossil shop next to La Criolla Plaza.

GOLF: Try the **Costa Azul Golf and Beach Resort** which features nine holes amidst 45 acres of greenery.

GASPAR HERNÁNDEZ: This town is mainly of note for its meat market. You can see carcasses hanging at shops that line the sides of the road. The area erupted in controversy in 1997 after some 125 families who been living on land in La Hermita in the Gaspar Hernández area, for over a half-century were evicted by some 200 Dominican soldiers. Family heads were arrested and held at the military barracks while their homes were destroyed by a power shovel. The citizens of Gaspar Hernández rose in protest and blockaded the road. A Spanish company is planning to build a tourism development here – thus the evictions.

The land is reportedly part of the "historic patrimony" of the Gaspar Hernández municipality, and no less than three presidential decrees have declared the land to be publicly owned. The Spanish company and the Instituto Agrario Dominicano have been locked in a dispute over the title in the courts. The head of the Instituto Agrario Dominicano has called the Spanish company's deed "toilet paper." President Leonel Fernandez has ordered an investigation.

Río San Juan

Located in the heart of the dairy industry, this typical small town has a sand-flea ridden beach and a lagoon. The best reasons to stay here are to savor the hospitality of the Bahía Blanca resort and to explore a small town.

SIGHTS: The town's **Grí Grí Lagoon** is an extremely popular tourist excursion. You'll find boats (labeled "Brugal" of course!) which will take you into the lagoon. If chartering your own boat, expect to spend around US$24 per boatload; each boat can hold 20. Reservations are unnecessary. If you are on your own,

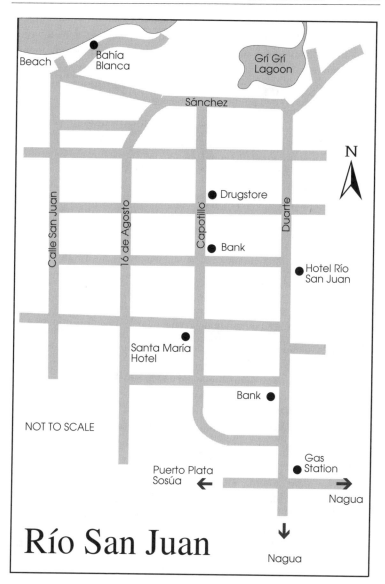

Río San Juan

you will have to bargain fero-ciously.

Boarding the boat, you spend a pleasant hour in the lagoon as you cruise past mangroves alive with cattle egrets, Dominican fisherboys, *grí grí* trees, flocks of seabirds, and bizarrely shaped rocks. The tour is highlighted by a visit to the **Cueva de las Golon-drinas**, a cave containing swal-lows. Located beyond the river's mouth and several miles along the rocky coast, the cave was cre-ated by an 1846 rockslide. Tidal conditions have to be right for you to enter. The prettiest part of the trip comes when you pass a lovely swimming hole.

NEARBY BEACHES: Caleton and Playa Grande are also nearby. Playa la Preciosa lies at the headland of Parque Nacional Cabo Francés Viejo, as does Playa El Breton; Playa Diamante and Playa Boba are farther on. **La Entrada** is another unspoiled beach in the area. Another attraction is la **Virgen de la Cueva**, a rock formation in a cave just off the road which is said to resemble the Virgin Mary.

PRACTICALITIES: On the main street, family-run 38-rm. **Río San Juan Hotel** (☎ 589-2379/2211) resembles a country inn; it has a restaurant, bar, lounge, tennis court, pool, nightclub, and disco. They can also arrange the boat trip. In Santo Domingo, ☎ 567-3325.

Set right on a bluff overlooking the sea, the **Bahía Blanca** (☎ 589-2562/2563, fax 589-2528), Gaston F. Deligne, is another alternative. The ambitious project of Quebec-born Lise Peineau, it has attractively furnished rooms. Its restaurant has both good food and ambience. People seem to like it here.

Also try the less expensive **San José** and **Santa Clara** hotels. Less expensive still are the **San Martín** and the **Caridad**. There are a few restaurants along the

street that has the Río San Juan Hotel. The otherwise attractive **Cheo's Café Bar** should be boycotted because it serves sea turtles on the menu.

DIVING: Check out **Grí Grí Dives** (☎/fax 589-2671).

Playa Grande

The recently established resort area of Playa Grande is 26 miles (60 km) to the W of Puerta Plata and an hour's drive from the international airport. Scheduled facilities at this mile-long beach include mammoth luxury villa hotels, apartment hotels, tennis courts, horseback riding stables, and an 18-hole, US$3.2 million dollar golf course.

The **Caribbean Village Playa Grande** is an Allegro Resort.

A US$3.2 million 18-hole golf course designed by Robert Trent Jone will be the only course in the world with 10 tees overlooking the sea.

Nearby are the **lighthouse** at Cabo Frances Viejo and the cliffs and bay of **Cabo Breton**, an area containing vacation homes of the elite, some of which are for rent.

The **Costa Verde Hotel** (☎ 476-8444, fax 476-8450) offers 94 rms. with pool, restaurant, disco, and boutique.

Three miles (five km) to the E of Playa Grande near Abreu, **Eden Bay** (☎ 809-582-6565, 800-366-3508; EPS-D-232, Box 02-5548,

Miami, FL 33102; www.edenbay-resort.com; e-mail edenbay.resort@codetel.net.do) is an all-inclusive naturist (nudist) resort set on 123 acres and includes 190 rooms and cottages, four tennis courts, volleyball, ocean kayaking, banana boats, shuffleboard, pool, fitness center, two Jacuzzis, horseback riding, snorkeling, and diving. There's not much by way of a beach. Rates run from around US$214 d.

Amazonas 2 is a "wildlife reserve" and butterfly farm of sorts. It lies right off the main highway near Eden Bay.

Nagua

The beach-lined fishing village of Nagua stands on the shores of the Bahia Escocesa. Get here before it's developed! It takes three buses and some 3½ hrs. to get here from Puerto Plata or 3½ hrs. from Santo Domingo. If changing buses here, the two terminals are in different locations so you may need to take a *motoconcho*; ask your driver.

Stay at low-budget **Hotel San Carlo**s (US$7 with bath, fan and power plant), **Hotel Familiar** (US$8, may not have electricity) or **Hotel Corazón de Jesús**. One

reader recommends **Hotel Mi Bahia**, toward the W end of town. It charges around US$10 for a room with a bath. At C. Duarte 81-A (the street running parallel to the ocean), friendly and unpretentious **La Escocesa** offers seafood, delicious fruit juices, and other local specialties.

Outside of town on the way to Río San Juan are **Las Brisas** and **Casa Blanca**.

In **Cabrera**, you can stay at the **Hostal Catalina**, the **Hotel Julissa** (☎ 589-6355), or the **Hotel Naranjo. Hotel Condo La Palmeral** (☎ 437-8389) is also here.

Cotui, to the SW, is one of the island's oldest towns, dating from the 16th century. It has a zinc mine. You may stay at the **Central, Eden** or at **El Rancho Del Lago** (☎ 696-0045), a comfortable hotel with horseback riding, French restaurant, and other facilities. It costs around US$60 d.

Samaná Peninsula

This beautiful 30-mile (48-km) peninsula, 75 miles (120 km) NE of Santo Domingo, is characterized by heavy rainfall and by a range of lush, forested hills, as well as coconut and banana plantations. Houses of locals are painted in pink and purple pastel washes, and fishermen in the bay cast for snapper from flat-bottomed boats. There are a wealth of activities for the adventurous here. You can snorkel at Cayo de Lavantado in Samaná Bay, at Rincón Bay, and at other locations.

FAUNA: Along the coast, you can expect to see wood storks, brown boobies, and white-tailed tropic birds. Plovers, rails, sandpipers, roseate spoonbills, terns, purple gallinules, and ibises are often found in marshy areas near the beaches.

whale watching: Whales may be seen along the mouth of the Samaná Bay during Jan. to late Feb. There are numerous trips available (see *tours*). Environmentalists are pushing to have the area declared an "environmental reserve."

A humpback whale sanctuary, **Sanctuario de Ballenas Jorobadas del Banco de la Plata**, lies 50 miles (80 km) from the coast, due N of Cabrera. This "Silver Bank," a 100-ft.-deep (30-m) lagoon, attracts some 2,000 to 4,000 migrating humpbacks from late Dec. to early March. Giving birth to their offspring here, the young are nurtured before taking off together for points unknown in the N Altantic. Sea turtles also congregate here. Scientists may make trips out here during the mating season.

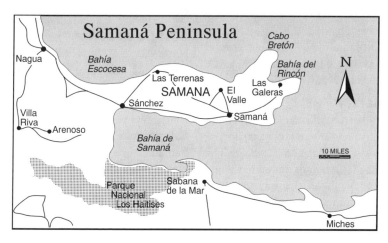

For information on joining the expeditions – which take seven-12 hrs. each way – contact the National Parks Office in Santo Domingo (☎ 682-7628), the Centro de Investigaciones de Biología Marina (CIBINA) at the University of Santo Domingo (☎ 668-8633), or the Fundación Dominicana Pro-Investigación y Conservación de los Recursos Marinos, Inc. (MAMMA) at Av. Anacoana No. 77, Apdo. C-4 or at Apdo. 21449 in Santo Domingo. MAMMA can assist in planning trips from Puerto Plata and Samaná.

ENVIRONMENT: As elsewhere, this peninsula has its share of environmental problems. The laws on the books are good, the enforcement lax. Environmentalists are pushing for more protection, both for the marine environment and for the mangroves. Although tourism is comparatively undeveloped here, it has caused its share of problems. Tourists craving exotic cuisine have ensured the extinction of the manatee in the area around Las Terrenas, and the local turtle appears ready to follow.

GETTING HERE: It's a 4½-hr. trip from Santo Domingo to Samaná via San Francisco de Macorís, Nagua, and Sánchez. The views going up to Sánchez are knockout; on the way you pass the home of a rich Dominican whose estate walls appear to go on forever. Take a bus from Caribe Tours.

The alternative is to take a bus or *público* to San Pedro de Macorís and then another to Sabana La Mar (stay at low-budget Hotel Sabana la Mar), and then cross by one of two often crowded boats per day (11 and 5; return at 9 and 3) from Sabana to Samaná. You should note that black marketeers have been known to buy up tickets on this route and motorcyclists have been ripped off by boatmen who load the bike from the ferry. (To board or land from Sabana la Mar, you will need to transfer to and from a smaller boat).

A 25-min. flight from Santo Domingo, brings you to out-of-the-way Arroyo Barril airport. The airport is planned for expansion into an "international" one, but a report has found 17 reasons why it is unsuitable. The government maintains that it will be open in 1998 or so, so time will tell.

GETTING AROUND: The entire peninsula can be explored by boat, but the local boatmen charge an arm, a leg, and a rudder. Not all the roads are paved. In the peninsula's NE, Rincón Bay can be reached by road from Samaná town, as can Limón village in the peninsula's center. Las Terrenas and Portillo beaches can be reached by paved road from Sánchez or by a much worse road from Limón. A road also extends to the up-and-coming resort village of Las Galeras, and public transport leaves from the market in Samaná for it and all other destinations.

Santa Bárbara de Samaná

Santa Bárbara de Samaná, Samaná's main town, is located on the peninsula's S side, overlooking a bay speckled with tiny islands. Big things were planned here, but they never developed. Once-beautiful narrow streets overhung by wrought-iron balconies were destroyed under Balaguer's first 12 years and replaced with ugly concrete structures and broad asphalt boulevards. These replacements were more sanitary but less atmospheric. Used primarily by pedestrians and *motoconchos*, the main street is a four-lane highway bordering the waterfront.

Still remaining is the small evangelist "*churcha*." A former English country church, it was shipped to Samaná and reassembled in 1901 by African Methodist ex-slaves from the US. This congregation was adopted by Wesleyan Methodist missionaries from the Turks and Caicos in 1837 after its minister passed away. Today it serves as the Dominican Evangelical Church. All in all, there's very little reason to visit the town except to use it as a base for visiting the peninsula's beaches by car.

HISTORY: On Jan. 12, 1493, Columbus is claimed to have arrived here and battled the Ciguayos; he named the bay the Golfo de las Flechas (the Gulf of Arrows). The remains of his fort still stand. The town itself was founded in 1756 by Gov. Francisco Rubio Peñaranda and populated by families brought from the Canary Islands to stave off conquest by French buccaneers from Tortuga, an island off Haiti's N coast. After Haitian independence, fleeing French planters arrived with their slaves. English-speaking blacks are a prominent if surprising feature of the town. There are conflicting stories as to how they got here. One maintains that Samaná was founded during the 1824 Haitian occupation when the *Turtle Dove*, a sloop carrying escaped American slaves wrecked in Samaná Bay. Swimming ashore, they founded a settlement. Another maintains that Haiti's leader at the time, Jean Pierre Boyer, made contact with abolitionist groups in Philadelphia and financed passage and resettlement of as many as they could send down.

Of the 5-6,000 sent, some died, while others were unable to adapt. Some 2,000 chose to remain. Under Trujillo, anyone

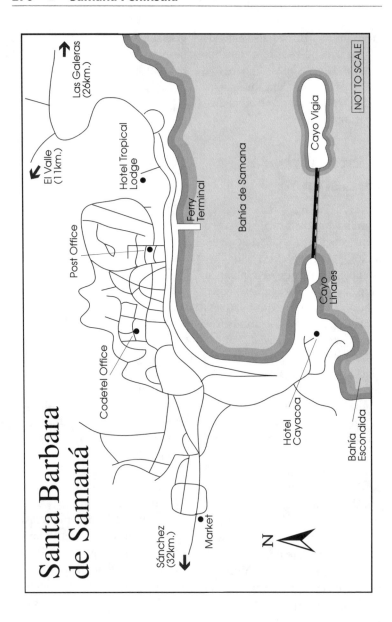

Santa Barbara de Samaná

Las Galeras (26km.)

El Valle (11km.)

Hotel Tropical Lodge

Post Office

Ferry Terminal

Bahía de Samana

Cayo Vigía

NOT TO SCALE

Codetel Office

Cayo Linares

Hotel Cayacoa

Bahía Escondida

Sánchez (32km.)

Market

N

heard speaking English publicly was beaten, and today all are bilingual. In any case, the language and culture of America's Old South are still very much intact here, and Browns, Joneses, Kings, Smiths, and Greens abound. They still have a rich cultural tradition – including tales of werewolves and vampires – although this is fading. In the 1870s, the town and the entire peninsula narrowly escaped annexation by the US.

THINGS TO DO: Samaná has a dramatic backdrop, but the town isn't what you would call wildly exciting. Given the extensive urban renewal, it lacks atmosphere, and persistent touts can make life unpleasant. A high bridge runs from a point near the town to an offshore island, where a restaurant was planned but never constructed. The most interesting thing to do is to walk out along the **"bridge to nowhere."** There are actually a chain of three connecting small islands. As you can see, it would've been quite a walk to dinner if the restaurant had actually been constructed. The structure might be considered a Zen statement on the futility of life or a comment on the insanity of unplanned development. In any case, there is definitely nothing like it anywhere else in the world. Allow an hour for the walk both ways. The entrance is on the grounds of the Hotel Cayacoa. It looks private but is not.

Also in the vicinity, but farther away from town at the bottom of the hill, is a small beach at **Puerto Escondido**. If you have your own wheels (or rent a scooter or bike) the town can be used as a base. A **waterfall** is on the Río Coco, a 15 min. walk from Km 7. Be sure to keep walking past the brook: it's not the waterfall! Finally, you can also visit Cayo Levantado or whale watch (see below).

ACCOMMODATIONS: One unfortunate aspect of town are the hordes of otherwise unemployed English-speaking young gentlemen who wish to show you a hotel and collect a commission. The best way to defeat them is to feign deafness and ignore them.

ultra-luxury resorts: Formerly named the Bahía Beach Resort and now run by Occidental Hotels, the 70-unit all-inclusive **Hotel Cayacoa Beach** (☎ 538-3131/3136, fax 538-2985) is dramatically set on a hill overlooking the bay. Rooms have cable TV, fan and a/c. It has a large garden, and shuttle service is provided to Cayo Levantado. Rates run around US$110 s, 190 d.

Newly opened in 1992 and also now an Occidental hotel, the all-inclusive **Hotel Gran Bahía** (☎ 538-3111, fax 538-2764) is a 110-rm a/c all-inclusive ultra-luxury resort some five miles (eight km) E of town. It has a small beach, two tennis courts, horseback riding, and a nine-hole golf course. Rates are around US$125 s, US$200 d.

Out on Cayo Levantado, Occidental Hotels also runs the all-inclusive **Hotel Cayo Levantado** (☎ 538-3141, fax 538-2985). It has a main building with 13 rms. (including four jr. suites), and nine three- and four-bedroom "villages" with a/c and satellite TVs. Rates are around US$125 s, US$200 d.

The Occidental Hotels may be reached in North America and Canada (☎ 506-877-3160, 800-843-3311, fax 506-877-3160), in Belgium (☎ 30-235-0373, 09800-14596), in Denmark (☎ 8030 1031, 45 87 00 08, fax 45 87 22 49/93 21 41), in France (☎ 05 00 11, 4071 2121, fax 4071 2131), in Germany (☎ 0180-231 21 21, 06151-905760, fax 06151-905750), in Ireland (01 6605 000, fax 01 6605 540), and in Switzerland (☎ 155 5583, 715 1616, fax 715 5583).

inexpensive: The French-run 12-rm **Hotel Tropical Lodge** (☎ 538-2480, fax 538-2046), charges around US$40. It's right in town and overlooks the bay. It has a library of books in French and is probably the best bet for comfort if you want to stay in town.

On the way out of town and across from Captain Morgan's, family-run **King's** (☎ 538-2352) offers rooms with fan and bath from US$15.

At Santa Bárbara and Colón, the inexpensive and hospitable **Nilka** (☎ 583-2245) has 10 rooms. Only the ones upstairs have a/c. The 14-rm. Hotel **Cotubanama** (☎ 538-2534) has rooms fro around US$30 d.

There are a number of others, including **Hotel Kiko** (☎ 588-2565), C. La Logia 4; **Hotel Docia**, C. Santa Barbara; or the **Casa de Huéspedes Tete de Casado**, C. Duarte 4. Owned by a teacher, it is good value if you bargain.

low-budget: There's really nothing basic here except the **Fortuna**, which is next to King's and is also rented short-time!

If you want to stay out of town, **La Tambora** (☎ 538-2066) is some five miles (eight km) in the direction of Las Galeras. It charges US$25 with breakfast for its seven rms. A bungalow is available for long-term rental.

FOOD: Typical dishes here include *pescado con coco* (fish cooked in coconut milk), gingerbread, and Johnnycakes. Heading E along the Malecón, you come to **La Hacienda**. Next, **Le Café de Paris** offers crêpes, pizza, and cocktails. Set on the corner of Parque Central, **La Mata Rosada**

and **Camilo** have local food. Others include **Chino's, El Nautico, Grant's American Café**, and **Don Juan**.

ENTERTAINMENT AND BARS: Yachtie types hang at **L'Hacienda. La Lobita, El Coco**, and the **Naomi Nightclub** are the two discos. The latter is on the waterfront.

SERVICES: Banco La Comercio is one place to change money. There are three **gas stations;** one is along the dock and two are at the entrance to town. A **post office** is behind the Camilo just off the Parque Central. Open from 8 AM to 10 PM daily, **Codetel** is at C. Santa Bárbara 6. **Cars** may be rented from **J.A. Rent-A-Car** and **Estilo Rent-A-Car**. Rent **motorbikes** from **Xamana Rent A Motor** (☎ 538-2556/2066), Av. Malecón 3 and 5. There are several other outlets. CEBSE (☎ 538-2042) is the most active environmental organization.

TOURS: Canadian Kim Beddall, a local legend, runs **Victoria Marine** (☎ 538-2494, fax 538-2545, Box 53-2, Samaná), a tour agency that conducts the best whale watching trips. Kim positively venerates the whales, and, as a marine biologist, is a highly informative guide. If you are here at the right time of year, this is an experience you should not to miss. **note:** Many of the local boat operators abuse the whales.

Word of this has gotten out among German visitors, and tour participants dropped from 30,000 in 1996 to 18,000 in 1997.

FESTIVALS: The *bambúla* and the mildly erotic *chivo florete*, traditional dances, may be seen at the local festivals such as the *fiestas patronales* of Santa Bárbara held on Dec. 4 and the ones for St. Raphael on Oct. 24. The *oli oli* is a men's dance seen in *carnavál* parades.

FROM SAMANÁ: *Caribe Tours* departs from its offices on the Malecón for Santo Domingo four times daily. A direct road between Samaná and El Limón has been built; it continues on to Las Terrenas and Sanchez. Roads also lead to Las Galeras on the coast (see below). A ferry runs to and from Sabana La Mar. (See *from Samaná Peninsula* at the end of this section for information on the ferry and other options).

Vicinity of Santa Bárbara de Samaná

Cayo Levantado

This is the most popular of the offshore islands and has a white sand beach. The island is suffering from the impact of pollution. It is often overcrowded with visitors. If you must go, the best time

Whale Watching

Whale watching is now a major source of revenue for the area. About 15,000 visitors turned out in 1995 to see some of the 1,000 or more humpbacks that visit the bay during their breeding season from mid-Jan. to mid-March. Be sure to obain a copy of Ken De Pree's booklet *Whales of Samaná*. Highly informative, it also makes a fine souvenir.

Although the official reserve is at Silver Bank (see page 267), this requires a grueling 24-hr. journey. The whales can easily be seen just 20 min. offshore.

is on weekdays during the off-season.

PRACTICALITIES: The cheapest way to arrive is by public boat from the Samaná dock. The other alternative is to take a *público* from town to the point where Transportes José and Simi Báez (also fishing, whale spotting) run boats to the island (RD$100 pp RT; min. 6) . They'll pick you up later. Bring your own food and drink. Planned excursions cost US$40 pd and up. Lunch is served by vendors, but is not especially cheap. Watch out if purchasing jewelry here; peddlars are notorious for selling fakes. Hotel accommodation is at the luxurious **Cayo Levantado Beach Hotel** (☎ 221-2131, fax 532-5306).

Sánchez

Once a prosperous seaport, this little town has 19th-century architecture and basic accommodations. It once had the nation's only railroad, which ran from San Francisco de Macorís and La Vega. This is the first town visitors will come to upon entering the peninsula. If you should need or wish to stay here, try **Hotel Restaurant La Costa**, ☎ 552-7275, C. Libertad 44 (doors lock at 10!); it has rooms with noisy a/c or fans. You may also try the less expensive **Hotel La Gran Parada** as well as **Hotel La Patria**, C. San Tome. Another alternative is to take a room in the aging yellow Victorian house. Eat at **Restaurant Las Malvinas** or other bistros.

Playa El Rincón

A 3,500-bed hotel is planned for this beach, one of the most glorious in the Republica. It will probably open sometime around the turn of the century. Currently, there is only a small restaurant here.

Playa Las Galeras

The half-mile beach of Las Galeras is in a lovely setting at the E end of the Samaná peninsula. There's no electricity or telephone here – only cellular lines and privately owned generators. Gone are the days when the village had only two hotels and a couple of restaurants. These days, Las Galeras is booming – not like Las Terrenas, but things are definitely picking up.

GETTING HERE: Driving, it's a straight shot from Samaná town. There are plenty of sights along the way. Otherwise, go to the market and wait for a *guagua* (US$1.40; one hr.), which will take you when it fills up.

Las Galeras is set at the end of a scenic road some 16 miles (26 km) from Samaná town. The paved road rises and falls along the coast. En route, you will pass coconut plantations, small beaches with crashing surf, fruiting papaya and tamarind trees, and limestone outcrops rising just as they do on the islands of Los Haitises. You might see a man holding two chickens on a donkey laden with netting stuffed with coconuts, a white stuffed toy bear jabbed into a barbed wire fence, or old men slapping dominoes on a table.

FOOD AND ACCOMMODATIONS: The award for the most spectacular design goes to the **Villa Serena** (☎ 696-0065, fax 538-2545; Apdo. 51-1, Samaná), one of the world's most impressive intimate luxury hotels. As you enter the main lobby, there is a breathtaking view of the grounds and the sea. A small palm-tree island lies out in the distance. You may play board games in the expansive lounge area or just sit and take in the view. Each room of this 11-rm. two-storey hotel has its own special design. Attractive prints, fabrics, and other objects from all over the world give them distinctive charm. Each large room has an overhead fan and most have a/c as well. Rooms have attractive balconies edged by tropical foliage. The staff are quite friendly and management is astoundingly multilingual. Your fellow guests will be German, French, and Quebecquois.

Villa Serena's restaurant provides gourmet meals. Breakfast offers your choice of eggs, French toast, juice, cheese plate, fruit plate, coffee and tea. You can choose the ingredients of your omelette.

The hotel has a small pool, and, while the hotel's property terminates in a rocky escarpment, you will find a small pure white sand beach to the R of the hotel's shoreline. The main beach is just a few min. walk away. Bikes and snorkeling equipment are for rent. Rates are around US$90 s, US$100 d, and US$135 t. Rates include breakfast; dinner plans are available at extra charge.

Samaná Peninsula

Right next to the hotel is the **Villa Lotus**, a two-rm. hotel run by a Swiss woman who is a painter. It has a great design and attractive backyard.

The next hotel you come to is the friendly German-owned and -run **Hotel Moorea Beach** (☎ 696-0424, reservations 538-2545, fax 696-0425). It has a breezy lobby/sitting area and attractive rooms with overhead fans.

They charge around US$35 s, US$50 with breakfast. Right next door is a pharmacy that has never opened and next to that is the **Marinique**, a set of slightly deteriorating one-rm. bungalows that rent for US$18.50 pn with a reduction to US$14 for three nights or more.

On the main road, the **Paradiso Bungalows** (US$18.50) are across from the **Pizzeria 2-10**, an Italian-run low-key restaurant which offers good food and large portions at reasonable prices. It is a local hangout, with a daily special. **Chez Denise**, which serves inexpensive French and other dishes, is right next door. Next to the Supermercado De Todo, **Un Poco** is run by an Italian. **Dilsa Rent A House** (fax 538-2545) is run by Dilsa Batista, who can can set you up with a house for four for around US$60 pn.

Across the road are the **Club Bonito** (☎/fax 696-0082, fax 538-2545; www.club-bonito,com;

e-mail glosos@pop.sannet.or.jp) and **Todo Blanco**. Both are under the same management (although this may change in a few years), and both charge the same: US$80 s, US$96 d for a/c rooms; rooms with fans only are around US$50. A total of 14 rms. are available, as is a restaurant. Of all the hotels it has the prime location, facing directly on the beach.

The next beach you come to (and one of the most beautiful on the entire peninsula) hosts the all-inclusive **Cala Blanca Beach Resort** (☎ 682-8913/6809, 223-0035, fax 682-8338). It offers 50 rooms including junior suites, restaurant, bars, disco, gift. shop, baby sitting, and horsback riding. Rates are around US$115 d all-inclusive, probably less if you get a package.

The Bancrofts (fax 538-2545), a retired English couple with stories galore to tell, reside in a magnificent home at the end of the beach. They have one room downstairs to rent out for US$18.50. If you are interested in politics, health issues, and the like, you will be taken in and possibly taken out sailing as well.

Up the main road, Italian-run **Villa Marina** makes good pasta dishes; they're open for dinner. They also have a bed and breakfast: around US$20 s or d.

Rancho Thikis (☎ 538-2044) is a horseback riding center and has five rooms priced at around

US$60 d with part-board. It is near the entrance to the village so it is not convenient for going to the beach.

FOOD SHOPPING: There are a few *colmados* around, notably **Super Colmado La Rubía** on the main road opposite the Salsa Bar. The **Supermercado De Todo Un Poco** is run by an Italian. It sells ice-cold beers, cheeses, and other delights. There are some other small restaurants, including the **Posada Las Galeras**. Meals are also served by local women at kiosks in front of the beach; they generally ask inflated prices for meals from tourists.

ENTERTAINMENT: Nights tend towards the quiet side. There's a billiard table in **Club Bonito**. The **Salsa Bar** is open for dancing after 9 PM. Cockfights are held in the **Gallera de Las Galleras** from 3-7:30 PM every Thursday.

SERVICES: If you have a phone card, you can use the pay phone in front of the Cala Blanca to make calls.

Cala Blanca rents windsurfing equipment and you may use their tennis courts.

There are a few souvenir shops around including **Artesania Acosta** and **Cocorico**. Both are on the main road.

EXCURSIONS: Dive Samaná offers a variety of dives (including Cabo Cabron) for US$35 on up. They also offer PADI courses.

Their office is across from the Hotel Bonito entrance. **Guayacan Tours** is headquartered in Hotel Bonito; they offer beach excursions at prices higher than charged by the local fishermen.

Near Villa Marina on the main road, **Rancho Thikis** (☎ 538-2044) offers horseback riding trips; it has been recommended by residents. You can also go fishing with local boats.

THE BEACHES: Las Galeras beach is fine, but **Cala Blanca** beach is truly spectacular: this white sand beach has calm blue-green water and swaying palms. The water is so still because the offlying reef breaks the waves.

There are a number of other beaches in the area which are more difficult to reach. To the E, **Playa Madama** is a lovely small beach ridged by rocks and crags. Taino petroglyphs can be found in some of the caves, and the water is good for snorkeling, You can go there by boat (RD$300 pp), horse (RD$350 pp), or on foot (one hr).

Playa Colorado is a lovely beach set amidst a verdant landscape. You can get there by boat (RD$400/boat), horse (RD$450 pp), or on foot (3½ hrs).

Playa Rincón. This deserted beach is 20 min. from Galeras by boat (RD$500 pp) or 40 min. by jeep along a rough track. Cliffs of the 2,000-ft.-high (600-m) Cape Cabrón flank its rear. One of the nation's most beautiful beaches, it will be the site of a huge hotel with thousands of rooms. The funding is coming from Spain. There is a small restaurant open here now. The turnoff is from the main road to Las Galeras.

Playa El Valle is a large, long beach with a small restaurant on it. Travel here is by boat (RD$400 pp) or by jeep (1½ hrs.)

Limón

This town on the river of the same name has a wonderful 165-ft. waterfall, **La Cascada**, which was declared a natural monument in 1996. To get a guide for the falls and to rent horses, inquire at the navy guard post in Limón or visit the **Casa Bercam** in the village, where you'll find a bar and restaurant run by a help-

---

66 Reader's Comment

"The El Limón Falls were indeed spectacular, but not nearly as memorable as the adventure getting there. We rode on a motoconcho from Las Terrenas for half an hour and then on a mule down the side of a mountain for at least another half-hour. There had been a lot of rain and at times the mules were up to their knees in mud and several times lost their footing. I recommend avoiding this trip if it has been wet, and trying to find a well-established guide if you do decide to go." – C.J., Toronto

---

ful Spanish expat; he has horses for rent. It stands perpendicular to the police station. The trip takes an hour along a steep one-mile trail. You'll have to wade two rivers; the water comes up to your knees. Needless to say, it's not an easy trip, and it's not advisable to bring children.

Pura Vida (cellular ☎ 707-7221, fax 240-6070) offers canyoning trips to the waterfall from Las Terrenas.

Las Terrenas

This long stretch of the N coast offers some of the nation's finest beaches. At low tide you can walk right out to the coral reefs. Although it lacks Sosúa's glamour, it also has less noise and hassle. The area is becoming more and more developed, but it still has the informality of a small village. These days you'll see idiots out on jet skis and tooling down the beach with all terrain vehicles. But, with a bit of effort, you can get away from all of this: Las Terrenas remains highly recommended as a place to go and relax. There are a large number of Swiss and French in the area, so if you speak the language, you'll feel right at home.

Secluded Playa Bonita is situated around the headland to the W, and the all-inclusive resort of El Portillo (with an airstrip) lies to the E. Humpbacked whales

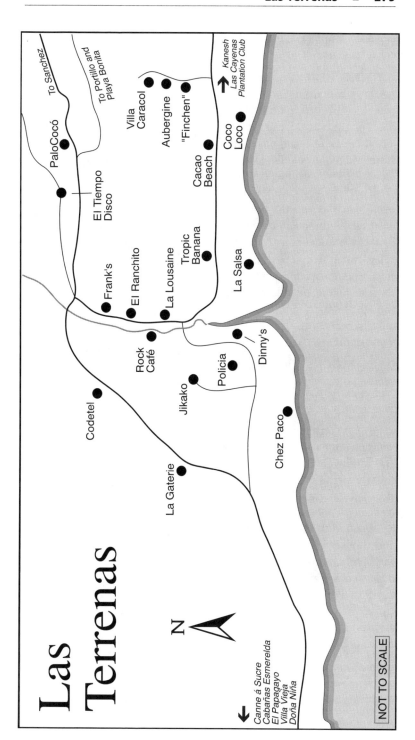

can sometimes be spotted off the coast in season.

GETTING HERE: A number of *carreras* run from Sánchez. Expect to wait a long time for the back of the pickup truck to fill. The 11-mile (17-km) paved road from Sánchez offers fantastic views – passing rolling hills covered with palms and marvelous overlooks – as you rise and then descend. A new direct road to Samaná is under construction.

by car: It would be difficult to find a better use for a rental car than to take it on this road. Although there are no gas stations after Sánchez until Las Terrenas, some homes sell it in gallon jugs.

ORIENTATION: The layout is pretty simple. A main road stretches all the way from Sánchez to Limón via Portillo. As you enter Las Terrenas, a side road leads off left to Punta Bonita, several km away. Pickup trucks terminate at the end of the village; the road straight ahead continues to Portillo. A branched loop road heads off to the L; the bulk of the guesthouses are down here along the beach and on the way. A few others are toward Portillo. As you head to Portillo, the beach becomes more and more beautiful and less frequented.

GETTING AROUND: You can generally get everywhere on foot, and there are no safety problems at present. *Motoconchos* charge

five *pesos* (40¢) during the day and 10 *pesos* (80¢) at night. Locals are charged only three pesos. These guys work so hard and so late because they've bought the bikes on credit and have to make payments or face repossession.

ACCOMMODATIONS ON THE MAIN ROAD: Attractive **Palococo** (☎ 240-6068, fax 240-6151) charges from around US$40 d. It has a pool and Jacuzzi. Dinners at its international restaurant are around US$12. **Dinnys** has plain but breezy rooms near the sea for around US$9.

ACCOMMODATIONS ON THE BEACH: A number of small hotels/guest houses, including **Louisiane**, are off the loop road and near the beach. Most guesthouses and hotels have backup generators; public electrical power is a recent development here.

Hotel Tropic Banana (☎ 240-6110, fax 240-6112; Apdo. 25, Sánchez, Samaná) has a pool and attractive rooms from around US$30 on up. It is popular with French and Spanish visitors and has a superb restaurant. In Montreal, Canada, ☎ 819-546-7010 or fax 819-564-8191.

With 190 rooms, **Cacao Beach** (☎ 240-6000) is the largest hotel and seems larger than the village. ☎ 565-2097 in Santo Domingo for information.

Off the main road past Cacao Beach near Coco Loco, attractively designed **L'Aubergine** (☎ 240-6167, fax 240-2401) charges around US$16 off-season and US$28 during the season. A good restaurant is downstairs.

German expat Kursten has three rooms above his **Finchen Restaurant** (☎ 240-6116, fax 240-0670). While the rooms are low priced and very attractive, they're best suited to nightowls because the restaurant stays open late.

Farther up the same road, **Hotel Villa Caracol** has rooms without bath starting at about US$9. Its best suites are around US$36. In Germany, contact DER Reise-Center Lippstadt GmbH, Markstrasse 3, 4780 Lippstradt; ☎ 02941 3185 u. 51 18; or fax 02941 59685. **Coralitos**, which has villas for rent, is the next hotel up the alley.

Another good place to stay is the seaside **Kanesh Beach** (☎ 240-6187, fax 240-6233). Rates start from around US$35 for rooms with overhead ceiling fans.

Atmospheric **Las Cayenas Hotel** (☎ 240-6080, fax 240-6070), which resembles an old Caribbean great house, is the brainchild of Marie-Antoinette Piguet, a Swiss woman who visited here on vacation. Fan and lights in the room are powered by solar panels. The downstairs is on the regular

power grid. Rates (which include breakfast and taxes) are around US$45 s and US$60 d. A bungalow is also available. Dishes are high quality, and a full breakfast is served. As one reader writes, "It is a charming small hotel... with chickens and pigs in the yard (and is) great value for a relaxing and tranquil visit. A possible drawback for some is that hot water is rare, and you can not use electric appliances here."

Newly opened in 1997, the **Hotel Loma Cerrada** (☎/fax 223-0034) charges from US$25 pn for its studios; it is the forerunner of a huge complex (with 50 rms. and 30 houses), which will have a golf course; look for it to open around the turn of the century.

Set back from the road along a track near the town center, the Swiss-run **Aloha Bungalows** are inexpensive and attractive.

PUNTA BONITA HOTELS: There are three hotels at Punta Bonita, which has a pretty beach. It is reached by a separate road. You may hike indirectly over the hills to Playa Cacao. The German-run 19-rm. **Atlantis** (☎ 240-6111, fax 240-6101; e-mail atlantis@code-tel.net.do) is one of the best places to stay in the area. It features an accomplished chef who once worked for the late French prime minister Francois Mitterand. Rates are around US$55 s, US$62 d including tax and service.

The **Acaya** (☎ 240-6161, fax 240-6166) has 16 rooms with ceiling fans and balconies, a restaurant, and a diving school. They rent for US$35 pn and sleep up to four. Also here, the **Casa Grande Hotel and Restaurant** (☎ 240-6070) charges around US$30. It is reputed to have good food. One final option is the **Punta Bonita** (☎ 240-6082).

ACCOMMODATIONS ON THE PORTILLO ROAD: Opposite El 28 on the road towards Portillo, **Los Piños** (☎ 240-6168, fax 240-6070) offers attractive bungalows and rooms for rent.

Cabañas Esmeralda is some 150 ft. from the road. Modest rooms with shower and mosquito net cost US$20/d. Bargain during the slow season or if you're staying for a few nights.

Owned by a Venezuelan, **El Papagayo** (☎ 240-6095) is right on the road to Portillo as well; it has a very pleasant atmosphere. Rooms start from around US$20-25. It has a restaurant and snack bar. Nearby, **Villa Vieja** rents a furnished two-bedroom apartment with kitchen for about US$25/night. The **Casa Robinson** (fax 240-6070) is a French-run hotel with inexpensive rooms with kitchens.

Aligio Beach Hotel (☎ 240-6255, fax 240-6169) is a modern Italian-run establishment which should appeal to creatures of comfort. Cabins have thatched-roofs and overlook a pool. Rooms have phones. Rates are around US$65 s, US$90 d, and US$180 t with breakfast and dinner.

Popular with Peace Corps volunteers, the lowest priced place is run by **Doña Niña** off the road to Portillo; ask around for directions. An old Dominican lady, she almost seems to have stepped straight out of a historical photo. Her place also seems to be a historical relic. She charges US$2 for a full breakfast and US$4 for a room. Doña charges standard rates for soft. drinks as opposed to the extortionate DS$10 (80¢) charged by most restaurants. Her favorite but rather suspect phrase is *"mi es pobre."* Whatever money she garners does not go back into maintenance, and stories are told about her wealth. There's an outdoor shower, and a manually flushed toilet. Be certain not to kill any tadpoles while flushing, or you might find yourself reincarnated as a frog. A large condo project (Villas las Flores) is planned for this stretch of road; it may or may have not materialized by the time of your arrival.

The **Hotel Castello Beach** (☎ 240-6311, ☎/fax 240-6312) is the last hotel before Portillo, a few km further. The 18 a/c suites have TVs and a small kitchen. They have pool and a dive shop, **Popy Divers**, who (unfortunately) also rent jet skis.

EL PORTILLO ACCOMMODA-TIONS: Head straight from Las Terrenas and follow a paved road along a beautiful beach for 2½ miles (four km) to find the simple but attractive all-inclusive **El Portillo Beach Resort** (☎ 240-6100, fax 240-6104), which has 171 rooms and cabañas, two restaurants, pool, two tennis courts, volleyball, bicycles, daily entertainment, and horseback riding. (Time limits are applied to some of these activities.) The scuba center offers PADI courses, excursions, and dives. El Portillo is popular with European package tourists; many are return visitors.

The resort is in an incredibly gorgeous and idyllic setting. The staff is low-key and have that glowing Dominican hospitality. Unlike many Caribbean all-inclusives, El Portillo has a wonderful beach with a coral reef literally within spitting distance. The cafeteria-style restaurant serves a wide variety of dishes. You may sign up for dinner at the à la carte restaurant. Appetizers and dessert are self-service, and you can order an expresso with your dessert. Evenings feature entertainment, and the disco opens at 11. A variety of tours and excursions are offered, but these (as with the scuba) are not included.

There are attractive large cabins (suitable for two couples) and sets of two-storey units, each of which has balcony or patio, overhead fan, desk, and bath. The lower units are partially camouflaged by greenery, and the diverse tropical foliage adorning the hotel grounds attracts a variety of birds, including iridescent hummingbirds. High-season rates run from US$100 s, $150 d.

❝ Reader's Comment
"I had never snorkeled before. Snorkeling at Portillo in Las Terrenas was the highlight of my trip. I could kick myself that I waited until I was 61 years old to do such a thing.... Please encourage people to bring along snorkeling equipment. It's inexpensive and light to carry. Who wants to be hitting around a stupid golf ball when he or she could be snorkeling!" – N.H., Dearborn, MI

FOOD: There are innumerable place to dine. **La Salsa** is a thatched-roof gourmet beach restaurant. Italian-run **Chez Sarah** serves dishes prepared by its French chef; it is just E of La Salsa and before the creek.

One of the most popular of the local gourmet restaurants, **Paco Cabana** serves seafood and other dishes in an attractive atmosphere.

La Brasserie, across the street in the small mall entitled El Paseo de la Costanera, serves pasta and other dishes at reasonable prices. Next door, **La Crepe-rie** offers a variety of crêpes as well as gourmet ice creams.

main road food and dining: If cooking for yourself, there's a small market and other vendors along the main road. The best bread in the entire peninsula is baked at **Panaderia Francesa** next to Comedor Polanco. The Dominican baker here learned his art from his French brother-in-law who came for a visit. High-priced **La Gateria** offers deli-type foods. **Comedor Economico el Zapote** serves up greasy Dominican dishes such as fried fish and plantains. **Pizzeria Las Cañas** is a friendly thatched-roof place with a good menu. The **Daxmax** is a pizzeria with lasagna, fish, and other dishes; it has a garden setting. **La Casa Azul** serves Italian dishes in a patio setting.

Portillo road dining: Excellent places to eat breakfast are at **Los Piños** and at (lower budget) **Doña Nina's**. **El 28** is a small gourmet French restaurant on the beach near the beginning of the El Portillo road; it serves fish, paella, and other dishes. **Casa Pepa** serves pasta, salad, and crêpes at inexpensive prices (starting at US$1.75 for crêpes).

en route to and near the beach: Rincón de Fleur is on the water. Near the beach, **Dinny's** is a reasonably priced restaurant. **Zuni's** has good seafood. The

German-owned **Tropic Banana** features gourmet cuisine. **Finchen Restaurant** serves Dominican and German food; it's also a very popular watering hole. Down the road, you can also dine at **Kanesh** or the attractive **Las Cayenas Hotel,** which has delicious food served outdoors on the attractive patio or indoors. There are a large number of local restaurants on this road, as well as some low-budget eating stalls where you can really revel in atmosphere. At the end of the beach strip, **Las Ballenas** serves French food. **L'Aubergine** has good pizza near the beach.

SNACKS: Two ice cream shops, **El Polo Heladeria** and **Heladeria Chumbo** are out on the main road.

ENTERTAINMENT: The **Kuh-Bar-Libre** is a German-style second-story bar with a motif that includes a display of cow skulls.

On the main road, the roar of *motoconchos* conflicts with that of blaring generators. The best disco is the French-run **Mambo.** A second is **Disco Terraza Nuevo Mundo,** down the street from Codetel. **Eclipse Discoteca** is across from the Nuevo Mundo. **Tibidabo** is another classy, popular joint. As usual, the German girls are throwing themselves on local lads; prostitution is growing here. Expect to have your crotch grabbed in the disco. In any event, plan on being out all night because the action seldom begins before midnight! If you want to get out of the tourist scene go to **D'Galah,** which is generally 100% Dominican!

Across from El Tiempo, **Arco Iris Video** shows movies nightly for 40¢. Six miles (10 km) towards Sánchez, **La Raquera** is hosted by an entertaining pistol-toting gentleman who resembles the Marlboro Man. At **Chichi** in the town of Sánchez itself, an old guy plays Latin classics.

SERVICES: There are now moneychangers galore along the main road. You may also change money at your hotel. A **Codetel** office (fax 240-6070; open daily 8-8) is on the main road; **Western Union** is also there. **Car rentals** (US$60 per day) are available near the beginning of the road to Portillo. There are a number of doctors; the best is **Dr. Polanco**.

RENTALS: Santa Klaus, on the main road, rents bikes and motorscooters.

DIVING: Hotel **Tropic Banana** has a dive center with a good reputation. **Popy Divers** (☎ 240-6312, fax 240-6311) are in the Hotel Castello Beach. The growing popularity of Las Terrenas has spawned an increasing number of dive shops. The **Stellina Dive Center** (☎ 240-6000, fax 240-6020) is a German-operated dive operation in the Cacao Beach Hotel. German, Italian, Spanish,

and English are spoken. In addition to two dive boats, they also have a glass-bottom boat. ☎ 01/531 18 09 or fax 01/431 02 57 in Zurich, Switzerland.

☞ *Traveler's Tip*
*There are two helpful sources of information. One is **Bahía Tours** (☎ 240-6088,/6298, fax 240-6297) which can confirm reservations and help you with travel. The second, **Sunshine Services** (☎/fax 240-6164), C. del Carmen, offers good information, as well as bike and mountain bike rentals, money exchange, and booking of trips, tours and hotels.*

TOURS: Pura Vida (cellular ☎ 707-7221) has canoe trips to the waterfall from Las Terrenas. They also have Hobie Cat rentals and lessons, at the end of the beach near Las Ballenas Restaurant. The open-air **Horse Center Las Terrenas** (☎ 240-6296) is next to the Tropic Banana, with rides from one (on the beach) to seven hrs (to the waterfall).

SHOPPING: Souvenir shops are on the main road. Also there, the Haitian **Caraibes Art Gallery** is worth visiting.

Leaving the Peninsula

BY AIR: Air Santo Domingo (☎ 683-8020, fax 683-8436;

www.g-air-europa.es/air_sdo;
e-mail info.air_sdo@g-air-europa.
es) operates between Herrera airport (in Santo Domingo) and
Punta Cana, Portillo (Samaná
Peninsula), Santiago, La Romana,
and Puerto Plata. Flights inter-
connect between destinations.
Rates are from RD$700 on up.

FROM LAS TERRENAS: Buses
(☎ 682-0021, 221-3029) leave
from the main road to Santo Domingo. In the past, transportation to Limón has been scarce; as
the road improves, this will
change. You must hire a *motoconcho*. From Limón you can go
on to Samaná. Otherwise, to get
to Samaná you backtrack to Sánchez. Both ways take about the
same time. If using public transportation, allow plenty of time –
around two hrs. from Las Terrenas to Las Galeras.

BY FERRY: As it has for years, a
ferry runs from Samaná to Sabana de la Mar. Departures are at
11 and 3, although this is subject
to change. After buying a ticket
(US$2.45), you wait in "line" to
board the small vessel. It is preferable to ride on top of the boat.
The crossing takes about 1½ hrs.
Watch for flying fish en route.
When you reach Sabana de la
Mar, the boat can't make it all the
way in so two leaky little boats
ferry passengers across to the
pier. One is free; the other costs
35¢. The boats are actually

☞ **Traveler's Tip**

*If you feel comfortable both with
your Spanish and being off the
beaten track, Miches would be the
place for a visit! The area has beautiful beaches devoid of tourists and
peddlars alike. The best snorkeling
is at Punta el Rey.*

pushed (not rowed) to and from
the dock. Owing to the missing
planks, the pier must be the "ho-
liest" place in the nation! Don't
worry, you won't fall in if you are
careful. *Motoconchos*, buses, and
taxis meet the ferry. You should
have no trouble getting a bus to
Santo Domingo and this could
save you as much as an hour.

FOR PUNTA CANA: If heading to
Punta Cana, you must first go to
Miches (US$1.75); the *guagua*
terminal is 1.2 miles (two km)
away and may be reached by *motoconcho*; **Pizzeria de Italiano,**
600 ft. (200 m) down the road
from the terminal, has rooms
and a disco. It's a rough road but
it serves as an excellent introduction to Dominican life. En route,
you see many villages and scenes
of village life – from laden don-
keys to men playing dominoes to
women weighed down with laundry. From Miches, you should
continue on to Higüey (US$2.80)
and then take another bus to
Punta Cana (US$1.40). This bus
passes by most of the major hotels.

The Southeast

Sugarcane is synonymous with Eastern identity. Towns such as San Pedro de Macorís, Higüey, and La Romana host huge sugar processing plants that refine the nation's top export. But the region is not all fields of waving cane: some of the nation's top resorts are here as well. King of them all is Casa de Campo near La Romana. Although the inland portion of the SE is flat and dry, the beaches along the "Costa Caribe" here are splendid white sand stretches. And, with some 9,000 beds available, there's never a shortage of accommodations!

EXPLORING: Buses run from Santo Domingo to San Pedro de Macorís, La Romana, and Higüey. Other locales such as Parque Nacional del Este and Parque Nacional Los Haitises are considerably more difficult to get to. Beaches are scattered along the Costa del Coco and the Costa Caribe. The most famous resorts are the Casa de Campo near La Romana, the hotels at Punta Cana on the coast to the E of Higüey, and those at Juan Dolio and Guayacanes on the S coast.

Parque Nacional Los Haitises

Located along the S shore of the Bahía de Samaná, Parque Nacional Los Haitises is the nation's second most visited national park (after Parque del Este). It covers 78 sq. miles (208 sq. km) and stretches for 15 miles (24 km) W from Boca de Inferno and Bahía de San Lorenzo to the mouth of the Rio Barracote at the W end of Samaná Bay.

Its name (Taino for "The Hills") befits a region where incredibly lush and verdant tropical limestone islands – up to 1,000 ft. high – appear like ships floating on the sea. Ordinarily this type of karst terrain accompanies semidesert vegetation, but rainfall of over 90 in. per year, combined with frequently overcast skies, have made the islands bloom, and tropical humid forest is the norm here.

It is a dramatic and spectacular trip as you cruise by these small islands. You'll see local fishermen ensconced on shelves in the islands. One may hold up a fish in hope of a sale.

The most notable is **Cayo Cacata**, one of many islands where birds nest. As you pull in by the island, nesting frigates and falcons fly overhead – an unforgettable sight.

There are three caves with pre-Columbian carvings and drawings. **San Gabriel** is the

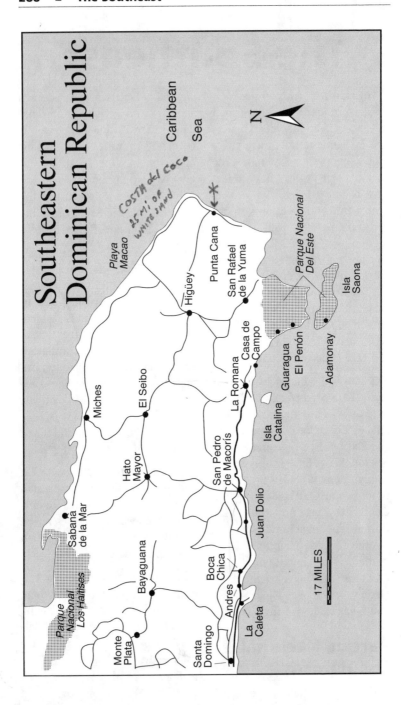

Southeastern Dominican Republic

SANTO DOMINGO 70 LA ROMANA 24 HIGUEY PUNTA CANA

most spectacular in terms of sta-lactites and stalagmites. One for-mation looks like a statue of St. Gabriel, thus the name for the cave. Another circular area ap-pears to have been used for cere-monies. Reputedly, Tainos also lodged in this cave. There's one small petroglyph.

Near the entrance to **La Linea cave**, you will find a long row of rocks. No, it is not a dam but the remains of a railroad. Some 50 yrs. ago it was built as part of a now defunct scheme to ship sug-arcane from the area. Out to-wards the sea are the remains of rusting metal posts that once held the pier. La Linea (named af-ter the railway line) is a large cave accessed by a narrow passage. The entrance is marked by a mangrove swamp, which gives the area a spooky ambiance. It has numerous pictographs, cer-tainly one of the best (if not *the* best) collections in the entire Caribbean. Unfortunately, these have been marred by Dominicans who have scratched their own names on the wall.

The ranger station (which has no brochures or other informa-tion – just bored rangers), stands at the entrance to the **Arena cave**. Just outside the cave are a few stone carvings of masks. Planks and plank walkways take you through the cave, which has little inside save some bats, but which makes for a dramatic visit.

FLORA AND FAUNA: Normally montane species such as bego-nias and mountain palms com-pete here with such lowland forest species as *copey, almacigo* (*gumbo limbo* or birch gum), and *balata*. Red and white mangroves line the reserve's shore. Crusta-ceans, mussels, and oysters clinging to roots are visible at low tide. Seabirds found here include snowy egrets, roseate terns, frig-ate birds, and brown pelicans. Other birds include ruddy ducks, least grebes, narrow billed-todies, white-cheeked pintails, and Ridgway's hawk. Farther up the river, northern jacanas, double-breasted cormorants, great blue herons, and coots may be found. Hutias and solenodons also re-side here.

TOURS: The park can only be visited by boat and by sea, a trip best undertaken in the morning. It is not for the queasy, taking at least an hour each way to cross the 12-mile passage, and seas can be rough at times. If you are not interested in seeing spectacular islands, birds, caves, and Taino pictographs, then you are better off staying at the hotel. Many tours depart from Sosúa and Cabarete and bring you to the pier. (Keep in mind that this will make for an extremely long day).

Pierre Fayet (☎ 552-7593/7695, fax 552-7399) oper-ates from his Malvinas Restau-rant in Sánchez. He goes out daily during the season (around twice weekly off-season) and will take you out for around US$35, including lunch back at the restaurant. Pierre has been doing this for years and clearly knows his subject. He also offers river tours, which are well worth going on.

Others offering tours include: **Transporte Maritimo Minadiel** (☎ 538-2556) in Samaná, Gary Hurtado of **Cruceros Nauticos** (☎ 538-2152, 240-6100), and Hector Talvarez of **Wega Tours** (☎ 556-1197, 682-6430) in Sabana de la Mar. **Wolf Wirth** (☎/fax 586-1201) in Puerto Plata can also help with trips.

For **independent charters** through the national park office (☎ 556-73333) at Sabaneta la Mar, you will pay around RD$500 for up to 12 passengers; the office will also arrange for a guide.

PARQUE NACIONAL NATURAL LAGUNA REDONDA Y LAGUNA LIMÓN: These two muddy lagoons, Redonda and Limón, are found in the nation's NE; they lie 11 and 17 miles (17 and 27 km) respectively from the village of Miches. The Laguna Redonda is connected to the sea by the Caño Celedonio. Limón can only be reached on foot or horse from the community of Los Guineos, 800 m to the S. The 22 species of birds found in the area

include the great egret, black-crowned night heron, northern pintail, and the roseate spoonbill.

A controversy now rages over whether the area's reserves should be reduced; local developers claim that the large extent of the reserve prevents them from building hotels, thus robbing them of income.

ACCOMMODATIONS: Swiss-run and adventure-oriented, **Hotel Punta El Rey** charges US$40 pd including meals. For more information/reservations call the Hotel Palacio in Santo Domingo at ☎ 682-4730; fax 800-687-5535; or write Apdo. 20541, Santo Domingo.

Near the village of Miches, stay at the **Coco Loco Beach Club**.

A final alternative is the Austrian-run **Cabinas Playa Tortuga** (☎ 553-5717) which are at Playa Laguna de Limón. Rates are around US$30 and US$40 (with kitchen). Taxes are additional.

TROPICAL PLANTATION: Set at Km. 20 along the Carr. Hato Mayor-Sabana de la Mar, **Tropical Plantation** (☎ 470-9693, 412-0971, 223-0056) is a working flower farm whose blooms are both exported and sold domestically. The grounds contain a botanical garden, tropical farm, orchid nursery, butterfly house, and many indigenous species of birds. Its restaurant is open 9-6 daily. Admission is DS$100 for foreigners and DS$50 for Quisqueyans and residents.

Higüey

Twenty-four miles (40 km) NE of La Romana, Higüey is the capital of the Province of La Altagracia. The area was first settled in 1494 by *conquistador* Juan de Esquivel, who later conquered Jamaica. The town was founded in 1502 on the orders of Frey Nicolás de Ovando. It began to flourish from 1502-1508 when Ponce de León served as administrator. The most notable features of Higüey are its churches. Using the town as a base, you might explore the palm- and sea grape-bordered beaches running along the coast from Bávaro 30 miles to Laguna Nisibón. Watch out for the strong Atlantic currents if swimming here.

SIGHTS: Most notable is the **Basilica de Nuestra Señora de la Merced** (Our Lady of Mercy), located on the spot where Columbus's forces planted their cross while fending off an Indian attack. Miracles are attributed to the soil here, which the Dominicans come to gather. According to legend, Columbus and his men, surprised by a Taino attack, were nearly done in when, lo and behold, a vision of the Virgin Mary appeared on the cross, frightening the Indians and allowing the Spaniards to repel the attack. Inside the shrine are kept two splinters of wood believed to have come from that original cross; it's said Columbus cut wood for it from the nispero tree nearby.

Replacing Nuestra Señora de la Merced (Our Lady of Mercy) as the nation's patron saint in 1922, La Altagracia (the Virgin of the Highest Grace) is credited with numerous miracle cures. In one, an aged and mysterious pilgrim (believed to have been one of the apostles) arrived in a small village in the E part of the country and begged food and shelter from a father with an ill daughter. Upon his departure, he gave a small picture of the Virgin Mary to the father. When the daughter gazed at the Virgin, she was cured instantly.

The modern **church** – shaped like a pair of 200-ft.-high hands folded in prayer – was constructed on the site where the picture was first admired, and an annual pilgrimage is made here on Jan. 21 and Aug. 16.

A little more than three miles (five km) to the E, **La Otra Banda** is an attractive village with pastel-colored houses. It was founded by immigrants from the Canary Islands. The homes are Victorian in style.

A small museum of Taíno artifacts, the **Sanctuario de los Tainos**, is on the road near La Otra Banda; it is open from 8:30 to 12:30 and from 2:30-6, Tues. through Sun.

ACCOMMODATIONS: There is really no reason to overnight in Higüey but, should you wish to do so, there are plenty of places to stay. Accommodations here include **Hotel Brisas del Este** (☎ 554-2312), Av. Mella; **Hotel Colón** (☎ 554-4283), C. Colón 46; **Hotel San Antonio** (☎ 554-2331), C. Colón 48; **Hotel Genesis** (☎ 554-2971), C. Colón 51; **Hotel Volcán** (☎ 554-3101); inexpensive **Hotel Restaurant Don Carlos** (☎ 554-2344/2713), C. Ponce de Leon; **Hotel Restaurante El Diamante** (☎ 554-2754), C. Santana 23; or more expensive (around US$40) **Hotel El Naranjo** (☎ 554-2277), C. Altagracia.

low-budget: These include the **Hotel Ana** (☎ 554-3569), Av. Hijo 48; **Hotel Presidente** (☎ 554-5990), C. Hnos. Trejos 136; and the **Hotel San Juan Plaza** (☎ 554-3518), Altagracia 40.

FOOD: Eat at **Restaurant El Gran Gourmet**, C. Santana 117; **Restaurant La Fama**, Arz. Nouel 2; and **Restaurante El Español Original**, Carr. Mella at Km 1.

Codetel is on Av. Bertillio.

Costa del Coco
(The Coconut Coast)

Stretching from Higüey up along the NE coast, the Coconut Coast covers more than 25 miles (40 km) of white sand beaches edging crystal clear shallow waters. Its beaches – Playa Macao, Playa Cortesito, Playa Bávaro, Punta Cana, and Punta Juanillo – have been groomed for the upscale tourist market, and there are now an increasing number of resorts in the area.

Punta Cana

Punta Cana is now the nation's most prominent tourist resort area. It is just minutes by overpriced taxi from the international airport of the same name. The area's major attractions are its beautiful beaches, some of the world's finest.

Punta Cana is not for the budget-conscious. Not only do "five star" resorts proliferate, prices in the shops are perhaps the highest in the entire nation. A large bottle of Presidente beer sells for US$3 here and US$1.30 elsewhere! You can find items such as Philadelphia cream cheese, but you will have to pay an extortionate US$6 for the pack! The shops can charge these exhorbitant prices because people are on vacation and don't care about prices. The nearest place for cheap shopping is Higüey, about an hour by bus (US$1.40). Ask your hotel where to catch the bus.

However, if you have the moola, you like large resorts, and want to get away from everything, this area may be what you are looking for. It is not for people who are interested in exploring the Dominican Republic, simply because its remote location makes it time-consuming or expensive (or both) to travel elsewhere.

While vactioning here – if you choose to remain within the hotel compound – is not the same as visiting the Dominican Republic, it *is* an international experience! You'll hear French, Spanish, German and English spoken, and many guests are from Argentina and Chile. Interestingly, it's the S Americans who complain to management because the German women sunbathe topless as they do in Europe! "My child is right nearby," they groan.

GETTING HERE: The vast majority of visitors arrive by international flight, and this is the only place they visit. For them, the resort is all they will see of the Dominican Republic. **Air Santo Domingo** (☎ 683-8020, fax 683-8436; www.g-air-europa.es/air_sdo; e-mail info.air_sdo@g-air-europa.es) operates between Herrera airport (in Santo Domingo) and Punta Cana, Portillo (Samaná Peninsula), Santiago, La Romana, and Puerto Plata. Flights interconnect between destinations. Rates range from RD$700 on up.

HISTORY: The Punta Cana Group built the first hotel, the Punta Cana Club, which opened with 10 cabañas in 1971. Club Med opened in 1981, and the Punta Cana International Airport followed in 1984, with the Punta Cana Beach Resort opening in 1987. The success of the initial Punta Cana properties spurred Spanish investors to construct a combined total of more than 10,000 hotel rooms in the area. New hotels are still under construction, and Oscar de la Renta and Julio Iglesias are now spearheading a vacation-home project. Sadly, much of this development has come at a cost, and many hotels have cut down mangroves, dumped in the Laguna Baváro, and indulged in other unsavory policies.

SIGHTS: Other than water-related activities, there's not a lot to do in the immediate area. If you are bored, you could perhaps tour other resorts. However, there is now one major attraction. Inaugurated in 1997, the **Manatí Park** (☎ 552-0807, 688-0720) covers an area of 74 acres (300,000 sq. m.). It was built by Inversiones Arrecife, a Spanish investment company who has invested some US$14 million. The park is still in its formative stages. Although its avowed intention is to create an environmental and education center, it is nowhere near accomplishing that goal and, at present, it is similar to a small, pricey zoo which will be best appreciated by young children.

There are two portions to the compact park. The left part has the animals and the Taino village. You'll find a flamingo pond, birds in cages, a duck surrounded by baby chicks, crocodiles sleeping on a yellow concrete sandbank. The best exhibit is the circular iguana pit. The guide will invite you in and show you poppa, momma, and son. (Babies hide under the rock piles.)

The replica of a Taino Indian village houses Dominicans in dress-up who demonstrate Indian crafts and lifestyle. During performances, a central thatched pavilion (which houses artifacts galore, as well as reproductions) has a slide show (with re-enactments of traditional activities), while in the nearby huts the village's inhabitants give demonstrations. "Tainos" carve statues with metal files; a girl bakes cassava bread; a man makes pottery; a man rolls cigars in a hut labeled *tobaco*; another Taino has climbed up in a tree whooping and hollering.

The other major performance is provided by the captive sea lions and dolphins in a pool area to the R of the entrance. The sea lions, Tibu and Toya, waddle out first. They are put through their paces in a five-min. show in which the duo clap their flippers in applause, demonstrate their balancing abilities with balls, and so on. Tibu kisses a beautiful

woman selected from the audience.

The six dolphins jump out of the water in time with the music, touch buoys suspended from a wire, don giant glasses, jump over ropes, and disco dance to the tune of Michael Jackson's "Bad" sung in Spanish. Except for a mention of how they vocalize, no explanation is given as to the dynamics of their physiology or lifestyle. And virtually nothing in the way of environmental education takes place during the show. It is hard to tell whether the dolphins – blessed by heredity with a permanent inscrutable smile – enjoy what they are doing. In any event, the fish tossed their way ensure that they cooperate.

Pure-bred Spanish stallions, similar to others found in Jerez de la Frontera in Spain and in Vienna, perform during the evening hours to a combination of lights and music. The "Dancing Horses," performances are Wed. and Sat. at 9:45 PM.

The park (☎ 552-0807) is open daily from 9-6. The shuttle bus is included in the entry fee. Prices are US$10 (two-12 yrs.) and US$21 (adults). "Swimming" with the dolphins – a short plunge in their company – is US$35, and the Dancing Horses are US$65. A "parrot show" takes place three times daily, the dolphins and sea lions show is held twice daily, swimming with the dolphins is done twice daily, and the Taino Village is open twice daily. Be sure to pick up a schedule from your hotel so you can catch the programs you are most interested in.

ACCOMMODATIONS: Hotels are listed in their order from N to S. Not all hotels are included, and new ones will have opened by the time of your arrival. Most hotels here book packages in advance.

At Playa de Arena Gorda, 360-room **Hotel Riu Taino** (☎ 221-7515/2290, fax 685-9537) is a luxurious German-run resort; its sister is the 374-room **Hotel Riu Naiboa** (☎ 221-2290, fax 685-9537). Rooms have phones, satellite TVs, a/c, and terraces.

Hotel Iberostar Dominicana (☎ 221-6500, fax 687-5356; www.iberostar.com; e-mail iberostar@iberostar.com) and the **Hotel Iberostar Bávaro** (☎ 221-6500; fax 687-5356; www.iberostar.com; e-mail iberostar@iberostar.com) are the two Dominican all-inclusive ultra-luxury links in the Spanish-owned Iberostar hotel chain. Set at Playa Bávaro, they largely cater to a European clientele. The 349-rm. all-inclusive Iberostar Dominicana has restaurants, a "Creole-style" shopping street, and a pool. Rooms each have a/c and fan, phone, TV, balcony or terrace, and refrigerator. The Iberostar Bávaro has 70 bungalows; each has eight a/c jr. suites with

TV, phone, refrigerator, and balcony/terrace. Facilities include restaurant, disco, shops, and minimart. It offers a half-board plan. Both cater to children.

Set on 100 acres, the **Punta Cana Yacht Club** (☎ 565-0011/3077, 686-0084) has villas and one-bedroom apartments, as well as a golf course, four tennis courts, disco, and boutiques.

The 340-room **Punta Cana Beach Resort** (☎ 221-CANA, 541-2714 in Santo Domingo, fax 547-2200, 541-2286; 800-972-2139) has four restaurants, bars, discos, and a pool. Rooms (set in three-storey pink towers) have a/c, TV, phone, and other amenities. A range of activities including watersports are available.

Comprising 750 suites, the **Melía Bávaro** (☎ 221-2311, fax 686-5427; 800-33-MELIA; www.solmelia.es; melia.bavaro@codetel.net.do)) opened in 1991. It has beautifully landscaped grounds with a nature walk and aviaries with parrots ("¡Hola!" they chirp), as well as peacocks and other birds. The mangroves have been left as part of the property, and pink flamingoes stalk for prey in a pool inside the health spa. The spa has two Jacuzzis, saunas, equipment, and massage room. Transportation is provided by motor trams so you can hop on and off at any point.

You can dine in your choice of three restaurants. If you opt for the half-pension plan, you may have buffet breakfasts and dinners in either the Chopin or the Hispaniola. Everything is included with your breakfast; all beverages (including water) are extra at dinner. The buffets encompass an enormous range of selections. Each suite (request an upper-level one for privacy), is a combination living-dining-and-sleeping area. A satellite TV receives numerous channels, and a fan over the bed provides an alternative to the a/c. There are 86 two-storey bungalows on the grounds; each has eight suites. A single building holds 80 jr. suites and two master suites.

Entertainment is offered every night, a disco pumps out sounds after 11, and the Chopin offers classical music concerts every night: A string quartet serenades you from a boat that circles around the canals to the rear of the restaurant. Bird calls add spice to the compositions. (Reserve a dinner seat for the best view.) Other facilities include two pools, four lighted tennis courts, watersports, a disco, and a snack bar and gourmet restaurant (where half-pension guests can dine for a surcharge).

The neighboring 96-acre (237 ha) **Melía Paradisus** (German for "Paradise"), is an all-inclusive resort which opened in 1995. It has 434-suites. Unlike many of the nation's all-inclusives, the resort has service and accommodations in line with Jamaican resorts such as the Superclubs chain. The 28 two-storey structures have attractive suites with balconies or patios similar to those at the Bávaro. There are five all-inclusive restaurants. The Pizzeria Dolce Vita serves great pizza and pasta dishes. The most popular restaurant is the a/c formal El Romantico which is often booked for days in advance. It has gourmet French cuisine and impeccable service. A tram will take you around the grounds and over to the Bávaro. Rates run around US$135-250 pp including taxes and service charges, depending upon the time of year and based on double occupancy.

note: In Europe, the hotels may be reached toll-free at ☎ 01 802 121723 (Germany), 0 800 41 31 65 (France), and 8000 282 720 (Britain).

Set on 70 acres, 320-rm. all-inclusive luxurious **Club Méditerranée** (☎ 687-2767, 686-5500/5532; 567-5228/5229 in Santo Domingo) offers tennis, swimming, beach, nightly entertainment, and watersports. Charters bound here depart from US and Canada. In the US, ☎ 800-528-3100.

The 324-rm. all-inclusive **Hotel Occidental Playa Real** will open sometime in 1998. It will offer three restaurants, three bars, two pools, tennis, and watersports. Rates are around US$110 s, US$170 d. The 536-rm. all-inclusive **Hotel Occidental** will also probably be open by the time you get here. It will offer six restaurants, four bars, two pools, tennis, and watersports.

The Occidental Hotels may be reached in North America and Canada (☎ 506-877-3160, 800-843-3311, fax 506-877-3160), in Belgium (☎ 30-235-0373, 09800-14596), in Denmark (☎ 8030 1031, 45 87 00 08, Fax 45 87 22 49/93 21 41), in France (☎ 05 00 11, 4071 2121, fax 4071 2131), in Germany (☎ 0180-231 21 21, 06151-905760, fax 06151-905750), in Ireland (01 6605 000, fax 01 6605 540), and in Switzerland (☎ 155 5583, 715 1616, fax 715 5583).

less expensive: There are a few budget hostelries in the area. **El Galeón del Pirata** (☎ 223-3497) has rooms for US$30 with breakfast; bargaining is possible. **El Cortecito** is a 20-rm. hotel for around US$50. **Las Corales** faces the beach and charges around US$130 d with half-board.

Macao: To get away from it all continue on to Macao which, save for a few *cabañas*, is relatively undeveloped. **Hacienda Barbara** (☎ 685-2594, 565-7176) is an exclusive family-style inn

☞ *Traveler's Tip*
If you are staying in this area and have wheels, head up past the Riü hotels and continue N along the coast. You'll find mile after mile of deserted beaches. Exercise caution: the waves can be large, with strong undertow.

featuring tennis, pool, and beach. It borders a 1,000-acre coconut plantation. In the US, ☎ 516-944-8060. The only low-priced place here is **Coco's Cabañas**; bargain to get a good price. Bring your own water, and watch out for stingrays and the dangerous undertow. To get here, take a *camioneta* from Higüey.

SHOPPING: Harrison's has a branch near Higüey. All of the hotels have gift shops. Shopping is also available at a small mall and at various stores. Prices are quite high.

TOURS: You can go to just about anywhere from the Dominican Republic: for a price! The best place to book a tour is at your hotel's tour desk. Tours are available to Altos de Chavon, Old Santo Domingo, Isla Saona, Rancho Cumayasa, Rancho Jonathan, Samaná/Cayo Levantado, Isla Catalina, and even to the Turks and Caicos. You can also go on a "4 x 4 wheel adventure tour," a jeep safari, and on a "fun buggy."

La Romana

Located 70 miles (112 km) from Santo Domingo, just under the E hook of the nation's S coast, this city – once noted only for its sugar production – is now better known as a vacation resort. Casa de Campo is a specially developed complex for upper-class tourists. Altos de Chavon, set up on a plateau above the Rio Chavon, is an artists' village (complete with museum) built in 16th-century Spanish style. This city of 102,000 also has the nation's largest sugar refinery; its name, meaning "the scales," came about because cane growers brought their crops here to be weighed and purchased.

GETTING HERE: Buses run from Santo Domingo or Higüey.

by air: Air Santo Domingo (☎ 683-8020, fax 683-8436; www.g-air-europa.es/air_sdo; e-mail info.air_sdo@g-air-europa.es) operates between Herrera airport (in Santo Domingo) and Punta Cana, Portillo (Samaná Peninsula), Santiago, La Romana, and Puerto Plata. Flights interconnect between destinations. Rates run from RD$700 on up.

ECONOMIC HISTORY: La Romana became a sugar town when the existing mill was built in 1917. The plant has grown over the years and now produces half a million tons per year – the bulk of the sugar exported annually. In the early 1960s, Gulf & Western entered the picture. Investment by this gigantic conglomerate grew to US$200 million and included sugar, cement, cattle, factories, and the tourist complex Casa de Campo. In an attempt to make La Romana into the "Showcase of the East," Gulf & Western poured an estimated US$20 million into the town. Although the corporation changed the face of the city, it employed administrators educated in the rough atmosphere of Batista's Cuba. Gulf & Western was charged with bribery and intimidation. The independent labor unions were destroyed and a company union substituted. The nearby free trade zone was also dominated by Gulf & Western.

ACCOMMODATIONS: In town are the **Hotel Frano** (☎ 550-4744), Pd. Abréu 9, which charges around US$15 for rooms with a/c; the **Hotel Bolivar** (☎ 550-2626), Pd. Abréu 61; the **Hotel Condado** (☎ 556-3010), Altagracia 55; the **Hotel Persia** (☎ 550-0816), G. Luperón 45; **Hotel Jupiter** (☎ 556-5906), G. Luperón 122; the **Hotel Rendy** (☎ 556-3540), Dr. T. Ferry 178; and the **Hotel Rincon Cri-ollo,**(☎ 550-5525). There is also the **Hotel Adamay** (☎ 556-6102/6202), which is less than a mile out of town en route to San Pedro de Macorís and priced around US$20. At Km. 4.5 on the way to San Pedro de Macorís, **Cabañas Tio Tom** (☎ 556-6212, fax 556-6201) has 72 comfortable rooms with a/c, a pool, and a disco. The stone and wood 58-rm. *bohio*-style **Dominicus Beach Village** (☎ 533-4897) has rooms with hammocks, raised platform beds, and cascade-style showers. It has a virtually private beach. Less than half an hour from Casa de Campo, **Apart-Hotel Casa de Campo** (☎ 566-7464, 567-2812) features swimming pool, bar, and restaurant.

SERVICES: Tricom is on C. Duarte and **Codetel** is in Parque Duarte. **Tropical Tours** (☎ 556-2636) is one local tour agency. **Banco Popular** is on C. Duarte and **Banco Nacional** borders Parque Duarte.

car rentals: Contact **Rentauto** (☎ 556-4181), **Honda** (☎ 556-2609/3835), **National** (☎ 556-2512), or **Nelly** (☎ 556-2156).

ENTERTAINMENT: The **Hollywood Plaza** theater shows current films.

Vicinity of La Romana

Casa de Campo

Spread out over 7,000 acres, this is the nation's preeminent tourist resort. It was remodeled in 1994. Accommodations are available in more than a thousand hotel rooms and villas. There are 17 tennis courts, two 18-hole golf courses, a marina, and two conference rooms. Visit Playa Minitas for watersports such as windsurfing, snorkeling, and sailing, including Hobie Cats. Also available are deep-sea fishing, a sunset sail, river fishing, charter boating, tennis, golf, riding, polo, shooting. The Fitness Center provides racquetball, squash, aerobics and a fully-equipped gym with a Jacuzzi and sauna. Transportation is provided by shuttle bus, horse-drawn carriage, and golf cart. Rooms run from around US$210 on up, with an off-season low of about US$100. A 10% service charge is added. ☎ 800-223-6620 or 305-856-5404 in the US or 682-2111 in the Dominican Republic.

Altos de Chavón

Designed in mock-Italian style and set on a hill eight miles (13 km) E of Casa de Campo, this US$40 million creation – a cobblestone village which appears timeless – is like a theater set brought to life. Actually constructed in the 1960s, it has been artificially aged: stonework and obelisks have been deliberately chipped. The "village" is wonderful to visit in the evening when lanterns illuminate the cobblestones. Silkscreen and photography are taught here, and paintings are exhibited. A free shuttle bus runs here from Casa de Campo every 15 min.

SIGHTS: Named after Poland's patron saint in commemoration of the papal visit, the **Church of St. Stanislaus** overlooks the cliffs towering above the Río Chavon. Opened in 1981, the **Archaeological Museum** (open daily 9-9) exhibits indigenous artifacts collected by Dr. Samuel Pon. There are stone hatchets, clay pots, griddles used for baking *casabe* (cassava bread), heart-shaped vases, equipment used in ball-games, beads, and shells. Some of the most intriguing items are found in the Mythology and Art section. Taino religious worship centered around three *cemis* (idols) – one for crops, one to ensure painless childbirth, and one to bring sun or rain. Sex in Taino art was seen as being divine and mystical rather than crude and distasteful. The *cahoba*, the principal Taino religious ceremony involving inhalation of a hallucinogen, is spotlighted in one display. Note the *cemi* with a plate on its head for *cahoba* powder. The spatulas were used to cleanse the body prior to participation, and *dujos* are the special seats used in the ceremony. The **Chavón Art Galleries** exhibit works by artists from the Dominican Republic and around the world. The 5,000-seat **amphi-theater** was inaugurated with a show by Frank Sinatra; Julio Iglesias, his Latin counterpart, has also appeared here.

ACCOMMODATIONS AND FOOD: The 10-rm. **La Posada Inn** has a pool. Two- and three-bedroom apartments are also available. There are five restaurants.

GETTING HERE: Buses and *publicos* run from Santo Domingo.

Boca de Yuma

Said to be the best place in all the Caribbean for blue marlin, the fishing village of Boca de Yuma hosts a deep-sea fishing tournament in June. From here a road runs inland to Higüey. Just over a mile N of San Rafael de Yuma is the restored residence of Ponce de León, where he lived from 1505-1508. Also visit **Cueva de Berna** (Berna Cave), which has Taino pictographs.

PRACTICALITIES: Club El 28 is an intimate Italian-run hotel which charges around US$30 d. It has a a pool and (of course) an Italian restaurant.

Isla de Catalina

One of the nation's top dive spots, this island is accessible by boat from La Romana marina. In recent years, it has become a target of cruise ships and an incredible 200,000 tourists now arrive annually! Naturally, the influx has been criticized by environmentalists.

If permission is obtained from the La Romana Naval Station in advance, one may camp here, but there are few facilities. Bring all of your own water and supplies. Offshore on the N side, there's a wall and reef.

Bayahibe

A small fishing village, Bayahibe is set on a small bay. Dive at the coral reef, which has a wide variety of sponges. Get here soon before it becomes overdeveloped!

PRACTICALITIES: It can be reached either by taking a bus from Higüey and then a *moto-concho* or by taking a direct bus from La Romana. The village has a disco and around half a dozen restaurants. A charter boat to Isla Saona costs around US$100 RT; it's best to get a group together to share the cost.

You can find lodging here with families for as cheaply as US$7 d. Accommodations include **Hotel Cabaña Milysade** and **Hotel Bayahibe**; both are priced at around US$15.

Casa Daniel (☎ 809-223-0622; fax: 550-1510; e-mail cbamert@codetel.net.do) is a small Swiss-run guesthouse which has a diving school. Room rates are around US$20 s or d; breakfast is US$5 addtional. In Switzerland, contact Mike Keller

(☎ 41(0)1-820 26 80, 41(0)1-830 44 39).

An all-inclusive AMHSA resort, the 600-rm. **Casa del Mar** (Santo Domingo ☎ 562-7475, fax 566-2436; 800-472-3985; www.world hotel.com/AMHSA; e-mail amhsa@codetel.net.do) offers tennis, horseback riding, bicycles, archery lessons, scuba lessons, pedal boats, banana boats,water skiing, and windsurfing. It opened in late 1997.

FOOD: Eat at the **Bahía**, which has excellent lobster, or at the **Bayahibe**, which has equally fine seafood.

Parque Nacional del Este

Set in the SE corner, this "National Park of the East" comprises portions of the mainland combined with oval-shaped **Isla de Saona**, which is separated from the mainland by the Catuano canal. Some three to four ft. wide by 14 miles long, the island has a few sandy beaches, tons of mosquitoes, and the two settlements of Adamanay (on the SW coast) and Punta Gorda (on the W coast) – but not much else. Adamanay was the settlement's original name; it was discovered by Michelle de Cuneo on Columbus's second voyage. Locals here survive through fishing and hunting pigeons and wild hogs. The park's beaches can only be reached by boat; Casa de Campo arranges tours. Bioluminescent **Bahía de Catalina** on the S coast displays orange and green whorls in its waters. Near Bayahibe is the **Guaraguao** area of the park where a number of caves have pre-Columbian carvings and drawings.

FLORA AND FAUNA: The area is comprised of tropical deciduous forest atop limestone. The endangered hutia and solenodon are also present. Manatees and bottlenose dolphins may be seen offshore. There are 112 species of birds. The endemic Antillean piculet is found in dry coastal areas, and the American oystercatcher lives around Punta Algibe on the mainland. Birds on Saona include the village weaver, the Hispaniolan lizard-cuckoo, the red-legged thrush, the black-crowned oriole, the black-crowned palm tanager, the palmchat, the limpkin, and the Antillean palm swift. Sea turtles and rhinoceros iguanas are also here.

ENVIRONMENT: A 1997 USAID-funded study concluded that "ecotourism" is causing definite harm to the park.

Visits by hundreds to the caves are damaging their internal micro-climates and disturbing the bat colonies. Motorboat landings on the beaches affect the dolphins, manatees, turtles, and iguanas. In addition, fuel and lubricant deposits are accumulat-

ing on the beaches. "Ecotourism" here is strictly "egotourism," and so far has failed to use the park as a vehicle for education or to enhance awareness of the importance of preserving the environment.

PRACTICALITIES AND HIKING: A ranger cabin and office is at the park's W entrance near Bayahibe. The park department offers daily tours as part of the entrance fee. A marked trail leads to a nearby cave that harbors bats and owls; rangers are available to guide visitors. Set near the town of Boca del Yuma, the E entrance has a ranger's cabin and a trail that runs parallel to the coast. Boats can dock at Adamanay on Saona. There are several trails on the island.

Isla Saona is now a major tourist attraction; the islanders' colorful homes and the pure white-sand beaches are powerful draws. Unless you arrive early in the morning or late in the afternoon, you can expect crowds. There are two ways to get to the island: by speedboat or by catamaran or trimaran. The speedboat will allow you to spend more time on the island.

San Pedro de Macorís

Just 40 miles (65 km) E of Santo Domingo, the placid seaport of San Pedro de Macorís (pop.

140,000) is set on the Río Higuamo, surrounded by the sugar plantations that support it and by baseball fields that have fostered the sport; local youths regard baseball as the key to prosperity. The town supports the Universidad Central del Este (UCE) – whose medical school is reputed to be among the nation's best and has attracted many US students. It also supports a baseball stadium. One of the largest Industrial Free Zones is also located here. A nickname for locals is Serie 23 after the numeric code found on the *cedulas* (identification cards) belonging to inhabitants.

HISTORY: San Pedro was founded by a mixture of Italians, Germans, and Arabs in the 1870s. During the days of high sugar prices (up to 22¢ a pound) it was nicknamed "the Sultan of the East." In those prosperous days, Pan Am flew its American Clipper hydroplanes from the US, landing in the Río Higuamo. Now the town has frequent electric blackouts. Never a favorite of Balaguer, as its inhabitants consistently backed his opponents, the town has remained undeveloped in comparison to Santo Domingo and Santiago. Most streets remain unpaved, and the overall feeling is one of being in a country village. There isn't much here to attract the casual visitor.

SIGHTS: San Pedro's neoclassically styled Church of St. Peter the Apostle serves as an orientation point; the bus terminal is right in front. The nicest place to walk is along the **Malecón**. Here, there are food stalls and you can watch the sea crash against the rocky crags.

A nearby sight is the **Cueva de las Maravillas** (Cave of the Marvels), which has a number of pre-Columbian paintings on its walls. It was declared the **Reserva Antropológica de las Cuevas de las Maravillas** in 1996. **Playa El Soco** is suitable for swimming, and there's good fishing at the river by the small village of Cumayasa.

ACCOMMODATIONS: Inexpensive **Hotel Macorix-UCE** (☎ 529-3950,) has 28 a/c rooms, pool, disco, and tennis courts. Located on G. Deligne, in front of the Malecón and near the medical school, it provides special packages for students. Rates run around US$17 s or d with fan and US$25 s or d with a/c.

Other hotels include **Hotel Datni** (☎ 529-4040), C. Toconal 6; **Hotel Macorís** (☎ 588-2530), C. Restauración 44; **Hotel Nuevo Central** (☎ 588-2304), C. San Francisco 49; **Hotel Olimpico** (☎ 588-3584); Av. Libertad (Carr. Nagua at Km 1); **Hotel del Jaya** (☎ 588-2705), San Francisco 40; and **Hotel Altagra-**

cia (☎ 588-6470), Av. Libertad 132.

FOOD: One of the more attractive restaurants is **La Roco** which is on the Malecón right near UCE. The **Restaurant Club Nautico El Puerto**, on Av. Malecón at Enrique Rijo, specializes in seafood and flambé. The **De Marcos Cafeteria** is right under the Hotel Independencia. Others include **Restaurant Don Luis** and **Restaurant Osteria** on Av. 27 de Febrero; **Restaurant Don Ernesto** at Av. 27 de Febrero 155; **Restaurant Arias** at C. España 9; and **Restaurant Independencia** at Independencia 148.

ENTERTAINMENT: Seaview Disco is right on the Malecón.

INFORMATION: Call the **Ayuntamiento** at ☎ 529-3600 or the provincial government at 529-3309.

SERVICES: The two **Codetel** offices are on Av. Independencia.

FESTIVALS AND EVENTS: *Guloyas* (Goliath), the local dance, was brought by the *Cocolocos*, immigrants from the Leeward and Windward islands. The dance known as *Momise* stems from the English mummer (masked dancing) tradition. Taking place on the June 29 *fiestas patronales* of San Pedro Apostol (St. Peter), as well as on other festive occasions, there are also three dance-dramas. Presenting a story similar to the St. George and the Dragon legend is *la danza del padre invierno* (the dance of father winter). There's also *la danza salvaje* (the wild dance), and *la danza de El Codril*, which features a troupe of dancers linked arm-in-arm and divided into two rows. Costumes feature innumerable beads and mirrors.

BASEBALL: The town is known for its ballplayers, and the winter league games are still held here from Oct. to Jan. at Estadio Tetelo Vargas, with San Pedro favorites, the Estrellas Orientales, playing. Of the 300 or so Dominicans currently playing in the US major and minor leagues, more than half come from here. The Hiroshima Carp, a team from Japan's Central League, has been scouting in town, and its owner has announced plans to establish a US$1.8 million baseball academy nearby.

Spanish Vocabulary

Days of the Week

domingo	Sunday
lunes	Monday
martes	Tuesday
miercoles	Wednesday
jueves	Thursday
viernes	Friday
sabado	Saturday

Months of the Year

enero	January
febrero	February
marzo	March
abril	April
mayo	May
junio	June
julio	July
agosto	August
septiembre	September
octubre	October
noviembre	November
diciembre	December

Numbers

uno	one
dos	two
tres	three
cuatro	four
cinco	five
seis	six
siete	seven
ocho	eight
nueve	nine
diez	ten
once	eleven
doce	twelve

trece	thirteen
catorce	fourteen
quince	fifteen
dieciséis	sixteen
diecisiete	seventeen
dieciocho	eighteen
diecinueve	nineteen
veinte	twenty
veintiuno	twenty-one
veintidos	twenty-two
treinta	thirty
cuarenta	forty
cincuenta	fifty
sesenta	sixty
setenta	seventy
ochenta	eighty
noventa	ninety
cien	one hundred
ciento uno	one hundred one
doscientos	two hundred
quinientos	five hundred
mil	one thousand
mil uno	one thousand one
dos mil	two thousand
un millón	one million
mil millones	one billion
primero	first
segundo	second
tercero	third
cuarto	fourth
quinto	fifth
sexto	sixth
séptimo	seventh
octavo	eighth
noveno	ninth
décimo	tenth
undécimo	eleventh
duodécimo	twelfth
último	last

Conversation

¿Como esta usted?	How are you?
Bien, gracias, y usted?	Well, thanks, and you?
Buenas dias.	Good morning.
Buenas tardes.	Good afternoon.
Buenas noches.	Good evening/night.
Hasta la vista.	See you again.
Hasta luego.	So long.
¡Buena suerte!	Good luck!
Adios.	Goodbye.
Mucho gusto de conocerle.	Glad to meet you.
Felicidades.	Congratulations.
Muchas felicidades.	Happy birthday.
Feliz Navidad.	Merry Christmas.
Feliz Año Nuevo.	Happy New Year.
Gracias.	Thank you.
Por favor.	Please.
De nada/con mucho gusto.	You're welcome.
Perdoneme.	Pardon me.
¿Como se llama esto?	What do you call this?
Lo siento.	I'm sorry.
Permitame.	Permit me.
Quisiera...	I would like...
Adelante.	Come in.
Permitame presentarle...	May I introduce...
¿Como se llamo usted?	What is your name?
Me llamo...	My name is...
No se.	I don't know.
Tengo sed.	I am thirsty.
Tengo hambre.	I am hungry.
Soy norteamericano/a	I am an American.
¿Donde puedo encontrar...?	Where can I find...?
¿Que es esto?	What is this?
¿Habla usted ingles?	Do you speak English?
Hablo/entiendo un poco Español	I speak/understand a little Spanish
¿Hay alguien aqui que hable ingles?	Is there anyone here who speaks English?
Le entiendo.	I understand you.
No entiendo.	I don't understand.

Hable mas despacio por favor.	Please speak more slowly.
Repita por favor.	Please repeat.

Telling Time

¿Que hora es?	What time is it?
Son las...	It's...
... cinco.	... five o'clock.
... ocho y diez.	... ten past eight.
... seis y cuarto.	... quarter past six.
... cinco y media.	... half past five.
... siete y menos cinco.	... five of seven.
antes de ayer.	the day before yesterday.
anoche.	yesterday evening.
esta mañana.	this morning.
a mediodia.	at noon.
en la noche.	in the evening.
de noche.	at night.
a medianoche.	at midnight.
mañana en la mañana.	tomorrow morning.
mañana en la noche.	tomorrow evening.
pasado mañana.	the day after tomorrow.

Directions

¿En que direccion queda...?	In which direction is...?
Lleveme a... por favor.	Take me to... please.
Llevame alla ... por favor.	Take me there please.
¿Que lugar es este?	What place is this?
¿Donde queda el pueblo?	Where is the town?
¿Cual es el mejor camino para...?	Which is the best road to...?
De vuelta a la derecha.	Turn to the right.
De vuelta a la isquierda.	Turn to the left.
Siga derecho.	Go this way.
En esta direccion.	In this direction.
¿A que distancia estamos de...?	How far is it to...?
¿Es este el camino a...?	Is this the road to...?
¿Es...	Is it...
... cerca?	... near?
... lejos?	... far?
... norte?	... north?
... sur?	... south?

... este?	... east?
... oeste?	... west?
Indiqueme por favor.	Please point.
Hagame favor de decirme donde esta...	Please direct me to...
... el telephono.	... the telephone.
... el excusado.	... the bathroom.
... el correo.	... the post office.
... el banco.	... the bank.
... la comisaria.	... the police station.

Accommodations

Estoy buscando un hotel.... that's...	I am looking for a hotel
... bueno.	... good.
... barato.	... cheap.
... cercano.	... nearby.
... limpio.	... clean.
¿Dónde hay hotel, pensión, hospedaje?	Where is a hotel, pensión, hospedaje?
Hay habitaciones libres? rooms?	Do you have available
¿Dónde están los baños/servicios?	Where are the bathrooms?
Quisiera un...	I would like a...
... cuarto sencillo.	... single room.
... cuarto con baño.	... room with a bath.
... cuarto doble.	... double room.
Puedo verlo?	May I see it?
Cuanto cuesta?	What's the cost?
Es demasiado caro!	It's too expensive!

Dominican Republic Glossary

agregado – refers to the sugarcane workers who, up until the late 1940s, labored under the feudal system wherein wages were paid partially in goods and services received.

anatto – A small tree whose seeds, coated with orange red dye, are used to color cooking oil, commonly used in the preparation of Caribbean cuisines.

areytos – epic songs danced to by the Tainos.

asopao – a soupy rice dish containing beef, chicken, fish, or other seafood.

bacalao – dried salt cod, once served to slaves.

balneario – a government-administered beach area.

barrio – a city district.

bohio – Taino Indian name for thatched houses; now applied to the houses of country dwellers.

bola, bolita – the numbers racket.

bomba – Musical dialogue between dancer and drummer.

botanicas – stores on the Spanish speaking islands which sell spiritualist literature and paraphernalia.

calabash (calabaza) – small tree native to the Caribbean whose fruit, a gourd, has multiple uses when dried.

callaloo – Caribbean soup made with callaloo greens.

callejón – narrow side street; path through the cane fields.

campesino – peasant; lower-class rural dweller.

canita – the "little cane," bootleg rum (also called pitorro.)

carambola – see star apple.

Caribs – original people who colonized the islands of the Caribbean, giving the region its name.

carretera – a road or highway (abbreviated Carr. in the text)

caudillo – Spanish for military general.

cassava – staple crop indigenous to the Americas. Bitter and sweet are the two varieties. Bitter must be washed, grated, and baked in order to remove the poisonous prussic acid. A spongy cake is made from the bitter variety as is cassareep, a preservative which is the foundation of West Indian pepperpot stew.

cays – Indian-originated name which refers to islets in the Caribbean.

century plant – also known as karato, coratoe, and maypole. Flowers only once in its lifetime before it dies.

cerro – hill or mountain.

chorizo – Spanish sausage.

compadrazgo – the system of "co-parentage" which is used to strengthen social bonds.

conch – large edible mollusk usually pounded into salads or chowders.

cuerda – unit of land measure comprising 9/10ths of an acre.

cutlass – the Caribbean equivalent of the machete. Originally used by buccaneers and pirates.

duppy – ghost or spirit of the dead which is feared throughout the Caribbean. Derives from the African religious belief that a man has two souls. One ascends to heaven while the other stays around for a while or permanently. May be harnessed for good or evil through obeah. Some plants and birds are also associated with duppies.

escabeche – Spanish and Portuguese method of preparing seafood.

espiritismo – spiritualism.

fiestas patronales – patron saint festivals which take place on Catholic islands.

guava – indigenous Caribbean fruit, extremely rich in vitamin C, which is eaten raw or used in making jelly.

guayacan – the tree lignum vitae and its wood.

güiro – rasp-like musical instrument of Taino Indian origin which is scratched with a stick to produce a sound.

langosta – spiny lobster (really a crayfish) native to the region.

lechon asado – roast pig.

naranja – sour orange; its leaves are used as medicine in rural areas.

padrinos – godparents.

pasteles – steamed banana leaves stuffed with meat and other ingredients.

pastelitos – small meat-filled turnovers.

personalismo – describes the charisma of a Latin politician who appears and acts as a father figure.

pinoños – deep fried plantain rings stuffed with spiced ground beef and other fillings.

plebiscite – direct vote by the people on an issue.

plena – form of dance.

poinciana – beautiful tropical tree which blooms with clusters of red blossoms during the summer months. Originates in Madagascar.

público – shared taxi found on the Spanish speaking islands.

sancocho (sancoche) – stew made with a variety of meats and vegetables; found in the Spanish speaking islands.

santos – carved representations of Catholic saints.

sea grape – West Indian tree, commonly found along beaches, which produces green, fleshy, edible grapes.

sensitive plant – also known as mimosa, shame lady, and other names. It will snap shut at the slightest touch.

surrillos – fried cornmeal-and-cheese sticks.

tachuelo – a variety of tropical hardwood.

taro – tuber also known as sasheen, tannia, malanga, elephant's ear, and yautia.

trigueno – ("wheat colored"). Denotes a mulatto and differentiates brunettes from blondes.

velorio – Catholic wake.

zemi (cemi) – idol in which the personal spirit of each Arawak or Taino Indian lived. Usually carved from stone.

Booklist

Travel & Description

Arciniegas, German. *Caribbean: Sea of the New World*. New York: Alfred A. Knopf, 1946.

Blume, Helmut. (trans. Johannes Maczewski and Ann Norton) *The Caribbean Islands*. London: Longman, 1976.

Bonsal, Stephen. *The American Mediterranean*. New York: Moffat, Yard and Co., 1912.

Hart, Jeremy C. and William T. Stone. *A Cruising Guide to the Caribbean and the Bahamas*. New York: Dodd, Mead and Company, 1982. Description of planning and plying for yachties. Includes nautical maps.

Morrison, Samuel E. *The Caribbean as Columbus Saw It*. Boston: Little and Co., 1964. Photographs and text by a leading American historian.

Radcliffe, Virginia. *The Caribbean Heritage*. New York: Walker & Co., 1976.

Sharpe, Kenneth Evan. *Peasant Politics: Struggle in a Dominican Village*. Baltimore: John Hopkins Press, 1977.

Ward, Fred. *Golden Islands of the Caribbean*. New York: Crown Publishers, 1967. A picture book for your coffee table. Beautiful historical plates.

Weil, Thomas E., et al. *Area Handbook for the Dominican Republic*. Washington, DC: Government Printing Office, 1973.

Wood, Peter. *Caribbean Isles*. New York: Time Life Books, 1975. Includes descriptions of such places as Pico Duarte in the Dominican Republic and the Blue Mountain region of Jamaica.

Flora & Fauna

Humann, Paul. *Reef Fish Identification*. Jacksonville: New World Publications, 1989. This superb guide is filled with beautiful color photos of 268 fish. Information is included on identifying details, habitat and behavior, and on reaction to divers.

Humann, Paul. *Reef Creature Identification*. Jacksonville: New World Publications, 1992. The second in the series, this guide covers 320 denizens of the deep. Information is included on abundance and distribution, habitat and behavior, and identifying characteristics.

Humann, Paul. *Reef Coral Identification*. Jacksonville: New World Publications, 1993. Last in this indispensable series (which is now available boxed as "The Reef Set"), this book identifies 240 varieties of coral and marine plants. The different groups are also described in detail.

Hoppe, Jürgen. *The National Parks of the Dominican Republic*. Santo Domingo: Dirección Nacional de Parques, 1989. A photographic guide to the nation's parks.

Kaplan, Eugene. *A Field Guide to the Coral Reefs of the Caribbean and Florida*. Princeton, N.J.: Peterson's Guides, 1984.

de Oviedo, Gonzalo Fernandez. (trans. and ed. S.A. Stroudemire. *Natural History of the West Indies*. Chapel Hill: University of North Carolina Press, 1959.

Stockton de Nod, Annabelle. *Aves de la República Dominicana*. Santo Domingo, Museo de Historia Natural, 1978.

History

Bell, Ian. *The Dominican Republic: Politics and the Dominican Republic*. Boulder, CO: Westview Press, 1981. An important book for understanding the nation.

Calder, Bruce. *The Impact of Intervention: The Dominican Republic During the US Occupation of 1916-1924*. Austin, TX: The University of Texas, 1984. This fascinating study expores all facets of the US invasion and its aftermath.

Crassweller, Robert. *Trujillo, The Life and Times of a Caribbean Dictator*. New York: Macmillan, 1966.

Cripps, L.L. *The Spanish Caribbean: From Columbus to Castro*. Cambridge, Ma.: Schenkman, 1979. Concise history of the Spanish Caribbean from the point of view of a Marxist historian.

Deer, Noel. *The History of Sugar*. London: Chapman, 1950.

Hernan, Edward S. and Frank Brodhead. *Demonstration Elections: U.S.-Staged Elections in the Dominican Republic, Vietnam, and El Salvador*. Boston: South End Press, 1984.

Hovey, Graham and Gene Brown, eds. *Central America and the Caribbean*. New York: Arno Press, 1980. This volume of clippings from The

New York Times, one of a series in its Great Contemporary Issues books, graphically displays Amnerican activities and attitudes toward the area. A goldmine of information.

Knight, Franklin W. *The Caribbean.* Oxford: Oxford University Press, 1978. Thematic, anti-imperialist view of Caribbean history.

Lowenthal, Abraham F. *The Dominican Intervention.* Cambridge, MA: Harvard U. Press, 1972.

Mannix, Daniel P. and Malcolm Cooley. *Black Cargoes.* New York: Viking Press, 1982. Details the saga of the slave trade.

Martin, John Bartlow. *Overtaken by Events: The Dominican Crisis from the Fall of Trujillo to the Civil War.* New York: Doubleday, 1966.

Rodman, Selden. *Quisqueya: A History of the Dominican Republic.* Seattle: University of Washington Press, 1964.

Ruck, Rob. *The Tropic of Baseball: Baseball in the Dominican Republic.* Meckler Press, 1991. Replete with anecdotes, this is a historical survey of the Dominican passion for its adopted national sport.

Sale, Kirkpatrick. *The Conquest of Paradise: Christopher Columbus and the Columbian Legacy.* New York: Knopf, 1991.

Slater, Jerome. *Intervention and Negotiation: The United States and the Dominican Republic.* New York: Harper and Row, 1970.

Szulc, Tad. *Dominican Diary.* New York: Delacorte Press, 1965.

Welles, Sumner. *Naboth's Vinyard: The Dominican Republic, 1844-1924.* New York: Payson and Clarke, 1928.

Williams, Eric. *From Columbus to Castro: The History of the Caribbean.* New York: Random House, 1983. Definitive history of the Caribbean by the late Prime Minister of Trinidad and Tobago.

Politics & Economics

Atkins, G. Pope. *Arms and Politics in the Dominican Republic.* Boulder, CO: Westview Press, 1980.

Atkins, G. Pope. and Larman Wilson. *The United States and the Trujillo Regime.* New Brunswick, NJ: Rutgers University Press, 1972.

Barry, Tom, Beth Wood, and Deb Freusch. *The Other Side of Paradise: Foreign Control in the Caribbean.* New York: Grove Press, 1984. A brilliantly and thoughtfully written analysis of Caribbean economics.

Black, Jan Knippers. *The Dominican Republic: Politics and Development in an Unsovereign State*. Boston: Allen & Unwin, 1986. A fine introduction to the nation covering history, government, and economy.

Blanshard, Paul. *Democracy and Empire in the Caribbean*. New York: The Macmillan Co., 1947.

Bosch, Juan. *The Unfinished Experiment: Democracy in the Dominican Republic*. New York: Praeger, 1963.

Diederich, Bernard. *Trujillo: The Death of the Goat*. Boston: Little, Brown, and Co., 1978.

Kryzanek, Michael J. and Howard J. Wiarda. *The Politics of External Influence in the Dominican Republic*. New York: Praeger, 1988. A sweeping, well-written overview of US intervention in the Dominican Republic along with history and recent economics.

Matthews, Thomas G. and F.M. Andic, eds. *Politics and Economics in the Caribbean*. Río Piedras: Institute of Caribbean Studies, University of Puerto Rico, 1971.

Mitchell, Sir Harold. *Caribbean Patterns*. New York: John Wiley and Son, 1972. Dated but still a masterpiece. The best reference guide for gaining an understanding of the history and current political status of nearly every island group in the Caribbean.

Roosevelt, Theodore. *Colonial Policies of the United States*. Garden City: Doubleday, Doran, and Co., 1937.

Wiarda, Howard. *The Dominican Republic: Nation in Transition*. New York: Praeger, 1968.

Wiarda, Howard. *Dictatorship and Development: The Methods of Control in Trujillo's Dominican Republic*. Gainesville: University of Florida Press, 1970. A brilliant treatise on the almost unbelievable methods and economic policies employed by the Trujillo regime.

Wiarda, Howard and Michael J. Kryzanek. *The Dominican Republic: A Caribbean Crucible*. Boulder, CO: Westview Press, 1982. Another fine introduction to the nation.

Art, Architecture & Archaeology

Buissert, David. *Historic Architecture of the Caribbean*. London: Heinemann Educational Books, 1980.

Gosner, Pamela. *Caribbean Georgian.* Washington D.C.: Three Continents Press, 1982. A beautifully illustrated guide to the "Great and Small Houses of the West Indies."

Music

Bergman, Billy. *Hot Sauces: Latin and Caribbean Pop.* New York: Quill, 1984. Includes a brief mention of *merengue*.

Index

Accommodations, *1, 95-98; the Cibao, 211-12, 215; Cordillera Central Region, 193-94, 195, 196-97, 199; Costa Caribe, 171, 173-74, 177-78; Puerto Plata and the North, 223-28, 236, 241-44, 250-55, 264, 265; Samaná Peninsula, 271-72, 274, 275-77, 280-83; Santo Domingo, 142-48; the Southeast, 290, 292, 295-97, 298-99, 300, 301, 303-4; the Southwest, 182-83, 184, 185, 186, 189-90*

Acuario Nacional, *138*

Agriculture, *50-53*

Aguas Blancas, *201*

Air travel. See Transportation

Alcazar de Colon, *125-26*

Altos de Chavón, *299-300*

Amazonas, *265*

Archaeological Museum, *300*

Armando Bermúdez National Park, *201-6*

Arts: *art and artists, 1, 67; art galleries, 163; and crafts, 67*

Bahía de Catalina, *302*

Bahoruco, *187*

Balneario La Poza, *196*

Baní, *183-85; Palmar de Ocoa, 184-85*

Banica, *187*

Banks, *1, 166-67*

Barahona, *185-87*

Basilica de Nuestra Señora de la Merced, *291*

Bayahibe, *301*

Beaches, *82-83; Costa Caribe, 176; Puerto Plata and the North, 222, 240-41, 264; Samaná Peninsula, 274-78; the Southwest, 184-85, 187*

Bible Park, *140-1*

Biblioteca Nacional, *136*

Black market, *103*

Boca Chica: *accommodations, 171, 173-74; beaches, 176; entertainment, 175; events, 176; food shopping, 175; map, 172; restaurants, 174-75; services, 176; shopping, 176; sports, 176; tours, 176; transportation, 171, 176*

Boca de Yuma, *300*

Bonao, *193-94*

Broadcasting and media, *101*

Business hours, *1*

Cabarete, *249; accommodations, 250-55; biking, 260; diving, 262; entertainment, 257-58; events, 250; food shopping, 257; golf, 262; health, 259; history, 249-50; horseback riding, 260; important phone numbers, 258; jungle river tour, 261; restaurants, 255-57; services, 258-59; shopping, 257, 262; transportation, 250; windsurfing, 259-60*

Cala Blanca, *277*

Calle las Damas, *126*

Calle Padre Billini, *131-32*

Cambita Carabitos, *182*

Camp David Ranch, *211*

Camping, *1*

Capilla de la Virgen de Rosario, *132*

Capilla de Nuestra Señora de los Remedios, *128-29*

Capilla de San Andrés, *132*

Capilla de San Gregorio Magno, *179*

Car rentals, *1*, *92-93*; *Costa Caribe*, *178*; *Puerto Plata and the North*, *233*, *248*, *259*; *Santo Domingo*, *123*, *165-66*; *the Southeast*, *299*

Casa Bercam, *278*

Casa Bonita, *187*

Casa de Campo, *299*

Casa de Caoba, *180*

Casa de Francia, *128*

Casa de las Bastidas, *128*

Casa de Tostado, *131*

Casa del Cordón, *130*

Casa Marina Beach, *240-41*

Casa Museo Generalisimo Máximo Gómez, *237*

Castillo del Cerro, *180*

Catedral de San Felipe, *219*

Catedral de Santiago Apóstol, *210*

Catedral Primada de America (Catedral de Santa Maria la Menor), *125*

Caveing, *1*

Cayo Cacata, *287*

Cayo Levantado, *273-74*

Cayos Siete Hermanos, *238*

Centro de los Héroes, *142*

Centro Turistico, *180*

Cerro de San Francisco, *187*

Chapel of the Third Order, *132*

Chavón Art Galleries, *300*

Church of St. Stanislaus, *300*

Cibao, the, *207*; *Moca*, *215*; *San José de la Matas*, *215*; *Santiago de los Treinta Caballeros*, *207-14*

Climate, *5, 7*

Clothing, *1*

Club de Comercio, *219*

Columbus Aquaparque, *241*

Conduct, *109-13*

Constanza, *198-200*

Convento de los Dominicanos, *131-32*

Coral reef ecosystem, *18-21*

Corbanito, *184*

Cordillera Central Region, *193*; *Aguas Blancas*, *201*; *Armando Bermúdez and José del Carmen Ramírez National Parks*, *201-6*; *Bonao*, *193-94*; *Constanza*, *198-200*; *Jarabacoa*, *196-98*; *La Vega*, *194-96*; *Reserva Científica Valle Nuevo*, *200-201*

Corral de los Indios, *187*

Costa Caribe: *Boca Chica*, *171-76*; *Juan Dolio*, *176-78*; *Parque Nacional Submarino la Caleta*, *178*

Costa del Coco, *292-97*

Cotui, *265*

Credit cards, *1, 106*

Cueva de las Golondrinas, *263-64*

Cueva de las Maravillas, *303*

Cueva del Paseo de los Indios, *137*

Currency, *1*

Customs, *108-9*

Diving, *83-84*; *Costa Caribe*, *176*, *178*; *Puerto Plata and the North*, *222*, *237*, *248*, *262*, *264*; *Samaná Peninsula*, *285*; *Santo Domingo*, *166*

Divorce, *102-3*

Economy, *42-46, 48-50*

Edificio del Centro de Recreo, *210*

El Conde, *124-25*

El Defiladero de los Amargados, *187*

El Higuero, *215*

El Museo de Amber, *222*

El Número, *184*

El Pato, *187*

El Pomier Archaeological Reserve, *181-82*

El Quemaíto, 187
Electricity, 1
Elias Piña, 187
Entertainment: the Cibao, 213; Cordillera Central Region, 195-96, 197, 200; Costa Caribe, 175; Puerto Plata and the North, 231, 236-37, 246-47, 257-58; Samaná Peninsula, 273, 277, 284-85; Santo Domingo, 154-58; the Southeast, 299, 304; the Southwest, 186

Faro a Colón, 138-40
Fauna, 12-21
Faxes, 1, 100
Festivals and events, 69-75; the Cibao, 213; Cordillera Central Region, 194, 198; Costa Caribe, 176; Puerto Plata and the North, 231-32, 237, 240, 250; Samaná Peninsula, 273; the Southeast, 304; the Southwest, 184, 185
Flora, 7, 10, 12
Food, 75-82
Fortaleza de San Felipe, 219, 222
Fortaleza Ozama, 126, 128, 129
Fuerte de la Concepción, 124
Fuerte de San Gil, 125

Galeria de Arte Moderno, 135
Gaspar Hernández, 262
Gazcue, 133
Goat Island, 188, 189
Government, 40-42
Grí Grí Lagoon, 262-63
Guaraguao, 302

Hacienda María, 179
Haina, 179
Haiti, 57, 191, 237
Hallucinogenic rituals, 111
Health concerns, 101-3, 166
Higüey, 291-92

History, 21-40; Cabarete, 249-50; important dates, 47; La Romana, 298; La Vega, 194; parks of the Southwest, 188, 189, 190; Puerto Plata, 217-18; Punta Cana, 293; San Pedro de Macorís, 303; Santa Bárbara de Samaná, 270-71; Santiago, 209; Santo Domingo, 123
Hospital-Iglesia de San Nicolas de Bari, 133
Hostal Nicolás de Ovando, 128

Iglesia Convento de Santa Clara, 131
Iglesia Corazón de Jesus, 215
Iglesia de la Regina Angelorum, 132
Iglesia de las Mercedes, 132
Iglesia de Piedras Vivas, 180, 182
Iglesia de San Antón, 132
Iglesia de San Cristóbal, 180
Iglesia de Santa Bárbara, 132
Iglesia del Carmen, 132
Iglesia las Mercedes, 195
Ingenio Boca de Nigua, 179
Ingenio de Diego Caballero, 179
Instituto de Tabaco, 210
Isla Cabritos, 188, 189
Isla de Catalina, 300-301
Isla de Saona, 301
Island Beata, 191

Jarabacoa, 196-98
Jardin Botanico Nacional, 136-37
José del Carmen Ramírez National Park, 201-6
Juan Dolio, 176-78
Jungle River Tour, 261

La Ataranza, 130
La Cascada, 278
La Ciénaga, 187
La Isábela, 235-36

La Orquidea de Sol, *222*
La Romana, *298-99*
La Vega, *194-96*
La Vega Vieja, *195*
Lago Oviedo, *190*
Laguna Enriquillo y Parque Nacional Isla Cabritos, *188-90*
Land, buying, *115*
Land features, *3-5, 8*
Language, *63-67; schools, 166, 246*
Las Terrenas, *278-85*
Limón, *278*
Loma Isabel de Torres, *222*

Malecón, *303*
Manatí Park, *293-95*
Maps: *Boca Chica, 172; Caribbean Islands, 6; Dominican Republic, 9, 183, 288; Hispaniola land features, 8; national parks and scientific reserves, 11; Puerto Plata and the North, 217, 220-21, 239, 263; Samaná Peninsula, 267, 270, 279; Santiago, 208; Santo Domingo, 121, 127, 129, 135*
Marine life, *13-18*
Marriage, *2*
Medical emergencies, *102*
Mercado Central, *211*
Moca, *215*
Money, *103, 105*
Monte Cristi, *236-37; Parque Nacional Monte Cristi, 237-38*
Monumento a los Héroes de la Restauración, *210-11*
Museo de Artes Folkloricos Tomás Morel, *210*
Museo de Historia Nacional, *136*
Museo de Jamón, *130*
Museo de la Porcelana, *132*
Museo de las Casas Reales, *129-30*

Museo de Trujillo, *141*
Museo del Hombre Dominicano, *134-35*
Museo Duartino, *125*
Museo Maritimo, *130*
Museo Mundo de Ambar, *133*
Museo Nacional de Historia y Geographica, *135-36*
Museo Numismatico, *136*
Museo Pre-hispanico, *141-42*
Museo Virreinal, *126*
Music and dance, *67-69*

Nagua, *265*
National Botanic Gardens, *136-37*
National parks and reserves: *Cordillera Central Region, 201-6; Costa Caribe, 178; map, 11; Puerto Plata and the North, 237-38; the Southeast, 287, 289-91, 301-2; the Southwest, 181-82; visiting, 118;* Nuestra Señora de las Mercedes, *195*

Packing, *113-15*
Palacio Consistorial, *210*
Palacio Nacional, *133-34*
Palmar de Ocoa, *184-85*
Panteón Nacional, *128*
Parks, *of the Southwest, 187-91*
Parque Independencia (El Conde), *124*
Parque los Tres Ojos de Agua, *137-38*
Parque Luperón, *219*
Parque Mirador del Este, *138*
Parque Mirador del Sur/Paseo de los Indios, *137*
Parque Nacional del Este, *301-2*
Parque Nacional Jaragua, *190-91*
Parque Nacional los Haitises, *287, 289-91*

Parque Nacional Monte Cristi, 237-38
Parque Nacional Natural Laguna Redonda y Laguna Limón, 290
Parque Nacional Sierra de Bahoruco, 188
Parque Nacional Submarino la Caleta, 178
Parque Zoologico Nacional, 137
People, the, 53-61
Photography, 115-17
Pico Duarte, 202-4
Playa Blanca, 185
Playa Chiquita, 184
Playa Colorado, 277
Playa El Rincón, 274
Playa El Soco, 303
Playa El Valle, 278
Playa Grande, 264-65
Playa las Galeras, 274-78
Playa Madama, 277
Playa Monte Río, 184-85
Playa Rincón, 277-78
Plaza de Cultura (Santiago), 210
Plaza de la Cultura (Santo Domingo), 134, 135
Population, 2
Postal service, 100-101, 165
Practicalities, 86-117
Pueblo Viejo, 184
Puerta de la Misericordia, 124
Puerta El Conde, 124
Puerto Plata and the North, 217; accommodations, 223-28, 236, 241-45, 250-55, 264, 265; beaches, 222, 240-41; Cabarete, 249-62; diving, 222, 237, 248, 262, 264; entertainment, 231, 236-37, 246-47, 257-58; festivals and events, 231-32, 237, 240, 250; Gaspar Hernández, 262; health, 234; history, 217-18, 249-50; important phone numbers, 233, 259; La Isabela, 235-36; maps, 217, 220-21, 239; Monte Cristi, 236-38; Nagua, 265; orientation, 218-19; Playa Grande, 264-65; rentals, 233-34; restaurants, 228-31, 236, 245, 246, 255-57, 265; Río San Juan, 262-64; services, 232, 237, 247-48, 258-59; shopping, 234, 247, 257, 262; sights, 219, 222; Sosúa, 239, 240-49; supermarkets, 230; tours, 232-33, 247; transportation, 218, 219, 234-35, 237, 238, 240, 248-49, 250
Punta Cana, 286, 292-97

Religion, 61-63
Reloj de Sol, 129
Reserva Antropológica de las Cueva de las Maravillas, 303
Reserva Cientifica Natural de Villa Elisa, 238
Reserva Científica Natural Laguna de Rincón, 187
Reserva Científica Valle Nuevo, 200-201
Reserves. See National parks and reserves
Restaurants, 2, 75-82; the Cibao, 212-13; Cordillera Central Region, 195, 197, 199-200; Costa Caribe, 174-75, 178; Puerto Plata and the North, 228-31, 236, 245, 246, 255-57, 265; Samaná Peninsula, 272-73, 274, 283-84; Santo Domingo, 130, 148-53; the Southeast, 292, 300, 301, 304; the Southwest, 183, 185, 186
Rincón Lagoon, 187
Río Caño, 187
Río San Juan, 262-64
Ruinas de San Francisco, 130-31

Safety, personal, 116
Salto de Biguate, 196
Samaná Peninsula, 267-70, 285-86; Cayo Levantado, 273-74; Las Terrenas, 278-85, 286; Limón, 278; Playa el Rincón, 274; Playa las Galeras, 274-78; Sánchez, 274; Santa Bárbara de Samaná, 268, 270-73 San Cristóbal, 179-83
San Francisco monastery, 195
San José de las Matas, 215
San Juan de la Maguana, 187
San Pedro de Macorís, 302-4
San Rafael, 187
Sánchez, 274
Sanctuario de Ballenas Jorobadas del Banco de la Plata, 267
Sanctuario de los Tainos, 291-92
Santa Bárbara de Samaná, 269-73
Santa Cerro, 194-95
Santiago de los Treinta Caballeros: accommodations, 211-12; entertainment, 213; festivals and events, 213; health, 214; history, 209; map, 208; orientation, 209; restaurants, 212-13; services, 213-14; shopping, 214; sights, 210-11; tours, 211; transportation, 207, 209-10, 211, 214; vicinity of, 215
Santo Domingo 2000 Project, 140
Santo Domingo, 119; accommodations, 142-48; air travel, 119-20, 169-70; buses, 168-69; car rentals, 123, 165; city layout, 120, 122; entertainment, 154-58; food stores, 153; history, 123; Malecón sights, 141; maps, 121, 127, 129, 135; metropolitan sights, 133-42; Old Santo Domingo sights, 124-33; public transportation, 120; restaurants, 130, 148-53; services,

164-68; shopping, 158-64; supermarkets, 154; taxis, 122; tours, 164, 165; transportation, 119-20, 122, 168-70
Santo Hoyo, 195
Services and information, 98-101; the Cibao, 213-14; Cordillera Central Region, 197-98; Costa Caribe, 176, 178; Puerto Plata and the North, 232, 237, 247-48, 258-59; Samaná Peninsula, 273, 277, 285; Santo Domingo, 164-68; the Southeast, 299, 304; the Southwest, 184, 185, 186 Shopping, 106-9; the Cibao, 214; Costa Caribe, 176; Puerto Plata and the North, 234, 247, 257, 262; Samaná Peninsula, 285; Santo Domingo, 158-64; the Southeast, 297
Sociedad Fe en el Porvenir, 219
Sosúa, 238; accommodations, 241-44; beaches and sights, 240-41; car rentals, 248; diving, 248; entertainment, 246-47; events, 240; food shopping, 245-46; important phone numbers, 247; language study, 246; map, 239; restaurants, 245, 246; services, 247-48; shopping, 247; sports, 248; tours, 247; transportation, 240, 248-49
Southeast, the, 287; Altos de Chavón, 299-300; Bayahibe, 301; Boca de Yuma, 300; Casa de Campo, 299; Costa del Coco, 292-97; Higüey, 291-92; Isla de Catalina, 300-301; La Romana, 298-301; Parque Nacional del Este, 301-2; Parque Nacional los Haitises, 287, 289-91; San Pedro de Macorís, 302-4
Southwest, the, 179; Baní, 183-85; Barahona, 185-87; Haiti,

191; *map, 183; parks, 187-91;*
San Cristóbal, *179-83*
Sports, *248, 262; baseball, 86,*
304; biking, 260; fishing, 85;
golf, 85-86, 262; horseback rid-
ing, 85, 176, 260; polo, 85; and
recreation, 82-86; sailing, 83;
scuba and snorkeling, 83, 84;
surfing, 84; tennis, 86; water-
sports, 82-85; windsurfing, 85,
259-60. See also Diving
Sugarcane mills, *179*

Taxes, *2; departure tax, 1, 90; ho-*
tel, 97
Teatro Nacional, *136*
Teleférico, *222*
Telephones, *2, 99-100; 165, 233*
Tipping, *2, 110*
Torre de Homenaje, *128*
Tours, *89-90, 92-93; Cordillera*
Central Region, 204; Costa Car-
ibe, 176, 178; Puerto Plata and
the North, 232-33, 247; Samaná
Peninsula, 273, 285; Santiago,
211; Santo Domingo, 122-23,
165; the Southeast, 289-90,
297; the Southwest, 190
Transportation: *air travel, 87-89,*
90-91, 119-20, 169-70, 214,
218, 250, 285-86, 293; boats
and ferries, 89, 95, 112-13;

buses, 1, 90, 91-92; the Cibao,
207, 209-10, 211, 214, 215; Cor-
dillera Central Region, 194, 196,
198-99, 200-201; Costa Caribe,
171, 176; driving, 1, 93-95; gua-
guas (vans), 1-2, 169; hitching,
95; internal transport, 90-91;
motoconchos (motorbikes), 2;
Puerto Plata and the North, 218,
219, 234-35, 237, 238, 240,
248-49, 250; Samaná Penin-
sula, 269-70, 273, 274, 275,
280, 285-86; Santo Domingo,
119-20, 122, 168-70; sea travel,
89; the Southeast, 293, 298,
300, 301; the Southwest, 180,
183, 184, 187, 189, 191; taxis, 2,
92, 122; walking, 95
Tropical Plantation, *290*

Universidad Autonomal Santo
Domingo, *142*
Universidad Católica Madre y
Maestra, *211*

Visas, *2, 97*
Voluntariado de Casa Reales, *129*

Water, *2*
Waterfalls, *196*
Watersports, *82-85*
Web sites, useful, *104-5*
Whale watching, *267, 274*